# PALACE COUP

## The Inside Story of
## Harry and Leona Helmsley

# MICHAEL MOSS

⚓
### DOUBLEDAY
New York  London  Toronto  Sydney  Auckland

PUBLISHED BY DOUBLEDAY
a division of Bantam Doubleday Dell Publishing Group, Inc.,
666 Fifth Avenue, New York, New York 10103

DOUBLEDAY and the portrayal of an anchor with
a dolphin are trademarks of Doubleday, a division
of Bantam Doubleday Dell Publishing Group, Inc.

Library of Congress Cataloging-in-Publication Data

Moss, Michael, 1955–
    Palace coup : the story of hotel magnates Harry and Leona Helmsley
    Michael Moss. — 1st ed.
        p.    cm.
    ISBN 0-385-24973-X
    1. Helmsley, Harry.  2. Helmsley, Leona.  3. Businessmen—United States—
Biography.  4. Women in business—United States—Biography.  5. Real estate
developers—United States—Biography.  6. Hotels, taverns, etc.—United States—
History.  I. Title
HC102.5.H45M67    1988
333.39'092'2—dc 19
[B]                                                                                          88-36759
                                                                                                CIP

ISBN 0-385-24973-X
Copyright © 1989 by Michael Moss
All Rights Reserved
Printed in the United States of America
*Book Design by Kathryn Parise*
April 1989
FIRST EDITION

For Ellen,
and for Bob and Vinny

# ACKNOWLEDGMENTS

I get the byline for this work, but the credit goes to many others. Only some can I name here. Jane Dystel, at the Edward J. Acton Agency, got things rolling and believed in a first-time author. So did Casey Fuetsch, my editor at Doubleday, who then kept me on track. Ilze Zvirgzdins, a friend and a fine reporter and writer, plowed and then smoothed an early rough draft.

A number of reporters shared their experiences covering some aspect of the Helmsleys. Among them, I'm most indebted to Ellis Henican of *New York Newsday* for a key introduction. Barry Meier helped me plot one particularly challenging interview. My current editors were more than generous in giving me time off. To Ellis Cose, a friend and fellow refugee from the Gannett Center for Media Studies at Columbia University, I owe computer literacy. With him there was Life Before and Life After Split Screen. And to the Center's director, Ev Dennis, I owe thanks for his boundless encouragement.

Journalists aren't worth red cents without librarians, and I leaned hard on Karen Van Rossem and Christine Baird at *Newsday*, who, as always, knew just where to go for even the most obscure information. In the same vein, the staff at numerous public archives and courthouses were also a lot smarter than I was in tracking down documents.

My family shored up the home front. And my better half, Ellen, put up with it all. But it was the Helmsley "family" to whom this book is most owed—the tenants, the brokers, the hotel employees, the home staff, their personal friends, contractors, and providers of various services.

It was not, by and large, an easy or pleasurable task for them to help me understand Leona and Harry Helmsley (who refused to be interviewed directly). To sort fact from rumor, I grew obdurate in challenging their recall. The vindictive appear in this book only when their accounts could be double- or triple-checked. The whining was weighed in the context of employer-employee relationships. Perhaps the most reliable sources were those very reluctant voices who anguished over their mixed feelings, knowing they were betraying someone who had betrayed them. Some chose to remain anonymous, for fear of reprisal, and of those I'm particularly indebted to Harry's closest aides for speaking frankly, if confidentially.

I owe thanks to many other people for extending me a helping hand—whether the assistance was an introduction to a source or simply listening to me mull things over. They trusted me to be accurate and fair, and to the extent that this book fails, it's my burden to bear.

Conversely, to the extent that this book succeeds in explaining matters complex and contradictory, I'm indebted to my many teachers and to the editors at the Pacific News Service in San Francisco, who fourteen years ago urged me to do two things if I did anything at all: spell people's names correctly and push especially hard to answer questions that begin with the word "why."

# CONTENTS

# PALACE
# COUP

# CHAPTER 1

# THE PALACE

A ROYAL CROWN ADORNS THE WROUGHT IRON, SPLITTING NEATLY down the middle when the gate is swung open. Brownstone pillars anchor the sides. A lantern hangs overhead, piercing the sky with arching spikes.

No guards stand at this regal entry to the Helmsley Palace. Rather, they watch from inside the hotel, relaxed until word comes that the Queen is headed their way. She's the one person whose mere appearance sets off alarm.

Out on the street, traffic flows uptown along Madison Avenue, pulsating with the lights. Four lanes of buses, cabs, and the omnipresent stretch limousines move through to the Upper East Side of Manhattan, the Silk Stocking district where shops grow more posh with every block before giving way to Spanish Harlem.

Noise from the scramble crashes through the gate, flooding the courtyard. This is, after all, the heart of New York City. The doorways of even the wealthy are awash with its frenzy. The din bounces off the high brownstone walls that lead to the Palace. Still, the courtyard is alluring. Four massive lead planters each holds a delicately leavèd linden. The marble flooring, a charcoal hue, is free of clutter and notably cleaner than the sidewalk just a few feet away. On this watched ground, leaves and litter never linger.

Most guests arrive through the hotel's side entrances on Fiftieth and Fifty-first streets, where doormen stand under double-tiered brass-and-glass canopies ringed with bare light bulbs like Broadway marquees. But the front gate serves up two special treats for those who walk in off the avenue. Centered in the courtyard is a thirty-two-foot mosaic of marble and granite, laid perfectly smooth in a concentric-circle design lifted from fifteenth-century Italian cathedrals. Then, straight ahead, just above the revolving door under the arches of the neo-Romanesque façade, is a picture-postcard reflection.

The mirrored view is of St. Patrick's Cathedral, which sits directly across Madison Avenue, and of the towering Rockefeller Center beyond. Two world-renowned landmarks, of the church and the state, bouncing off the hard polished glass.

The courtyard mosaic is remarkable for another reason. Its tones are light and dark browns, set apart by rings of off-white stone. And except for the nearby brownstone walls, which would easily blend with the pine and granite rock faces of Yosemite Valley, the mosaic is the only earthen thing about the Helmsley Palace.

To walk through the revolving door is to be stunned by the gilt and the gilded of a dainty Versailles. The air is hushed. People move with a slight spring across the thick burgundy carpet. Except when the guards have raised their alarm, the only distraction is the hotel itself. It resounds with ornament draped over ornament, gold leaf dusted with gold, dangling crystal reflected in crystal.

Stairs with golden banisters lead from the lobby area to the ballroom and the dining and sitting areas, where room after room is filled with chandeliered charm. One, christened the Music Chamber in 1888 when it was built, is now called the Gold Room, smothered in gilt as if some minstrel traipsed through with a wand. A vaulted ceiling arcs two stories overhead. Delicate stained-glass windows draw light from the courtyard. A shallow golden balcony holds a golden harp. Along other walls, garlands of golden foliage are draped in relief. Tea and scones can be taken sitting on upholstery done in a light beige that compounds the golden hue. Gold even dominates an oil mural of a chatty Roman scene.

Above all that garnish and glitter rises fifty-one stories of brand-new hotel. The opulence peaks at the top, where four corner suites form the penthouse apartments. Real sheiks and real princesses stay here, as do those with acquired royalty like Imelda and Ferdinand Marcos and their pal the arms dealer Adnan Kashoggi. They ride up in their own elevator. They lounge in a two-story-high, glass-walled living room. They can use either a circular staircase or a private lift to reach the rooftop sun room and open-air garden, and every one of their rooms has a breathless view of the Manhattan skyline.

Below are a few dozen multi-room suites and a few hundred more basic guest rooms, done in French pastels and antique white furnishings with a gentler silver- and gold-leaf trim. Window boxes neatly tuck in the drapery. And each room—whether it costs $225 or $1,800 a night —receives the same starter kit: a tray with two toothbrushes, a lint remover, tiny plastic bottles of coconut shampoo and moisturizer, a shoehorn, a matchbook sewing kit, a bottle of Saratoga spring water, and plastic ditty bags of sundry sizes and functions.

Each bathroom also holds an oversized bar of soap, a swing-armed magnifying mirror, and the huge, thick, fluffy towels that Leona insists on for each of her guests, as she does for herself. Be pampered, they're told in effect, and rest assured that the bed quilt will never, ever come wrinkled—or one of the 156 maids will pay.

All that is the Palace Hotel that Leona and Harry Helmsley share with the world—proudly, boastfully so.

They hand out glossy booklets to tell how they saved—without regard to budget—the public rooms from abandoned century-old mansions.

They eagerly spread Leona's commercial image as the Palace Queen: hostess and provider extraordinaire of overnight lodging. A grinning Leona dressed in a black-and-red ballroom gown and silver crown has appeared in so many ads that she's become to hotel rooms what Frank Perdue is to chickens—an image that sells, however campy or crass. Her heart-shaped face, arched eyebrows, and stretched, practiced smile have become recognizable to millions, and as easily lampooned as the grin of Jimmy Carter.

The Helmsleys even gladly admit to the world her fitful inspections. Having the Queen dress down a doorman for leaving a dropped cigar butt unattended is good for business, she and Harry decided, so she dons a sneer for the cameras. She practiced the display of fury shown in a CBS *60 Minutes* segment that aired in 1985 and again three years later. The show also secured the Helmsleys' position as public figures basking in the fruits of their lifelong labors. With Harry's profits they bought an airliner and remodeled it into a flying penthouse, they bought a twenty-one-room country estate, they bought a mountaintop retirement retreat in Arizona, and they threw the famous black-tie "I'm Just Wild About Harry" birthday parties that have sent thousands of VIP guests skipping home with ditty bags full of favors including the ubiquitous "Wild About Harry" music box.

And in case anyone missed them on TV or in the magazine ads, Leona has her staff place every night in every Helmsley hotel room—from Hartford to Orlando, New York City to St. Louis—a freshly reprinted glossy, royal-red-covered magazine article that profiles her as the Queen, tyrant to the careless employee, gushing matron to Harry, and hostess to the spectrum of Manhattan society open to the new—business magazine centerfold—rich.

All that is the authorized public image of Leona and Harry, whose net worth has topped one billion dollars and is bounding for two. But it's just so much illusion, crafted to mask a private world that is steeped in personal and corporate intrigue.

Their account of how the Palace was created is pure revisionist. Amidst the onyx and marble is the true record. The Helmsleys started the Palace with both feet on the bottom line, and without any appreciation for history or art or even the church across the street until it was clear those things would make them a buck. They then foundered in their own greed.

Their image as the endearing tycoon couple who found new love in old age is also misleading—as was the temporary affection they once showed to their daughter-in-law, the ceiling in one of their smaller

New York hotels that collapsed and killed a sleeping guest, as misleading as their official account of the "burglar" who entered their Palm Beach penthouse to put a twelve-inch knife into Leona's chest. Few doubt that Leona and Harry came to love each other, in some fashion. Indeed, their relationship may well have been nurturing, given Harry's social blooming after they married. But their mutual adoration was more complicated below the surface, where Leona and Harry came to feed on a virulent trauma that eventually fed on them.

And the image of Leona's practiced smile, notwithstanding her conduct as an effusive, doting Jewish mother who calls people "baby" and "sweetheart," is as misleading as her biographical account of her life. Behind the smile lies the force of a tyrant that erupts time and again, as it did one midday in 1981.

It was near peak lunchtime and the dining room of the Helmsley Park Lane Hotel in Manhattan was filling with guests. The Park Lane, where the Helmsleys live in a penthouse duplex, is more stately and subdued than the Palace. Its elegance is of a Fifth Avenue class, like the Plaza Hotel next door. Its ad campaign features Leona as the refined society matron, penning courtly responses to guests who have written her to praise the hotel or share some quaint experience.

The diners that day, typically, were part upper-class tourists, part business people. At one table in a corner not far from the kitchen doors sat a sixty-one-year-old woman, accompanied by a younger man who appeared to work for her in some executive capacity. As they conversed, her words grew louder, more heated, until she was verbally lashing out at the man.

The staff on hand couldn't tell what had made her so angry, but the more furious she became, the more he cowered.

She had ordered a tuna sandwich, a low-fat, low-calorie specialty of the house, dressed in a dab of mustard and chives. Not too wet. Not too dry. With toast triangles and pickles on the side. She had ordered the same for the man. And now, having taken a huge bite, her cheeks bulged. The tuna oozed from the corners of her mouth, foaming up all white and green. So too did foul words pour out. They were more than foul. There were "fucks," and "shits," and what seemed to be one of her favorites, "cocksucker," in combinations that were either particularly crude or nonsensical, and only ever so slightly garbled by the mash, which she seemed unable or unwilling to swallow.

None too mild revulsion spread through that corner of the room. "The language on her," recalled a dining-room staffer who turned to flee.

There were guests sitting near her. A man at an adjoining table called over the maître d' and asked, "Why does Mrs. Helmsley let people like this in the hotel?"

"He was pissed," said a waiter who witnessed the scene. "They had two children, a boy and girl, at the table. They were all dressed up. The man is paying three-fifty for a piece of toast. And there's this truck driver sitting next to them."

The man again asked the maître d', "How can you have a lady like that in here?"

And the maître d' answered, with the most proper straight face and softest voice he could muster, "That's no lady. That's Mrs. Helmsley."

From that day on, the dining-room captain would never, ever let anyone sit near Leona's table. Rather, they blocked out the adjoining tables when her appearance was anticipated. The waiters with that space just had to forgo their tips.

That same year, 1981, when Harry Helmsley turned seventy-two, he had his own memorable lunch in the Palace Hotel.

It had been a trying year for the master of real estate. The Palace initially got rave reviews. But it had a $20 million problem. That was the sum that the hotel, suddenly and mysteriously, came in over budget. Harry should have been shocked. Never before in his life had he let his ledgers get so out of hand. But, in effect, he shrugged his shoulders and composed a nice, tidy letter to his investors asking them to help foot this unexpected, but most worthy bill.

They didn't buy it. And they didn't buy it big. Another decade with another set of investors, Harry's ploy might have worked. But these were sophisticated, wealthy men and women who played their own hardball games—fiscally conservative Germans, suspicious Arabian lords, an American industrialist and a shopping-mall magnate, and another American group of savvy investors that included Barbara Sinatra, Frank's wife. Most were in for a million bucks or so.

The investors balked and hired a big-gun attorney to sue. Harry beckoned them to the Palace to keep all the cards from tumbling down.

"It was a very elegant, boozy lunch," recalled the investors' attorney. A couple dozen representative investors were present, along with Helmsley executives who corroborated what happened next.

At 2 P.M., Harry stood up at the lectern, facing the horseshoe-shaped table. He spoke of the marvelous hotel that had just opened. He stressed the restorations, and the painful sight of union-wage artisans using toothbrushes to restore the brownstone walls. He pointed out the praise from architectural and hotel industry critics, the better-than-expected room rates, the likely profit to come rolling in.

Then, his voice grew louder, only slightly, but ever so out of character. "I've heard that a number of you are unhappy with my request," he said with grand understatement. "That those number of you are thinking of filing a lawsuit. That they are ungrateful for all the work that we've done. Well, I have built them the finest hotel in the world. I am a man of principle. AND I WILL NOT BE HAD."

But Harry Helmsley had been had. And not long after that meeting, a private investigation launched by the investors turned up the very same sort of evidence—mysterious invoices, unaccountable charges, expenditures for other hotels billed to the Palace—that seven years later got the Helmsleys in trouble with the state and federal tax collectors.

That government trouble stemmed from their alleged doctoring of invoices to make Helmsley businesses pay for improvements to their weekend retreat in Greenwich, Connecticut. Federal prosecutors are alleging that the Helmsleys thereby avoided paying $1.2 million in personal income taxes over a three-year period. It's a sum that even their critics concede is petty compared with the $140 million in taxes they did pay. A good many taxpayers couldn't stand up to that margin of error of less than 1 percent. But however insignificant the sum is to the Helmsleys, or unexceptional it is to the public norm, the charges carried penalties of huge fines and years in jail, and the government cranked up its prosecutorial machinery to prove its case, which was assigned to a prosecutor who, six years earlier, had helped win a tax-fraud conviction against the Rev. Sun Myung Moon. A dozen staffers pored over tens of thousands of private Helmsley documents. Seventy-eight sworn witnesses were lined up against Leona and Harry.

The Helmsleys recoiled at the shock waves. They pulled back into themselves. And there, in the inner sanctums of the Palace and Helmsley Enterprises, a private war developed that overshadowed even the government trouble. Harry had been duped, but not by his investors. He'd been taken by the one person in his life he would refuse to blame, and when others around him whose opinions he once trusted pointed the way, Harry stood back and let loyal aides fall as they may. The wounded piled up around the Helmsleys like so much trash after one of their banquets. And that, his closest, most enduring friends could never understand or forgive.

It wasn't always that way. For six decades, Harry Helmsley danced on the lawful side of right and wrong, playing the edge like an astute gambler to amass one of the most incredible real estate empires this country has seen—a $5 billion sweep of towers and hotels from the Empire State Building to a thriving merchant's mart in Los Angeles. Skylines in cities throughout the nation bear his imprint.

He built himself into one of the richest, most respected, most trusted entrepreneurs. He defined consummate deal-making before Donald Trump was born. With a high school education he devoured the federal tax code. Then he flexed his skill, time and again, plying a world where the most secretive dealers, the ones whose names seldom appear even in business pages, wield the most power. In a city of real estate barons, he was crowned the dean.

And then he met Leona.

Theirs is the story of a driven and finally reckless man succumbing to a beautiful but manipulative woman who craved power as few others have craved it.

He came to need her attentions. She went after his crown. And as they danced, she slipped into his empire and pulled him over that fine line between right and wrong that he had so deftly straddled. Along the way, their most devoted were cast off, their closest friends were embittered. Yet, it's not quite the classic case of one corrupting another, because both Helmsleys are blamed.

Leona may have accomplished one of the more cunning coups in contemporary American business. But the world she invaded faults none other than her Harry, who stood by and let it all be.

## CHAPTER 2

# THE CHASE

CHASE NATIONAL BANK, WHOSE NAME LATER CHANGED TO CHASE MAN-hattan, did not, in its early years, have a large interest in real estate. It was a commercial lender. It fueled, primarily, those companies whose business it was to make things. By contrast, its portfolio of mortgage loans—that is, money it loaned out to people in exchange for a lien on their property—was rather tiny.

Its mortgage business grew somewhat in March 1930 when Chase merged with the Equitable Trust Company. The preceding decade had been meteoric for Chase, as it was for its rival, the National City Bank, which later became Citibank. Both institutions bulged with the huge profits of the 1920s. Their rivalry also flared. Both claimed ties to the same prestigious family: John D. Rockefeller's brother William helped found National City in 1901, while his son John Jr. bought heavily into Chase, appointing a director for his 3.8 percent holding. But the merger blew National away for a time. Chase became the world's largest bank in terms of its total resources, which neared $2.7 billion.

The Equitable that merged with Chase dabbled in commercial lending. But it was primarily a trust, making money by managing trusts and estates. On behalf of its clients, Equitable would invest in real estate by buying mortgages. More commonly it would put its clients' funds into what were called mortgage participations, or pools of mortgages that specialists would assemble in order to sell off shares. Thus were the huge mortgages of large office buildings or apartment houses made accessible to the small investor who might want to buy only the equivalent of a few rooms.

In hindsight, of course, the small investors who bought into mortgage participations would have been better off with savings accounts. Because when the stock market crashed in 1929, that rock-solid thing called real estate value started collapsing. An office building in 1932 was no longer worth what it had been in 1928. Value was a thing of demand, and after the crash, the "demand" was selling red apples and pencils on Wall Street. On the other hand, mortgage participations might have seemed a solid deal since the companies issuing them guaranteed payment to the investors, as to both interest earned and principal gained as the real estate value rose. As it turned out, it was the mortgage participation firms that got hit first when values plummeted.

With the collapse, the mortgage participation companies could no longer guarantee the promised payments. They folded, by the dozens. And the whole mess was taken over by the New York State Insurance Department, which in most cases swept in with its own management teams to "rehabilitate" the mortgage firms and to salvage the ailing investment scene.

Thus, Equitable, as it merged with Chase, suddenly found itself steeped in a troubled mortgage business in a bigger way. Even so, Chase with its new Equitable holdings was not an exceptionally large real estate power. A good many other trust administrators were in the same game, scrambling to sort through their portfolio and wring the most from every property.

But what happened next made Chase the biggest mortgage player by far. Because so many people were in distress from the failed mortgage companies, a group of smaller banks eventually combined all their mortgage accounts into a new state-backed entity called the Mortgage

Certificate Loan Corp., which would make loans for a percentage of the investments made by individuals in mortgage participation certificates. After a few years, Chase bought the whole kit and caboodle.

Now Chase had masses of property revolving through its hands. Some it would keep. Much it would not. And one of the most eager customers for the discards was a very young and driven Harry B. Helmsley.

So little has been written about Harry Helmsley that barroom biographers could easily joke about starting Harry's biography with the line: "He was born in a log cabin, which by the time he was two he had subdivided."

Even Harry's real name is not widely known. He was born Henry Brakmann Helmsley, taking his mother's maiden name for his middle name. He quickly swapped Henry for Harry, using the latter in high school and on all but his first deeds and incorporations. Eventually, he would sign everything Harry Helmsley, or more commonly, Harry B. Helmsley. The calligraphy of Harry's signature in his early days included elaborate H's, with extraneous curls and crossings.

In later years, his brokerage firm and his public relations man, Howard Rubenstein, turned out a progression of résumés, but they divulged little of Harry's distant past. None mentioned his parents by name. They did say he was born in northern Manhattan, which was true. Harry was born in the Inwood section—a middle-class suburb isolated in the far northern tip of Manhattan. But they neglected to say that he was raised mainly in the Bronx, where he also plans to be entombed in a family cemetery vault. If he wanted to hide that association, the explanation most likely lies in the stuff of social standing by address. The Bronx was not an unseemly place to call home earlier in this century. But it was an association he might have wanted to dump in light of the borough's serious economic degeneration through the 1960s. The librarian of the Bronx high school where Harry graduated joked when the school discovered it no longer had any copies of his graduation yearbook: "Harry Helmsley bought them all up so people wouldn't know he came from the Bronx." Only to the tenants of his huge Bronx housing complex did he freely admit his roots, and he did so eagerly to soften their anger in what became Harry's longest-running landlord–tenant war.

Harry's was not a pure rags-to-riches rise, but it was cotton-to-cashmere. His parents were middle-class, as was much of the Bronx, where they moved shortly after he was born on March 4, 1909. The Bronx generally lies to the north of Manhattan, separated by the Harlem River.

In the late 1980s Tom Wolfe could write about fear-struck whites working at the Bronx County courthouse feeling they had to emerge en masse at dusk to collect their cars parked a few blocks away in the largely black neighborhood. Newspapers in July 1988 carried stories about a twelve-year-old who took a handgun to summer classes at Harry's high school, but their interest was casual and linked to a rash of city school violence; a twelve-year-old with a deadly weapon in a public place is not on its face a headline-making occurrence. But the Bronx, through this century's first three decades, was going through what historians call its awakening. "The decades from 1890 to 1925 were the innocent years in the Bronx," wrote Lloyd Ultan and Gary Hermalyn in their book documenting that period. "The Bronx grew from an area of small villages and farms to a borough of the nation's greatest metropolis, housing more than one million people. This rapid growth and the changes it brought in its train were almost universally looked upon by the area's residents as signs of progress. The Bronx was on the move, and the future was promising."

Villages formed along ethnic lines. And Manhattan's famed boulevards grew northern extensions. Germans gathered in Morrisania and Melrose, whose main street was called "Dutch Broadway." The Irish chose Kingsbridge, Riverdale, and Mott Haven, where they primarily worked in a foundry and coal yard; Irish physicians concentrated along Alexander Avenue, giving it the nickname "Irish Fifth Avenue." Black families made homes in Williamsbridge and near 163rd Street in Morrisania. Jews settled in Mott Haven and Hunts Point.

The Bronx was farm country, interspersed with industry, through the turn of the century. Villages were no more than a few blocks in size—hamlets surrounded by farmland and orchards and wild fields. Streets were improved for only short stretches. The houses were wood frame. There were few renters; most people owned their homes. Few people could be described as very poor. The borough's rich mostly congregated in Riverdale alongside the Hudson River two villages north of Manhattan. Suburbia, however, moved in fast, bringing adventuresome entrepreneurs like Harry's maternal grandfather, who made a good living buying and managing apartment buildings.

Harry lived for a time with his parents at 1478 Grand Boulevard and Concourse near 176th Street, on the edge of the village of Tremont. The Grand ran north-south, an extension of Lexington Avenue in Manhattan. Opening farmland to the city's sprawl, it was paved the year Harry was born and became a major artery, splendid with its stately rows of Art Deco homes and apartment buildings.

Harry is the son of Henry Helmsley, a notions buyer for a wholesale dry-goods firm, and Minnie Brakmann, the landlord's daughter. Their religion was Lutheran.

Harry has spoken little of his parents, to either friend or reporter. But two references he has made reveal his attitude toward them in hindsight. Harry liked to say that the reason he bought his first building in 1936 was to provide his dad employment superintending the building. "I was supporting him anyhow," Harry told *The Wall Street Journal*. "One of the reasons I wanted to buy the property was so he could get a job."

Harry's father may have been an embarrassment to Harry, who throughout his own life measured success—in friends and strangers alike—only in dollars. Frederick Papert was head of the Municipal Art Society and worked closely with Harry in the late 1970s during the tortuous planning of the Helmsley Palace, into which Harry was finally persuaded to incorporate the brown sandstone landmark houses built by the journalist and railroad magnate Henry Villard in 1884. Villard accomplished a great deal in his lifetime, but he had a wild entrepreneurial streak that caused him to die rather poor. "When it was all over I said to [Harry], 'There can't be any question that you're going to call the hotel the Villard Hotel,'" Papert recalled. "But it was the one thing with which he disagreed with me and he stuck to his guns. He said he would not name a hotel after a failed businessman."

By contrast, Harry credited to his mother, Minnie Brakmann,

nothing less than his whole career. "The best advice I ever got was from my mother," he told *Good Housekeeping* magazine in 1983. "It was simply, 'Buy real estate.' And like a dutiful son I bought and bought and continue to buy throughout this country."

Harry had one sibling, a brother named Walter six years his junior, whom Harry took under his corporate wing. Walter worked for his older brother for twenty-six years. He became a vice president-treasurer of Harry's real estate brokerage firm. He bought into Manhattan properties with his older brother. And he managed as many as twenty-five buildings at one time before retiring to Delray Beach, Florida, in 1966. Walter Helmsley died in 1974.

Harry's terrible eyesight kept him from a number of things, including going to war. He had to wear thick heavy glasses. Moreover, his eyelids drooped, forcing him into a permanent squint and giving him Asian-looking eyes to go with his large, squared head. Harry eventually had his eyes widened through surgery—a part cosmetic, part medical operation that improved his sight—but not until he was in his late seventies.

He attended Evander Childs High School on Gun Hill Road, the second upper school to be opened in the Bronx. According to school officials, Harry did quite well for himself. His Regents exams showed particularly good scores in economics, advertising, law, and French. "I used to go to football games, when I was a kid, at the Catholic Prefectory grounds," he recalled once, adding, in case the reporter misinterpreted, that he only watched. "I'm not a football player."

Though the *New York Post*, in its biographical snippets of Harry, preferred to say he dropped out, he did in fact graduate from high school in 1925 at age sixteen. Indeed, he was one of two dozen kids, out of a class of more than 125, who received their "diploma awarded with honors," according to the Evander Oriole yearbook. Harry's name is on a darkening brass plaque for the school's honor roll. It was not unusual to succeed out of Evander at the time. Many of Harry's classmates went to New York University, Columbia, or other good schools. Although he took college courses, particularly in history, through the extension services of New York and Columbia universities, as well as from the YMCA, Harry did not attend college. He went to work to help support his family, and like other young men at the time, he blanketed the city with letters of application for work.

The New York that Harry Helmsley stepped into was undergoing a boom. The 1920s were awash with good fortune for many, and the city—especially Manhattan—was bursting with new development. The frenzy translated into steel and cement, and height. "The city is in upheaval," *The New York Times* editorialized in 1926. "In not more than half a dozen years the skyline of midtown Manhattan has been lifted a hundred feet. . . . American vision, daring, restlessness, engineering skill have all been properly read into this marvelous transformation from brownstone in Babylon."

The boom was mainly in office buildings, which were in big demand after a construction halt during World War I. "Business rules the world today, and as long as business can best be served where many offices are concentrated in one small area . . . business architecture will be supreme," Sheldon Cheney wrote in *The New World Architecture* in 1930.

There was a myriad of reasons why the construction industry suddenly went rampant: expanding companies needed more space, corporations saw a promotional boon in putting their name on a new headquarters, and spiraling land values and taxes drove property owners to replace their underdeveloped properties with bigger buildings that would generate more cash every month.

The speculation that poured through the stock exchange spilled over into land and buildings, especially as buildings came to be included in the new consumerist mores that encouraged the replacement of everything grown obsolete. One-eighth of the national income was spent on buildings in 1925, and there developed what's now known as the real estate "flip," wherein a piece of land or building changes hands in rapid succession with the chain of owners doing little more than finding new buyers who'll pay more than they did. When it comes to apartments, flipping usually devastates the tenants, since the short-term owners don't care about upkeep or the building's long-term future. In land and commercial developments, flipping means higher prices and higher rents.

Of course, the stock-market crash of 1929 changed all that. As in the October 1987 plummet, there was a delayed reaction to the '29 crash in real estate circles. Things entrepreneurial did not immediately close down. Much of the construction that had begun continued. For several years after, skeletons of steel were still going up in Manhattan. The gaudy, commercial Art Deco-styled Chrysler Building in midtown, the Cities Service tower on Wall Street, and several bank skyscrapers all went up after the crash. Even the limestone-and-granite Empire State Building in lower midtown Manhattan didn't open until May 1, 1931. And then the frenzy stopped, like a party spoiled by a fight, and a dread quiet fell over the city.

Harry Helmsley played a small role in that drama, taking a job with Dwight, Voorhis & Perry, one of several hundred real estate firms operating in Manhattan during the boom. Harry joined the company in 1925, and his first task, at $12 a week, was running errands during the upward-spinning 1920s. He learned on the ground how unlimited numbers of unsophisticated investors would willingly risk their life savings in real estate, and that they would do extraordinarily well as long as property values rose. Even terrible buildings—that is, those whose operating costs exceeded the income from rents—were winners if their value went up. The Roaring Twenties covered up a lot of mistakes.

But then very quickly the young Helmsley tasted the downside. He saw investors lose all they'd gained and more. He'd see even the best buildings—those whose rental income exceeded the cost of heating and maintaining the structure—slip-slide in value as the market sank. Pennies suddenly counted where dollars were plentiful. Harry saw the owners scramble to squeeze the most from their tenants, and tenants maneuver to make ends meet every month when the bill collectors called.

Gathering rents in person was a common and necessary chore in those days, especially after the crash. Not everyone was cashing in on the 1920s, and the biggest bill also was the most tempting to put off. The majority of rent collectors packed a pistol, with a city permit, though most never had to brandish their guns. The bank was lenient with its tenants. It had to be. For many people there was simply no way to pay on time, and for a long while there were few evictions, in large part because a slow-paying tenant was better than none at all. The rent collector's job was to encourage gently, and be there before others came to be paid.

"These were difficult times," James Bloor recalled. Bloor was twenty-five years old when he began collecting rents for the Chase National Bank in 1932. His turf was Harlem. "People were in need. They tried to pay the landlord after the grocery bill was paid. So you had to be persistent and keep after them or else they'd run you five or six months' rent and you'd have to evict. You had to be tough, but sympathetic as well. It was an interesting experience, but short-lived, thank God." Bloor, though hardly unkind or unsympathetic to the tenants, abided by formal and rather strict rules. Though at times he would be beseeched with travails of some sort or other, usually honest accounts of family hardship, he did not play the social worker. "I stayed away from that. I was up there for one purpose, to collect the rent," he said.

Among the routine, Bloor experienced the bizarre. His Harlem turf was a mixture of Spanish, Italian, and Asian families. "We took over a house on 109th Street, on the East Side. I still remember the address," Bloor recalled in his Manhattan office, where, in 1988, at eighty years old he was still working—as the court-appointed trustee of a huge real estate bankruptcy. "Everybody was Spanish-speaking, so I got the superintendent, because I wanted to be introduced under proper auspices, so people would know who I was and what I looked like. We started ringing doorbells, and I came to one apartment and somebody called out from the farthest reaches in Spanish. The superintendent responded in Spanish and he turned to me and said, 'We have to wait a while.' So after a while I heard somebody unlock the door, and I started to go in, and he said, 'Wait, wait.' So we waited until we heard somebody call out from the apartment's far end again and we went in. There was no furniture at all in the living room, dining area, and kitchen. Then we went into the bedroom and there were two or three chairs, a trunk, and a bed with two men in it and a woman between them. What the relationship of these people was, I had no idea and didn't ask."

Harry Helmsley's turf included Hell's Kitchen, a square mile of

Manhattan's far western flank filled with freight yards, factories, warehouses, stock pens, and tenements. Just prior to Harry's arrival on the scene, Hell's Kitchen suffered under the country's toughest gangs, and had a reputation as the most dangerous real estate. The area was named for a gang organized in 1868, and even the Hell's Kitchen that Harry entered was extraordinary for its grime and poverty.

Harry also worked the garment center and the flower and fur districts, which lay to the east between Hell's Kitchen and Broadway, stretching north from Twenty-fifth to Forty-first streets. Though still bustling, the garment center today is a mere shadow of the frenzy during the 1930s. Then it was New York City's largest industry, ranking fourth in the country, and the streets were vibrant with commerce.

There were a lot of young rent collectors in those days, and as might be guessed, young Harry worked harder than anyone else. In the afternoons a pack who plied the Hell's Kitchen area would make off to a movie theater near Madison Square. But not Harry Helmsley. He had other things on his mind, recalled Allan Taub, a real estate broker. "I once said to him, 'I notice you don't go with the others to the movies. What are you doing with yourself?' And he said, 'I'm studying real estate in the afternoon so I can be a broker.'"

Two things happened to Harry Helmsley in those rent-collecting days. One, he made friends with people who would later sit in very high places, and they would share a close bond from having met in hard times, like buddies who met in a war. And two, he learned how to size up a building. Both things he did probably better than anyone else, and both things helped make his career.

The friends Harry made were the bankers and other financial-institution types whose property he would manage, or buy and sell, through the Depression. Harry ingratiated himself with them, collecting rents and then turning deals that made sense and money for everyone involved. At the time the friends Harry made were just low-level staffers. But Harry had a keen sense for others who were driven like him, and he drew himself to those he felt were going places. They did. Even as Harry built his empire, they built theirs, becoming the chief executive officers and board chairmen of the world's great financial institutions. "He's had great relationships with these people and they have the highest regard for him as a person of the highest ability and integrity," said Peter Malkin, a partner in the firm, Wien, Malkin & Bettex, which hammered the legal points into many of Harry's real estate deals.

One such contact was James Bloor, who graduated from rent collecting to managing Chase National's burgeoning portfolio of property. It was through Bloor's office door, starting in 1936, that a smiling, friendly, and ever so smart Harry Helmsley would stroll, looking for deals.

Harry was learning to play the matchmaker. Chase was usually looking to sell a piece of Manhattan, having acquired foreclosures or forced its own. It would post a weekly listing of properties it wanted to unload. Others were looking to buy. But this was the Depression. Investment money was scarce and suddenly much smarter than it had been in the 1920s. So Harry acquired his second skill—one perhaps even more critical to his empire building than the contacts he made. Harry learned how to look a building up and down and appraise its value to within cents. But more than that, Harry learned how to see potential in buildings to which others were blind.

In those days he mostly brokered what looked like mongrel dogs: second- and third-rate buildings, often worn down on the outside and lacking in either status or tenants. But he would see their inner charm that would make all the difference to a canny investor. Sometimes the advantage would be its location. Harry would find some way to capitalize on a building's proximity to a railroad depot or manufacturing plant. Sometimes it would be the tenants. He would look at the rent rolls and figure out ways to find better-paying renters. Always he would look at the cost side, figuring ways to cut heating bills or slim down the superintendent staff. And the result would be that he would discover buildings on which owners could make money—not much money by 1920s standards, but enough in the Depression. The buildings would be ones that hordes of other brokers would pass over.

"He had superman powers, to see through walls and see what was there, [what] people with normal vision couldn't see. He was just one of those people," said one of Helmsley's closest aides, a veteran real estate attorney and broker who asked not to be identified because he now handles several key and delicate projects for Harry.

Bloor was also impressed by Harry Helmsley, on both business and personal levels. "He was a very persistent guy. He would come into the Chase and say, 'What are you selling today?' so to speak. Or he would learn through the public records or the grapevine that we had foreclosed, or had acquired title to a piece of property in some way or other. And he would inquire as to what our price was, what we were looking for.

"Then he would go out, look at the property, analyze the income operating certificates. He would attempt to find a buyer for the property. And occasionally he met with success. Or occasionally as far as Chase was concerned. I'm sure he was calling on Mutual of New York and Metropolitan Life and the others who were overburdened with foreclosed real estate."

Helmsley's business morals also impressed Bloor. The first thing out of Harry as he walked through the door was a smile—a simple, honest smile. "He was a real estate salesman, but he was not pushy in that sense," Bloor said. Moreover, not once did Harry Helmsley engage in any of the ethically questionable practices that were as common in those days as they are today. Bloor, in fact, was a stickler to the point that he would not even lunch with brokers.

"I made it a practice and have always in my business life never to put myself under the obligation of anyone I was doing business with," said Bloor, whose associates point to his court appointeeship as proof of his purity. "Harry walked in the door, discussed with me or other people I worked with what we had for sale. Or he would make an offer for a piece of property, and would then go on his way. I can't recall a single incident in connection with Mr. Helmsley where there was anything under the table. Never."

Harry took his contacts, his sixth sense about property, and his straight, easy way with people, and with them he ran.

Harry became an infrequent voice in the short items that appeared in *The New York Times*'s real estate section, whose semi-advertisement articles were in those days even more aligned with the real estate community than they are today. The real estate sections of the *Times* and to a lesser extent the other dailies were the only places outside of the industry papers where a real estate man or woman would want to be seen. After all, serious news coverage invariably would drag in such untidy matters as the interest that tenants or the community and tax-payers at large might have in a development.

Harry made a wide range of real estate news by weighing in on the day's debate. In July 1930, amidst the first stirrings for new laws to control rents, there was Harry B. Helmsley unloading some different opinions about city tax policy during the Depression. Everyone would be much better off if the owners of unprofitable buildings would be allowed to simply close them down and not have to continue paying taxes, he argued. "It costs almost as much to operate a building that is 30 percent rented as to operate one 95 percent rented," he was quoted as saying. "It is, therefore, obvious that the greater percentage of rentals in a building will mean a greater profit to the landlord. If, therefore, certain non-productive buildings were closed, the tenants would go to the buildings that were open and so would enable those owners to carry their buildings and to pay their taxes promptly."

A few years passed before his next appearance in the *Times*, in 1936, when he fought a decision by Langdon Post, the Tenement House Commissioner, to enforce the law requiring apartment-building hallways to be fireproofed. Helmsley warned that the unwanted result would be slum clearance. "The effect of this legislation will not be the expenditure of large sums to modernize slums but it will tend to force owners of tenements into foreclosure or will force them to close their buildings," Helmsley said. He predicted spiraling rents, as people moved out of their $1-a-week fire-hazard apartments and drove up the demand for non-lethal space. He also foresaw the advent of public housing, which he viewed like a farmer seeing locusts. "As soon as this situation becomes acute, the result will be government low-cost hous-ing. Perhaps that was the purpose of the enforcement of the act," he said.

Twelve months later, with Langdon Post now starting to build low-cost apartments as head of the new city Housing Authority, Helmsley was trying to explain away rent increases on higher operat-ing costs and municipal spending on public services. "It is through the law of supply and demand that rents eventually find a level which will pay taxes, operating expenses and a fair return on investment," Helmsley said. "As the proportion of the tax burden to the total expense of real estate increases, it is obvious that rents must also increase. This increase of rent will be of no value to the owner, as he will act solely as a collection agent for the city. Rent payers in New York must realize that the rent they pay includes municipal service, and as they obtain more service from the city they must set aside a larger proportion of their income for rent. If the present tendency toward a greater service continues, there will be a new yardstick as to the amount of rent that should be paid. Instead of 25 percent of the income, there will be 33 percent budgeted for rent."

In 1940–41, reporters rang up Helmsley for expert opinions on Twenty-third Street, where he bought his first office building in 1936, and on commercial lofts on the West Side of Manhattan from Chelsea to Hell's Kitchen, where after collecting rents he began brokering buildings. "Not since 1927," he said authoritatively, "has the situation in the loft market been so bright. Naturally, this is due primarily to the expanding defense program." The average occupancy rate in his company's buildings was 93 percent, said Helmsley, who was eager to help with the war. "New York, with its thousands of small manufacturers, will at last be given a chance to prove that it, too, can produce for the defense of the country and will convert its machines to war production. All this effort will require loft space which can be provided in New York at fair rentals," he said in January 1942.

Also to help with the war effort, Helmsley urged the razing of the last standing sections of the Second Avenue El, the elevated tracks. The El was essential transport, especially for the city's working class. It was as fast as the subway and had far nicer views. But it was also the bane of adjacent property owners, and Harry Helmsley had no trouble choosing sides. "This eyesore, which long ago ceased to have an indispensable value, is going to be torn down eventually anyway," he told the *Times*. "Under ordinary circumstances there might not be any hurry about it, but with the urgent need for metal the job should be done immediately." He went on to complain about the El's "cost per passenger being 15 cents whereas only 5 cents is paid. This causes a drain on the city finances. All luxuries of this type at this time should be eliminated."

Helmsley then attacked the tax assessor for what he and many in the real estate industry felt were unfair assessments. And he attacked by counterpunching with a pair of his own suggestions. One idea would have forced the assessor to lower his assessments by requiring the city to buy any private property that the owner felt had been assessed too high. The other was to link real estate taxes to income—the income, that is, of the entire city. Taxes thus would more neatly rise and fall with wage levels, he argued, unburdening the landlord during times of economic depression.

The news stories also chart Harry Helmsley's initial corporate rise. He had no title in 1930. By 1936, he was cited as secretary in his firm. Two years later he was vice president, of a firm with a new name: Dwight, Voorhis & Helmsley. Of the partner he replaced, Perry, Helmsley said to *The Wall Street Journal,* "Poor John Perry, he was such a great salesman, such a wonderful man. Three years went by without his making a penny in a commission on a sale." And in 1943, the Harry Helmsley being quoted was company president.

The same years Helmsley was winning a place on his company's doorplate, he made two big personal moves. He acquired his first deed, and he married, for the first time. Both steps plunged Harry Helmsley into the life of a hardworking, tightfisted, conservative industrialist.

The Religious Society of Friends, or Quakers, whose members now number several hundred thousand, dates itself to the year 1652, when George Fox stood on Pendle Hill in northern England and had a vision of "a great people to be gathered."

The New World was rough going for the new Quakers. Puritans in Massachusetts rejected them outright as they began arriving in the late 1650s; four Quakers were hanged in Boston. Their welcome was only slightly less inhospitable in New York City, where the Dutch under Peter Stuyvesant rebuffed their advances. The reaction was understandable. The Quakers then were the brimstone-and-fire evangelical Christians of the New World, and felt it their mission to proselytize and convert everyone in sight.

Their common name, Quaker—which Friends have never adopted

but don't consider a term of reproach—was itself a poke at what others saw of their early ways. It derived, according to a seventeenth-century chronicler of religions, "from people's shaking and quaking that received them and their doctrine." The Quakers were known to be plain dressers, with some rather stiff body language. Ofttimes they could be separated in crowds for not wearing periwigs. They were not big on parties. Rather, they were industrious. As one observer wrote, their code was to "maintain none of their poor who can work in idleness." They rebelled against authority. And they were pacifists. They fought no official wars, and worked at keeping their own personal lives free of combat. The big guns on ships that failed to discharge were named after them.

Quakers today, especially through the American Friends Service Committee, are perhaps best known for their deep commitment to making peace and helping those hurt by war. AFSC members accomplish an extraordinary amount of work toward those ends. But for much of United States' developing years they were its foremost industrialists and builders. And it was the most conservative branch of the New York Friends chapter that Eve Ella Sherpick Green joined in 1934 after the death of her first husband. Arthur Green had graduated from Lehigh College and was bound for success. "He was a very fine man," said Eve. "He had a business job, I don't remember just what. It was a very good one. It took us to Boston." Arthur Green died in an auto accident, and Eve returned home to New York.

Eve and Harry Helmsley were married on February 25, 1938. It was a very plain Friends Meeting House ceremony. "It was the simplest sort of thing possible," said Eve. "People go to the Friends Meeting House, and then you marry each other. There's nothing special. Before we became married, I had been a member and he became interested in Friends." Two years later Harry was accepted as a Friend into the conservative Twentieth Street Monthly Meeting by Eve's nomination.

Harry's work with the Meeting House was predictable. He became the auditor in 1948, and then worked on a charitable fund that spent money helping blacks, American Indians, and the poor in general, and on distributing books "tending to promote piety and virtue and the truths of Christianity." Its assets hovered around $50,000. Harry was its treasurer throughout his marriage to Eve. Harry also served on another library-supporting fund.

Serving with Helmsley on the Murray Fund was Eve's brother, Eugene "Ship" A. Sherpick, who died in 1964. Ship Sherpick was a successful and influential attorney. He was a law partner of U.S. Court of Appeals Judge Harold Medina before Medina's appointment to the bench. He served as a special referee of the state Supreme Court. He became president of the New York County Lawyers Association. Sherpick handled some of Harry's very first real estate buys.

Helmsley worked on Quaker business with James Wood, the son of attorney L. Hollingsworth Wood and a rising power in the Bank of New York. Now retired, Wood continues his work for the New York Monthly Meeting as a fundraiser. He called on Helmsley in 1983 for several thousand dollars to purchase a new air conditioner for the records room. But there's reason to believe that Helmsley's pockets for the Friends will go much, much deeper upon his death.

Eve and Harry Helmsley's first home was an apartment in a building at 55 Tiemann Place, a short, two-block street just north of Riverside Park in Manhattan's Upper West Side, in a neighborhood dominated by Columbia University housing. They then moved to Gramercy Park.

Gramercy was for many decades one of the city's most exclusive neighborhoods. It was built for exclusivity. Its creator, Samuel Ruggles, was one of the first real estate entrepreneurs who realized there was premium money to be made in offering exclusiveness. So atop the marshland that the Dutch in the seventeenth century had named Krom Moerasje, or "little crooked swamp," he laid out in 1831 an English-style square of paths and greenery and gave it to the city with the proviso that it be held forever for the exclusive use of Gramercy Park area residents. A heavy black iron fence was put up to surround and insulate the park. The nightly northward flow of Bowery bums, the tens of thousands of homeless men who alternately stayed in ten-cent dormitories and roamed about the city at night keeping warm or hunting for dawn bakery giveaways, would just have to pass by Gramercy. The golden keys that were first handed out to buyers of Ruggles's adjacent sixty-six lots were replaced with simpler metals, but the effect remains today: steel gates and eight-foot-tall fencing keep the public out.

Among those who still lived on Gramercy when the Helmsleys arrived were Joseph Day, perhaps the world's largest real estate operator at the time, and John Gregg, owner of the Gregg School of Shorthand. Just a block away on Nineteenth Street was a colony of artists and writers living in a group of remodeled houses, including Ida Tarbell, the corporation-slaying journalist, Clara Fargo Thomas, the muralist, and sculptor George Julian Solnay. A few stately red-brick homes remained on Gramercy, but most of the large old brownstone homes were replaced in the early 1930s with seventeen- and eighteen-story apartment houses. The Helmsleys moved into one at 45 Gramercy Park North.

Their apartment faced south, with a view of the park, and soaked in sun on those cold winter days when Harry would be off to the office and Eve would go about her own work at home and with the Quaker Meeting House.

"Eve was very friendly with my mother," recalled Peter Krulewitch, a third-generation New York real estate entrepreneur who moved to 45 Gramercy with his parents in 1946. The Krulewitches lived three floors up, in a similar eight-room apartment. "We moved out in 1960 when they co-oped the building, because my father thought the price—$280,000—was too high and he was going to show the owner." Of course, the apartment's worth has long since shot past $1 million.

"I remember we used to get postcards from Eve from all over. And it was funny, because she would never send letters. They cost more. She would always send postcards instead. She was a dear, sweet lady," he said.

Louise Addis, another 45 Gramercy resident, also remembered the Helmsleys, though she was a working career woman with children and her interaction with the Helmsleys was only occasional. With Harry gone early and back late, she would mostly meet and greet only Eve in the elevator. "I knew them only slightly, but I admired her terribly, and always wondered what happened to her," Addis said of Eve. She recalled one encounter in particular. "Everyone had maids then. And my daughter, who was five or six, came home and rang the doorbell and the maid [must have been] doing something because she didn't hear her. Well, Mrs. Helmsley took her and cared for her until the maid or someone came home. That was so typical of how thoughtful she was."

Charming and delightful. Kind and thoughtful. Caring. Educated and very attractive-looking. That's how Eve was remembered by Addis and others in those days. Eve herself remembers it only vaguely, but pleasantly. "The park was lovely," she said. "And the Meeting House was right across from us."

Harry had to walk but three blocks from Gramercy to his office in one of the city's most famous buildings. It was originally named the Fuller Building. But that soon gave way to a nickname, the Flatiron, whose tall triangular shape has graced thousands of black-and-white postcards of the city. Because Broadway sweeps up the narrow island of Manhattan at a slight angle, it forms a half dozen little triangles of land when slicing across the other north-south-running avenues. Most often the wedges were made into parks. In 1902, the twenty-one-story Flatiron went up on the triangle formed by the intersection of Broadway, Fifth Avenue, and Twenty-third Street.

The Flatiron marked a turning point in structural engineering. Rather than height being limited by a ratio of bulk between the floor area and thickness of walls, the Flatiron's innovative steel frame carried the weight floor by floor. The steel permitted new heights, or in this case, a very narrow building. At its bow, the Flatiron has only a twenty-one-story string of curved windows.

Just to the north of the Flatiron was Madison Square and the first two sites of the entertainment Garden. (It later was renamed Madison Square Garden when it moved uptown.) It was here that William Jennings Bryan won the Democratic nomination for President, Bill Brennan was floored by Jack Dempsey for the heavyweight title, and John Ringling put on his circus shows. But Harry Helmsley would have been more interested in the old Garden's successor, the New York Life Insurance Company Building, which opened just before the stock-market crash. Even closer to home and his office, the Metropolitan Life Insurance Company had already built its fifty-floor headquarters on Twenty-third Street. Both places Harry Helmsley would visit weekly looking for foreclosure bargains.

Helmsley got to know the area intimately, and what he saw he liked, or at least boosted to others. "Improving 23d Street Area: H. B. Helmsley Sees Progress Enhanced by Many New Buildings," read a headline in *The New York Times* in the winter of 1940. But it was in the modernization of older buildings that Harry had taken a particular interest.

From his small office on West Twenty-third Street, where he moved after working out of the Flatiron, Harry roamed the area hunting for deals. "In 1940, there were really only a few of us working in the office at 137 West Twenty-third Street," said Alvin Schwartz, who left Harry's side in 1949 but returned to become one of his two key associates. "Harry was the management man, but he was also running the office inside and doing some brokerage too. It was about this time that he started buying buildings."

Harry and Eve both bought into the Flatiron Building, acquiring three-sixteenths and one-sixteenth, respectively, in 1951, when Harry also became the treasurer of the partnership that owned the building. Five years earlier he found an older loft building on Twenty-second Street just a block from the Flatiron, and it was purchased by a foursome split evenly among Eve, his brother Walter, Eve's sister-in-law Nelle Sherpick, and Dorothy Schwartz, the daughter of Helmsley's longtime partner Leon Spear and the wife of Helmsley's longtime associate Alvin Schwartz. Harry was the broker. Eve's brother, Eugene Sherpick, handled the papers through his law firm, Sherpick & Medina. Sherpick also helped Helmsley set up the first of the hundreds of dummy corporations he would use to buy and hold his property— Random Realty, incorporated in 1941 and dissolved in 1946. (It was at Random that Helmsley used his given name, Henry, on official documents for the last time.)

Harry bought his own first building in 1936. He walked by the building—across from Met Life—every day and often he would stand out front and count the number of people who went into its ground-floor store. What he saw, of course, were walking dollar signs and the positive side of the cost/benefit equation that would indicate whether operating the building could earn him money.

Harry belonged to the Twenty-third Street Association, and once when they met on a rotating basis at the famous Schrafft's, Harry talked excitedly about the building. Harry decided to take the plunge when he discovered he could get the aging ten-story loft building for a steal. He paid a mere $1,000 for a building with a $100,000 mortgage because the owner was in grave danger of being foreclosed on, and went about fixing it up. It was in this building that he installed his father as the elevator operator and super.

It's unclear where Harry got the $1,000 stake. Other brokers later came to believe it was Eve who bankrolled Harry, though they weren't married until 1938, two years after he bought the building. More than one Manhattan real estate magnate got his start by marrying someone with money. Eve did have money, and Harry gained access both to it and to the political influence of her attorney brother when he married Eve. "They became friends, we became connected," said Eve, who couldn't recall how the Twenty-third Street building was financed. Harry told a reporter once that he used his mother's savings.

In any case, it became one of his favorite stories to tell reporters. "They were willing to let me buy their mortgage for $1,000—my only $1,000—and I took over the building's debt," he said once. Here, he learned with his own investment at stake how to squeeze a solid building for everything it was worth. "I watched the building's expenses, such as fuel, electricity, and the payroll. I made sure that there wasn't one extra man on the staff. One extra employee could cost $3,000 in those days, and that made the difference as to whether I could pay the mortgage. I also knew the building had vacancies that I could fill." He roamed the area for new tenants to fill every space.

It was a devoted approach to a timeworn equation: increase the benefit and decrease the cost. He did what he was learning to do best. And then he learned firsthand another vital lesson that affected the way he would build his empire: he held on to the property until the time was right to sell.

He sat. He waited. And then, just after the war, he got his price: $165,000, for a net gain in ten years of about $100,000. Harry Helmsley was on his way.

## CHAPTER 3

# A HATTER'S DAUGHTER

IF HARRY HELMSLEY WAS SHY ABOUT HIS FAMILY AND EARLY YEARS, Leona Helmsley has tended toward the evasive, even the misleading, in discussing her pedigree with friends or in public.

The reason is not self-explanatory. Few would find fault in her for her distant past. But even when forced into court and subjected to oaths, she prefers to trim her past to a tight one-verb sentence, as in this July 1983 response: "I was a model, married woman, divorced woman, real estate, senior vice president, and in real estate of my own firm, and hotels."

She rarely admits her age. She actually lies about her birthplace, claiming to be a New York City native. She never speaks of her second divorce and a third separation. Nor does she ever speak of her parents or siblings. "She just doesn't discuss her family," her publicity agent would tell reporters flatly. Most intriguing about the mysterious Leona is her name, or rather, her succession of names.

Some facts about her birth are revealed by official records. She was born on the Fourth of July 1920. The time was estimated at 6 A.M. The locale was the High Falls district of Marbletown, a hamlet due north of New York City in hilly Ulster County. The birthplace was home, registered on a certificate by a doctor four days later.

But one item on Leona's birth certificate was left very unclear: her name. It reads "Lena Rosenthol." The surname is almost certainly misspelled. There are few, if any, Rosenthols in the world. There are many, many Rosenthals, and that's the spelling Leona used for a time. But Lena might have been listed correctly. Her parents were new immigrants. Both Lena and Leona were names used in the Old World, with Lena being the more common of the two.

At any rate, it didn't seem to matter to Leona just how her first name was originally spelled. At other times in her life she would use Leni, and the nicknames Mindy and Lee. Her legal signature is something else again. The first letter is a large, looping sweep of an *L*. Then follows what looks like a lowercase *l*, open-looped and distinct from the capitalized *L*. Next comes a normal-shaped *e*, followed by a distinct *o* and *n* and *a*. The second *l* appears regularly, and baffles both handwriting experts and her own staff. She uses the middle initial M.

If Leona wanted to hide the basic facts of her birth, she couldn't have picked a better place to be born. New York State has the strictest of laws regarding the privacy of birth certificates, census records, and marriage licenses and divorce papers. It treats them as state secrets.

There was one file, however, that Leona could not legally seal. Not only did it contain the only public copy of her birth certificate. It held something even more intriguing: the court order permitting Leona to officially change her surname from Rosenthal to Roberts.

That move in itself is not unusual. Untold numbers of Jews were forced to change their last names to avoid persecution in America. What is odd about the filing is that she waited so long to make her adopted name legal.

～

Marbletown was booming in 1920. Construction of the Delaware-Hudson Canal had brought thousands of laborers up from New York City. They were mainly Irish, Italian, and Polish. The cement mills were the big employers, turning out a first-class, superior binder known as Rosendale Cement, which builders would use in their finest projects or in others, sparingly, to upgrade lesser cements. It might have been Harry and Leona's one little quirky connection to the past—she having been planted in the very spot in the world where he derived the very essence of his empire.

The day Leona was born, the Fourth of July was celebrated with a parade, big marching bands, and a picnic to while away the afternoon.

The town was peaceful, pleasant, and very Old World in its village ways. Shopping entailed a visit to half a dozen shops—the butcher, the bakery, and, now and then, the hatter. "Oh, they made beautiful hats at that time," said Margory Quick, whose father ran the Rockcliff Hotel in High Falls, the section of Marbletown where Leona was born. "My Aunt Rose made hats, and people in Kingston made hats too."

Morris Rosenthal was a hatter, though he seems to have taken up the more mundane ends of the business, specializing at one point in army caps. Rosenthal, a Polish immigrant, was thirty-two when Leona was born. His wife, Ida Popkin, also Polish, was thirty. She listed her occupation as housewife, and she cared for two other daughters and a son.

Leona confided in very few people about her parents. Her long-time personal secretary, Maryann Eboli, said Leona seemed to be more fond of her father, but spoke little of either. "Her mother was a tyrant. That's how she described her," said Eboli. The Rosenthal children gravitated toward their father, who was soft-spoken and almost shy around his wife.

Leona's family was plagued by poor health. Her father died at age fifty-two of heart disease. Several of his children led sickly lives to varying degrees. One of Leona's older sisters, Sylvia, was very obese, diabetic, and wheelchair-bound in her later years. Her younger brother, Alvin, had a brain tumor in his later years and gained enough weight at times so that Leona was constantly after him to diet.

Leona had neither her father's heart disease nor any other ailment that afflicted her siblings. She grew up strong—the strongest in a physically weak family. Leona and her sister Sandra had the best looks; Sylvia and Alvin grew up rotund, with bulbous faces. But Leona always thought Sandra was at least a shade prettier than she, and a jealousy festered. She eventually turned on both her sisters, accusing Sandra of abandoning her when Sandra married a man with money at a time when Leona was scraping, and spurning Sylvia for not taking care of herself. With neither sister was she on good speaking terms when they died in the early 1980s. She refused to attend either funeral, and though she did pay for annual memorial services for her sisters, she stopped attending those after a couple of years. But Leona always did care for her little brother, Alvin, getting Harry to bring him into the Helmsley business and treating him a notch above other aides.

Sometime after Leona was born, Marbletown began losing its economic fire. The big change was the inevitable completion of the D & H Canal. That sent the engineers and laborers packing, and hurt the local economy throughout.

The Rosenthals left Ulster County for New York City just before Leona would have started school.

They moved to the borough of Brooklyn, to its far southern reaches that touch the Atlantic Ocean, where Jews as far back as the late 1800s congregated to pool their collective meager resources.

The Rosenthals never settled. Leona popped up in half a dozen places in the first eighteen years of her life. The Rosenthals first lived on Mermaid Avenue on Coney Island. The street runs the length of the island one block inland from Surf Avenue, where the beach meets the Astroland Amusement Park and its famed landmarked wooden Cyclone Roller Coaster. Mermaid is not now, nor was it then, a place where anyone wanted to live. It's always been one of the first stopping places for immigrants—very poor, very shabby, very isolated socially and economically. The high-rise low-rent apartment buildings are interspersed with rubble-strewn vacant lots and junked cars. Many residents, including old Eastern European Jews, do not speak English.

From Mermaid the family moved to West Thirty-third Street, and then to several other homes in Coney Island and adjacent Bensonhurst. Bensonhurst then was the next step up from Coney Island, and today it's a neighborhood right out of the television sitcom *All in the Family*. The area surrounding Leona's elementary and junior high school is pretty and very residential with tree-lined streets and two-story brick or aluminum-siding houses with porches. The school, Seth Low, is and has been almost entirely Jewish. It's also poor.

Leona attended Abraham Lincoln High School, but only for a semester or two. Her family moved to New Jersey, and then to Manhattan, where, she has said, she was drawn to Hunter College like many young sixteen- or seventeen-year-old girls who couldn't afford private school. The school was founded by Thomas Hunter, who liked to say that he arrived in New York from Ireland in March 1850 with nothing more than a box of books and his health. He established the college twenty years later, calling it Normal College; its name was changed in 1914 in his honor. It was the women's branch of the city college, and Hunter honed its intent into one sentence: "The main purpose of this college is to raise the daughters of the poor to the highest plane possible."

Leona has said she attended Hunter for two years before dropping out. She says she studied English. If she was there in 1936, she would have been in the first class allowed to enter a general liberal arts program. Until then, almost every student was directed toward teaching.

It's certain she did not graduate. The school yearbook from Leona's class is filled with all the typical stuff of college—clubs, special project groups, along with pages of graduates' pictures in alphabetical order. She did not make that or any other Hunter yearbook. Nor did she stand out in any way, according to class leaders who would have known her. In all, it's unclear whether Leona actually attended. College officials will not say. Perhaps more importantly, if she did attend, the education did not make a lasting impression. Leona in later years would rarely read a newspaper. "Who has time?" she once remarked. She never gained an appreciation for books, as one incident in her Palace decorating would show. And those with whom she conversed typically felt a void where there might have been factual context or depth from a sense of history.

Educated or not, she married at age eighteen.

Little is known of Leona's first husband. He was an attorney named

Leo E. Panzirer, born in 1910 and trained at St. John's University in the borough of Queens. He was admitted to the bar in 1933, and continued to practice on his own in Manhattan through 1988. Panzirer refuses to speak publicly at length about Leona, except to acknowledge that he was, indeed, the Leo Panzirer who was married to Mrs. Helmsley. At home, his second wife, Zelda, runs a hard interference, telling reporters that he won't speak, and if he did, he would say only "nice things, good things" about Leona.

Although he fathered her only son, Jay, Leona also refuses to speak at length about Panzirer even to friends. She once told *New Woman* magazine that her lawyer husband (she didn't name him), who had come from a family in hotels, turned out to be her complete opposite socially. "He was tone deaf and I love music, which gives you an idea of our relationship," she said.

But the mere mention of Panzirer's name on one occasion sent her into a fit of anger. Seymour Rabinowitz, her longtime attorney, who developed an equally close legal relationship with Harry in the 1980s, said he once got a call from Panzirer. Leona's former husband bluntly asked for a business favor, making it clear he expected help because he was once married to Mrs. Helmsley. Rabinowitz passed the request on to Leona. "She was not at all pleased," Rabinowitz said, understating her reaction.

Jay Panzirer, who was born to Leo and Leona in 1942, also seemed to have lost touch with his father. Jay didn't speak much of him to friends or spouse. Nor did he introduce people to Leo. And that was unusual for the easygoing, friendly Jay. But Leona had exorcised Leo from her life, and Jay willingly maintained the same forced distance that Leona demanded from other relatives at various times when she had had a falling-out.

After a marriage of some years, Leona was divorced from Panzirer. The timing grows vague. Leona either left Jay with Leo to go and make her way in the world. Or she took him with her, burdened by the adolescent. At any rate, at some point Leona did not speak to Jay. That may have occurred in his teens, or later when he left home to attend a private academy and then college. In any case, she lamented to friends about the separation and it came back to haunt her with heaps of guilt feelings that surfaced in Jay's later years. "There was a lot of guilt there," said Eboli, who also got to know Jay through casual dating. "She had to leave him, and never got over that."

Shortly after divorcing Leo she got married again, to Joseph Lubin, a garment industry executive. It was, by secondhand rumor, a very bad marriage that survived five hard years. What is known is that Leona and Lubin divorced and remarried before breaking up for good. Jay Panzirer knew his stepfather only vaguely, having left home for school.

Leona claims to have modeled at some point, using the name Leni Roberts. She said she posed as a Chesterfield cigarette girl. If so, it likely occurred just after she left high school. In the late 1930s and early 1940s, Chesterfield had a "girl next door" campaign in *Look* and *Life* magazines before moving on to famous stars. Leona also says she worked as a sales floorwalker, modeling furs. There's reason both to believe and to disbelieve her claims about modeling. Much later, at least one of her ad agents noted that she appeared relaxed and professional behind the camera and never complained of long, tiring sessions. On the other hand, Leona's collections of scrapbook pictures—she has boxes of them—contain not a one of her modeling, say two people to whom she has shown her collection. And her former husband Leo also seemed to express surprise at her claim, exclaiming very briefly over the telephone, "Modeling? I don't know anything about that." Searches of *Life* for the years 1939 to 1943 turned up no ads with models resembling Leona or named Leni Roberts. (Models were identified in the ads.)

Leona had worked for Lubin in the garment center. Details of that time in her life are gone. The man who hired her away in 1962, Robin Nederlander, has died. But others at Nederlander's firm, a real estate company called Pease & Elliman, after its founding partners, recall that she came from a sewing factory, where she worked in some secretarial-administrative capacity. Interestingly, Leona has said on at least one occasion that she faked her typing test to land her secretarial job with Nederlander.

She revealed another trick to *New Woman*. To get Nederlander to hire her in 1962, she subtracted five birthdays from her forty-two years.

At Pease & Elliman, Leona Roberts worked as a secretary until the firm was sold in 1964, when the purchaser promoted her to a bona fide real estate broker. She needed to take no special test. The company just added her to its brokers roll and she got her company license. "Who had time to study? My son and I had to eat!" she later said, referring to Jay, who then was twenty-two.

Through the mid-1960s in the United States, city dwellers did not own apartments, except in New York City, where there was a unique and rather novel breed of apartment called the cooperative. In a co-op building each tenant owned a share of the entire building, and the share would permit residence in a specific apartment.

Leona's first assignment selling cooperative apartment units was at 175 East Sixty-second Street. She then worked a succession of other posh East Side apartment buildings, including the Park V and the Victorian. Leona also worked the St. Tropez, a brand-new thirty-five-story high rise on the far East Side of Manhattan that became the city's first condominium.

The condo, like the co-op, involves ownership. But instead of buying a share of the whole building, the condo owner buys a unit. In most cases condo owners also buy a share of the hallways, basement, and other common areas, though sometimes the developer will lease back those areas to the condo owners. Procedurally, the condominium operates differently too. Unlike co-ops, condominiums have no board of directors that approves new residents and makes other key decisions. Everything is spelled out in the condo contract, and condo buyers usually are free to sell to whomever they want. In fact, condo buyers often are mere investors, who won't live in their unit but will rent it out.

There also are some intriguing condo mutants. Quite often in New York City today apartment buildings will be divided into two sets of condominiums—one set consisting of the residential and common-area condo units, and another separate single condo unit for the retail-store space on the ground floor. Sometimes that retail condo is then leased back to the residential condo owners as a moneymaker. Also, entire commercial buildings have been divided up into business condos.

It didn't take long for the condo to catch on. There were 5,000 units sold nationwide in 1969. Five years later 220,000 condos were sold. Many involved resort-area beach town homes or mountain chalets. But a good many were big-city apartments or suburban town houses. Abuse and fraud were rampant in those early and entirely unregulated days as developers worked all sorts of tricks. One was to underestimate the maintenance fees condo owners would have to pay, so that a year after they moved in they would be paying as much for maintenance each month alone as their neighbors on the block were paying in rent. Another was to lease back the common area and charge exorbitant fees for recreation facilities. One Florida attorney told *The Wall Street Journal* that he knew a developer who was getting $250,000 a year from a pool that he leased to a condo building for ninety-nine years.

Perhaps most painfully for buyers, there sometimes would be long delays between the time they made large deposits on a condo purchase and the time they could actually move in. Construction delays could take many months, even years. "Condominiums: New Rip-off," headlined *The Nation* in 1974. And the head of a Chicago mortgage company said that same year: "The condominium concept is no flash in the pan, but so many have been built in the last three years that many inexperienced developers got into the business. Consequently, some terrible things have been pushed down buyers' throats, and in today's competitive market the selling pressure and abuses are bound to get worse."

All of that came after the St. Tropez conversion, where Leona Roberts's main problem was explaining to people just what a condo was. The St. Tropez moved very slowly. More than two years after it opened, 135 of its 300 apartments remained unsold. The building was blamed for setting back other condo sales in the city, giving them a bad name in the industry. But the St. Tropez more likely was slow because of its location way over on First Avenue and the relatively high price of its $80,000 three-bedroom suites in the upper tower. A quarter of a century later those suites were selling for $800,000 to $900,000, but that kind of inflation wasn't to be guessed at when they were first sold.

"I was the best real estate woman in the country," Leona would later recall. "I did the first condo in New York when nobody knew what a condo was."

But herself soured by the St. Tropez, Leona Roberts was no condo booster. She stuck with co-ops thereafter, and got a big break when she was put onto 980 Fifth Avenue at Seventy-ninth Street, perhaps the most luxurious and expensive new co-op building in the city. It brought her a good sum of money, a reputation, and a close dating relationship with the owner, Gus Ring, who has since died.

Her former associates at Pease & Elliman remember a hard-driving woman who mixed some Yiddish humor in with her long hours. But she was not a company woman, said her superior. "She was hardworking, diligent, and meant well, but she worked full-time for herself," he said.

She also, he added, began to display a capricious temperament. "She was funny, sociable, just unpredictable." Leona would erupt in anger as easily as she would soothe a harried associate.

Leona was not a slim woman then. She was big—big-boned, big-fleshed. Some of her peers considered her fat. In published pictures she appears chunky, fleshy-faced. If she had cheekbones, they were hidden below. She wore makeup in prominent colors and prodigious amounts. Her black eyelashes were extra long. And her posture was bad.

Leona had a one-of-a-kind slouch that one of her closest executive assistants would imitate, sending his audience of others who knew Leona into stomach-grabbing fits. Her shoulder would be thrown back and down. Her stomach bulged like a little kid's gut. Her whole torso slumped backward, and if she had a fur coat it would be draped over her right shoulder, dragging on the floor. Poised she was not. And she flushed her good health with nicotine—three or more packs a day. They gave her a gravelly, husky voice for the rest of her life.

"She was big, physically big, not how she is now. And tough. And those black eyelashes were a foot long," said one Manhattan apartment broker who knew Leona in the mid-1960s. Still, Leona could strike a seductive pose. She smoked her cigarettes in a long, slender black cigarette holder. She wore fine clothes, getting them from Martha Inc., a Park Avenue shop with a hostess and guard at the door.

Leona was big-breasted too. And she was proud of her breasts. Time and again in later years, she would be talking to aides or to a woman reporter while trying on a new gown for that evening's party, and she would bend over to check a hem or fiddle with a fold, pridefully exclaiming something like these words that once made print: "If I lean over, my husband will kill me."

~

Leona knew about leverage, as did Harry, and she developed her own ways to obtain things she couldn't buy.

Manhattan real estate was a sly game in those days. An entrepreneurial spirit flourished. People without money on the hunt for their fortunes did the next-best thing: they traded and bargained away what things they did have. Often that thing was a mere word—a word to apartment buyers that so-and-so was the carpenter they should get to remodel their cabinets; a word to a landlord that the law firm of such-such-and-such knew the condo rules better than anyone else; a word to wives that this beautiful dress could be bought at so-and-so's boutique at a remarkable bargain. None of that was illegal, unless somehow the exchanges affected the apartment sales price. Rather, it was mere bartering for the American Dream, Monopoly played with the "I help you, you help me" edition.

Some around Leona were convinced she was a walking salesroom. She wore clothes they thought she could ill afford. Jealousy may have tainted their observations. But they didn't fault her for doing so. If she got them for free or discount in exchange for promising to wear them like an ad, even her critics would call that tenacity. She was a three-time divorcée with a son and there were millions of people in Manhattan trying to make it.

Two people could recall firsthand how Leona played the word game with them and others. In 1961, Leona retained Joseph Catania, an interior decorator who had done the offices of her dentist. Over the next twenty-six years, Catania became one of Leona's closest confidants, getting as close as she permitted. "She was given good breaks on everything, in exchange for her promise that she would do something for you. That's certainly how she hired me," said Catania, who first decorated a succession of Leona's apartments.

In 1967, not long after she had left Pease & Elliman and joined another real estate firm, Sutton & Town, Leona wanted to form her own subsidiary with which to handle residential real estate sales. Seymour Rabinowitz at the time worked at the firm of Stroock, Stroock & Lavan.

"She was smart about it," Rabinowitz said. "She came to me and said, 'Your firm has a tremendous reputation in the co-oping field and in the business world. Your name attached to a co-op gives it a semblance of respectability. I'd like you to represent me. I cannot pay you. However, I would recommend your firm to do the co-oping on any building that I get.'

"It turned out to be a good arrangement," he said. "The fees that we were [later] paid made up for the free advice we gave her."

Through the subsidiary she created, Sutton & Town Residential, Leona innovated a remarkable accounting method for making the most of converting rental apartments into co-ops. Later, others quickly adopted the method, so that it became an industry norm.

Until then, real estate companies relied on the telephone to sell apartments in buildings they were converting. Salespeople would ring up the tenants, or other prospective buyers, and then set up appointments to meet them at the apartment. The salespeople would act as brokers, getting paid solely by hefty commission they would make in a sale.

Leona thought up a better way, and it would make her a lot more money. Rather than rely on commissioned brokers, she hired her own salespeople and trained them herself. Then she set them up in a model apartment in the building. And they would call on the tenants, regularly, and between calls bump into them in the hallways or elevators or as they lounged in the backyards. Her sellers then would become friends with tenants, doing little friendly things such as helping to carry in groceries. And they did very well. Her staff turned apartment buildings faster than anyone else in town.

But the magic in Leona's method came on payday. Instead of

giving her sales crew part of the sales commission, she would pay them a salary. And it was a very fine salary at that, with a big bonus at the end of the year. Her staff would be making $15,000 to $18,000 a year, which in those days was very good money, and then they'd bring home a $4,000 bonus. They were happy, and so was she, because even the big salaries and bonuses were easily paid for out of the huge commissions, the better part of which Leona would keep.

She steamed through conversions, setting up, selling out, and then rolling her staff over to another project just as the finished one wound down. Often she would act as the closer.

Apartments initially have to sell themselves. If a prospect doesn't like an apartment or can't afford it, no seller in the world can make that sale. But if prospects walk in who *sort of* like it and *think* they can afford it, usually it takes a little extra touch to actually sell the apartment. Leona Roberts had that touch. She would talk all the right talk —about the tax savings in owning a co-op, the hedge it would be against inflation, and the soaring property value it undoubtedly would enjoy. She even argued against the city's new rent stabilization law (which worked against her by making renters feel more secure against rent hikes) by warning that landlords might start cutting back on services if they couldn't recover the cost in higher rents.

But she had two particular tricks, aside from the usual strategy of "talk kitchen to the wife and talk maintenance fees to the husband." Leona would turn things around so the buyers would believe they could not afford not to buy it. And when possible, she'd drop her voice, fold her hands gently, and talk woman to woman. She used both those tricks on a resident of Sutton Place who asked not to be identified.

"I was in business, with IBM, in management, and I had my mother with me, and I was traveling a lot on business," said the prospective buyer. "She called me, and I went down to her office. It was on the second floor, where they have the current building office. She was most ingratiating. And she was the overbearing type of salesperson. You know, the type who tells you to put a dress on and it looks terrible, but they say it looks beautiful. But what she really did that I remember is talk to me woman to woman. It was like she wanted to help me, to show me how this was just for me, and how I could be owning this apartment that I was paying rent on, and how it would be a wise business decision for a woman in my situation."

Leona's role as a woman in the business was rather intriguing. She was not the only woman by any means. In 1962 Agnes Nolan became president of her real estate firm, which specialized in helping tenants find apartments. "There was no problem being a woman," Nolan said recently, sitting in her Madison Avenue office with a view of the southern end of Central Park. "Women have been in real estate for a long time. And if you're good at what you do, you'll find people will respect you."

Beatrice Kaye, who left nursing to sell town houses, told an industry paper in 1965 that women may even have an advantage with some clients. "I think the public, particularly the woman in search of a house, an apartment, or an investment, welcomes a realtor who understands the woman's point of view," Kaye said.

But as Leona's reputation spread, she gained a rare foothold in the male-dominated, higher-stakes segment of the real estate industry covered by *Real Estate Weekly*. Hers often was the only female face in the paper's lampoon issues, where in September 1969 she was pictured in bed with Arthur Levitt, who later became president of the American Stock Exchange. "This Medicare is terrific!" read the caption under the doctored photo, showing Leona and Arthur clinking glasses of booze under the bedsheets. "Miss Leona M. Roberts, in charge of condominiums, marvels at the VIP treatment she's getting. And it's from an actual VIP, too—N.Y. State Comptroller Arthur Levitt. Some taxpayers DO get service!" ("I only knew her indirectly," Levitt would later quip.)

But she was also taken seriously, getting profiled the previous year as the "Man of the Week." "Miss Roberts Sees Switch to Co-ops Speeded as Values Continue to Climb," read the headline next to a mug shot of her in a tight bouffant, pearl earrings, pearl necklace, and bare shoulders. "We are making history today in this area of real estate, and that's why it's so exciting," she was quoted, going on to explain that cooperative apartments would take over the city in the next five years as apartment-building owners realized they could make a lot more money selling their structures to their tenants—much more than they could merely selling the whole thing to another landlord.

Most of those who bought apartments from Leona Roberts were well-to-do. Many were wealthy. Some had substantial power. She liked to tell reporters in later years that among the buyers was Larry Tisch, the financier who in the 1980s gained control of CBS. But maybe the most important person Leona ever sold an apartment to was Leon Spear.

Leon Spear was one of the Three Old Men in real estate to last into the 1980s. The other two were Henry Baker, who at ninety years old in 1980 was the nation's oldest working broker, and Henry Forster, an octogenarian at the end of the 1970s whose biggest deal perhaps was the 1959 conversion of the Pierre Hotel into cooperative apartments.

Manhattan developer Lewis Rudin, whose late father, Sam, was of that same Old Guard of real estate entrepreneurs, credited its ranks with having nothing short of an extraordinary, innate vision. "I'm sure that Leon probably had a very intuitive sense," Rudin said when Spear died in 1986. "That's something that men of that era had. They had an intuitive sense about our business that not too many people have today. It was operating from the seat of their pants. They didn't make market surveys and they didn't bring in experts. They felt it, they sensed it. They went around and made decisions based on gut feeling."

Spear was an endearing sight in his later years. At work, he roomed with another executive and roamed about with his father's gold-headed cane. Spear's father was Jacob Rabinowitz, an Orthodox Jew who manufactured paper boxes and raised his family in Manhattan's historic Lower East Side. His older brother, Aaron Rabinowitz, founded the Spear Company, giving it their mother's family name, and Leon Spear —who changed his own name to his mother's—took over its management of $100 million worth of property in 1928.

Herbert Silverman was Spear's office mate for twelve years prior to Spear's death, and his account of Leon's time there is a window into the world where dozens of brokers acted independently. "He was still arranging deals, getting buyers and getting sellers, and was able to generate a fair amount of commission for himself. He was just amazing. He knew everyone in the business, and everyone would refer matters to him because of their love of him. A lot of people in real estate would never talk to anyone but Leon because he was a man of the highest integrity or character in advising to buy or sell," Silverman said.

Spear kept a lighter on his desk with a revolving ball on top that had the names and birthdays of his eleven grandchildren and eight great-grandchildren. He was frequently making calls to one or another, but included Silverman in his family. "I sort of had a little father complex because my father died very young. He was as close to a father to me as I could have had. He gave you an extra dimension in life. If I ever came in with the least bit of a long face he'd say, 'Now, now, sonny, as long as you wake up in the morning feeling well that's all you need in life.' When I went on a trip he would hug me."

In his spare time Spear would do paintings by the numbers. He did one of a poodle to match Silverman's real dog. He followed golf tournaments, tennis, baseball, and football, and had a television next to his desk. He was an avid reader, but would borrow Silverman's *Wall Street Journal.* "He figured, why should the two of us have a subscription?" said Silverman. "He was poor as a child, and very conservative about money. When he got a doctor's bill that seemed unreasonable he'd always ask me."

Spear also would not hesitate to comment on sundry affairs. Like others of his generation, he became astounded by the escalation in property values and the money to be made in real estate. "Young salesmen have had a field day for ten years," he once said. "They rent a full floor in some buildings, they make a commission of $40,000—if I got $300 my father would give me a special dinner. Of course, they have to share it with their partner, Uncle Sam."

But to Leona Roberts, Leon Spear was special in another way. He was a partner of Harry Helmsley. Actually, they were partners only in name. The office Leon occupied up to his death was on a lower floor in Helmsley-Spear's headquarters on Forty-second Street, and was more honorarium than functional.

In fact, Harry bought Spear's firm in 1955, but not for its good name and clients, as most service firms are bought and sold. Harry absorbed it, paying Spear $500,000, to acquire Leon Spear's brother-in-law, Alvin Schwartz. Schwartz had become a trusted right arm to Harry before he left to work for the family, and Harry discovered that the only way to get him back was to buy the whole company.

Leona Roberts knew that story. And she knew well who Harry was. She even said so, gushing in print after they met that she fully appreciated that he was the top real estate man in the country, "Mr. Real Estate."

So when Leona sold Leon an apartment in the Brevoort at 35 Park Avenue, she asked, very sweetly, for one of those "words" or favors. She asked the kindly old partner of Harry Helmsley for an introduction. And she got it.

## CHAPTER 4

# THE SYNDICATOR

HARRY HELMSLEY DID NOT INVENT THE REAL ESTATE SYNDICATE. NOR did he first use the concept of rounding up a lot of small investors to buy something very big. That credit goes to Fred French, a swashbuckler of sorts whose brainstorming enriched an awful lot of people he never even met.

Born in 1883, French was raised into a family with a branch related to President Millard Fillmore. He was educated at Princeton, then reeducated by cowboys on a ranch in Mexico. He returned to New York in 1905. After starting his own company from scratch, he came up in 1921 with what he immodestly called the Fred F. French Plan, which he first used to build the high-rise, Old English-style Tudor City on the eastern edge of midtown Manhattan.

French built Tudor City with money from hundreds of people who chipped in as little as $100 apiece. It was the first time something private and so large was built by people with so little, and it broke open the world of real estate that until then was exclusive forage for the wealthy.

"Never before, as far as we know, has the man with $100 to invest been given the same terms as the man with $100,000," French wrote in *The Real Estate Investment of the Future,* published in 1928. "Never before have the public been permitted to participate in the erection and ownership of income producing buildings and obtain their rightful share of the profits."

The idea caught on.

Dozens of entrepreneurs went about setting up similar investment pools in the 1920s. They drew middle-class investors who were too scared of stocks yet too hungry for income to be satisfied with mere interest from banks. The Depression cooled that scene, but real estate pools came back even stronger, and in 1943 an insurance company came up with an amazing twist. According to attorney David Clurman, who researched the matter for his book *The Business Condominium,* the insurance firm devised a scheme in which the owners of a Gimbels in Philadelphia sold the department store to a pool of investors and then immediately leased the store back from them. No one had heard of such a thing. But the arrangement did two very nice things. It handed the store owners a new supply of capital. And in the eyes of the IRS it made the pool of investors exempt from high corporate taxes because they were not involved in running the store.

The deal came to be known as the lease-back. And such investment pools came to be called limited partnerships, because the shareholders had very limited roles in the businesses they bought. They couldn't vote. They couldn't make decisions. Sometimes they were asked permission to dissolve the entire deal; sometimes not.

At about the same time, a young student attorney at the Ivy League Columbia University in Manhattan was poking his way through case law. And he made a similar discovery based on an obscure Ohio case. The attorney was Lawrence Arthur Wien, and his discovery led him to become one of the country's wealthiest promoters of real estate syndicates. Founded by him in 1929 when he was just twenty-four, Wien's sixty-lawyer firm now represents a stellar corporate clientele heavy in banks—Chemical, Irving Trust, National Westminster, First American, Apple, Dollar Dry Dock, European American, Connecticut, Norstar. It also represents Merrill Lynch, British Airways, Seagram, and the Tennessee Valley Authority.

But for a good long time Wien and his partners—they now include his son-in-law, Peter Malkin—were kept busy working on his own proliferation of real estate deals. Wien kicked off his real estate ventures in 1931 with a partnership that bought a Harlem apartment house for $8,000. Once he discovered lease-backs, he was able to cast much larger nets to collect much bigger investors.

But as good as Wien became in hunting up money, he lacked one whole aspect of the real estate game. He didn't have a sixth sense for buildings. He couldn't walk down the street and look at an office or manufacturer's loft and feel instinctively whether it was a good deal or bad. In fact, this son of a wealthy silk manufacturer would rather not walk the streets at all. It wasn't that Wien was pure silk stocking. He and his wife rode the subway. It was just that he had other interests. Instead of carrying home pounds of papers each night that might have told him what the building at hand would produce in operating profits, he preferred to socialize, to go out with his wife or meet with investors and work on his many philanthropic projects. Wien spent a good part of his career life giving time and money back to Columbia University.

Moreover, by instinct he was not a technician. He was a promoter. He liked to create deals, not manage them once they were done. So it was business love at first sight when he met Harry Helmsley in 1949 in a deal over a small building at Columbus Avenue and Sixty-seventh Street on Manhattan's West Side, near Central Park.

Harry was the broker. Larry was buying for friends. They fit together like some Chinese yin-yang, except the meditation was over money and enlightenment was wrung from the cutting of pure white light deals in which everyone involved did rather well. "Wien was such a good fundraiser. He had a very, very high personality," said Seymour Durst, a doyen of Manhattan real estate entrepreneurs who developed around Times Square. "And Helmsley was a very smart investor and manager. So it made a great team."

When he wasn't roaming the streets looking buildings up and down, Helmsley's world was his office. He moved into the Lincoln Building, on Forty-second Street across from Grand Central Station, soon after he and Wien bought it in 1954 with one of their early syndicates. And he stayed there, on the fifty-second, fifty-third, and fifty-fourth floors.

Friends would marvel at how small Harry's office was, considering the corporate domain he ruled over. It was tiny, really. It had a sofa and some chairs. The view wasn't bad. Harry could look south to lower midtown and beyond to the canyons of Wall Street downtown. But six people would make it cramped. One had to sit up straight during meetings in Helmsley's office as much to fit as to stay alert. Flanking Harry's are the equally austere offices of Alvin Schwartz and Irving Schneider, the other real estate men who joined Harry early in his career and became his partner in several big deals.

Helmsley learned to communicate through three secretaries, who stayed with him for decades. He kept all three busy with calls and letters, which he wrote out in a stylish longhand on white or sometimes yellow legal-sized pads. "If I was a girl, I'd be pregnant all the time," Helmsley once said. "When someone comes in with a good deal, I can't say no."

Harry's "Dear Larry" letters became famous among his circle of friends and business associates. They're exquisite, incisive analyses of the sort few business people have matched. "He could put together a letter describing the pros and cons of a particular piece of real estate in a better manner than anybody I've ever seen through my life. Those letters were truly masterpieces," said Steve Brener, a former longtime Helmsley aide.

Helmsley would pen out "Dear Larry" and then dive into the deal at hand. As it was usually a building, he would spell out its physical features, its strengths and weaknesses. He'd explain how the acquisition would occur. And then he'd gaze into the future to give Wien some sense of what could happen—what the tenants might do, how it fit into the overall market.

What was particularly special about Helmsley's memos was that he approached most deals both as a technician and as a principal. That is, he'd look at them with the cool, detached eye of any expert appraiser, and then he'd also see them as an investor with his own little piece at stake. Significantly, most other real estate people are either technicians or principals, and they lack the synergy Helmsley could spin out of the combination.

Helmsley's deal letters came to be considered priceless, and his executives kept copies of those involving them, sent by Harry's secretary Augusta Helm via the Helmsley-Spear couriers in red coats and black slacks. They studied his method because Helmsley would ask for much the same back from his staff. The "Dear Mr. Helmsley" memo had to be ordered like a newspaper article, with the most important facts up high. Helmsley would want to know the location, the size of the building, and how much the building was making. He'd want to know about the rent roll, about the financing that was available, and what it might be purchased for. Only with all that would a decision be made.

Helmsley organized all that data into loose-leaf binders, one for every property, and he put them right behind his head. Even today there are rows of them, stacked the way an attorney might keep law books, organized alphabetically, and the sight of Helmsley swiveling around in his chair to reach for one of his black, brown, or green property books has always been a riveting experience for his cadre of executives, who would then watch as Helmsley's mind turned over.

He kept meticulous track of his empire as it grew. Seymour Rabinowitz, who became the Helmsley-Spear in-house attorney ten years after he worked for Leona, was astounded by the degree to which Helmsley monitored his property. "I went to Harry's office once," Rabinowitz recalled, "and as I went in he was reading and initialing rent applications on commercial space, which basically was a form that his agents would have to submit if they wanted to make a lease in an office building. It would indicate the name of the tenant, the building, the amount of space they were taking, the last rent paid for that space, the new rent paid for the space, a short pricing of lease terms, the cost of putting the tenant in, how much for brokerage, etc. And if Harry said O.K. to the deal, he would immediately put his three initials— HBH—on the bottom and send it back to the agent. No commercial space could be rented unless there was an HBH at the bottom of that application.

"I didn't know he did that, and I said, 'I guess you do that on big deals?' And he said, 'No, I do it on every deal, whether it's for five hundred feet or a million feet.' And I guess I looked amazed, because he went on and said, 'If you're a jeweler, you have an inventory, you know every piece you have and what it's worth. My inventory is space. I have to be as aware of what my inventory is worth as a jeweler has to be aware of his, and know what his expenses are and what his projected profit is.' "

Helmsley littered his binders with handwritten notes, which Augusta Helm or Ceil Fried would type up for him. But he could always find what he needed, and fast. "I will go in to see him with twenty-five different questions and I'll be out of there within fifteen minutes with the answers to all of them. He's fast because of his ability to keep countless aspects of our business at his fingertips," William Lillis, a Helmsley-Spear vice president, once said.

Those near Helmsley believe that if he had had a personal computer, he and his little electronic mouse could have handled twenty times the work he did. Helmsley and his empire, they're convinced, was limited only by his memory and by shelf space for those property binders.

But Harry Helmsley did not have the kind of access to money that Larry Wien did, and they would compete to heap praise on one another. "I've never seen anyone who could isolate the one or two key factors in a deal and figure exactly what they're worth as Harry can," Wien would say of Helmsley in 1965. "He's the canniest negotiator you'll find anywhere. I think he's the best real estate man in the United States. I'm fortunate that we're together." To that Helmsley responded of Wien, "He's ingenious. When the going is tough, and the financing gets difficult, he makes a decision and fights it through. That's when he shines."

And when they went on the hunt, it was Helmsley for property, Wien for investors.

In later years, they would restrict their partnerships to a handful of investors. "That keeps everything private and eliminates the red tape of registering an offering with the Securities and Exchange Commission," the industry paper *Real Estate Weekly* explained in 1965. They developed a stable of fifteen investors who, as the wealthy directors of large companies, were eager to invest their money in low-tax deals. But in the beginning Helmsley and Wien crafted large syndications, in the style of Fred French, and their first decade together produced nearly 100 public syndications involving 15,000 investors.

In each, the deal was largely the same. Helmsley would find the property and negotiate with the seller. Wien would write up the legal paperwork and then round up the investors. Then they'd turn the building over to Helmsley to manage, and they'd sit back and rake in the rents. Most of those deals were successful, and continue to make money for Helmsley and Wien.

But the big one, the deal that would bring them fame not only in the real estate world but in the world at large, by putting their names on the front page of *The New York Times* as deal-makers extraordinaire, came in 1961 when the owner of the Empire State Building finally, after three years of negotiation, was prodded to sell. The prodder was Harry Helmsley. The syndicate designer was Larry Wien. And it was at the time a double superlative that made large headlines— the most complex deal, for the world's tallest building.

"The story of the Empire State Building deal," an annual Helmsley company report would later boast, "is one of bulldog tenacity, never-ending patience, new ideas to deal with unique situations and 'cloak and dagger' secrecy."

The Empire State grew from a rash of super building dreams that arose in the late 1920s. The most extravagant was posited by the real estate firm of Noyes-Schulte, which claimed to have found two whole blocks of downtown Manhattan on which it would build a 150-story tower. The promoter, architect-entrepreneur Raymond Hood, maintained that the design was no problem. "Some time ago I got our engineers to figure up just what would be the theoretical maximum height for a skyscraper," Hood said later. "The formulas that the present building laws allow to use for steel would enable you to build a tower 7,000 feet high. The elevator companies are ready." But Noyes-

Schulte's assemblage was not. It turned out that the firm couldn't get its hands on all the necessary leases until 1937, and the dream died.

The dream held by former Governor Alfred Smith did not. He had the site—a midtown Manhattan block where the defunct Waldorf-Astoria had sat losing its prestige and clientele to newer hotels. He had the go-ahead—the Waldorf had been purchased for $14 million only to be demolished for a fifty-story loft building that didn't go up. And he had the energy—the site changed hands, as did the investors involved, and Smith took charge.

The Empire State was made of superlatives. It broke records with every material that went into tall buildings—60,000 tons of structural steel and as much weight of stone, 10,000 tons of marble, 10 million bricks; 2 million feet of wiring, 100 miles of pipe, 350,000 bulbs plugged into as many sockets, and 6,400 windows with varying views of the city. There were 85 floors of office space, with observatories on the 86th and 102nd floors. And it went up very fast, in eighteen months. Upon opening in May 1931 the building won mixed reviews.

Clearly, the world's tallest tower was impressive for that fact alone, admitted Lewis Mumford, who covered architecture for *The New Yorker*. "It really is tall. From almost every part of the city it bulks so large that it almost looks as if it belonged to a different race of structures from the thirty- and forty-story Lilliputians that make up the foreground." Others granted the Empire State its own special charm, including George Sheppard Chappell, who preceded Mumford at *The New Yorker* using the pen name "T-Square." It was "obvious," he wrote, "that here was a structure worthy of consideration not because of its altitude or acreage but because of its sheer beauty . . . [its] long bays of windows in unbroken, gleaming lines."

But the Empire State was built at the end of an era dominated by heavy cement, and others were keen for the transition to the modern sleek tower. "Our tall buildings all progress backward," Douglas Haskell, critic for *The Nation*, complained. "From the picture of free open volume given by the bare frame they work back to that of solid 'mass,' which is surely more primitive. Or is it archaeology that has been sped up? Our architects no longer wait for their buildings to be buried by the past. They entomb them in stone before they are even done. They subject them to creeping petrification. The finest Empire State was buried a year ago. It was the Empire State of the skeleton stage. No steel frame had been quite so fine before. This was because of the vertical strips of nickel steel that now serve as guides to the columns of windows. All that was needed then was glass, and what a boast of the future would have been made then and there. What gives this building its special character is this: that it was caught at the exact moment of transition—caught between metal and stone, between the ideal of 'monumental mass' and that of airy volume, between handicraft and machine design, and in the swing from what was essentially handicraft to what will be essentially industrial methods of fabrication. No New York building of the current season has been so basically progressive, or half so fascinating as a problem."

Of course, it was the view of metropolitan New York, not the architecture, that brought four million people to the top observatory in the first five years it was opened, and on this too there was some brilliant criticism.

Among them was F. Scott Fitzgerald, who marveled at the irony of the tall tower going up after the stock-market crash. "From the [economic] ruins, lonely and inexplicable as the sphinx, rises the Empire State Building and, just as it had been a tradition of mine to climb to the Plaza [Hotel] roof to take leave of the beautiful city, extending as far as the eyes could reach, so now I went to the roof of the last and most magnificent of towers. Then I understood—everything was explained: I had discovered the crowning error of the city, its Pandora's box. Full of jaunty pride the New Yorker had climbed here and seen with dismay what he had never suspected, that the city was not the endless succession of canyons that he had supposed but that it had limits —from the tallest structure he saw for the first time that it faded out into the country on all sides, into an expanse of green and blue that alone was limitless. And with the awful realization that New York was a city after all and not a universe, the whole shining edifice that he had reared in his imagination came crashing to the ground. That was the gift of Alfred E. Smith to the citizens of New York."

The Empire State Building, of course, would bring much more to the whole world. When it opened it had a mooring mast for blimps, and two actually docked there for a few minutes in very high winds before Smith admitted the whole idea was silly. Two years later RKO released the legendary monster movie *King Kong,* in which a giant ape (actually eighteen inches tall) clambered about on top batting off planes. In 1945, the real thing, a World War II bomber, smacked into the 79th floor and killed a building elevator operator by snapping her cable and sending her plummeting to the ground. A few people have jumped. More than a few birds have crashed into the side. Hundreds of thousands of people each year stand in long lines to take elevators to the top, while a few dozen in February every year race up the 1,860 steps in times of twelve minutes or more. In 1983 for the ape's fiftieth anniversary an eight-story nylon balloon version of King Kong was flown from the observation tower. He flopped when workers couldn't get him blown up properly and when they did he sprang leaks. The newspapers poked fun. So did a few tenants who were doing battle with Helmsley in one of his apartment complexes. Their picket signs pictured Kong and Harry and the words: "Two of a kind."

None of that history likely mattered to Harry Helmsley, except in its effect on how much rent the tenants would pay, or how much gate the tourists would bring, or how much NBC and others would pay to keep their antennas on top of the city's highest roof. On the downside, what mattered to him as he looked at the Empire State from his own office window, or as he stood outside on Fifth Avenue looking straight up, or as he wandered around inside poking into the cupboards, was how much electricity would be needed to keep all those bulbs shining and those elevators running. His mind was on how many of the original 580 building employees he would need to keep.

And the Empire State had some drawbacks. Because of its height, fully one-third of its inner space was taken up by a huge core of functional innards—sixty-nine passenger and six freight elevators, sundry utility lines, and, of course, a dozen or two of the longest-ever version of those glass chutes that whisked letters into the building's own post office branch. Moreover, it hadn't been air-conditioned, so the best offices were all near the windows and rents plummeted as one stepped away into the building.

As in every deal, Harry took his tours, made his notes, added up his numbers. Then he went to Robert Crown, whose father, Henry, had added the Empire State to his Chicago-based empire in 1951, and started to talk sale. Three years later the deal was done, but this was no simple contract.

It might have been just a straight sale had the Prudential Insurance Company been permitted by law to pay more than $50 million for any one thing. Prudential already had purchased the land below the Empire State for $17 million in 1951, and the company wanted the whole show. But it could not tap its coffers for more than $50 million, and Crown wanted $65 million for the building. In stepped Wien with his extraordinary deal.

He would buy the building for $65 million, and then immediately sell it to Prudential for $29 million. In return for that deal, Wien would get a 114-year master lease good for both the building and the land. That's where Prudential bowed out of the picture and 3,300 people stepped in. To make up the $36 million shortfall owed Crown after subtracting the $29 million from Prudential, Wien set up a general partnership syndicate and offered the world a piece of the action in $10,000 chunks.

But what's even more intriguing, and revealing of the way he and Harry were doing business, Wien set up yet another layer of investors. He created the Empire State Building Co., giving himself a quarter share, Helmsley a quarter share, the shipping magnate D. K. Ludwig a 37.5 percent cut, and the Martin Weiner Realty Corp. a 12.5 percent share, all in return for a proportionate sum of money that supplemented the smaller investors' pool. This would be the functional operating entity, and it would shield the Empire State Building Associates —who were Wien, Malkin, and a third partner, along with all the small investors—from heavy corporate tax. The Company each year would pay the Associates a certain rent. The Company's incentive to do well was that it would keep a 50 percent share of the profit on top of that minimum. The small investors were lured with the qualified "promise" of a 9 percent annual return, or $900 per $10,000 investment. While tax status varied from person to person, only slightly more than half that amount would be reportable to the IRS as ordinary income. The rest would be considered return on invested capital, and was thus a huge tax write-off.

The state, once they figured the deal out, let the big boys like Ludwig fend for themselves. But regulators in the state attorney general's office became alarmed about the chance that the small investors could be held liable for more than their investment. In limited partnerships, the partners have just that: a limited role. They don't have a say in managing the property, nor do they have any liability to the bankers or other creditors should the deal go bad. They're in it for the sum of their $5,000 or $10,000 or whatever-sized investment, and that's all.

The Empire State, however, was not a limited partnership syndicate in which the investors were unquestionably immune from legal liability should anything go wrong. Its investors were considered to be general partners, which by definition made them more broadly liable. That worried David Clurman, an attorney in the state attorney general's office, who became the world's leading expert on regulating real estate syndicates. Wien and the other creators of the Empire State deal felt they had dealt with the liability factor, but Clurman was worried enough to fight for some written warnings in the normally bland prospectus that offered shares in the syndicate. So on the front page of the offering, in relatively medium-sized print, was an exceptional warning to turn to page 12 for more information about "certain individual liabilities." Participants, page 12 warned, "may be liable" under New York law for any obligation that Wien and his two other general partners may develop.

The Empire State had some other risks. Its net income had dropped from 1959 to 1960, falling from $6.4 million to not quite $6.1 million, mainly because of rising observatory expenses, an increase in nonpaying tenants, alterations to tenant space, and miscellaneous operating expenses. Moreover, there would soon be a problem with the tenants themselves. Most of the firms renting space in the Empire State were small merchants. There had been, for most of its history, about 850 tenants, with about the same mix as there was in the 1980s—302 men's wear shops, 74 shoe sellers, and the rest a wide variety. But in 1962 almost one in four tenants, using a quarter of the building's 1,753,000 square feet, would have their leases expire. That could be good, if rents could be raised. That could be bad, if everyone decided to move out.

All of that was spelled out in the prospectus. But in reading the document today it seems unlikely that all, or even many, of the small investors would have understood the risks. Peter Malkin today still considers the Empire State prospectus a "model of clarity," and compared to many others it was. Clurman, who helped shape it, said he believed then that most investors could read it and understand its contents. But he questions whether they bothered to read it, and whether, if they did, they gave its warnings any more credence than smokers do the cautions on cigarette packs. Even syndicate creators tended to be blinded by the riches to be made and ignored the fact that real estate values do not always go up. "The offering plan might not have been that difficult to understand, but the problem was in its projections into the future. A good real estate deal has got to have good projections into the future, and there's no way in the world other than guess. It is a speculative business," Clurman said.

"The real danger in real estate syndication was that people thought real estate was absolutely safe," he continued. "And those were people who were living on social security. People were taking money out of the bank or out of municipal bonds and were investing in this for a regular return. And there were problems beyond the economics. One was where to resell the units. Today, with the massive markets on Wall Street, you sell them like stock. But in the ordinary syndications, you may have great danger in not getting your money back when you need it."

Clurman is convinced that real estate syndications in general would not have captured so much investment money as they did if all the dangers were known. "A lot of people would not have invested had they recognized that [about selling the shares alone]," he said. "No matter what was in the plan, or how many times it was pointed out, if people had recognized that, they would not have invested. They should never have bought real estate syndications, but they were attracted by the higher return. It was greed here; as [the minimums for investment] got smaller and smaller, to $2,000 and less, it was easy to put money in. And it was thought by everyone that real estate only went up. A lot of people lost money, because some of these guys were wild, they didn't know what they were doing. They would buy apartments in areas where you had transients moving in, and there was no security for a regular flow of income."

However revealing, the Empire State prospectus was persuasive, and as Clurman noted, Wien by then had developed a reputation. "Nothing breeds interest more than respect. Wien, especially at the time of the Empire State, had done a number of syndications, and they were mainly successful, and he had a following, because he did well most of time."

The Empire State did not fail, and the investors have never been called into court to help make a pile of bad debts good. The deal likely will stand as long as Wien and Helmsley remain solvent. But the insecurity of real estate syndicates is underscored by the fact that even in the grand Empire State Building, things did not go well at first.

Unforeseen in the prospectus, its clarity notwithstanding, two big tenants moved out in the first year. The 97 percent occupancy rate in 1961 fell to 86.6 percent in 1964, and Helmsley had to scramble. He stepped in as an iron-tough manager. He cut costs by first slowing and then automating the elevator service. He slashed employee overtime. He installed air conditioning and then, of course, jacked up the rent. He also courted the 850 tenants, who were mostly small men's wear and shoe-selling firms.

In 1965 Helmsley was taking out full-page ads in *Real Estate Weekly,* soliciting tenants for the "Front Office of the World," and the tenant flight was turned around. Occupancy rose to nearly 100 percent in 1970, dipping to 90 percent during the recession in 1975, and climbing again to nearly 99 percent, according to Helmsley-Spear figures.

Perhaps the most difficult aspect of real estate syndicates is the issue of profit—profit to the investors, who put in their little bundles of cash; profit to the promoters, who put in their skill. Neither group could do it without the other, but at times that is hard to see from within the deal.

Fortunately for the promoters, syndicates are written by them and for them. As one attorney told *Forbes* magazine in 1984, "We try to write an insurance document for the general partner, not a document designed to help somebody evaluate the real risks of a deal." Again, the Empire State deal exemplified the quandary of what profit for whom.

Over the years, the Empire State investors did far better than the promised 9 percent minimum. In 1980 Malkin estimated that year's return at 20 percent. Federal records for 1987 showed the investors got back even more—a whopping $4,963 per $10,000 originally invested. There had been a very steady gain in earnings: 1983, $2,530; 1984, $3,068; 1985, $3,303; 1986, $4,446.

Yet Helmsley, by comparison, along with his three other general partners in the managing Building Company entity, have consistently counted their annual earnings in millions, not thousands. In 1986, the Empire State made an overall profit of $28.7 million. By arrangement, the Company gave back half of that profit over $1 million to the 3,300 small investors, or $13.9 million. That left Helmsley's group of four with $14.8 million. Helmsley's share of the Empire State profit for 1986: $3.7 million.

That's not all he made, however. Besides being a general partner in the Building Company, Helmsley was designated the Empire State office cleaner, and in recent years the firm he set up to do that has received a $4 million annual fee—a job that one outside estimator told a business reporter they could do for one-quarter less. Helmsley received $90,000 per year for generally managing the building, while Wien received the same for legal services. Significantly, each year Helmsley has also received the standard rate of brokerage commission each time a tenant renewed a five- or ten-year lease. With the rent roll in 1987 at about $62 million, Helmsley's annually computed commission would have totaled $2 to $3 million.

Opinions vary among investors, depending on who's asked. "It's been marvelous. They are wonderful. I would invest my money with them anytime," said Pearl Abend, a middle-class retiree who is living off the several $10,000 pieces of the Lincoln Building and other Wien-Helmsley syndicates that she bought as a young woman. Julien Studley, a professional real estate developer who bought into the Empire State, is not so sure it's been a good deal.

"This building and others aren't being run aggressively for the investors," he told a New York business magazine. "The [senior] partners send out a sheet that says, 'You're getting a 48 percent return on your 1961 investment.' No big deal when you think of how real estate values have gone up. For Mr. Helmsley and Mr. Wien, the properties are just a stream of money. The buildings are the investors' property, but the [senior partners] think of them as theirs."

Unlike real estate sophisticates like Studley, few investors probably ever realize how much money the senior partners in their deals are making. Records that report those amounts can be tracked down. But the annual reports sent to investors usually list only their own limited profits. Even if they did learn of the general partner profits, and became disturbed, investors in syndicates would be ill-advised to take legal action. There are too many disincentives to sue. In fact, a more lawsuit-proof deal has never been structured.

Such litigation inevitably will be lengthy and costly, since the syndicators can be counted on to amass a strong defense. Deep pockets are needed, far deeper than most people with $10,000 to invest likely have. And even if the small investors sue and win, there's the grave danger that the investors themselves will become liable for the partners' losses. At the minimum, actually winning a suit will force the dissolution of the syndicate, and that type of dissolution is heavily taxed by the IRS. The suing investors would likely lose all that they would have gained in the award. It would have to be a suit on moral grounds.

The savviest investors will instead challenge their partners and settle before reaching court. With the syndicators' reputation at stake, there's a good bet they will settle for whatever price the investor is asking, within reason. And if the syndicate creators react with a shrug, it's because the settlement cost is shared by all the investors as just another expense of the syndication. As Wien said casually of one such challenge that was settled out of court, "There are some people who feel no matter what they got, it's never enough."

But Wien, and initially Helmsley, were not so fortunate in 1981 when an investor got angry enough to take them to court.

Jeffrey Kahn had just turned twenty-one when his father made a birthday present out of the elder Kahn's $10,000 share in the Berkeley Building, an office building on West Forty-fourth Street in Manhattan next door to the Harvard Club. Fifteen years later, just after Christmas

1980, Kahn was one of eighty-six investors in the Berkeley Building who received a "Cordially, Larry" letter from Wien announcing that he wanted to sell the building, which was purchased in 1953 for $3.1 million and had provided a string of very nice dividends. Wien said he could get a minimum of $9 million, and he laid out some good reasons why they should sell. The building was getting funky in its seventy-five years of age, and needed some turning to avoid getting bedsores. "The cost is likely to be very great," he wrote of those modernization requirements. Second, a buyer was waiting where there was none before. "This may change," he warned. Third, the building could secure only a secondary share of the rental market and had been the first to suffer when vacancy rates fell citywide. "It may happen again," Wien said. And fourth, the economy was uncertain. "Financial problems of tenants could create a serious situation in the future," he wrote.

Then he spelled out the details of the sale, using a $9 million sale as a hypothetical. The eighty-five investors collectively would get 37.5 percent. Another 37.5 percent would go to the entity that leased the building, much as the Company did in the Empire State deal. In this case, the entity was formed with Wien, Helmsley, Helmsley's brother Walter, and five others. Helmsley held 70 percent of the group. And the rest, or 25 percent of the sale price, would go to Wien's law firm. In comparison to those millions, which Wien in his letter left only as percentages, he carefully spelled out that each $10,000 investor would get no less than $26,471 in cold, hard cash.

Wien needed 75 percent of the investors to say yes. He got 85 percent. And in July 1981, he collected, not $9 million, but $19 million for a building that from the sound of Wien's letter was ready to croak. Each investor was to get $70,588 for each $10,000, not $26,471 as Wien suggested. But, of course, his own share also almost tripled.

But Kahn was unassuaged by Helmsley's brilliant brokering in getting $19 million for a building that he, Kahn, felt the syndicate should hang on to. He filed suit, and in 1982 it was certified a class action. Wien would have to fight his way out of this one, or settle with all the investors.

After three days of trial in 1985, things must have appeared bad to Wien's legal eyes because he chose to stop the proceeding and settle.

The deal they cut was this: The sale would not be contested if Wien would offer $2 million of his profits back to the investors. He only had to offer. They didn't have to take. Under the settlement terms, Wien would get to fire off a new letter to the investors, spelling out the situation as he saw it and giving them the chance to take a share of the $2 million or leave it to him. It was a masterful letter, mixing modesty with self-congratulation, poking at Kahn while praising the other investors, and like prospectuses themselves, revealing all that the court forced him to reveal, but ever so subtly. "My law firm and I have always worked diligently for the benefit of all the participants," Wien wrote, again substituting his usual formality with a "Cordially, Larry Wien."

The court prescribed a period of "free speech," which in law terms translates as a free-for-all in which both sides could lobby the investors. Bette Snetman of Miami Beach was among several investors who were put off by Wien's letter and the subsequent calls from his office.

"Dear Sir," Snetman wrote to the court on the Fourth of July. "I purchased a participation in this building when I was a young girl and have held it until the recent sale. I felt the court should see the enclosure I received on July 1st with the court papers. On the same day Mr. Wien's office called asking me to tear the letter up. I still don't understand whether he meant his letter or the forms to be returned to the court, but I have received other calls from the office through these proceedings asking me not to join the 'class' and expounding Mr. Wien's generosity and brilliance, and telling me how he deserved all the money he was receiving.

"I am a recent widow of modest means, supporting 2 children and 2 grandchildren. The money awarded means a great deal to me, the amount I will have to pay in legal fees will be important.

"I do not understand why Mr. Wien's office should be allowed to put this kind of pressure on me and I resent the fact that though he totals the amount of money I received over the years he neglects to total the many millions of dollars he received which, he forgets, he did receive only because I and others invested our money. Yours truly."

But what happened finally in the Berkeley case can only be counted as a victory for Wien. Of the eighty-six investors who were offered a share of the $2 million, only fifty-three chose to take the money. For reasons unknown, the thirty-three others took nothing, letting Wien keep almost $800,000 of the $2 million.

Just as remarkably, another testimonial to the respect Wien wielded among lay investors came as the judge dismissed the jurors after three days of intricate trial that labored on amortization and depreciation and the other terms of syndications. Jane Gordon covered the trial for the now defunct news weekly *CityBusiness,* and she was startled by the jurors' only question when their part was over. She wrote that all they wanted to know was: "How could they themselves invest with Wien?"

It's that kind of blind faith that drove Helmsley's syndications. And while, in the words of W. C. Fields, he may not always have given a sucker an even break, he did give them returns. Indeed, Harry Helmsley was only beginning to make a lot of money for a lot of people.

## CHAPTER 5

# EMPIRE BUILDING

ON A MUGGY JULY MORNING IN THE EARLY 1960s, HARRY HELMSLEY and two aides trooped off to southern Florida to look over some beach frontage. They might as well have taken Jackie Gleason along for all the slapstick.

With Helmsley was Steve Brener, an admitted workaholic who joined Helmsley in 1952 with a Purple Heart and sense enough to realize he was stepping into a new sort of minefield—the Helmsley corporate inner sanctum. Brener retreated to his own ground and developed the lodging business for Helmsley. "I backed into hotels because the competition in Helmsley-Spear was much too good or strong as far as I was concerned. I did not see myself being competitive with guys like Alvin Schwartz or Irving Schneider," said Brener, now one of the hotel industry's leading consultants.

Also along was Jim Earley, who had been with Helmsley since

1947 and directed Helmsley-Spear's maintenance programs. By 1969, when Earley was named a vice president, he had a 1,800-member staff and the care of 203 apartment houses and office buildings in Manhattan. "He was a big guy, tall, like a football player," recalled Brener, who was dwarfed by Earley and the six-foot-three Helmsley.

The trio headed for La Guardia Airport, where they had booked first-class seats on National to give the big men some leg room. They were early, so they went to the coffee shop and promptly chatted their way to missing the plane. "Everything was just wonderful, you know. We were sitting and talking and drinking coffee and the plane just left," said Brener.

They managed to get on the next flight—in coach, so Helmsley and Earley had their knees for lunch on the three-hour flight.

They were headed for Palm Beach, where an old school friend of Brener's had told him about a hotel for sale. But with the Palm Beach airport still undeveloped, they flew into Miami and rented a car for the two-hour drive back north along the coast. They got the biggest car Hertz had, and Earley, the engineer, checked it all out. Stepping off the plane they had gotten a blast of the Florida heat. So Earley made double sure the car had air. "Really great air conditioning," said Brener, " 'cause in those days you didn't get great air conditioning and it was hot."

"I was in the back. Earley was driving. Helmsley was in front. And I'm dying. They're dying. We're all dying," said Brener, remembering the drive through the flat Florida savanna in 100 degree steaming humidity. "Jim Earley, the great engineer, Harry Helmsley sitting next to him, mopping his face and neck, and me in the back. They're up there turning knobs and pulling levers, and they just couldn't make the air conditioner work. Eventually, sometime before we got there, we figured it out. We had turned on the heat."

They made Palm Beach and found the Ambassador Hotel, next door to the Sea Breeze. Helmsley bought both. But along with the Sea Breeze came a boat by the same name. It apparently was used to ferry guests. "So we had to go to the boatyard and find the thing, and it turned out to be this enormous boat, fifty-six feet or something like that, and Harry is standing there, looking at it, up and down," said Brener.

Helmsley looked, in his squinting way. He mulled. And then in no big hurry he turned to his aides like a man who had never been off the island of Manhattan and said, "What do we do with this?"

Harry sold off the boat. Indeed, it was a good long while before he bought another hotel and paved the way for Leona to step into her hotelier mien. He was wary of anything that didn't involve commercial tenants and a ten-year lease.

Larry Wien had an even greater distrust of hotels. So for the balance of their relationship, Helmsley stuck mostly to office towers in creating his empire. And create he did. Over the course of three decades, but especially in the twenty years following his meeting Wien in 1949, he acquired dozens of properties across the country, and then even built a few in Manhattan himself.

Harry and Larry started their buying spree before they did the Empire State deal. They began in 1950 with a big brawny garment center building on Seventh Avenue. Three years later they wove a syndicate around the Berkeley Building on Forty-fourth Street. In 1954 they got another vast group together to buy the Lincoln Building on Forty-second Street, where both Helmsley-Spear and Wien's law firm moved and remain today. In 1957 they added a trio of combination buildings—lofts and offices—on Seventh Avenue. They also bought the towering Equitable Building on lower Broadway, near Wall Street.

Almost every Manhattan tower has had some effect on the city. But the Equitable all by itself revolutionized real estate in New York when it opened in 1915. Though Harry was just starting school then, it primed the city for the Helmsley empire to rise.

For one thing, the Equitable transformed the old skyline. It went up like a rock wall, stealing light and air from the city as it rose a staggering forty-four stories. Hundreds of windows in adjoining office buildings went dark in its shadow. And Manhattan's first skyscraper canyon was born. The resulting public outrage prompted the city to enact the first rules forcing developers to angle their buildings back as they go up, pyramid style. Today, when the city ponders an architect's plan, it puts the design to a light and air test that puts a cap on how much of the sky a building can steal.

More importantly, the Equitable ripped up the traditional real estate calculations, handing the owner new levels of profit by squeezing money from stone. Suddenly, with ample light and air provided to more of *its* tenants, the Equitable owners could charge much more for rent. It formed the prototype for what Harry Helmsley came to trade in—the city's equivalent of an entire town, thirty vertical acres where every workday 16,000 people streamed in to eat, shop, and conduct business. They paid rent by the window and the view. And there was record-breaking profit to take to the bank, as the rent roll far exceeded the expense of keeping the lights burning and elevators running.

Helmsley was perfecting his eye for property in all that hunting with Wien, and he came to be known as one of the industry's best appraisers. But Helmsley was learning something else too that proved equally important to his investing.

Spiraling inflation is no longer the mystery it once was. Nowadays, even Young Turks in the real estate business can learn in business school what to do when prices and values start climbing wildly. In short, they're taught to buy property with a whole lot of borrowed money, especially when the money can be borrowed at fixed interest rates. That way, when everything soars—interest rates as well as property values—the deals that were cut with fixed interest rates soar only in property value. Steady goes the cost of money. Up goes the property value. The resulting gap is all for the smart investor to take home. And it only widens as inflation gets worse.

Three or four decades ago, however, that was a new and wonderful discovery shared among only the best and the brightest in real estate deals, and no one learned it quicker or better than Harry Helmsley.

Helmsley did so well during times of inflation that it's said by some that he liked a rousing inflation. He never let on to his closest friends. He was too much the booster. Admitting a lust for inflation would be an economic sacrilege. It also would be like buying gold, which he felt was to bet against oneself and against the country's economy. And though Leona once invested in gold—she once took an icy bath in Canadian Maple Leafs—Harry Helmsley never did.

"He didn't consider inflation a necessity," said his longtime friend and fellow New York developer Larry Silverstein. "He always referred to inflation as having established the fortunes for all of us, because as a result of inflation, values rose to a remarkable extent. Without the ravages of inflation I'm not sure wealth would have accumulated so quickly and to the extent that it did."

Peter Malkin, the Harvard-educated partner in Wien's law firm, speaks with the formal and precise words that clients pay part of their fortunes to hear. "I never heard Mr. Helmsley say it was important to have inflation. But he certainly said that if you owned hard assets and there is inflation, you're likely to do very well," Malkin said.

"He and other people who became involved in real estate during a generally inflationary period—if they were cautious in their original acquisition, and did not overfinance, and operated efficiently—would get the benefit of having their property values rise up with the general inflationary trend," said Malkin. That was especially true "in the old days when you could get half or two-thirds of your acquisition cost financed with long-term mortgage financing with fixed interest rates that did not fluctuate with inflation. Then, of course, you would have a leverage advantage. And you would get an even higher benefit from inflation on the equity that you owned because you would get the benefit of inflation on the entire property, but you would only have part of the money invested. The balance of the money would be fixed return money that would not reflect inflation."

What syndicators like Helmsley have done during recessions, of course, is flip that ploy around. When interest rates, production, and wages all fall, that is the time to pour money into good buildings. And they should be bought for cash, without any mortgage loans at all, since the value of money is likely to drop faster than real estate will. In the meantime operating profits will keep rolling in.

Again, the notion of bending with a recession is the stuff of textbooks nowadays. But that chapter wasn't written in Harry Helmsley's days. And he wasn't in school to read it if it was. Helmsley learned it on the street, using real money and with a real career at stake, where figuring things out meant not good grades but putting food on the table. And he couldn't have picked a more sobering time to get street-wise about economic havoc.

From the wild and wicked 1920s to the dour Great Depression, Helmsley was dunked into this century's greatest economic swings. He saw firsthand the reams of money made hand over fist in the seven years that followed the post–World War I depression. He noticed, and the company he was working for thrived on the subsequent crazed rush to invest that money. He later saw too that that money had gone into a good many schemes that had no protections and no guard against the possibility of more sober days ahead.

Helmsley experienced the subsequent great stock-market crash as the 1920s closed. He tasted the drying of capital. He felt the poverty that hit those who were left unprotected. Climbing out of the Depression, he then passed through a succession of lesser recessions and expansions—World War II, reconversion and the 1949 recession, the Korean War and the bumpy stagnation of the Eisenhower years, the Vietnam War inflation, and the mid-1970s fall. And through them all he perfected his ability to sense, and then react to, the ups and downs by keeping his nose in the air. It was as if he could sniff out the economic seasons. In the winter of recessions he would wrap himself up against the sleet by making tight, insular deals with lots of cash. Then with the expanding warmth of inflation he'd loosen up, reach out, and spread his money by taking big fixed-interest mortgage loans.

Helmsley was like the canny, God-fearing farmer who somehow knew just when to plant after the last frost and when to harvest to beat the first lashing storm. Too, he knew what kind of crop to plant to get that year's best market. And usually it was something his neighbors weren't yet planting. Real estate is not unlike farming, in that everyone eventually reacts to the cycles, en masse, destroying the market prices by oversaturation. Helmsley learned to be there first, maybe a season ahead. Exclusivity was his best game.

A few people were privy to Harry's strategy. As many as ten executives in his corporate flagship, Helmsley-Spear, made their first million dollars by participating personally in Harry's deals, or by being allowed to do their own, which he in turn would then ride for a share. One of those was Seymour Rabinowitz, Harry's in-house attorney for nine years before he was shoved from Harry's side in May 1986. "He once told me his philosophy," Rabinowitz said, sitting on his living-room couch in Fort Lee, New Jersey, where residents look back on Manhattan over the Hudson River. "Unquestionably there are cycles. In bad times, he would try to invest as much as he could. If a building cost $5 million, he would put up $5 million. In times when prices were very high, he would make an investment. But he'd invest very, very little money. He would buy with mortgage, heavy mortgage, so if the building didn't turn out, he would let the building go." Harry was not above bailing out. His pride never stood in the way, and his banking friends understood.

Helmsley also became the master of tax law. "He was way ahead of the field, and did things that people who wrote tax law didn't know you could do. Like paying large amounts of advance interest, when paying advance interest was legal," said Steve Brener.

But Helmsley remained largely devoted to equity, and to real estate, while a good many other syndicators in the early days were really securities people. They were playing Monopoly, but it might as well have been any other game with a bank. "Somebody once said that during the 1920s, these wild guys setting up real estate pools, they were buying real estate to sell securities, rather than selling securities to buy real estate," said David Clurman, who wrote the country's first syndicate regulatory law.

But this was all underlying, long-term strategy. What really mattered at any one moment were the individual deals, and Helmsley was learning to make deals like no one before.

~

Bernard Mendik, now one of the wealthiest Manhattan-based real estate entrepreneurs, was just starting out in the business when he and Larry Silverstein approached Harry about a building on East Forty-seventh Street near the United Nations that Helmsley wanted to sell. "It was an old loft, and I think really he had outgrown the building," Mendik said. "But for us it was the Taj Mahal. We were looking up to it and he was looking down on it. He had set a price on it, $925,000. So we went up to see him. There were three of us—myself, Larry, and

Larry's father, Harry Silverstein. And we went to his office, in the Lincoln Building, and the three of us sat in front of his desk and started to negotiate with him. I think we said something like $800,000.

"Now, in those days Harry Helmsley was not the man that he is these days. He was a very taciturn person. Very, very quiet. Very reserved. He didn't say much. He was a tall man, and successful, and he was someone to look up to, especially when you're twenty-six or twenty-seven years old. He was the big man. So after telling him we wanted to pay only $800,000, all he did was harrumph. So we had a little conference, and we went up to $825,000, and he harrumphed again. And we kept going up as he kept harrumphing. And finally we got to $925,000, which was his asking price, and we were lucky to get out of there without having to pay more."

If Mendik hadn't started to study Helmsley by then, he certainly did afterward, as did Silverstein. They both would spend weekends reading and analyzing the prospectuses that Helmsley and Larry Wien would prepare for their syndicates. And Mendik endeared himself as a protégé to Helmsley, and even more so to Wien, who taught him not only how to make money but how to give it away as well.

"Harry had a unique way of negotiating," Mendik continued, sitting at a coffee table in an office three or four times the size of Helmsley's and furnished far better. "I had heard of it and saw it in action when we negotiated that first loft deal. He was known for something that I don't think anybody has ever matched. I've never run into it. It requires an enormous amount of self-confidence and resoluteness. When anybody wants something bad enough they will bargain for it and negotiate. He never seemed to want anything so terribly that he would give up his style.

"When he was selling something, he would set a price, and you couldn't get him down. Now, a lot of people do that. They'll say, 'I'll sell when I get a price.' But that wasn't his style. He didn't say, 'I'll sell when I get a price.' He decided to sell, really decided to sell, and then he waited until he got his price. There's a distinction between that, because he really intended to sell. Some people don't really intend to sell, they just want to see how far they can go."

Helmsley also knew value was transient. He considered a deal undone one day to be dead the next. An offer unmet was history. Observers like to think there's a science in appraising real estate. But there isn't. Helmsley knew better than anyone that value was totally subjective. Any piece of property is worth something different to different people, and on any given day it's usually worth something different from what it was the previous day or what it would be the next day. Observed one of Helmsley's top aides: "A fellow I used to work with once said, 'A sale of real estate never takes place unless the seller and buyer disagree on the value.' And that's probably true."

The aide outlined the recent history of a little more than fourteen acres of New Jersey at the foot of the George Washington Bridge in the town of Fort Lee. Helmsley had bought it to develop a luxury housing project. Helmsley never developed the land, but he did collect a string of unsolicited offers. "That property was valued at fifteen million dollars, and a few months after we bought it Harry was offered twenty-five million, and he turned it down. He said he wouldn't consider anything less than thirty. A while later he had an offer of thirty, and he said he wouldn't consider anything less than thirty-five. And he had an offer of thirty-five and he said he wouldn't consider anything less than forty. And he had an offer of forty and he said he wouldn't consider anything less than fifty. And recently we had an offer of seventy-five and he said he wouldn't consider it."

Those numbers were increments of ten million dollars. Almost anyone else in Helmsley's position would have gone weak-kneed and grabbed. There are few people even in Helmsley's rank that could casually turn down the higher bidding. Harry Helmsley could, without effort. And he reacted in the same cool, collected way in his earlier days when the increments were in thousands and he needed the commission.

In buying property Helmsley would strike an even calmer pose. At times there was a line of salesmen out the door or on hold trying to get past Ceil Fried to talk to Helmsley. It wasn't that they thought he would pay any more than another buyer. It was simply that they knew he would pay. In a business fraught with hemming and hawing, Helmsley was always good for a deal on the spot. He wouldn't have to be wined and dined. One needn't dawdle in social niceties, or even discuss the property. Helmsley already knew it. He wanted to know the asking price and the basic terms. That was it.

Continued Mendik: "Let's assume the seller wants ten million. Harry Helmsley would have looked at it and analyzed it first. And let's say he thinks it's worth eight. Now, that's not that far away from ten. He didn't come in and say five. He said something that is below the asking price but what he wants to pay, and so the seller comes back and says, 'I'll give it to you for nine.' That's it. Harry doesn't negotiate anymore. He's off the deal. You either come back and sell it to him at the price he wants or he's not going to buy it.

"Now, that puts the seller in a very, very unusual position. First, you know that you have a responsible buyer in Helmsley. Two, you know you have a man of his word. If he says he is going to buy it at that price, he will buy it at that price. He may get tough on the contract, but the business deal is done. So you have a very tough decision to make. You sell it to Harry at that price and not go to the marketplace, or you risk not having him as a buyer after the first round. He made many, many great deals that way. A lot of properties he bought before they really ever got to the market. People would go to him right away. He'd look at it, make an offer, pay the price, and nobody else ever got involved."

Helmsley's charm in all his years of deal-making has been effuse, not superficial. His invariable greeting has been a smile, a warm handshake, a word about the family. But his intentions, by all accounts, have been sincere. Helmsley smiles because he wants to smile, not because he thinks it will build some instant rapport that will smooth the way to making money. James Bloor saw that sincerity in the 1930s when Helmsley walked into his office at the Chase National Bank and quietly asked what he had for sale. Four decades later the San Francisco hotelier Bill Kimpton saw that Helmsley sincerity when Helmsley met with him to consider building a luxury hotel in Hawaii. "He is very straightforward in what and who he is. He doesn't try to sell himself," said Kimpton.

"You've seen a mongoose and a cobra," Kimpton added. "The mongoose keeps circling and circling until the cobra gets all tied up, and then it attacks. Well, he taught me that you make an offer and then you wait. Maybe two years, maybe five years. I have properties that I've been waiting for five, six, seven years. You let the cycles work the price back."

Harry learned other plays. Some were tricks. Some were just direct approaches to doing business. All of them set him apart. One of the most effective was probably just his natural demeanor as a listener. He was a very good listener, and people respected him for the trait, which they'd consider a heartfelt courtesy. He would hear, and then weigh, ideas from everyone. But in the throes of a tense negotiation, Harry the listener would be frightfully unnerving. More than one person on the other side of his desk vividly recalled Harry sitting back and saying nothing—not a word—for fifteen or twenty minutes. With millions of dollars at stake, or at least hundreds of thousands in commissions, those were very long minutes.

He would place his right hand across his chest, to his left shoulder. And then he would tap, slowly, with his fingers. Tap. Tap. Observers would swear they could hear his mind turning, working through the numbers.

It was the fool who would talk and not take careful note.

Once, when his syndicate still owned and managed the St. Moritz Hotel on the south side of Central Park, he was approached by an executive vice president for the Simon & Schuster publishing company, whose president was living atop the hotel in a penthouse. The executive was there to renegotiate the lease, and according to Helmsley attorney Rabinowitz: "The guy was absolutely demanding. He would say, 'Okay, see? Okay, see?' And then he would want this, that, and the other thing. And say, 'Okay, see?' And Harry wouldn't say a thing. Not a thing. And when he was done with his 'okays' and 'sees' and all his demands, Harry said, 'Okay, and I see. And the answer is no.' The guy never even got it he was so wrapped up in himself."

A couple of hours later a Simon & Schuster attorney who was present called Rabinowitz and laughingly said he was shocked Helmsley hadn't just blown up at the buffooning executive. But Harry never exploded. He only very rarely let deals or people goad him into losing control. Indeed, that "Okay, and I see" was actually one of Helmsley's subtle one-liners. He rarely told a joke, but he would flavor or punctuate his remarks with a few precious words that were hilarious in the context of the sober, dour discussions on hand. The real estate newspaper industry in its lampoons gave Harry a nickname that never caught on, but it fit: "Chuckles."

Harry is very quick. One aide was doing a deal in Passaic, New Jersey, the eastern end of the industrial Rust Belt, and Harry casually asked what the site looked like. The aide had to confess that he hadn't had time to go see it, and, in fact, had been to Passaic only twice in his life, most recently for a funeral. "I know," said Harry without missing a beat, "the whole town died."

In negotiation, Helmsley would leave his competitors dumbstruck, and they naturally would think they were beaten by raw brilliance. But Helmsley was not born with a computer mind for real estate deals. He bought it. And the price was his life with Eve.

They were married, but they weren't.

"Until recently, until the last few years, his whole life was his work. It was totally absorbing," said one Helmsley executive. "He was like a composer or an artist, or someone in business in any field. He had no other interests as far as I could tell. His sole interest was real estate."

Harry spent vast amounts of time at the office. Only the workaholic Brener was there earlier each morning or later into the evenings. Yet Brener lived in Manhattan, just a few blocks from the office. Harry commuted over two hours each day, catching the train at Grand Central Station to his and Eve's home in the Westchester County town of Ossining, alongside the Hudson River.

They lived alongside the eighteenth green of a golf course, which Harry seldom used. "He was a social golfer," said Charles Urstadt, a former state official and a close friend. Harry could go the required rounds when he had to, as at the occasional business outing. He once played with Urstadt and Nelson Rockefeller at the governor's club, but it meant business to him, not sport. "If I was a better golfer I might be more interested in that game," Helmsley told a reporter once. "But, for me, real estate is the best game around—and when you're ahead in a game you like to keep playing."

The Helmsleys' house sat on a ridgetop. It was an odd-looking house, with a high-peaked roof and a screened porch dominating the front. But it had a spectacular view of the Hudson, and off to one side was an undeveloped hillside down which deer would amble.

Harry was apologetic to friends about the simple swimming pool he built, not wanting to seem like he was putting on wealthy airs. But throughout his life swimming has been his mental and physical therapy. On the road he would make a beeline for the pool or the ocean to do his strokes. At home he would rise before dawn to swim before driving down to the train station in his aging rear-engine Corvair.

But it wasn't just the vast amount of time he would spend away from home that interfered with their personal lives. Even when Harry was home he was not always there for Eve. He forwarded his telephone calls to his home, so that people ringing his office could be switched to him without their knowing.

Harry and Eve did do things together. They even gained a reputation among other real estate people as being somewhat adventuresome when they took up skiing. Most times they would merely drive up to a tiny resort along the Hudson that had a twenty-second ski run. Occasionally they flew to St. Moritz, Switzerland, or to Aspen, Colorado. Up on Buttermilk, or Aspen Mountain—Eve isn't quite sure anymore —Harry broke a leg.

Most times, however, Eve was left to play tennis with her friends. She loved the game and played frequently most of her adult life until she fell and broke a hip. Eve and Harry never had children. Eve's only child, which she had with her first husband, Arthur Green, died very young. But after a time Eve spent her days caring for her mother, who moved into one of their home's three bedrooms after her father died.

Eve was tight with her money, as was Harry, but to a lesser degree. But Eve was thrifty, not stingy. And friends say one oft-cited incident has been misinterpreted in recent press accounts. Eve and Harry threw only occasional parties at home, not being part of the suburb's dance-and-dinner-and-drinking crowd. And at one, Eve limited guests to one hard drink.

But that likely was her Quaker conservatism, which Eve took seriously. She went regularly to the meetings and participated in its various enterprise work, especially the American Friends Service Committee. In later years Eve adopted a special caring for impoverished children, and she donated time and money to various poverty-fighting causes.

The Helmsley empire ran on Harry's neglect of Eve. It ran on his sweat equity. One deal in particular seemed to set Helmsley in motion through the decade before he got into hotels. It would be his biggest, and last, large public syndicate. And it won him two kinds of fame.

The deal was the 1969 acquisition of the real estate trust owned by Morris Furman and Herman Wolfson. The trust, whose shares were traded on the American Stock Exchange, held about thirty buildings nationwide. It was a nice mixed bag, including office buildings in Houston, Los Angeles, and Des Moines, Iowa, as well as several in Manhattan and the tallest office tower in Newark, New Jersey. Two stars in the portfolio were the forty-nine-story One La Salle Building in Chicago and 1440 Broadway in New York City. The trust also held shopping centers scattered across the country.

The sales price effectively was $165 million, including $88 million in mortgages Helmsley would have to assume. But it was the cash that mattered. Helmsley needed about $80 million, having offered to buy the 4.6 million outstanding Furman-Wolfson shares for $16.46 apiece. Helmsley turned to his old friend the Chase Manhattan Bank and got an astounding show of corporate confidence. He received a $78 million loan, based on nothing more than his signature. And it wasn't even his legal given name. It was his nickname, Harry B. Helmsley. It was the largest unsecured signature loan ever. Helmsley proudly inserted a mention of it into his business résumé, though he hardly had to remind his peers. Word of the loan swept through the real estate world, elevating Harry Helmsley to the deanship of Manhattan's elite entrepreneurs.

But it was in crafting the new trust under his name that Helmsley set a second record of sorts. He designed a limited partnership syndicate that in terms of profits for him—the promoter—would rival all other syndicates. He renamed the trust Investment Properties Associates, having dipped into its holdings and picked out about ten properties for his own disposal. And then he offered shares to the world, filing a sixty-two-page offering prospectus with the federal Securities and Exchange Commission. There were 81,700 shares, at $1,000 each. And the buyers were offered a deal not unlike the Empire State: a 9 percent annual return and a 50 percent share of all the operating profit over that amount.

Where the deal took off from the Empire State was in Helmsley's take and his investment, or noninvestment, as it was. He promptly repaid his signature loan with the shares, which sold in a matter of hours. And then, with none of his own money at stake, he sat back and let inflation take its toll. The golden nugget in this deal was that as rents in the twenty office buildings rose with inflation, the 9 percent guarantee was minuscule compared to actual profit earnings of 15, then 20, then 25, then 30 percent. And everything over 9 percent was Helmsley's to split with the small investors. After he took out his brokerage commission and management fees and cleaning fees, of course.

The Furman-Wolfson deal also displayed what, more than any other single factor, came to characterize Harry Helmsley's empire. He built his fortune on something called depreciation. It's a vague and scary-sounding term to the lay person. But until the 1986 tax reform, depreciation was a very powerful tool—and a very corrupt one, in many eyes—which the rich would use to become richer by doing absolutely nothing.

For years, Congress was hammered to do something about the low taxes paid by the rich. So it raised the tax rate, higher and higher, until the rich in America were among the highest-taxed rich in the world— in theory. But at the same time the federal government devised its now infamous tax loopholes, allowing the careless person with wealth to escape the high rate completely. Among the biggest loopholes was the real estate depreciation. Depreciation was the amount of value that a building would lose as it aged. Of course, office buildings for a good long while in their lives don't lose value. They gain value, as rents go up and new buildings cost more to construct. But for tax purposes, and to provide the loophole, the IRS declared that buildings lose value, and that owners could deduct that book depreciation from their taxes as if they were actually losing money on their investment.

That's why realtors talk about "cash flow" when they forecast a building's fiscal future. The profit investors make will be a combina- tion of the building's operating profits and its tax depreciation. Say a building cost $15 million. The normal depreciation rate would have it losing 10 percent of its value per year, over fifteen years. So every year for fifteen years the owner would have $1 million to deduct from or otherwise alter his or her taxes. That meant that if the building also produced an operating profit of $1 million per year—that is, if rents would exceed maintenance and other costs by $1 million—all of that operating profit would be completely tax-free.

The same procedure worked for syndicates, with the share of ownership a ratio of the amount of participation. A person with a $10,000 share in a building would be deducting 10 percent of that $10,000 each year for fifteen years. And if the building was earning an operating profit of $1,000 per share, the entire share's annual earning would be tax-free. In many cases, using other tax law, syndicate investors—big and small—could invest in a dog of a building that barely broke even, and then apply the depreciation they'd get to their other income. They would thereby make substantial profit by lowering their overall taxes. With the Furman-Wolfson deal Harry Helmsley made both an equity-based and a tax-based syndicate work to its finest degree, and he was there to reap the profit and finance his next ventures.

Wien did not join with Helmsley in that syndicate deal. The only other general partner was Helmsley's close and longtime associate Irving Schneider, and it made Schneider enormously wealthy.

Schneider has a blocky, jowly face. And he's often described as the tough guy in the Schneider-Schwartz duo. Both men are described by friends invariably as warm, friendly, and entirely giving men. In matters of business, however, if Alvin Schwartz would smooth and stroke Helmsley-Spear's clients, Schneider would hammer. But then, in Schneider's piece of the Helmsley empire the only way to win was to hammer. Schneider worked the garment district. For Harry Helmsley and, increasingly, for himself, it was a tough neighborhood.

The garment center formed in the early 1920s when fashionable Fifth Avenue folks pushed the clothing manufacturers out. "The pants pressers were walking Fifth Avenue when the garment district was on both sides of it, between Twenty-third and Thirty-fourth streets, so the women couldn't go shopping," the aging Leon Spear, of Helmsley-Spear, recalled in 1980. "The big department stores said, 'Find another site.' We chose West Thirty-fifth to West Forty-first streets, between Sixth and Ninth Avenues—it was all low buildings then, not much more than a red-light district. By 1925, new buildings covered 80 percent of the new garment district and we managed most of them."

Six decades later the district faced innumerable problems. Manhattan, in its infatuation with white-collar service industries, was no longer hospitable to manufacturers. The trend to convert manufacturing lofts into residential condos continued strong. And the business itself was changing in ways that would mean less needed space. Even famous private labels are now using generic stock from other countries to which they merely affix their names. Where there once was clatter from sewing machines, there is silence. Where there were hordes of youngsters wildly pushing carts crammed with coats and dresses, there are empty side streets. As the greatest portent of a troubled future, city officials and others are weighing the notion of a Garment Center Protection District to save what can't stand on its own. "There's been a whole transformation. It's a different business," Schneider told several hundred real estate brokers and entrepreneurs in the summer of 1988.

"It's a very volatile area," Schneider said, his voice gravelly as he warned of a continuing residential encroachment and urged other landlords to brave out the incursion and maintain their property for the garment industry. "To give you an idea, in 1978 we were negotiating to buy a building that some people in this room were negotiating to buy. It was 1384 Broadway. In 1978 there was a first mortgage and second mortgage on it. Both being foreclosed on. The building was mostly empty. The previous owner was trying to get a variance to rebuild the building as an apartment house. Sounds incredible to some of you younger people. Sounded incredible to us. We bought it. Of course, we changed it, spent a lot of money, and it has become a vital part of the garment district. We at Helmsley-Spear are not concerned about the garment center disappearing. We are more concerned that other owners like us do what we've done to upgrade their buildings."

That rallying call to arms notwithstanding, for three decades from 1950 on Schneider played one of the better hands in the fiercest aspects of the real estate game, one that continues with office space today: musical tenants. Every time a lease came up, or sometimes even before, almost every landlord would try to steal the leaseholder. Sometimes it was theft by seduction, sometimes by coercion.

Things got so wild that Lawrence Wien went on a campaign against what he called tenant "piracy." In 1967 Wien rewrote his lease contracts to make it a breach of contract for tenants to move out before the lease expired, regardless of whether they paid for the remaining part of their lease. The problem for landlords was that empty space bred empty space. Prospective tenants would turn away at the sight of a lot of vacancy in a building. Explained the attorney: "It is very prejudicial to an existing building, and to the other tenants in it, to have firms moving out before their leases expire."

But as Schneider recalled, there was also a natural progression of tenants on which the smart landlord would seize. "You have to understand that buildings are characterized by the kind of business that is done in that building. For example, a dress building might be a popular-price-dress building. So that in the old days if the wholesale price was $5.75 to $8.75, no manufacturer making [higher-priced dresses] would come into that building. The owner wouldn't let him in. The owner wouldn't let a sportswear manufacturer in the building. The west side of Seventh Avenue could just as well be a mile away from the east side of Seventh Avenue. The buyers are different. The owners are different. The west side of Seventh Avenue is for the higher-priced-garment people. But all of the people as they [progressed in quality] would move. So that the person in 1375 Broadway would want to go to 501 Seventh Avenue, and when they priced up, they would want to go to 1400 Broadway, and after that they'd want to go to 498 Seventh Avenue, or 530 or 550. These are numbers that people in the garment center know, and that's the movement that took place." And Schneider, of course, or his managers would be there to encourage that flow, because there would always be more than one building in the same category, and there would never be enough tenants to take all the space.

Up to the mid-1960s Helmsley was strictly a manager and a buyer —whether for syndicates or, as he accumulated his own wealth, for himself. And his empire expanded by leaps. Only little paragraphs would make the New York papers, but the purchases were significant, and they added up. He bought lofts throughout the garment center, offices throughout Manhattan, and both commercial and residential property around the country—Philadelphia; Washington, D.C.; Greenville, North Carolina; St. Louis; Chicago; Houston; Los Angeles; and San Francisco.

Helmsley considered managing a building—to make the rent roll exceed costs—his first love. "Some real estate companies look on management almost as a stepchild," he once explained. "They may take operational responsibility for a building as the price of obtaining the rental agency and the lucrative leasing commissions involved. We are interested in those commissions too, but we also know that if we do a good management job for the owners, we will not only have the rental agency but the insurance brokerage and the sales commission if and when the building changes hands."

But as owners approached Helmsley-Spear looking for it to manage their properties, Helmsley would usually be offered, or he would ask for, an ownership share. "If their properties have potential we tend to take an ownership position in them, often through a relatively small syndication in which our principals will participate," Helmsley once explained.

He continued racking up shares or whole properties through the 1960s. Between 1967 and 1969 he bought the following: two shopping centers—the Fairview Shopping Center in Decatur, Illinois, and the Southgate in Fort Wayne, Indiana; the Carlton House, a luxurious residential hotel in Manhattan, from the British branch of the Astor family; the Insurance Exchange Building, Chicago's largest office building, with more than two million square feet of floor space for 330 life insurance and casualty tenants, in a deal that Schneider negotiated and then managed, adding it to his Helmsley-Spear chores in the Midwest; the twenty-story Boatmen's Bank Building in St. Louis, where Wien already owned the 691-unit Georgetown apartments; 857 units of garden apartments on Inwood Street in Houston; 1,223 apartments in Drexel Hill, Pennsylvania; and more in his own neighborhood: twenty buildings of apartments totaling 1,828 units in Queens, New York. Other deals took him into Philadelphia and Milwaukee, and Helmsley-Spear set up eighteen branches throughout the country.

Leon Spear would become somewhat baffled at the frenzy of his partner-in-name. "We can't keep track of him, with all his projects and acquisitions," Spear once said, somewhat tongue-in-cheek. "I say, 'For God's sake, when are you going to stop? What do you need this one for?' And Harry will say, 'Don't spoil my fun—when I get into a deal and it's full of machinations and complications to work out, it's like you having a grandchild.' "

Harry Helmsley on the prowl for property was an intimidating sight. "I remember that I went to look at a building once on East Twenty-third Street," Mendik said. "I took a cab and just as I was getting out of the cab, I noticed that across the street in front of the building there was a green Cadillac limousine, and I said to myself, 'Aw, shit.' Out steps Harry and I just got back into the cab and went home, 'cause there was no way you could compete with the guy when he wanted it. 'Cause he was going to get it."

For each of his purchases he would set up dummy corporations to hold the property. That was common industry practice. He simply did it more than almost anyone else.

His secretaries Augusta Helm and Ceil Fried were on more boards of directors than Lee Iacocca. Eventually Harry started incorporating in the state of Delaware along with everyone else, since Delaware had the fewest regulations, and it's believed that Helmsley eventually came to have as many as 400 separate incorporations with oddball, meaningless names, often based just on the property address.

Realesco Equities Corp., for example, which Helmsley set up and kept in New York State, was later expanded in a mass merger, for a $60 filing fee, to include the following corporations: 53 East 93rd Street, IFC Capital, IFC Syndicate, Invesco Manhattan, Invesco Properties, 9780 Airport, Springfield, 200 East, Dengro Realty, Dodvi Realty, Herne Realty, Parken Realty, and 8484 16th Street.

In the mid-1960s Helmsley also acquired two whole real estate companies that greatly expanded his realm. One was the Charles F. Noyes Co., which took him into downtown real estate in a big way. The other was Brown, Harris, Stevens, Inc., an apartment brokerage and management specialist. Helmsley-Spear, Inc., itself, according to company records, grew from a long chain of real estate firms, starting with S. B. Goodale (1866); S. B. Goodale and Son (1890); Goodale, Perry & Dwight (1914); Dwight, Archibald & Perry (1919); Dwight, Voorhis & Perry, Inc. (1925); Dwight, Voorhis & Helmsley, Inc. (1938); Dwight-Helmsley, Inc. (1946), and then the merger with Spear & Co. in 1955.

Harry Helmsley's entire empire—including the separately managed firms of Noyes and Brown, Harris, various Helmsley-Spear subsidiaries in Florida and other states, the hotel and office supplier Deco Purchasing, an office cleaning firm, and other subsidiaries—came to be known as Helmsley Enterprises.

When deals were done, and a new property was acquired, Helmsley then made a point of hiring the attorneys who'd been involved with the building before. So when it came time to challenge the tax assessor's reassessment, which Helmsley would invariably do as a matter of business practice, Harry would be represented by lawyers who'd been through it before. They knew the property. They knew the assessor. They knew the assessors' assistants. Helmsley aides ascribed to that policy a deep Helmsley loyalty, but it was more cleverness than loyalty. He was an expert employer in that he knew how to get the best out of every employee.

Above a certain level in the real estate world, as in other businesses, the top players are people of their word. Their employees might lie and cheat and backstab their way to profit, but after a certain point the big people—the Bill Zeckendorfs, Seymour Dursts, Donald Trumps, and Bob Blasses—have reputations to save. And rarely is reneging on an agreement to make any one deal worth a tarnished reputation. Word gets around. But Harry Helmsley's word was exceptionally good.

The Empire State Building deal, for example, was enormously complex, and set new parameters for deal-making. Over a hundred attorneys were involved—a huge number at the time—in formulating a contract that ran four hundred pages long just for the lease. Like a wedding party, the parties had to get together twice before the actual signing just to practice, and even then the real thing took a good part of a day. Most other Helmsley deals in those early empire-building days could be done overnight, with just a couple of people handing documents back and forth. But, big or small, at some point in the negotiation it all came down to a "yes" or a "no." And when Harry Helmsley said "yes," that was it on his part. His word was sterling.

"The real estate business is a tough game, and I have never met anyone or heard of anybody who had an unkind word about Harry," said Robert Wagner, a former New York City mayor who met and befriended Harry after he left office in 1965. "He was always a good man, a man of his word. His handshake was his bond."

Many of the people he transacted with have a "Harry's word" tale to relate, but Seymour Rabinowitz tells two of the best. One time he had brought to Helmsley a deal to unload some property in New Jersey. Helmsley considered and approved the sale for $5 million. But before they signed any papers someone else phoned and offered $7 million. Helmsley told Rabinowitz the $5 million deal would stand, and Rabinowitz called the original buyer, who was dumbstruck.

"He told me," recalled Rabinowitz, " 'You know, I heard a rumor that there was somebody else competitively looking to buy, but I didn't think it was serious. You know, we didn't sign anything. You could have gone with the $7 million.' " As it turned out, Rabinowitz even offered to pass along the name of the higher bidder to the $5 million buyer, so he could score an instant $2 million profit—minus a Helmsley-Spear brokerage commission, of course.

Another time and with another New Jersey property, a deal had been done, signed and sealed, but in the closing Rabinowitz had done an audit and discovered that Helmsley-Spear had miscalculated the selling price—to Helmsley's disadvantage by several thousand dollars. "So I went to Harry and told him and he said, 'Write them a check.' But what he didn't know was that I already had written the check and sent it out. I knew that's what he would say," Rabinowitz said. Rabinowitz then called the buyer, who represented a public corporation, and coyly told him there was something wrong with the sales price. The buyer sank into a mild depression, saying he just couldn't go back to his directors and ask for more money. Rabinowitz made his day by then saying the balance was his and a check was on its way. That kind of honesty awed Helmsley's peers, and stories like that would precede his next dealings. He was a publicity agent's dream.

Not every handshake worked out.

J. Myer Schine was a maverick entrepreneur, a "rugged individualist," one newspaper typecast him. Born in Latvia in 1892, Schine emigrated to America with his parents and hit the shore running. He candy-butchered on trains, selling sweets between stations. He sold dresses. After failing in a business in Syracuse, he settled in Gloversville, New York, and started to build a chain of motion-picture theaters. There were 250 Schine houses when federal prosecutors flexed their antitrust laws after World War II and forced him to dispose of all but 60. But Schine had picked up some real estate along the way with his ticket sales, and it was an estimated $150 million estate that Helmsley and Wien negotiated to buy in 1965.

The estate had some fine pieces: a twenty-three-acre tract under and surrounding the Ambassador Hotel on Wilshire Boulevard in Los Angeles; eleven other hotels nationwide; the 60 remaining Schine theaters in six states; and, above all, 3,000 acres of pristine, undeveloped ocean beach frontage in Palm Beach and Boca Raton, Florida, just waiting for condominium projects or estate homes to lap up on its shore.

On July 19, 1965, Wien and Helmsley proudly announced they were buying the Schine estate. The price: about $64.4 million. It was a rare advance story out of Helmsley or Wien. Helmsley especially was wary of any publicity spoiling a broth, and never spoke before or after to reporters in any meaningful detail. The Schine announcement made the front page of *The New York Times* the following day. But six weeks later the *Times* ran another story. This time it was Schine doing the announcing, and the word from him was that he was selling the estate's holdings for $69.5 million to another group. Helmsley and Wien were shocked. They had had what Helmsley considered to be a deal. "We shook hands on it," Helmsley told a reporter, "and then we went to work to prepare the contract. It runs to two hundred pages."

Schine never said publicly what changed his mind. Harry and Larry likely thought it was simply the $5 million extra that the second bidder, Realty Equities, offered to pay. Miffed, and with egg on their faces, they sued Schine asking for a sales commission of nearly $2 million. It seemed they had structured the deal much like any other—

the $2 million would have come from the roundup of Wien-Helmsley investors who would have been obligated to pay Helmsley a 3 percent commission for managing the transaction.

But even the Schine fiasco couldn't be blamed on Harry. His reputation was unsullied, and Helmsley's good word continued to win him extraordinary deals. His "true to his word" reputation also won him the best form of flattery: lampoon. In the annual spoof issues of *Real Estate Weekly*, the editors substituted real estate people for actors in stills of popular movies, and Helmsley was mercilessly poked at.

One of the doctored photos showed Helmsley in top hat and coat, addressing another real estate man, Adrian Phillips, who had a young woman on his arm. Read the caption: "Joshingly warning the lovely lady against Helmsley, Phillips told her to beware of him 'because he'll try to put one over on you!' But the gal was smarter than she'd been given credit for. 'He may be a big real estate operator,' she cracked, 'but he's an honest man. I can tell by his hand. They are in his OWN pockets.' "

The contacts Harry made in his early days also started to pay off.

Twelve years after the Chase loan deal Harry bought the remains of a huge real estate enterprise called the Investors Funding Corporation of New York. IFC had gone bankrupt six years earlier after a string of bad luck piled up. It bought a $20 million brewery for what turned out to be very unprofitable beer. It got smacked by the 1974 recession. Its founder and other company officers were indicted for offering bribes to the city fathers of Fort Lee, New Jersey, where IFC had been pinning its hopes on developing a tract of land at the foot of the George Washington Bridge. The only trouble was, the land had come cheap because it needed a change in zoning to allow the development, and the town, to IFC's mounting frustration, kept saying no.

IFC went into receivership, and there began the monumental task of dismantling the company to pay off the creditors, not to mention the many investors. IFC had some 200 properties coast to coast. It had 30,000 creditors. And there were fourteen banks with a stake in its assets. The court had to scrutinize every minutia, and the records of the deal—which in 1988 was still being wound down—filled 200 or more four-drawer filing cabinets that cost $12,000 a year just to warehouse.

Every property required an intense examination. There were third and even fourth mortgages to untangle, a very rare thing in the world of real estate loans.

But when Helmsley stepped in and offered to buy what remained of the IFC holdings—about 61 properties—for $70 million, it was as if the federal government itself had spoken.

No one had to ask who Harry Helmsley was. And no one needed anything more than his word. None of the fourteen banks. None of the 30,000 creditors. Not even the court raised a question about Harry Helmsley. Of course, Helmsley wasn't about to mess around with the deal if he wasn't serious about buying, the bankruptcy trustee pointed out. Still, there likely was no one in the world at the time who commanded such utter respect among the players, particularly the banks, all of whose board chairmen Harry knew.

And it didn't hurt that the bankruptcy trustee was none other than James Bloor, the Chase National Bank man. "I certainly knew who Harry Helmsley was without having to look into his accounts," said Bloor.

It was one thing to know Helmsley would be true to his word in buying a building. It was another to know he would follow through on a more complex deal, and it was Harry's good word that eased him into the next phase of his career.

Many real estate entrepreneurs will switch hats sometime in their careers to move from playing the simple investor to one who develops raw land into buildings. It's a difficult step. The developer has to pull off several tricky tasks. If the building site is not whole, it has to be knit together with smaller parcels whose owners might not want to sell. An architect and the actual builder/contractor must be hired. Prospective tenants usually must be lured, unless the whole building is to be done on speculation. And financiers must be convinced it will all happen so they will lay their cash down up front.

In the mid-1960s, Helmsley started to make that switch to developer, adding a new decoration to his spartan office: hard hats, inscribed with his name, one from each building he built. There were only a few because he never became a major office builder. He saved that skill for his hotels.

Helmsley's first building grew from a site down on Broadway, right next to the Equitable Building. He put up a sleek, fifty-two-story tower on the full-block site. Though very modern in its steel-and-glass structure, the building had spandrels in its design that helped it fit into the older, more ornate neighborhood. Former Helmsley-Spear executive Tom O'Keefe told a business reporter that the real estate market was slumping when the building opened in 1967. "It was a tough project. We were really feeling our way around at a time when the market wasn't advantageous for us. We had a hell of a time learning about escalation clauses and the like," O'Keefe said.

Helmsley found tenants. The Marine Midland Bank took nineteen floors and got to put its name on the building. The investment banker Donaldson, Lufkin & Jenrette, Inc., took another ten. The prestigious law firm of Palmer & Wood also moved in.

At the same time Helmsley began planning another building—a fifty-two-story tower in the western reaches of midtown Manhattan just north of Penn Station and the city's third Madison Square Garden. It eventually was raised to fifty-seven stories, and opened in 1971. The deal required a $100 million mortgage—one of the largest such loans ever made—from Helmsley's old friends at the Metropolitan Life Insurance Co. and the Equitable Life Assurance Society.

Bill Lehy, who spent forty-six years with Met Life before retiring, was handling its real estate division at the time. "He was an intense negotiator, and as they say, a man of his word," recalled Lehy. "But what was important in doing something like One Penn Plaza, or 22 Cortland, another building we did with Harry, was negotiating with people who knew what they were doing. If you succeeded [in striking a deal] with someone who doesn't know what they're doing, you don't succeed, because they don't follow through and perform." Helmsley said he would build, and he built, to the budget agreed upon.

Chase Manhattan participated in another temporary $90 million construction loan. An all-day signing session with thirty attorneys in Chase's headquarters left Helmsley exasperated. Putting the deal together took a year "from the time we shook hands to the time we signed," Helmsley said in July 1970. "I'm glad to get back into the real estate business and stop watching lawyers work at $100 a day."

Helmsley built two other office buildings in downtown Manhattan, as well as a nine-story merchandise mart in downtown Los Angeles for wholesale jewelers. And then, in the late 1960s, he high-stepped into the lodging business by putting up the first luxury hotel in Manhattan in almost a decade.

But first Helmsley would lose a partner.

One of Larry Wien and Harry Helmsley's last interactions was a long-drawn-out political fight against the proposed mammoth World Trade Center in downtown Manhattan.

The twin towers, each bigger than the Empire State Building, had been proposed by a bistate transportation agency, the Port Authority of New York and New Jersey, as a way of bringing new international commerce to Manhattan.

But Larry Wien and a good many Manhattan real estate players saw it differently. They saw it as a government incursion into their private turf. Indeed, the Trade Center was socialized development. The Port Authority would be given exceptional tax advantages that would enable it to charge rents far lower than the market rate in Manhattan. In effect, the towers would suck tenants from other buildings or force other landlords to lower their rents.

Moreover, they argued, the $3 million in payments the authority would make to the city in lieu of taxes compared poorly with the $15 million in property taxes that private developers would pay if they were building that much space.

Wien, Helmsley, and the small investors in the Empire State Building had another problem with the World Trade Center. They stood to lose the hundreds of thousands of dollars paid each year in rent by the forest of radio and television towers that perched on the Empire State. Most would have to move to the taller World Trade Center to maintain their broadcast range.

So Larry Wien, joined by Helmsley, went on the attack. They attended some thirty public meetings and hearings to air their complaints. Some of those present for those meetings recall that Wien did most of the talking. Helmsley was there largely in silent support.

Ironically, Wien and Helmsley chose Paul O'Dwyer, brother of a New York City mayor and an activist Irish attorney who handled a number of populist causes, to fight for the lawsuit they filed when they lost the political battle. O'Dwyer said he considered the pair, their millions notwithstanding, to be the underdogs against the Authority. "The Port Authority paid absolutely no attention to what we were doing, and before they were [legally] able to move in and take title to the land, they moved their equipment in and blocked off the streets and acted like what they were in those days, Nazis. They had the courts in their back pockets, the editors in the front pockets. They were the most powerful machine in the United States," said O'Dwyer.

Indeed, Wien and Helmsley badly lost their fight against the Authority, even though their case went to the state's highest court.

Not long after that, Wien and Helmsley stopped doing deals together. In 1982, Wien actually withdrew from a partnership with Harry in a Queens housing project. They remained inactive partners in other investments, and Wien's law firm continued to represent Helmsley-Spear. Wien never explained the break. There likely were several reasons. Wien never acquired the taste for hotels that Harry did. And unlike Harry, he began to shift from accumulating money to giving it away, from which he seemed to derive much pleasure. He spent his later years being philanthropic and working hard on several nonprofit boards. On that level, they simply grew apart.

But more than one mutual business associate speculates that the suave, sophisticated, but very low-key Larry Wien did not care for Leona at all. No one incident ever popped up to bring any such dislike into the open, though during the Helmsleys' legal troubles, Wien, in his few public remarks, pointedly left Leona out of his praise for Harry. But Wien certainly had a style and attitude toward life that would have clashed with hers.

If Larry Wien was born with class, Leona aspired to hers. They wouldn't have shared the same social circles. They couldn't have held an intelligent conversation. And in the tiniest of differences, they even approached moving around in the world from a different vantage.

Wien and his wife were of a class of wealthy New Yorkers who could easily afford a stretch limo but didn't mind taking the subway. It is, after all, the fastest way to get around Manhattan when traffic is bad.

One of Leona's former attorneys recalls meeting her downtown in her early business days, before she met Harry. "We both had to get uptown," he recalled, "and we couldn't get a cab. We tried for about five minutes. The subway was out of the question. And so I walked over to one of these standing limousines you see there today, and I asked, 'Are you available? We're going uptown.'

"And she looked at me in this most incredible way. All I did was get us a ride. It cost maybe twenty dollars. But all of a sudden I turned into a very classy guy in her eyes, because we were riding uptown in a chauffeured limousine."

There came a time when Leona began needing attorneys like the one who knew how to snag a limo.

# CHAPTER 6

# THE HARD-SELL CO-OP

ON NOVEMBER 30, 1971, LEONA MADE AN INTRIGUING REQUEST TO THE New York State court.

She wanted to change her name. Or, rather, she wanted to make legal the surname, Roberts, that she'd made up and used for much of her adult life.

Such a request to the court was not unusual. It recalls the story, said to be true, of a succession of embattled Jews who, upon arriving at Ellis Island, all changed their last names to Anderson. Suddenly, one family head decided to write Andrews on the registry papers. "What's wrong with Anderson?" the Andersons asked. "It sounds too Jewish," Andrews replied.

What's intriguing about Leona's name-change request, however, is the timing. It came just weeks before she married Harry. And it came as she was embroiled in three legal battles, one of which threatened to collapse her career in real estate.

The first fight stemmed from some carpentry done on her apartment on West Fifty-fifth Street in midtown Manhattan. At the time, Leona was climbing income brackets like an Olympic torchbearer running up so many little steps. Since she had been scraping along on a secretary's salary only a few years earlier, the press and her critics liked to scoff at the sums she claimed to be making in 1971.

She told one astonished interviewer, and repeated it later, that she had earned $450,000 in one three-month period alone. Those were 1971 dollars, when a million was still a million. Disbelief still abounds.

Indeed, had Leona only been selling apartments, she could have made but a fraction of that sum. The most expensive apartment in New York City in the 1960s cost $300,000 to $400,000. A typical 6 percent commission on that would be $25,000, which would have to be split with the brokerage house. To make nearly half a million dollars in three months at that rate would require the sale of forty such super apartments, or ten times that amount in average apartments. Neither she nor anyone else came anywhere close to that volume, more the work of a decade than a year's quarter.

But Leona Roberts was not merely selling apartments. She was converting whole buildings from rentals to co-ops or condos. She worked floor by floor, building by building, not unit by unit. Moreover, she was using her unprecedented sales arrangement, in which the crew's cut was greatly diminished.

"The cooperative pot is boiling. And the chief cook serving the tasty dishes of both cooperative selling and cooperative living is Leona M. Roberts, one of Manhattan's most imaginative and exciting real estate brokers," an industry paper gushed in a profile that ran on her birthday, July 4, 1968. "Miss Roberts, affectionately called Mindy by her affluent clientele, has established an enviable record of having sold millions of dollars' worth of cooperative apartments over the past five years."

"We are making history today in this area of real estate," Leona was quoted. "And that's why it's so exciting."

She was also, as she claimed, raking it in. Just converting the apartment building that Leon Spear bought into, the Brevoort, brought $750,000 in sales commissions, of which Leona kept the better part. In the five years preceding 1969, it was reported in an industry paper, Leona was "responsible for more than $150 million in cooperative sales."

So for work in her apartment, she could afford to hire a good carpenter. But Nick Pantazis of Long Island City didn't seem to meet her desires. He billed her for $4,485. She sued him for $50,000.

Her legal claim makes it seem like the Three Stooges had done the job. Among other things, she accused him of choosing defective materials, causing a building-wide flood by hammering a water pipe, mismatching the wood in a bookcase, crafting a buffet counter so that the "drawers continually fall on the floor," screwing up the bathroom tile job, mislaying the kitchen floor, mangling the bedroom closet tracks, banging up the front door, failing to line the foil paper in the bathroom, incorrectly installing all the electrical outlets, ruining the bedroom carpet, and failing to deliver a toolbox for the terrace and chains for the doors.

It couldn't be learned from the court papers how the case was resolved. The attorneys involved, as well as Pantazis, couldn't be found. But the $50,000 in damages she was asking for came to almost two-thirds the sum she received for the entire apartment, which she sold a year later.

Sol Friedman, a shoe-manufacturing executive, bought the nineteenth-floor apartment and moved in on Thanksgiving evening in 1972. He never met Leona personally. The transaction was handled by attorneys. The apartment was turned over to him in something less than terrific form, remembered a now retired Friedman, laughing. "It was not left in the worst of shape, but not the best. On a scale of one to ten, I'd give it a seven. But like my wife said at the time, it was the apartment we wanted and that's all that mattered." They cleaned up and tossed out an old bookcase left in the den, as well as a bedroom dresser.

Leona was seldom seen around the West Fifty-fifth Street building, where she had moved after living uptown on Eighty-fifth. "I'd see her on the elevator and would say hello, but that was about it," said Tom

Takubo, a neighbor. But she did maintain an office there for a time, and worked on the building's conversion to co-ops. Another tenant remembered her as a manager of sorts. "She was the one who checked me in," said Henny Youngman, the English-born stand-up comedian who lived in Brooklyn for most of his life until moving into the Fifty-fifth Street building. "She took the deposit. I remember it was one month's rent, $425. I met her later and she said, 'Remember me? I checked you in.' "

Leona was very busy in those months she worked as Sutton & Town's residential arm. But she soon got even busier after joining the firm that Harry Helmsley bought in 1965—Brown, Harris, Stevens, Inc.

The story she and Harry tell of their meeting has varied from time to time and in the retelling. But it goes something like this: Harry spotted her fantastic sales technique and said to an aide, "Go get her."

There's at least one reason to question that public account. Leona never in her life waited for something or someone to come to her. She had hunted Helmsley down as an employer, as she hunted him down as a spouse, those close to them both believe. She, and not Harry, had asked Leon Spear for the introduction. Even her public statements seemed pointed. "Miss Roberts," read one industry newspaper profile in 1969, "says she finds only one thing more exciting than her immersion in cooperatives: the opportunity to be part of the excitement and challenge that is generated by being identified with the activities of the person she regards as 'Mr. Real Estate'—Harry B. Helmsley."

On the other hand, it's clear that Harry valued her services. Seymour Rabinowitz negotiated Leona's first-year contract with Brown, Harris. He couldn't remember the details, but he did recall once casually rounding out her anticipated earnings in the first year at Brown, Harris and they were about $1 million, including bonuses. "And she was worth it, just for the first conversion she did that year," her attorney said.

Leona, probably in reaction to the widespread rumorings that she was gold-digging, also has repeatedly said that she possessed $1 million in cash three years later when she married Harry and that she turned the money over to him. She said she needed to do that to show him that she now completely trusted him.

Harry Helmsley made Leona Roberts a senior vice president, the highest-ranking woman at Brown, Harris. And he put her in charge of co-op sales.

That first year she had a dozen conversion projects underway at the same time. There was an incredible boom in Manhattan, and she rode it hard until the slump of 1970. Not only did business go bad. Leona was hit by two government challenges to her conduct, and the conduct of those for whom she was responsible, in selling apartments.

In the first case it's difficult to assess the integrity of the government's claim. The case record is gone. The hearing officer said he could not remember details. Leona's defense attorney, Joseph Forstadt, recalls some extraneous political factors that worked against her, but they don't appear in the transcript and could not be verified.

These are the facts: A man named Ittelson and his wife had purchased apartment 2C in a building at 525 East Eighty-sixth Street. The building was jointly owned by Harry Helmsley and his associate at Helmsley-Spear, Irving Schneider. Leona Roberts was directing a small staff trying to sell the apartments. Ittelson paid $38,640, and he and his wife moved in in March 1970.

A problem arose a few months later when the Ittelsons decided they would rather live in New Jersey, and made a down payment on a home using their expected proceeds from selling the apartment they had just acquired. But the Ittelsons then learned a real estate axiom the hard way, that a deal one day does not another make. The market, just in those months after they moved in, had slumped and no one was moving anything easily. The Ittelsons were told by Cornell Harra, one of Leona's sellers, that they'd have to take a bath in order to move their apartment anytime soon. There were other units in the same building being offered at deeply discounted insider rates, and even they weren't selling.

The matter might have ended there, but then the Ittelsons discovered something that won the court's favor. Their apartment actually had been sold to them by an existing renter in the building who had snapped up several units at the insider discount when Helmsley and

Schneider decided to convert the rentals to owned co-ops. And the renter, who then moved into another unit, pocketed the 30 percent difference in price the discount provided. The Ittelsons weren't told, and they might well have been able to negotiate a better deal if they had been. Instead, they were led to believe the building's units were all going at about the same relative price.

When apprised of the facts, two real estate attorneys opined that the Ittelsons simply should have been smarter. They were buying in an unregulated market—a private resale, between private parties—and weren't privy to the rules and regulations that governed the conversion of the building into co-ops. Had they been, the state clearly would have forced the converters to show them a prospectus on the conversion that listed everyone's prices and profits.

However, the Secretary of State's Division of Licensing Services came down hard on the sellers. Harra was reprimanded and warned to be "more circumspect" in his conduct. Another salesperson more closely tied to the transaction, Marion Terr, had her license suspended for three months and was fined $150. And Helmsley-Spear—Leona, Harry, and Irving were not found personally at fault—was forced to give the Ittelsons a refund or forfeit its brokerage licenses. The Ittelsons got their refund.

But the next case—far more serious—was against Leona directly. Indeed, she came within the drop of a judge's gavel of losing her entire career, and possibly even her future with Harry.

Leona's specialty in apartment sales was the closing. She had a killer instinct. All a salesperson needed to do was bring prospects to her. She then would home in on just the thing that would convince them to buy. It might be one spouse's infatuation with the kitchen. Or it could be another's concern about payments. Or she would sense that both people dreaded street noise, in which case she would turn on a drowning fan, keep the windows shut, and marvel at how that apartment wasn't washed with the honking, sirens, and yells of Manhattan. Above all, it was her attitude. She wasn't selling: she was giving people the investment opportunity of a lifetime.

With a string of successes under her belt, the fifty-year-old Leona was put in charge of converting an apartment house on East Fifty-sixth

Street into cooperative apartments. She was a logical choice for the job. It wouldn't be easy persuading the 172 renters in the twenty-story building to buy their apartments. The country's economy was hurting. And as far as co-ops were concerned, Leona herself would later testify in an unrelated case that things were bleak. "The bottom fell out of the market," she said.

So the owners gave their apartment house on East Fifty-sixth Street a fancy name, Sutton Place. Leona went to work on it with all her expertise and energy. And what ensued, according to state prosecutors, was one of the most heavy-handed conversions they'd seen. In short, the record shows, she and the building owners turned up the pressure on the tenants until they bought their apartments.

Sutton Place was a pressure cooker, and Leona was said to be the one turning up the flame.

The case brought against Leona was brutal. She and two salespeople were charged with muscling the Sutton Place tenants into buying their apartments. On and on the charges went, citing names and dates and circumstances. Several dozen tenants were named as victims. The coercion ran the gamut of dirty tricks, but one, described in the court records in more cryptic form, would have run something like this bad "knock-knock" joke:

"Who's there?"

"Leona, dear, your friend from the office downstairs."

"What is it?"

"I've come to see how you're coming along in signing those papers."

"Well, I just don't know if it's right for me, you know. The rent is so low, and the future's not bright, and owning is just so complicated with those mortgages and all."

"Oh dear, I'm so sorry to hear that, because Joe Schmo, who is living in a dreary Brooklyn apartment, and is just desperate to move into Manhattan, and is just drooling over this building, well, he just gave the owner a fifty-dollar deposit to buy your apartment."

The apartment conversion law was tough on tenants back then. Renters got first dibs on their apartments. But if they didn't buy, they were out. Eviction city. It didn't matter if they had lived there twelve months or twelve years. It didn't matter if they could afford their apartments or not. Hand over the keys. Out. So there was some hard thinking to do when Leona dropped the bomb about there being another person ready to pay up and move in.

Fact was, the state discovered, neither Joe Schmo nor his fifty dollars existed. They were mere figments of a saleswoman's ambition.

Just how Sutton Place came to New York State attorney general Louis Lefkowitz's attention could not be determined. The working files in the case—those with the prosecutors' notes and memoranda that explain their thinking process—were lost by the attorney general's office. Neither Lefkowitz nor his assistant, David Clurman, were comfortable discussing the case without reviewing those files.

It may have been that the attorney general's office simply got telephone calls from the tenants who suspected something was not right. Leona's defenders at the time now believe the state was drawn to the matter by a private attorney of the breed called a "shark"—a lawyer who chases apartment-building conversions by reading real estate ads to find clients, much like an aggressive probate attorney might read death notices.

In the case of conversions, the shark would feed on landlords by stirring renters to fight for the lowest possible apartment purchase price. Sutton Place would have attracted attention. It was a big, twenty-story building. The assessed value of the 172 apartments, as co-ops, was more than $10 million. With prices ranging from $15,000 to $85,000, the moderate-income Sutton Place residents who couldn't afford to buy their apartments certainly would have been spilling the blood to lure such a shark.

Or it may have been that Lefkowitz was flexing his political savvy. The case had some very good elements. There was a star female broker. She had a tycoon boss with whom the attorney general was wrestling on another controversial apartment conversion. The middle-class and, in some cases, aging tenants were under siege. The whole city, in fact, was awash with largely unregulated apartment conversions and the public was alarmed. If the attorney general sensed a good story, he was right. The press gave the story good play, and it wasn't long before Leona's attorneys were warning her that the whole thing could easily explode onto the front pages.

However it jelled, the months of investigation by Lefkowitz's staff led them to conclude that Leona's approach was so heavy-handed they'd have no problem winning in court. They stacked their complaints into several categories, charging that the building owners or Leona had: met the state requirement that at least 35 percent of the apartments have committed buyers by "loading" the building with "sham" sales to the owners' friends or speculators who weren't and never would be occupants; coerced at least eleven tenants to buy their apartments by threatening them with fake outside offers; harassed tenants by sending them eviction notices based on false allegations that the tenants were refusing to show their apartments to interested buyers.

The major perpetrator [of the false match offers] "was and is defendant Leona M. Roberts," the state charged. For instance, Doris Goldstein, a tenant in 3B, got a letter from Leona in September 1970 saying that Roland Earl Lee II had bid to buy her apartment. Goldstein didn't match the offer. But instead of selling the apartment to Lee, records showed Leona gave him his deposit back.

Asher Salwen in 4E got a similar letter a year later, but in his case the person supposedly offering to buy his apartment never even sent in a deposit. Nor did he, of course, buy the apartment when Salwen didn't match the offer. Bad checks from mysterious bidders also popped up. The man said to be eager to buy Charlotte Scott's 17G, bounced a deposit check so high it was never retrieved.

Just how hassled the tenants were is unclear. Many of them eventually bought their apartments more than a decade later when a brandnew offering under new ownership was approved by the state. Today, most of those named in the state case against Leona said they could not recall their encounters in any detail. Still, Lefkowitz had a tight case. He even had the motive. What with slumping co-op sales, it was clear Leona herself was under great pressure to make Sutton Place go.

Leona was in a fight for her life. She bought the best legal help she could. But the case against her was solid, and the court completely outlawed the Sutton Place conversion, forcing the building's owners to wait several years before trying again.

She turned to Seymour Rabinowitz. Rabinowitz, no litigator, in turn got Charles Moerdler, the Paris-born son of German refugees and one of the city's most respected legal battlers. Moerdler had come to be known as a bomber in the legal industry for his style. If some attorneys ply their craft with the precision of sharpshooters, Moerdler by contrast would rather fly over his target like a B-52 and open the bays.

His reply to the charges brought by Lefkowitz was to smoke the attorney general, counter-accusing him of fabricating the charges and using the press to nail his client in public. Indeed, his defense of Leona was to bear an uncanny resemblance to another Leona stance. The theme in both: she was being picked on in court and in the press because she was successful and a visible target, and Harry was even more famous.

"The Attorney General [has] embarked upon a publicity campaign of incredible proportions," Moerdler wrote in his court arguments. "On radio, on television, in the press and at news conferences he leveled charges even beyond those which are before this Court, and he engaged in that extrajudicial publicity campaign notwithstanding the high legal office he holds.

"The home addresses of the defendants suddenly found their way to the media and, I am told, an avalanche of obscene telephone calls predictably followed. Miss Roberts was likewise inundated for several days with a steady stream of obscenities. Additionally, I understand that each of the tenants in the apartment house in which Miss Roberts resides [on West Fifty-fifth Street] received from some unknown source a copy of a newspaper clipping reporting upon the Attorney General's charges. The defendants have not only been injured in their personal lives, they have also been professionally injured . . . they have been forced to cancel numerous appointments for business transactions involving other buildings . . . in one building in which defendants were engaged to convert the apartments to condominium ownership in the near future, copies of one of the above-mentioned newspaper articles were distributed to the tenants, thereby seriously impairing, if not completely destroying, the ability of the defendants to convert the building."

At an initial stage in the proceedings in November 1971, the court had temporarily banned Leona from acting as a broker on any project. That effectively froze every conversion project she was involved in, and Leona then was in charge of Harry Helmsley's apartment conversions, juggling perhaps a dozen major projects. Moerdler won two things for Leona. Just forty-eight hours after the injunction was imposed Moerdler got it lifted and freed Leona to continue working on anything other than Sutton Place.

Something even worse than losing that commission threatened Leona. The state wanted her license. And in the end it got it. But in a cunning legal move, Moerdler persuaded the state to let her turn in her license voluntarily. That way she could later simply reapply and there would be no state law to deny her a new permit. Moreover, there'd be no blot on her record. She had only to promise she would never do business again as a broker.

Still, she would not have been pleased with what Moerdler won. He declined to discuss the matter, but other attorneys who worked for Leona said they felt certain she would have concluded that Moerdler had failed her.

As one said in describing another incident: "She had a very low tolerance for mistakes. And to her a mistake was anything less than absolute perfection."

The case embittered Leona Roberts toward prosecutor Clurman. Not long after it was resolved, Clurman recalled being at a Real Estate Board of New York dinner when Seymour Rabinowitz came to his table with word that she wanted to see him. (Rabinowitz said he could not remember doing so, but neither did he doubt Clurman's recollection. "So many things go on at those dinners," he said.)

Clurman, it seems, had met Leona Roberts sometime earlier when she came to his office wanting him to autograph her copy of his book *Condominiums and Cooperatives*. Recalled Clurman, "She entreated my secretary and talked her into letting her see me so I could autograph the book. She came in and was very charming, very friendly. She was effusive, in fact very flattering, and I didn't know this woman from a hole in the wall. But I wrote in the book, 'With best wishes,' as I always do when signing a book, and I signed my name.

"The next time I saw her was at this dinner. Mr. Rabinowitz came over to see me, and he asked me if I would talk to her. I said I didn't think it was appropriate, because of the inquiry, and he said, 'Well, it's not about that,' and I said, 'Well, all right. I'm here.' I was a sitting duck there at the dinner. So he brought her over and she said, 'The reason I came over here is, I want you to buy back your book.'

"To put it mildly, that was about the last remark I expected from her, and I was nonplussed. Then I thought a little while and I said, 'By the way, what did I write in your book?' and she said, 'With best wishes,' and I said, 'You know something, I want to buy back that book.'

"So she said, 'I changed my mind.' And she walked away."

## CHAPTER 7

# WILD ABOUT HARRY

ONE OF HARRY HELMSLEY'S FAVORITE QUIPS IS ON THE JOY OF EMPER-
orship. "When I sit down," he learned to say with a twinkle, "the
board of directors has arrived."

He's used the line to explain why he never took himself public.
The sale of stock would have handed him a nice infusion of cash. But
such a move has strings. It would have exposed him to the attentions of
government regulators. Lights would have been shined into corners of
his affairs that were purposefully kept dark. He'd have been stuck with
a real board of directors. It's been far better for his sensitive enterprises
that he created cash cows out of private syndicates, in which his investors have no voice.

The quip also nicely describes his control of the Helmsley empire.

There is only one person at the top: Harry B. Helmsley. He is the
board of directors, the chair, the president, all wrapped up in one very

tall, straight-backed body and a mind utterly devoted to the business. He can reach anywhere in his $5 billion empire and act instantly without proxy. All he needs to do is spin around in his chair and grab one of his property books. Then he can punch up Ceil Fried on the intercom and have her ring up an Arthur Cohen or a Larry Silverstein or a Fred or Donald Trump. And a $1 million, or a $10 million, or a $100 million deal would be done, just like that.

But there is paradox in the quip. The man at the top in total control of himself does not, in fact, control all those around him. Helmsley Enterprises, especially its sales subsidiary of Helmsley-Spear, is a loose accumulation of fiefdoms in which the basic unit is a single self-driven, self-motivated, and self-regulated broker.

Until recently, Helmsley drove himself hard, yet he did not dictate to others. He rarely, for instance, asked aides to work into the night. More rarely still did he disturb them at their homes. Helmsley may have kept meticulous track of his property, counting and labeling and updating every square foot. But he did not keep track of his employees, rarely mentioning their ranks when he rattled off his millions of square feet and thousands of apartment units in hard assets.

The building managers who collect rents, fix heaters, and keep the elevators running may be a tightly knit group, as a corporate report claims. "One doesn't ordinarily think of a 10,000-employee company as a 'family.' Yet it is precisely the longtime, continuing emphasis on personal contact on every level that has helped Helmsley-Spear to become the country's leading real estate service company."

Not so with the brokers—the people out raking in huge commissions by buying or selling those buildings. Helmsley has not even liked to consider them his to direct. They work for his empire, in that he pays them wages in return for taking the major share of whatever they pull in. But they mostly work for themselves, dependent on commissions to buy their new cars, pay off their home mortgages, and otherwise amass the sums needed to live comfortably in New York.

Nor has Helmsley delegated managerial chores to others. His top aides, Schneider and Schwartz, have kept busy doing their own real estate deals. Helmsley, in fact, has made it a point to let numerous aides invest in their deals, acting both as brokers and as principals. As many as ten Helmsley men became millionaires in that way. It was a clever move, of course. It allows him to keep wages down—Helmsley salaries are minuscule by Wall Street standards, measured out annually in tens of thousands rather than hundreds of thousands of dollars. And it keeps their minds on business, albeit partly their own business. But there's a downside. It has moved them at times to put off whatever company obligations they might have. And internal management has not been a Helmsley-Spear strong point. Many a broker works there for months before feeling that anyone notices his presence. The year-end holiday party has often been the only time for interaction.

More importantly, the high standards of decency toward other dealers that Helmsley held himself to have not been enforced, or even encouraged, down the ranks of Helmsley-Spear. Brokers are free to fight for sales as best they know how. Except for Helmsley buildings, every property in the city, the country, the whole world for that matter, is fair game.

"He bred killers," said one former Helmsley broker.

On its face, Helmsley's hands-off approach to his brokers has not been a bad thing for business. He may breed killers, but they kill for him. Only the sharp-toothed have done well working for Helmsley. Only the best, in that sense, have stayed.

There are some highly ethical, highly moral, and very decent Helmsley brokers, to be sure. Then there are those who appreciate no ethical bounds. And they tend to set the pace inside the Helmsley empire, turning it into a microcosm of New York City business at its most vicious.

Hot leads aren't pooled. If they were, someone at Helmsley would grab them and run, adding them to their "cold-canvassing" rounds. And if the timing was right, the deal was theirs. The most telling indication of paranoia running rampant throughout the Helmsley brokerage houses is the locked desk. Every time brokers leave the office they pick up their Rolodexes, place them in a deep drawer, and then lock their desks.

Harry Helmsley's reaction when he has been asked to mediate fights among his brokers has been to turn to the loser and shrug, as if to say, "Why did you let that happen to you?"

Mike White says he got such a response from top Helmsley management when the man leading his group cold-canvassed his client and stole a deal. White moved from San Francisco to work for Helmsley on Forty-second Street in Manhattan in the late 1960s. He was a broker in Helmsley's loft sales division. "For a gentle kid like me, New York City in those days was the Vietnam for businessmen. You came out of there, and the rest of your life you have Agent Orange in you.

"Helmsley-Spear was a carbon copy of what was outside the door. It was like a jungle, in that there were snakes and people would shoot at you. Nothing was [considered] unethical. The guy sitting next to you could turn out to be your enemy. If you didn't have a strong psyche, Helmsley would develop a criminal paranoid mind. I couldn't trust anybody for ten years after I got out of there."

White thinks he might have overreacted, or been more sensitive than a native New Yorker might have been. But several other Helmsley brokers who left after a time say much the same thing. Helmsley Enterprises *is* like New York City—a great place to be if you caught the breaks and constantly won; a very rough place to be if you lost, or had other values in life.

That was the battleground onto which Leona Roberts stepped in 1969. And she thrived.

Not long after joining the Helmsley subsidiary of Brown, Harris, Stevens to direct its co-op apartment sales, Leona was bubbling with the kind of optimism that keeps the real estate world spinning. "Right now we are planning the cooperative sales campaigns for a dozen buildings, more than half of which are conversions. And it's only beginning," she told an industry paper. "More and more owners are studying the advantages of conversion."

Three years later, in March 1972, she was penning her own name to guest editorials. "We have actually arrived at the point in New York where, if one mentions that he lives in a Manhattan apartment house, he must still add whether it is a cooperative or rental building. It was not too long ago when living in a co-op was a novelty to be mentioned first. Today, co-ops—both newly built and converted from rental format—are a way of life for many thousands of New Yorkers. And they have become big business for those who have made a specialty of selling and managing cooperatives," she exclaimed, going on to list all the tax advantages that treat co-ops like the single-family suburban house.

If the real estate world was tough, and Helmsley-Spear was the toughest, Leona was, well, at least a match.

One attorney who first worked with her in the late 1960s paused from his filet of sole lunch to tick off a list of positive attributes. "These are the things you cannot take away from her," said the attorney.

"One, boundless energy and dedication to achieve. In the real estate business there probably is no woman her equal in that regard, and very few men. Bear in mind the discrimination and time frame. It was unique for a woman to be in that position at all. Two, she understood the nuances of real estate, especially the co-op market, and she was light-years, light-years ahead. And three, when she wanted to turn on the charm, there was no one remotely her peer. Those were the pluses. To say, then, that she was tough is again a gross understatement. She was extremely operative. Extremely competent. Extremely tough."

But Leona was also establishing herself at Helmsley Enterprises in a more personal, softer way.

Giordano is a moderately priced northern Italian restaurant in the Hell's Kitchen section of Manhattan, tucked out of the way on the far western flank of the city, near the Lincoln Tunnel. The neighborhood is part industrial, part tenement. An invasion by the illicit drug trade is the most visible change from the days when Harry collected rents. Well-dressed diners take seriously the establishment's offer to valet-park cars in a protected lot.

Inside, there's a full and formally attired staff of reservationist, maître d', headwaiter, roast carver, wine steward, waiter, and waiter's assistant on hand. But they are not doting. They keep their distance unless beckoned, because for the most part the diners are couples with their faces pulled close, whispering, hands touching hands.

On each candlelit table is a folded business card that says in a swirling red script, "Let's Have an Affair . . ."

And that's just what Harry and Leona had, in the transitional months of his separation before he divorced Eve and they were married.

Robert Wagner and his wife, Phyllis, who became friends with Leona and Harry, all had a laugh one evening at the Helmsley's Connecticut home when they discovered that both couples had dated at Giordano. "We used to kid each other about it, but it was just a coincidence," said the former New York City mayor.

Leona Roberts and Harry Helmsley also dined at the Joe & Rose on Third Avenue, an elegant restaurant five blocks from the Helmsley office. And they met on at least one occasion at her apartment on Fifty-fifth Street. Harry, who owned the building, had given her the apartment, perhaps as an outright gift, perhaps as part of her compensation for directing its conversion to co-ops, according to Seymour Rabinowitz. It was the best apartment in the building. There was one floor higher up. But her view, from the penultimate nineteenth floor, was equally good and she had a much larger balcony. Leona and Joseph Catania had decorated it in a bright green-and-blue motif.

Rabinowitz has forgotten the occasion for celebration. It was a business deal of some sort. He, Leona, and Harry all went to her apartment to toast with champagne. Harry, meanwhile, began spending weeknights in Manhattan, carrying two briefcases of work to an apartment at his St. Moritz Hotel.

Those intimate times together may have stirred some affection. But Leona likes to remember that there was one special moment when she fell in love with this six-foot-three-inch squinting, white-haired tycoon, who was once deftly described by *Wall Street Journal* reporter Randall Smith as a giant white rabbit. The moment came at a real estate industry dinner, out on the dance floor, where Leona's head would rise just above Harry's shoulder. They "just fit together," Leona later remarked, adding that Harry serenaded her with romantic songs having words he made up.

Their dating was not all smooth. Leona has only alluded to what might have been wrong, saying the trouble helped her to lose weight. "During a time in our courtship when we were having problems," she told *New Woman*, "I lost a pound a day for twenty days—twenty pounds I lost for my Harry, and I kept it off."

Leona also adhered to her beauty regimen, which included one little trick she pressed upon friends—men and women alike. It's called a Buf-Puf, a little spongelike scrubber that takes away dead skin and opens the pores. Leona believed in the Buf-Puf and the lotion she used with it. But more than one skin expert expressed surprise at Leona's recommendation. "Buf-Pufs, oh yes, you can buy those at Duane Reade [drugstore]," said an aide to Georgette Klinger, a Madison Avenue skin-care specialist. "But I don't know why she would use that. It's an abrasive. Like sandpaper. No one would use sandpaper on their skin unless they had a lot of what we call exfoliation [dead skin and other waste that sloughs off]."

Seymour Rabinowitz keeps his Buf-Puf in a closet at home. "I guess [Leona] thought I needed it," he said.

Curiosity abounds over whether Leona has had face lifts, and if she did, how many. Some who know her say she doesn't have the wide-eyed, permanent smile that characterizes some plastic surgery. But Leona's face is plumper, facial experts noted, and wouldn't suffer the pulled-back look. Helmsley's private foundation has given huge sums of money to the foundation set up for the Orentreich Medical Group in Manhattan—a specialist in skin care. Orentreich receptionists described the Helmsleys as "patients." The owners, Norman and David Orentreich, declined comment. The company, according to its tax filings, is also connected to research programs that deal with Alzheimer's disease.

But one person was privy to Leona's health care—Maryann Eboli, who was Leona's executive secretary for six years starting October 1979. Leona befriended a host of doctors. She preferred hand-holders, men she could see regularly, once a week or more. She would go whether her problem was physical or simply mental stress. Leona paid weekly visits for a time to Norman Orentreich to receive shots of collagen—a fibrous animal extract that skin doctors use to smooth out wrinkles. Eboli made the appointments and routed the bills. Another Manhattan doctor performed plastic surgery on Leona's eyes to remove the bags and tighten the skin.

But that more serious battle against aging occurred after she met Harry. Leona told *New Woman* a story about their courtship that relates back to her first real estate job and the secretarial application. She said, "I told him, 'Harry, you're not being very nice. I loved you so much that I made myself five years older for you when I first told you my age, so you'd feel more comfortable—and what other woman would make herself older for a man?' Sure enough, Harry hotfoots it back to the office, pulls out my original records where I'd said I was younger, and comes back to me, touched beyond all measure that I'd make myself older for him. It wasn't till after we were married that I admitted I really was five years older than the records showed."

The trouble Leona refers to may well have stemmed from Harry's thoughts about Eve. He anguished over the breakup, those around him at the time came to believe. It was more than a man dumping his wife of thirty-three years for a much younger woman. (Eve was even his senior by three years.) He was betraying her in a business sense too.

Eve had done business with Harry in a way nobody else had. She may have bankrolled him. She gave him her brother's business and legal connections. She even invested in some of his deals, and invited others to do likewise. And now, for the first time in a career that's been so lauded for its integrity and loyalty, Harry was getting set to abandon his original partner.

But Eve was not there for Harry in one crucial way. He couldn't drag home his real estate business and expect her to listen to his talk about mortgages and points and tenant/square foot ratios. Leona offered an ear to a man who was dying to talk, believes Rabinowitz. "Harry was always one to listen. He would listen to me, to anyone who would have had something to say. He would listen to all of them. And the idea that he could then go home and talk his problems out with Leona, even if she just listened, would be a major attraction," the attorney said.

Eve also might not have been there sexually for Harry. Eve had grown stout through the years, and an admirer says she reminded one of Wilhelmina, the late Netherlands queen. "She was a very fine lady, very polite and correct," said the admirer, Herbert Peters, a longtime Helmsley management-level employee at the Park Lane Hotel.

Eve and Harry began living apart just as he started to embark on the phase of his career that would bring him so much fame: luxury hotels.

The Park Lane, which he built on Central Park South, was more than a hotel to the Helmsleys. Eve said she helped Harry design the hotel, and its conservative, stately decor reflects her personality far more than it does Leona's. It was to be their new city home. On the top two floors, high above Manhattan, Harry put in a duplex penthouse apartment, replete with pool and patio with a spectacular view of Central Park.

The Park Lane opened on May 1, 1971, with all the fanfare and celebration appropriate to the first hotel to open in Manhattan since the Regency seven years earlier. Workers had been frantic getting everything done on time, but the party came off with a flourish. There was a formal reception line, with Eve and Harry at the head of the well-wishers.

But it was on this opening night that Eve confided to her closest friends that the Park Lane was not meant for her. That was the first and only time they would see her there, she told them. She wouldn't be living for long in the penthouse with Harry.

For some of Harry's associates, that night was the first and last look they had of Eve, who had never played a public role in Harry's business affairs in the thirty-three years of their marriage. Among those in line for the Saturday evening reception was Seymour Durst, not a close friend of Helmsley's but a longtime Manhattan developer who had done some business with him and who moved through the same banking and social circles. Harry and Eve were in the lobby receiving guests. Many brought gifts.

"I guess I knew he was married," recalled Durst, "but I had never seen her or heard much about her. And then they were divorced."

Eve used her late brother's legal connections to hire one of the best family-dispute specialists in the country, the London-born Manhattan attorney Louis Nizer. The size of the settlement Eve won was never made public. Rumors have been reported that peg it at $7 million. Some scoff at that sum. But Met Life's Bill Lehy, who had had access to Harry's financial statements at the time, said such a settlement was within his means. "At that point he could well afford to turn loose $7 million," Lehy said.

Eve moved first to the Carlton House, a Madison Avenue apartment building that Harry still owns. Robert Wagner, who also lived there after his first wife died, saw her occasionally at the elevator. She then moved to Fort Lauderdale, Florida, to be with her friends and former tennis partners. "They wanted me to come down and join them there," Eve said. Then she moved back north to New Jersey, where she lives in a retirement home for the wealthy.

Her friends there describe her much as others did during her three decades with Harry. "She's attractive. She wears fashionable, lovely clothes and lovely jewelry," said one neighbor. "I've had dinner with her, but she does not come to the dining room regularly. She's more than pleasant. She's friendly. In every way she's discriminating. We chat, and then she goes darting off."

Eve has a kitchen and cooks for herself. She has access to a car and driver and makes regular trips into the city. She has several close women friends who visit. "If you've got to be alone in the world, there couldn't be a better place," said one elderly resident. "The staff is extremely nice. They take care of you. You're around educated and nice people."

Still, for many there, it's a life in exile from their former lives. "No one is entirely happy when they're put out to pasture," the resident continued. The accepted conclusion at the home is that Eve "has had a pretty tough time, being discarded by someone. No woman likes being shoved out of the way for someone else."

Eve and Leona never met. At least once, though, Leona inquired after her in a naturally competitive way.

Rabinowitz, representing Harry, met with Eve once. Harry was selling some property that Eve had invested in and he needed her signature. Rabinowitz had lunch with Leona a week later and mentioned the encounter. Leona perked up. "What's she like? What's she like?" Leona asked.

"Leona, I wouldn't worry about it," Rabinowitz recalled replying.

"No, no. What's she like? I'd really like to know," Leona insisted.

"Well, she probably was once a very attractive lady. Now she's a little older, probably not as trim as she once was, and she wore a polyester pantsuit." The now trim, always fashionable Leona looked relieved.

Eve said she held no animosity toward either Leona or Harry. "I can't think of anything that is unamiable about any connection in our life. The separation? I don't know what I could say. That was also amicable. I don't have anything bad to say about it. It's all just ancient history," she said.

As Eve faded, Leona grew more intense. And Harry too changed.

After a quiet wedding that went altogether unreported in *The New York Times* social pages, and a honeymoon in Europe, Leona Helmsley moved quickly into the hotel business. In the very first years after their marriage, she acquired 10 percent of the stock in Helmsley hotels, helped change the very name of the hotels to Harley (an awkward contraction of their first names that they would both later regret), and took the first steps toward removing her most immediate rivals.

Her corporate footing, secondary only to Harry's, became such that she came to revise his quip about being the whole board of directors. To a business reporter she said, "The board of directors meeting [is] over when we get out of bed." And to another: "All I need is a mustache and glasses and I'll be Harry Helmsley."

She also got comfortable in their Park Lane penthouse with the spectacular deck and view of Central Park. Every morning after Harry went to the office, her private hairdresser would arrive to paint her nails and fix her hair. But first she would run through an exercise program and swim.

Leona became as devoted to swimming as Harry, but her reasons were more vain. She swims to keep her figure. Thirty minutes. Forty minutes. Sometimes longer. She hired a trainer and concocted some games with her hotel staff to give her encouragement.

She had one of the house servants stand at poolside with a gleaming platter full of glistening, freshly cooked shrimp. "It was a big tray, silver and polished," the staffer recalled. "The captain had me stand at the end of the pool, and each time she came around, I offered her a shrimp." They were Leona's rewards for doing her laps.

"So I would bend down, and she would take it or not. And if she took one and cocktail sauce splattered, I would have to take the whole tray back to the kitchen to be cleaned up. And I'd have to do that and get back in time before she made her lap. Now, I don't know if that was her or if it was just [the captain's] paranoia or what. But I'd be running and we'd be laughing as soon as I got back. When she'd be at the other end, we'd be sneaking a shrimp."

The shrimp story amused the entire hotel staff. Herbie Peters, now retired, opened the Park Lane Hotel and worked various managerial positions for sixteen years. "The shrimp? Oh yes, the shrimp," he said in his thick German accent, bending over into a laugh.

Most of Leona's gowns were done by a private seamstress Leona retained and set up in an office in Harry's Graybar Building, adjacent to Grand Central Station. But her pair of closets held dresses by Valentino, Diane Von Furstenberg and Pauline Trigère. Leona prided herself on her shopping prowess. "I remarked on the simplicity of her shoes," Jane Maas, who held the Helmsley advertising account for a short time, wrote in her book *Adventures of an Advertising Woman*. Leona told Maas, "The Fenton last at Saks. I buy them by the dozen and have them dyed." Continued Maas: "Leona does not believe in paying retail price for anything. One way is to buy in quantity. The other way is to bargain. Leona Helmsley deals with the great shops of the world as though they were souks of Jedda. 'Learn from me, darling. If you pay the asking price for anything, you're being robbed.' "

Joyce Beber, who built the famed Queen Leona advertising image and became a friend to Leona, also went shopping with her. "She would walk into Bill Blass's office and say, 'I am Mrs. Helmsley, and I will send all the people I know to buy dresses from you.' And she got all her clothes wholesale. It wasn't just to save money, it was to get the best deal. And the best deal was to make sure someone else didn't have a good deal."

Leona clearly was enjoying her life, but the first visible changes appeared in Harry's personal life. Harry the quiet, shy, workaholic introvert was to try on a third dimension.

For one thing, there was new sensuality and sex.

Both Harry and Leona have liked to remark upon their sex lives to friends, who came away with the impression that it was vigorous for people of any age. Harry, in his self-revelations, has tended to be indirect, adopting the bravado of a semi-embarrassed schoolboy. He might raise an eyebrow or smile in such a way that other men understand that his references about having a "second wind" do not refer to his laps in the pool. "I think married life is a great way to live," Harry said in an interview, laughing at the next question. "What do I like best about being married? Oh, come on. Besides . . . uh, I guess it's the partnership aspect, that you're not doing things alone, you're doing things in partnership. I think that's *so* important."

The only off-color remark a longtime buddy could remember Harry ever making before he met Leona was a joke with a punch line involving a sex change. Harry told it only in private. But he has more recently even let loose with sexual teasers, however innocent, in public.

To illustrate Harry's quick wit, his friend Larry Silverstein recalled having Harry talk at the Real Estate Institute at New York University. "It was packed to overflowing, with a hundred and fifty people in the class, and people would proceed to ask a broad range of questions with respect to hotels, office buildings, apartments. Harry handled the answers with extraordinary command of the real estate spectrum. Finally, at the conclusion of the evening, one young woman in the audience raised her hand—and I might add she was a very attractive woman— and asked Mr. Helmsley, 'In light of all your experiences, your accomplishments, is there anything left that you would like to experience?' And he looked at her, and his immediate response was: 'What are you doing after class?' Everybody laughed and Harry quickly said, 'Don't tell Lee,' and he did this with a twinkle in his eye. It was his ability to respond electrically and quickly but always with humor."

Leona was more straightforward to her women friends. Time and again she would pull one aside and exclaim that Harry's seven decades had done nothing to diminish his sexual strength. "At parties she would go on and on about how sexy he was, how great their sex life was," said Liz Smith, gossip columnist for the *New York Daily News.* "She would always say, 'Isn't he the sexiest? Isn't he the best-looking?' Which, of course, he wasn't. It was in the overkill department."

"He was swept off his feet," said Helmsley friend Carrie Rozelle, wife of National Football League commissioner Pete Rozelle. "I really see how she could mature a man's life." She laughed, adding, "I sure wouldn't want her going after my husband."

In some ways, Harry seemed to pull inward, or at least put some distance between him and his friends for inexplicable reasons. At times he would don a formality that wasn't common in the Helmsley-Spear owner whose employees were encouraged to say, "Hi, Harry," if they met him in the elevator. To hotel staff it became strictly "Mr. and Mrs. H."

Bernard Mendik recalled having a naturalist come to him long after Leona and Harry were married with hopes of using the roof of a building Mendik owned in Manhattan as a breeding site for birds. "We said yes. The mayor came up. There was a big public ceremony," Mendik recalled. "But then they wanted a building in the area where they could have a spotter, someone to watch the birds with glasses. They wanted to use the St. Moritz Hotel, because it was perfectly positioned. So I called Harry to ask him and he turned me down. I couldn't believe that he would have turned me down."

Mendik believes that might just have been the leather-tough side to Harry that has regularly popped up in his business dealings throughout his life. But, ironically, before meeting Leona, Harry had shown an extraordinary fondness for birds. At the National Audubon Society's request, he had taken to dimming the Empire State Building flood-lights in those weeks when migrating birds flew by. He did so to keep them from slamming into the building, attracted to the lights. True, that might have spared him some cracked windows. But had careening birds been an appreciable financial drain, Harry Helmsley would have thought of it first.

Much later, Harry would pull away from his friends and associates in far more important matters.

Generally, though, the new Harry that astonished the real estate world was a fun-loving, frolicking, easy-to-laugh man out on the town. He and Leona swept out onto dance floors from New York to Palm Beach. There were charity balls at the Waldorf-Astoria; charity balls at the Breakers. "Harry loved to dance," Rabinowitz said. "The two of them looked beautiful out on the dance floor. Tall, with good figures. It was ballroom dancing, and people were amazed by them. You could understand why they loved it."

Said Leona: "We like to do the Ginger Rogers–Fred Astaire dances best, but we can do all the others too. My husband is a great disco dancer."

Silliness reigned at some real estate parties. At one in April 1972, the month they were married, there was a musical floor show to flatter the real estate men. Sung to the tune of "Matchmaker, Matchmaker," one refrain went:

> *Samuel Lemburgus, lend us a loan.*
> *Don't let us lose—all that we own.*
> *We got a mortgage and it's coming due,*
> *And that's why we come to you.*
> *Kaufman and Wiler might need ten mill-i-on,*
> *Ed Malloy, he might need only three,*
> *Helmsley—hell, give him a bill-i-on.*
> *He's buying the Statue of—*
> *Aw! you know what.*

Leona began filling the extra closets Harry built into their Park Lane penthouse with the requisite new gown for every appearance. Even Harry supplemented the two suits he wore for most of his years with evening attire. Among the biggest and best parties were their own.

Before Leona, Harry's birthday celebrations tended to be all male, all business, almost unmemorable. Bill Lehy recalled parts of one— possibly Harry's sixtieth—at the St. Moritz Hotel. It was black-tie. A Rockefeller was on hand. There were lots of speeches.

Leona moved the parties to the Park Lane. And she invited men and women from the social and political Who's Who guest list. Among the chosen two hundred, besides Harry's real estate friends, were several former governors, including Hugh Carey, who drank so heavily that he once crashed over a table; several former mayors; and a host of celebrities, from Gregory Peck and Cliff Robertson to Mike Wallace and Dan Rather. A fourteen-piece orchestra played a lot of

"Love in an Old-Fashioned Way." But every fourth number would be the party's theme song, "I'm Just Wild About Harry."

Guests would wear buttons that said the same thing: "I'm Just Wild About Harry." And Harry would wander about with the biggest button of all, which read: "I'm Harry."

This was Leona's opportunity to show the world how much she loved him. And vice versa. The next line in the song, of course, is: "And he's just wild about me."

"Oh, here's gorgeous," she would gush when Harry walked up to her.

"Isn't he beautiful?" she would croon.

She and Harry would be the first on the dance floor and the last to leave, sometimes well into the morning.

Leona labored to make everything special, everything right. The rooms were decorated with streams of balloons. On the walls were heart-shaped posters with her and Harry's faces. The flowers were all white, and spectacularly arranged. One year each table got a gold-dusted replica of the Empire State Building, replete with a miniature King Kong. Once, a huge, expansive cake held replicas of all of the Helmsley buildings.

The guests were given music boxes that played the theme song. At the end of some parties ditty bags filled with assorted gifts were handed out at the door.

And yet, even in organizing Harry's birthday parties Leona could be petty and mean. In 1983, Joan McElroy began to help out with the parties with the utmost enthusiasm. Now she only shakes her head at a long, strange year in her life.

McElroy is a friend of the Helmsleys' interior designer, who was in charge of decorating the birthday parties. The designer had done some table centerpieces, but for Harry's seventy-fifth birthday in 1984 he wanted something special. So he and McElroy came up with a splendid idea. They would take Ken and Barbie dolls and dress them up as famous couples. But instead of the appropriate faces, they would substitute likenesses of Leona and Harry.

McElroy was perfect for the job. Though she never played with dolls as a girl, McElroy studied art and textile design and grew fond of dolls in her adult life. She'd become something of an expert. In 1974 Knopf published her definitive dollhouse guide, *Joan McElroy's Dolls' House Furniture Book.*

Five months before the party, they pitched the idea to Leona. She loved it, and over a series of three meetings they perfected the designs. McElroy also got a firsthand look at the Leona "power entry," in which she would use her mere appearance to put aides, clients, contractors, sellers into a cold sweat. "We were there in her office once, talking and waiting," McElroy said, "and suddenly everyone said, 'She's coming! She's coming!' Everyone tightened up. People—women, grown men—were afraid of her."

They needed to set eighteen tables, and they settled on Cinderella and Prince Charming, Rhett Butler and Scarlett O'Hara, Diamond Jim Brady and Diamond Lil, Fred Astaire and Ginger Rogers, Tarzan and Jane, King Kong and Fay Wray, Lieutenant Pinkerton and Cio-Cio-San (Madama Butterfly), Louis XV and Madame Du Barry, John Smith and Pocahontas, Li'l Abner and Daisy Mae, Antony and Cleopatra, Napoleon and Josephine, Romeo and Juliet, and Harry's favorite, the King and Queen of Hearts.

The only design problem came with Adam and Eve. Leona balked at their state of undress. They were to wear only fig leaves, and Eve was to be topless, of course. "I thought they were wonderful, but she threw a fit," said McElroy. Leona never said what she thought wrong about Eve. McElroy assumed it was Barbie's bare chest, but it wasn't at all clear whether Leona thought it immodest or Barbie's breasts too big or too small. Leona did insist that on all the dolls Barbie's cheekbones be made more prominent.

Then McElroy got to work. December came and went. So did January. She recruited artistic friends. "Napoleon's costume was copied from a portrait of the Emperor by Gérard, but we had to do surgery to get his arm into his vest," said Egan Sagik, who specialized in the tiny jewelry.

A visiting poet, Pamela Hadas, spent two weeks cutting out bronze-colored sequins for Pocahontas's Indian dress. Ben Fether, an industrial designer, was corralled into making all the wire glasses for Harry's look-alikes. Ken's eyes also were made to squint like Harry's.

McElroy slaved over the project. She even dipped into her daughter's closet to find in a blouse just the right fabric for Cleopatra's blue pleated dress. "It definitely was the most ridiculous thing I've done," McElroy said. "But at the time I was quite serious."

The March deadline loomed. "I used to sit up in bed at 4 A.M. in a panic. All the dolls sat on my windowsill, naked, as if to say, 'When are you going to dress us?' "

And then it was done. And for producing thirty-six twelve-inch dolls, for untold hours of work, and for suffering through a panic-stricken winter, McElroy received from Leona about $4,500.

McElroy picks no bone about the pittance. She was not a professional contractor or consultant, and wasn't experienced in such financial dealings. She thinks she cheated herself by applying herself so deeply to the dolls.

The next year Harry would turn seventy-six, and Leona asked McElroy to come up with something even bigger and better. She and the interior designer thought and thought and finally came up with a spectacular series of centerpiece scenes depicting the Spirit of 1776 for Harry's seventy-sixth. Again, the faces of Harry and Leona were to grace the bodies of famous people.

There was to be Harry dressed as Ben Franklin at his printing machine, Harry as George crossing the Delaware. Leona would appear as Betsy Ross sewing the flag. McElroy drew up a budget, figuring she would have to open a small shop and hire a staff. After much research and thought she presented a bill for $16,000 to one of Leona's assistants, Geoffrey Lerigo.

"He swallowed hard and took it to Leona," McElroy recalled, "and the message came back: 'Who does she think she is?' "

Leona didn't get the Spirit of '76.

Indeed, for her own sixty-sixth birthday party at their Connecticut house the very next year, Leona had to settle with the best her own designer could muster: a series of miniature Statue of Liberties with Leona's face plastered where Liberty's should have been. There was some astonished snickering in Greenwich that summer.

But behind the public scenes of the "I'm Just Wild About Harry" parties, Leona saved her best act for Mayor Edward I. Koch. Just what made her angry at the mayor is unclear. But year after year his presence was banned. "He was not to be put on the birthday party list," said Eboli, who had charge of the invitations.

Helmsley staffers recall Koch aides calling as many as ten times one year to secure an invitation. Nothing doing, Leona insisted. And that evening she told the Palace guards to watch for the mayor, as if he might decide to crash the party.

All of the dancing, the parties, and the sex must have distracted Harry Helmsley. Because in the next few years he would don a new business hat, and make some colossal mistakes.

## CHAPTER 8

# LANDLORDING

ON A WINTER DAY EARLY IN 1974, VIRGINIA PEET WAS WALKING BY
the Helmsley headquarters in New York City when a thought occurred
to her.

What if, she mused, the man who owned this building and seemed
to be embroiled in so much controversy over condominium conversions out here in New York, what if he had the same sinister plan in
mind for her apartment?

The sixty-nine-year-old Peet, who was only visiting Manhattan,
had taken note of the bulky Lincoln Building on Forty-second Street
just across from Grand Central Station, because right on its stone side
at eye level was a "Helmsley-Spear" plaque. She didn't know about
this fellow Spear. But she realized that Helmsley must be the same man
who had recently bought the Parkmerced housing complex in San
Francisco where she and her husband lived with 3,500 other families.

Peet was no fool. In fact, until she died three years later, she was a savvy political organizer in the Golden State, holding the presidency of the California Association of Older Americans.

Even worse for Helmsley, her husband was the Rev. Ed Peet, a fiery, activist minister who'd raised hell in a number of parishes before finding his niche with the socially conscious Glide Memorial Church in San Francisco. And worse still for Harry, when Virginia Peet got home and told her husband about the Helmsley building, and about how she was reading in the papers about this New York tycoon forcing his tenants in the Bronx to buy their apartments, the Rev. Ed and Virginia Peet got fired up.

It turned out that at about the time Peet was looking up at the Helmsley building having her troubling thought, Judge Joseph Karesh was reading Herb Caen's column in the *San Francisco Chronicle*. And there, amidst the restaurant raves and the theater pans and the I-saw-so-and-so-at-the-opera's, he spotted a little item on Parkmerced, about how Helmsley was contemplating a move to convert the apartments into condos but how that appeared to be down the road a good piece. But like Peet, the Carolina-born Karesh, also in his late sixties then, who had sat on the Superior Court bench for several decades trying criminal matters such as the racially explosive Zebra Killers case, was no fool. He too got fired up.

So now the judge and the minister and the Older Americans president went down to the San Francisco Planning Department and took a look at the Helmsley petition, which turned out to be a rather technical move to alter the Parkmerced subdivision plan. And underneath the verbiage about metes and bounds they saw that his intent wasn't vaguely similar to the deal in the Bronx where Helmsley was messing with the Parkchester complex. They saw it was an identical ploy. Helmsley, they realized with a shock, and it was clear there in black and white, was out to sell their 3,500 apartments as individual little condos. He was out to do it as fast as he could. And if they didn't buy, he'd round up others who would. Now the Peets and friends really got moving. Within hours they put together a mass meeting of their neighbors. Thereafter ensued the Great Helmsley Parkmerced War.

Even more remarkable, the Peets and Karesh and their troops linked up with others who were fighting the same fight 3,000 miles away. Within days of their discovery, the Rev. Peet flew to New York City. He met with the people battling Helmsley over the conversion of Parkchester, a sister community in the Bronx four times the size of Parkmerced. Peet also met with people who were fighting Helmsley to preserve two small parks in Tudor City; Helmsley wanted to enlarge this high-rise apartment complex in Manhattan by plunking down a huge new tower on top of the cherished parks. Peet met too with people across the East River who were fighting Helmsley over the expansive Fresh Meadows housing project in the borough of Queens.

They compared notes. They strategized. Peet told some of his other war stories. They developed an organized, energized, coast-to-coast anti-Helmsley coalition of the sort that no single landlord in the country had ever encountered. They even called it "Hands Across America," a decade before the catchy phrase was used in a more famous poverty-fighting crusade. It grew so powerful that the embattled Helmsley, one day when he seemed to be losing on too many fronts, shook his head slowly and insisted to a tenant-newsletter editor, "I don't understand why the people hate me so."

Harry Helmsley the rent collector, the building buyer, the syndicator, the office builder, had become Harry Helmsley the landlord, and he was getting whomped.

It's curious that Helmsley ever allowed himself to get into landlording in such a big way, because his first experience must have left a very foul taste in his mouth. In 1969 he paid $1.25 million for an option to buy the elegant, double-towered San Remo apartments on Central Park West—the boulevard that forms the western edge of Central Park in Manhattan. Two decades later some of New York's star apartment brokers would still drool over the San Remo. "If you stand in the foyer of these one-to-a-floor penthouse apartments, you can see through the dining room, the library, the kitchen, and living room in all four directions. It's superb," said one. "If you're star-struck," said another, "the San Remo is where Broadway and Hollywood types tend to nest."

Helmsley's idea was to buy the San Remo, nests and all, for $12 million. He would then sell the individual apartments for a collective $15 million, pocketing the difference for his trouble in arranging the conversion. The tenants rose up in legal arms. They didn't object to the conversion per se. They just didn't like Helmsley's price, or his profit. They also were mad because they had tried to buy the building themselves before Helmsley stepped in, and had been turned down for not having their financial act wholly together. So they went to court.

Helmsley almost forced through the conversion, but the tenants gained two things to their side: in 1971 the city passed a rent stabilization law, which meant if they did nothing and just continued to rent, life would remain affordable; and the same co-op market crash that hit Leona Roberts hit Harry Helmsley. Simply, 1970 was a bad year to move co-ops. Helmsley's plan was turned down, he lost his $1.25 million investment, and the building went co-op two years later only when the tenants finally bought it, for $10.8 million. Rejoiced one tenant: "We've beaten the best man in town."

So why did Helmsley the real estate dealer become a landlord? More than a few people have wondered over the years. To some extent, he'd already made the move, and was immersed in landlording by the time the San Remo went bad. Maybe, too, he merely considered the San Remo a fluke, thinking only of how very close he'd come to pulling it off.

Harry was slow to catch on to the fact that something extraordinary was called for in dealing with people's homes. He thought he could merely transfer his tightwad management skills to apartment houses and get by with spending the bare minimum for safety and comfort. "Just because he became a landlord didn't mean he would give away things for no reason," said a former executive of Brown, Harris, Stevens. One year the daughter of Harry's associate Alvin Schwartz moved into a Helmsley building. The appliances were aging. "So I asked Harry, 'Should we give her a new stove?' " recalled the executive. "He was a thrifty guy. He said no." The first Monday after that year's Thanksgiving, however, Harry called the aide back and said, "I guess we better get that stove." Her turkey had burned up.

Harry never seemed to differentiate between buying someone's office and buying their home. As long as it had tenants, a building was a building, he told real estate reporters who got curious about all his residential buying in the late 1960s and early 1970s. "Each deal stands on its own. If it's a satisfactory deal, it doesn't make any difference what kind of a property it is—residential, an office building, or a shopping center." And there were some very good deals in housing, because some key players wanted out.

Just after World War II, the country's insurance companies jumped into middle-class housing in a very big way. It was good public relations. The country badly needed affordable housing. Better still, it was good for business. All those grateful renters would need policies.

Two decades later, however, they were ready to bail out. They needed the cash. The projects were losing their tax benefits. So when Metropolitan Life decided to sell the biggest complex of all, the mammoth Parkchester in the Bronx, an old trusted friend, Harry Helmsley, the man who four decades earlier had first knocked on Met's door to take foreclosed buildings off its hands, was there to buy with a $90 million bid.

By all accounts, Metropolitan Life was a benevolent landlord. After all, it was there to please, if not coddle, its customers. From 1940 to 1968, Met Life kept the rents low, the grass green, the walls painted, and the crime rate almost nonexistent. Moreover, it worked to keep the complex all white by giving legacies, or first rental rights, to the relatives of tenants. Parkchester became a Waspy enclave in the Bronx, surrounded by largely black and much poorer communities.

Parkchester was, as its residents liked to say, a city within a city. Built on open land once owned and occupied by the Society for the Protection of the Destitute Roman Catholic Children, it sprawled over 130 acres. Half the area was left green grass or developed into wading pools, ball courts, and playgrounds. It had dozens of stores, its own four-screen movie theater, its own branch of Macy's. "If you wanted to, you could live your whole life here and never have to leave," one tenant leader said.

Helmsley the condo converter had no intention of filling Met Life's shoes. He didn't need the tenants. He wasn't selling insurance. Really, he wasn't even interested in landlording, except as it was required in transition. The residents, once they realized who he was and what he had in mind, turned ferocious as only organized New York City tenants can. "There was no reason to fight Metropolitan Life on anything. No issue," said Helmsley's biggest nemesis, a Parkchester native named John Dearie. "Then all of a sudden, instead of the paternalistic Metropolitan Life, we've got a real estate guy here who's out for the dollar."

The six-foot-four-inch Dearie made a formidable opponent to Helmsley's plans. Born in Parkchester the same year the complex opened, Dearie became a local basketball hero on the Parkchester courts, making all-city before going on to study at Notre Dame and earning his law degree from New York University. He then landed a job with the United Nations Secretariat before deciding in 1973 to run for the state assembly seat that covered Parkchester's 40,000 residents. Dearie and a resident named John Whalen would spend the next decade and more fighting Helmsley.

The housing was divided into four quadrants, totaling almost 12,300 units in 58 buildings. Helmsley drew a line through the complex, calling 4,000 units the North Quadrant, and it was this smaller portion that he proposed converting into condos. That was not Dearie's only fight with Helmsley. Parkchester residents also staged a rent strike and used other tactical maneuvers to get better police protection, improved recreation centers, and, above all, protection from rent hikes. At issue in the latter case was how much of his operating costs Helmsley would be allowed to pass on to the renters.

They also fought him on various maintenance issues, and charged him with keeping a large number of apartments vacant to ease the conversion to condos. Helmsley had no monopoly on that ploy, dubbed "warehousing" by tenant activists. But when his warehoused apartments reached 1,000 empty units, public officials exploded with anger at this particularly insidious move in view of the city's desperate need for affordable housing. San Francisco officials reacted the same way when the Rev. Peet brought the term "warehousing" home to paint on Parkmerced residents' placards. Helmsley backed down on that issue, in both cities, and was forced to rent apartments he would rather have kept empty until they were sold.

But Helmsley did not back down on the residents' biggest concern: conversion to condos. There were some setbacks. For example, he had to forgo his legal right to evict tenants in exchange for getting a lower threshold of tenants willing to commit to buying an apartment. New York's condo conversion law at the time required converters to get 35 percent of the tenants to pledge purchase of their apartments in order for the condo conversion plan to get state approval. Only 15 percent were needed if the converter agreed not to evict those who chose not to buy. But Helmsley used even this critical delay to his plans to his advantage, repeatedly pointing to it when he feigned incredulity at the hostility directed at his plans. "I'm not evicting them," Helmsley would tell the Parkchester newsletter editor.

All the attention given to his plans also forced Helmsley to let loose with some numbers, and defend his profit-taking. Helmsley could count on only a very few people reading the detailed financial statements he was forced to make. Fewer still would understand them. He and his fellow investors stood to get $55.9 million from converting the North Quadrant alone, indicating that the entire Parkchester complex, for which they paid $90 million, was worth $170 million as condos. But Helmsley was adamant in refusing to publicly discuss that profit, or even to concede that it was the business of his tenants. "It's true that I'm selling for more than I paid, which seems only proper in a profit economy," he told them. "I bought what I consider to be a $300 million property for $90 million. Met Life was so glad to get out of the real estate business that it settled for the highest bidder."

Helmsley bristled when tenants questioned his calculations or complained about their share of the profit. He drew an analogy to someone buying a loaf of bread. "People don't ask the baker how much it costs to bake the bread and what the baker's profit is, and then decide whether to buy the bread," he admonished the tenants. "It's a great buy."

But for many of the Parkchester residents, to buy or not to buy was a monumental and anxiety-filled decision. Among them was Margaret Feely, an Irish hotel cook, whose situation was profiled by a newspaper covering the conversion in 1973. Feely was paying $155.02 a month rent for her three sun-filled rooms totaling 654 square feet. "The two cents," she laughed in her County Sligo brogue, "I don't know what that's for." Helmsley was asking $11,655 from her to buy her apartment—$13,860 minus 10 percent because she was an insider and minus another 10 percent because she could pay cash.

The problem at Parkchester, however, as with so many other condo conversion deals, came in calculating the maintenance fees. For her $155.02 Margaret Feely had received free water, gas, electricity, and good service from Met Life. But in buying her 654 square feet she would also be buying a 0.0225 percent share of the common area—the hallways, the garbage chutes, the water pipes and electrical wiring in a building thirty-two years old that needed air conditioning. Her estimated monthly bill for maintenance and real estate taxes: about $91, or almost two-thirds her rent.

Helmsley, of course, would argue that the very essence of condominiums—ownership versus renting—would work over time to keep maintenance costs down. Indeed, he pleaded in various public forums that converting to condos would spare New York City the havoc that rent control threatened to bring. "It will help stabilize neighborhoods. The exodus from the city will be stanched because people will have more interest in their neighborhoods. This is the only way New York is going to be saved," he said.

The real estate industry shared Helmsley's enthusiasm. "The implications of this are marvelous," said another converter. "The buildings will be kept better, the tensions between landlord and tenant will be ended, the tenants will be able to run the project the way they want to and they will be free to spend to fix up their apartments."

It was a bone that David Clurman, the assistant attorney general, couldn't pick with Helmsley. "There is no question that properties are better maintained after conversion," he said in 1973. "In a rental situation, people just don't care as much. When they own their own homes, they take an interest in the neighborhood. This is a means of conserving New York's housing stock."

But neither Helmsley nor the state could say in any definitive manner how much it would cost the Parkchester buyers to maintain their new homes. When buyers like Feely signed their names on all the "X"-marked lines, Helmsley had to confess by law that he could only guess that the smallest apartment would have a $62.80 monthly maintenance charge. He could only guess that its real estate taxes would be

$22 a month and that the monthly carrying charge on a loan would be $22 and that mortgage interest rates would not rise above 7 percent. For people on tight budgets, who spaced their trips to Macy's, who had lived in Parkchester all their lives completely free of the worry about big rent hikes, and who never had to deal with the complications of ownership, those were very large uncertainties indeed.

Parkchester residents also quietly fretted over who would be joining them on the park benches. Many believed condo conversion would bring the biggest racial invasion since the Civil War, and it probably didn't do anything for their nerves when Stokely Carmichael told the Bronx that Martin Luther King, Jr., was too mild-mannered. Until 1968, Met Life had allowed only two dozen minority families in Parkchester, and it was charged with "deliberate, intentional, systematic, open and notorious" exclusion of blacks and Hispanics by the city's Commission on Human Rights. Pressure from that ruling, along with conversion, would bring dark faces to white Parkchester and many people were scared.

The North Quadrant of Parkchester sold, but ever so slowly. Slightly more than half of the 4,000 units were still being rented a decade later in the mid-1980s. Helmsley didn't offer the South Quadrant for sale until 1984. Dearie and state attorney general Louis Lefkowitz, through Clurman, fought Helmsley hard on the North Quadrant plan, bringing sundry lawsuits and getting legislation that tightened the condo conversion law.

Much the same issues erupted in San Francisco, where Helmsley bought Parkmerced in 1971—from Metropolitan Life again—for $40 million. But this time Helmsley's arguments about the value of ownership didn't fly at all, and the residents were ready. The Rev. Peet had learned some tricks from Dearie and others, picketing in front of Helmsley's brand-new Park Lane Hotel just a few weeks before the spring of 1974.

Lesson number one: "You've got to organize," Karesh said. "That's one thing it taught us, you've got to organize."

So after a first explosive meeting in the early afternoon of February 21, 1974, when twenty-four hours of door-knocking and leafletting by Karesh and his children produced several hundred Parkmerced residents at the Planning Commission meeting for item number R118.73.26, the judge and the reverend held an organizing meeting on March 7. More than 700 residents turned out for the first gathering of PRO—Parkmerced Residents Organization. They included Michael Carroll, a young and eager attorney, who took the group's chair, and George McCadden, a former United Press International reporter, who took charge of the newsletter.

Calling it the *Insider,* they ran off 4,000 copies of the first six-page issue, which reported on the group's formation, on the Peets' trips to New York, on a previous state legislative effort to permit California cities to regulate condominium conversion which was vetoed by then Governor Ronald Reagan. In his address, chairman Carroll exhorted other residents to join a robust cross section of middle-class America: "three attorneys, a clergyman, a medical secretary, a saleswoman, a labor leader, a department-store executive, a retired military man, a semi-retired newspaperman, three retired business executives, a retired executive secretary, and five housewives active in community affairs." But it was the *Insider*'s second issue that really got down to business. On the front was a picture of Harry Helmsley. And next to that, PRO ran a scorching, no-holds-barred article entitled "Helmsley Game-Plan Works Like This in Parkmerced."

The Rev. Peet was, perhaps, the least moved emotionally, simply because he'd been fighting for social causes since he was born from progressive roots in Wisconsin. "The idea of winning or losing never entered my head," Peet said, sitting at his living-room table, sorting through a scrap box. A green shag carpet covered the floor in his Parkmerced apartment. A metal pole held a couple of houseplants. A row of clay Hummels sat near the big picture window. Outside, dirty gray fog from the Pacific hid the big trees that ring Lake Merced (Spanish for "mercy"), but a basket of strong-scented blue eucalyptus leaves sat on a coffee table, letting a visitor know this was California. Peet, eighty-six years old in 1988, wore brown glasses and spoke softly over the cuckoo-clock chimes.

"I was coming from a pastorate of activism for thirty-nine years. That was my job, to be an activist, a drummer for peace, for these causes. And it never entered my mind whether we would win or not, we just did it," Peet said, adding that it was an easy jump from his task at Glide Memorial Church to organize San Francisco's elderly, since more than one in three Parkmerced residents were retired on fixed incomes.

For Karesh, though, the Helmsley War was new and captivating. As a judge, he was barred from speaking out on public issues that didn't concern him very personally. So the rousing speech he would give to the City Council urging it to severely restrict condo conversions was his first public stand, as was the battle in total, and he went at it like a young, blood-painted warrior.

"Their argument, of course, was that it was a deprivation of property without due process," Karesh said in his three-bedroom garden town house. White columns out front mimicked those on a Southern mansion. A metal-frame door led onto the back porch. "So I said, 'Take property. What are you talking about?' You can say in a certain area that you can't build high rises. You can say in a certain area you can have only certain kinds of business. You can say, for another example, that you can have only so many houses in a certain area. Of course it was constitutionally right."

Then he sat forward in his chair and recalled the first meeting when he was asked about the troops. "Somebody said to me, 'Get out the troops. Can you get out the troops?' " he said, nearly leaping out of his chair as he punched the air. "And I said, 'Get out the troops? Of course we can get out the troops. You bet we can get out the troops.'

"You know," he said, "you can talk about national politics, the Republican convention, the Democratic convention, and the races for mayor and governorships, and I'm telling you, there was no campaign, and you can forgive me for boasting, there was nothing like this, what we did. And I'm proud of it. And that's the truth. And when I think about it, it makes me feel younger.

"No one thought we would win," Karesh said finally. "We were going up against big people."

It took some months, but win they did. The state finally allowed municipalities to enact condo regulations, and San Francisco did just that in 1975, dubbing theirs informally the "Helmsley Law" because it effectively blocked his plans by limiting the number of apartments that could be converted each year.

The reasons Harry Helmsley lost in San Francisco are several. He was an outsider, and from New York City no less. He had been too open about his financial success in the deals with Met Life. PRO read into the public record excerpts from a 1973 *New York Times* profile in which Helmsley blurted out, "If you're a real good player, you get rich," and concerning his profit-taking in condo conversions, "I buy wholesale and sell retail. I'm entitled, like everyone else."

"Harry Helmsley was the perfect landlord for us in this situation," said PRO's first leader, the attorney Michael Carroll. "He wasn't a resident of the city or the state. He was a very notorious landlord, primarily because of his office holdings. And he had become very acquisitive over the years. It was very difficult to feel sorry for him if he was unable to achieve his goal."

Parkmerced had 6,000 diligent voters, and they went to the polls as a block. Judge Karesh discovered this back in 1960 when he barely survived a primary and won the general election only because in the interim he had moved to Parkmerced and let everyone know he now was local.

Helmsley had no political connections in San Francisco. But his biggest mistake was failing to do the next-best thing: buy those who did. Helmsley used local counsel, but his attorneys were not from the office of Willie Brown, the flamboyant and powerful state legislator, or from the two or three other firms that were politically connected at the time. "He ran through the motions, but it very quickly became a political battle he couldn't possibly win," Carroll said.

That was a lesson learned for Helmsley, and it wasn't long before he'd apply it back home in the biggest, most eruptive political battle he'd ever face.

Back in New York, Helmsley was having all sorts of landlording problems. He had just purchased the Park West Village apartments on the western edge of Central Park in 1972 and already the 2,700 families were getting nervous, speculating about what he might have in mind for their homes. If it was paranoia, their concern was understandable. Not only was there Helmsley's own history to consider; there was the project's. Park West, between 97th and 100th streets, was called the Manhattantown Urban Renewal Project. It went up in the 1950s so slowly and plagued by such fraud that it became the nation's tarnished example of how not to renew urban areas. Helmsley, the residents were sure, would only continue that infamy with his condo conversion plans.

Across the East River, the 8,800 residents of his Fresh Meadows housing project were readying the first case in their litigation against Helmsley that would extend for two decades.

Much of the Fresh Meadows battling has been over rather ordinary landlord-tenant disputes—rent levels, evictions for nonpayment, the level of service, personal injury. That's not to belittle the fights. Most of the dozens upon dozens of cases in state court involving Fresh Meadows tenants appear to have been legitimate arguments and of vital concern to the people involved. Thousands of such cases are filed against landlords in New York City each year. But one Fresh Meadows case in particular stood out.

It was brought by the NAACP, and the issue was racial discrimination. Doug Turetsky followed the case for *City Limits,* a monthly Manhattan newsmagazine that covers housing from the tenants' perspective but with an even hand. The suit, filed in 1983, had some biting affidavits. "I rarely, if ever, saw black people in the Fresh Meadows housing complex," Valerie Stroud, a police officer, testified. "It was my understanding that . . . Fresh Meadows did not rent to black people."

Helmsley and the NAACP avoided a costly trial by agreeing to a settlement that both prohibited Helmsley from refusing to rent on the basis of race and required him to take a number of steps to encourage minorities to apply. A year later the NAACP was back in court, accusing Helmsley of violating the agreement by trying to convert the apartments into co-ops. Helmsley again settled the matter, and since then has complied rather well. The Open Housing Center, a nonprofit citizens group monitoring Fresh Meadows, estimated that the number of black families rose from less than 1 percent to the 30th percentile. "It is a limited success story," said Alissa Kampner, an attorney with the Manhattan law firm representing the NAACP.

Helmsley himself was in revolt. As chairman of the Citizens Tax Council, Helmsley cautioned the state against giving cities too much power in taxing landlords and other businesses. "A number of major industrial firms have announced plans to leave New York to set up headquarters in suburban areas," Helmsley wrote *The New York Times*. "There is no question that high taxes were an important factor in their decision. We will witness an even greater exodus of business firms— large and small—if the city manages to obtain unlimited taxing powers."

On February 1, 1975, he stopped paying taxes on the 190 residential buildings in New York City that he owned or managed. With incredible gall, Helmsley announced that he simply didn't have the money in his pocket to pay the $1 million quarterly bill because the price of oil had gone up. "We stopped paying taxes because the properties just had no money," Helmsley told a business columnist. "Sure, I'm aware of the penalty [a 1 percent monthly fine]. But what can we do? The cupboard is bare. The fuel costs, up 200 percent in the last year, are just strangling us. About 80 percent of Helmsley-Spear's residential buildings are running in the red, and we just can't keep up with that damn excess in fuel costs."

The Fresh Meadows residents had a far different perspective, but of that project Helmsley said, "It got in trouble about a year ago. Fuel and electricity costs skyrocketed in a relatively short time and we started to run into very heavy deficits. Losses of $500,000 a year in recent years suddenly turned into a cash deficit of $1.8 million in fiscal 1974 and the owners paid that $1.8 million out of their own pockets to cover the taxes and mortgage payments. But there's just no way you can continue to do that."

If true, it certainly would have violated one of Helmsley's economic mores. He may have tolerated some break-even housing deals in anticipation of reaping profit in the conversion, but he wouldn't tolerate losing any sum of money in the interim. If Fresh Meadows was reaching into his pocket to any extent, and not withstanding his eventual profit-taking, the frugal Helmsley would have clamped down. And that would mean cutting expenses and services to the tenants.

The move against the city might only have been a ploy to get its help in fighting for lower oil prices, because three months later Helmsley led forty-six other landlords in a legal charge against the eleven big oil producers. The suit asked for $145 million in damages from the producers, charging that they met secretly to fix heating-oil prices and manipulated foreign commerce and violated the Sherman Antitrust Act to create the 1973–74 energy crises that forced millions of automobile drivers to sit in lines to get gas.

That same spring of 1975, Helmsley completely reversed his tax stand against New York by joining Lewis Rudin, a second-generation developer and president of the Association for a Better New York, in prepaying his taxes to help the suddenly very sick city. It was at Rudin's home that Mayor Abe Beame broke the bad news that Washington was going to let New York totter on fiscal bankruptcy, and Rudin's reaction was to round up a $600 million loan from the real estate community.

As a landlord, Helmsley dabbled in housing policy, but he didn't play any major role in landlord groups, and he never reached for a more encompassing perspective. Housing was never an emotional issue. Throughout the city there were hundreds of people each month who couldn't amass enough money to pay their rent, and they ended up on the streets. But Helmsley viewed homelessness and housing shortages in strict economic terms—terms not terribly unlike the broader Reagan trickle-down theory. He saw investors fleeing the housing business, citing the rise in foreclosures and abandonments and the complete dearth of new construction. And he considered the landlord—no matter what one thought of the species—to be endangered. "Residential housing is a disaster area, and it's going to get worse," he said. "Under the city's present policies, residential housing must collapse."

And why not? he thought. With the city giving away deep and unprecedented tax breaks for office and luxury housing builders, one would have to be silly to invest time and money in housing. So to fight homelessness, Helmsley believed, the city should do more to help landlords stay in business. Whenever asked, he would suggest an immediate 15 percent hike in controlled rents so landlords could more easily pay their bills. They would then, he assumed, apply more money to maintenance and service.

Of course, that was a losing idea in New York, in no small part because tenants had more votes than landlords. Raising rents wouldn't help the most visible victims—those without homes. In the short term, it wouldn't even help those with homes. And housing activists took immediate issue, accusing him and other landlords of lying about their economics. Their regular calls for an escape from rent control were met with an even louder collective "Open your books." Helmsley realized he was on the losing political side. "I just don't see that happening," he said of his proposed rent hike. "The votes are with the tenants, not the landlords. I just don't think that anybody cares about the deterioration in this city."

But for all his concern for the city, Helmsley knew he was safe. Indeed, there was one aspect to the mid-1970s chaos that gave the entrepreneur in him an advantage: private lenders were in an even tighter bind. Helmsley knew that the banks and insurance companies would bend over backwards to avoid taking possession of apartment buildings they had no expertise in managing, so he was able to let his mortgage payments slip with no complaint from the banks. In short, Helmsley the landlord was buying lots of free time until the market was ready for him to move. And his move, of course, was to bail out of landlording by converting to condos—buy wholesale, sell retail.

Helmsley's transient attitude toward housing perhaps explains why he never seemed to grasp that buildings containing people's homes were different from buildings that held their offices. He never caught on that they were far different creatures. Business managers could think objectively about the space they rented. They simply took the number of their employees and multiplied by the appropriate factor to get square feet. If they were printers, they knew they needed lots of thick electrical lines. If they had big equipment, the elevators had to be wide. If the address mattered, that too could be given a dollar value and factored in.

But renting an apartment, especially in New York City, is to seek a refuge from the assaults of urban living at its most extreme. And Helmsley has never seemed to understand that people will go to extraordinary measures to protect their apartment once they have one.

Perhaps he never made the simple connection that an apartment—
however small compared to his in the Park Lane—was, after all, a
home. Even the plight of an eighty-two-year-old woman couldn't
convince him of that.

---

**CHAPTER 9**

---

# TROUBLE IN
# TUDOR CITY

THE ESSEX HOUSE IS ONE OF ELEVEN BUILDINGS THAT FORM THE TUDOR City apartments in midtown Manhattan, not far from the United Nations and Grand Central Station. There's a doorman. A cloth marquee reaches out to the curb. The decor is medieval Old English. Gargoyles leer from on high.

Irene Phillips lived in the Essex for thirty-one years. And then suddenly, at age eighty-two, she didn't anymore.

Phillips moved into the Essex in 1940 after her husband died. Charles Phillips, an Englishman, was an internationally known stamp collector and dealer, counting among his clients King George V. After his death, Irene supported herself as a fashionable dressmaker.

Paying only $169 a month for her six-room Essex apartment, Irene Phillips was a product of the rent-control laws that Harry Helmsley and other landlords had come to loathe. As long as she stayed put, her

[ 145 ]

rent could go up only very, very gradually over the years. Her newer neighbors paid double or triple the rent she paid. Not until Phillips moved out could her landlord charge that much for her space.

Phillips might have lived out her life in the Essex, but she developed a problem in her later years. She began failing to pay the rent. So did her guardian, Dorothy Wilson, an elderly niece. It wasn't for lack of money that they kept missing the due dates. Rather, as both ladies confessed, they had a "tendency toward carelessness" about their finances.

Rudy Kratt was the Tudor City general manager at the time and he spoke poorly of Phillips. "I have a file on her two inches thick," he told *The New York Times.* "Three times she was brought to court about not paying her rent, but each time the judge sympathized with her. This time he didn't."

Phillips, two months overdue, was evicted. It was a pitiful scene that Thursday morning, November 11, 1971. Out on the sidewalk her belongings were stacked: tables and chairs and furniture of all sorts; china, ivory, and other items that her husband had collected from around the world. Four venerable white Chinese hand-painted vases sat precariously, waiting to be picked up. A framed photograph of King George leaned against a tree trunk.

Gertrude Cohen, Phillips's attorney, rushed to the scene. So did Wilson, who said she had obtained the two months' rent. It was too late. The payment was rejected, as was Irene Phillips. She moved in with her niece. It couldn't be learned how long she lived after the eviction, but Cohen at the time said Phillips had a "serious heart condition."

If the landlord, Harry Helmsley, saw another side to the eviction he never said so publicly. Indeed, he escaped vilification. Helmsley-Spear, Inc., was named the responsible entity, and manager Kratt took the heat from reporters who rushed to the scene. But the eviction of Irene Phillips was a portent of the trouble Helmsley would stir for himself in Tudor City, trouble that would lead him to be picketed, hanged in effigy, and battered in the press as never before.

Fred French built Tudor City on a bluff called Corcoran's Roost, after the infamous Paddy Corcoran and his Rag Gang. The view below was of a wasteland of foul stockyards, breweries, gas plants, and glue factories stretching along the East River. Only years later did the United Nations complex replace all that. Meanwhile, the Tudor City buildings were given what today seems a rather odd design: he turned the buildings, windows and all, inward toward midtown Manhattan.

Tudor City was an experiment in urban redevelopment for the middle class, which, it was feared, was fleeing Manhattan for the outer boroughs and suburbs because the city had grown too exhausting. Tudor City offered affordable rents, as well as some precious environmental solace to its 10,000 middle-class residents. French built or obtained for Tudor City a hotel, a restaurant, a post office, and a store. He also promised and delivered a little oasis: two small parks in the center, which he landscaped like English gardens.

"Directly opposite these first two units the French Co. have set aside a plot of approximately 128 by 500 feet to be planted in lawn and shrubbery. This will be for the exclusive use of Tudor City tenants and is one of the few private parks in America," the firm announced in 1927. Indeed, only the iron-fenced, lushly planted Gramercy Park where Helmsley lived in the 1940s could also make that claim.

French put in a miniature golf course in the southern park, and again he was quite proud. It had eighteen holes up to sixty feet long, sand traps, bunkers, water hazards, and lights at night. French boasted that it was the only such course in Manhattan. But it eventually disappeared, and the park reverted back to a garden, which was equally rare in that part of Manhattan, a long two miles from Central Park and a short three blocks from Grand Central Station with its city throb of cement, dirt, and noise.

The parks came to be revered. Tudor City residents would come down from their stuffy apartments on warm or cool days, weekends or weekdays, with their canes or with their children, and sit on the benches. At their feet would be gravel or wood-chip-covered walks. Alongside would be flowering, shimmering foliage. All around was a magnificent forest. Two dozen sycamores, or London planes, lined the parks. They were joined at the curbsides by a couple of flowering cherries, ashes, and ailanthus. Inside the perimeter, there were small-leaf lindens, Norway maples, pin oaks, flowering crab apples, catalpas, and magnolias.

The parks were private, and the custodian had a clever way to sort out outsiders. He would ask their apartment number, knowing Tudor City had a unique combination of numbers and letters that most people couldn't just guess. Down one level toward Forty-second Street, which cut eastward toward the East River through Corcoran's Bluff, were two smaller parks that were public.

The first hint of what Helmsley had in store for the parks came in June 1970 when the French Co. announced it had sold Tudor City to a Helmsley syndicate for $36 million cash and the assumption of mortgages totaling $7.5 million. *The New York Times* story discounted rumors that Helmsley wanted to demolish all of Tudor City and replace it with commercial development linked to the UN. But paragraph three had these words, which rang just as loudly through Tudor City halls: "He noted, however, that the property included vacant land only part of which is deeded to the city for park purposes. Construction of additional buildings on the open space, either by the new owners or another developer, is a possibility, Mr. Helmsley said." A few months later he was quoted as saying, "We are certainly exploring all possibilities. We have explored the idea of building on the parks. I can't afford to keep a park. I can't afford to buy a park and keep taxes on it."

Actually, Helmsley already was drawing up plans for not one, but two gigantic office towers to be placed on the parks. But what was most interesting about those first newspaper stories is that years later Helmsley himself would be referring to the parks as "vacant land," and therein lay the crux of the fight. What was oasis to the tenants was raw land to Helmsley. And what they considered their amenities he considered his to do with what he pleased. And technically, Helmsley was right.

French may have thought his parks were comparable to the private, inviolable Gramercy Park, but he failed to write that down in black and white in the property's deed. Look as they might, the tenants could not find covenant or other reference to the parks where it legally counted. They had only French's original sales pitches, which wouldn't go over in court. But they would do just as well in public and political forums, so that's where the Tudor City tenants took their fight against Helmsley, as had the Parkmerced residents.

The tenants quickly organized, led by a World War II PT-boat veteran named John McKean, who was drawn into Democratic party politics after meeting Jack Kennedy at an officers' reunion. McKean also happened to own his own real estate firm and knew a good bit about property.

McKean was primed for Helmsley. A couple of years earlier he had had a warm-up fight with Tudor City's western neighbor, the Ford Foundation, which wanted to buy Tudor City and convert it into a United Nations housing enclave. Ten thousand people did not want to move, but Ford had some key allies—the mayor, the governor—and McKean knew he'd lose that political fight. He needed a technicality, and he seemingly pulled one out of the air by calling a staffer with the congressional Ways and Means Committee who discovered that Ford's unique tax status would make buying Tudor City a very bad deal, if not illegal. That was in 1968, and McKean would again turn to Washington for some technical help in his fight against Helmsley.

His first step was to fire off a round of letters. Some were filled with masterful prose of persuasion. To the governor, Nelson Rockefeller, he noted Helmsley's involvement in the governor's pet project, Battery Park City, an office and apartment complex to be built on nearly one hundred acres of landfill. And he subtly warned that it would be dragged into the bad publicity if the parks were razed. "You must foresee the potential tumult on the day his bulldozers arrive to push over trees and shrubs that have been an adornment to the community for 45 years. At that time effective and articulate people will speak out. But by then the confrontation may be ugly and complex.

"He is getting his Tudor City investment back at a great rate and should, if only for the content of his biography, be prevented from looking on his two refreshing parks as just another pair of undeveloped lots."

McKean wrote other public officials, including Ed Koch, then a Manhattan representative in Congress, who sent back a robust pledge of support. "As you know, I am opposed to this proposed construction and I have joined in asking for the down-zoning of the park area so as to prevent the construction. Rest assured that I will continue to oppose this plan which I believe to be highly inappropriate."

McKean even heard from Monsignor Eugene V. Clark, who replied from the Roman Catholic archdiocese offices on Madison Avenue, where Helmsley, eight years later, would build the Palace Hotel. Clark apologized, saying Terence Cardinal Cooke never signed petitions. He added, however, that Cooke "is very much in favor of keeping the maximum amount of open space in our city." A prize in the correspondence came from the great builder himself, Robert Moses, who had been bruised by his own park-bulldozing episode years earlier in the course of laying almost every major highway in the New York City region. For all his tyrannical ways, however, Moses was a lover of parks and McKean softly reminded him of his role in dedicating the Tudor City parks in 1927. Moses wrote back on the letterhead of the bridge authority he had created to run his public empire building, and told McKean in May 1972: "Of course I agree and recall the dedication." Moses also referred McKean to several potential allies, and encouraged him to write Helmsley. "Have a talk with Mr. Helmsley. I don't know the value of the plots as real estate. He might donate one of the two plots, especially if he got some zoning benefit or concession as to the height of buildings, setbacks, etc. He is public-spirited, and I am sure approachable."

But McKean had tried Helmsley directly. In fact, McKean's first move was to ask Helmsley for a summit. On December 1, 1971, Helmsley dictated this note: "Dear Mr. McKean: I do believe that our plans for the parks will be very interesting when they are finally announced as we are preserving as much as possible. However, it is my opinion that if parks should be preserved, this is a function of the City government and it is hardly possible for private owners to be expected to support this. Perhaps the City should condemn the land and make the land into parks. At this time, there would be no point in discussing the plans."

McKean began holding rallies. One in late July 1972 drew a parade of public officials, including Percy Sutton, president of the Manhattan borough, and Koch, who again declared, "It'll be an outrage if the park is demolished to make way for a high rise. This matter concerns not only Tudor, but is really a fight for the whole city—that we make it clean and open."

McKean's goal of making it a citywide issue was catching on. "All we need is public understanding that this building is not merely a neighborhood problem. What happens in Tudor City may well be the pattern for ruthless development and environmental degradation everywhere in the city." But things would have to heat up for officials to actually act.

With both sides threatening suit, the city's first move was to suggest alternatives to Helmsley's threatened plunking down of two huge office towers atop the parks: build on just one park or build in between on a new platform constructed over the sunken Forty-second Street as it cuts through the bluff. Big easels were placed in the Planning Commission hearing room to hold the rough sketches, as Tudor City residents packed the gallery and Helmsley's representative scowled on the side.

Helmsley might have gone for the overpass, which would have, incredibly, allowed him to completely block off Manhattan's busiest crosstown boulevard with a huge steel-and-cement tower. But the idea that won official support was the first of several out-and-out swaps. In this case, the notion was to make an official little park district and hand Helmsley the right to build a larger-than-legal building somewhere else in midtown. The city approved the deal in late 1972, and Helmsley cried foul after adding up the numbers. He was trading a new forty-five-story tower for the right to build 20 percent higher than normally permitted on some other site he owned. Helmsley balked at the notion and filed the first suit.

Tudor City residents also realized they were treading on thin ice by getting the city involved. In creating the park district, the city would have declared the parks to be public. That prompted one nervous resident, fearing an invasion of "derelicts and winos," to write a newspaper: "I am afraid [that] would provide a cure that would be worse than the disease. The tiny parks would then attract an element that the mostly elderly tenants now using the parks would have reason to fear."

In 1973 Helmsley filed the first condominium plan for Tudor City. But he moved very slowly, asking the state to approve only ninety-five units. And Helmsley stopped with that first offering. Emotions were simply too strong in Tudor City for him to step in with his wholesale/retail business. He would have to resolve the parks battle first.

Meanwhile, McKean also filed suit. He had gone back to Washington looking for another technicality and found Representative Bill Green, who suggested they use the city's tough rent-control laws. "It was just a flash of genius," Green said. "It seemed there was sufficient evidence that the parks had been promised as an amenity to the tenants historically, so that the use of the parks for construction would mean a reduction in amenity, which would allow tenants to go to court and demand a reduction in rents." So McKean filed suit on those grounds. It would, at the least, severely complicate Helmsley's plans.

Six years passed. The city's economy floundered, or it might have just purchased the parks from Helmsley. Tudor City residents gained a new appreciation for the parks, and both usage and maintenance were up. Helmsley lost his suit, but did get a zoning change allowing him to build apartments on the parks, and that's what he proposed doing in 1978. Two years later, in 1980, all hell broke loose on Memorial Day weekend.

Anne Lowenstein was lying in bed when, at about 8 A.M., she heard John McKean's voice booming up through her windows. "He was yelling, 'Everybody out! Everybody out!' and literally we ran outside grabbing our sweatshirts or whatever we could grab," Lowenstein recalled. "Our oldest, Mimi, was only two or less at the time, so it was unwieldy getting out there."

Many people were out of town for the holiday, but Tudor City came alive as several hundred residents poured into the street where McKean was parading up down with a bullhorn.

McKean, in turn, had been awakened by an elderly woman named Lisa Ericsen, who lived right next to the north park. She had been up for hours when at 7 A.M. she noticed truckloads of lumber and twenty workmen pull up to the park. They started building a wall around the north park, and Ericsen frantically called McKean. "I normally wouldn't answer that early," McKean said. "There are thousands of people here and they all have my number. But I took the call, and she said, 'John, there's something very strange going on. I don't know, but you better come down and have a look.' "

McKean did, and confronted the men. The one in charge said he was there to build a fence. "Well, it wasn't too hard to figure out that this was preliminary to sending the bulldozers in. So what do you do? You can't fight it alone. You can only do it with numbers. And I got my bullhorn and started walking up and down the street, yelling, 'Emergency! Everybody out! Everybody down!' People started looking out the windows, like, what is this crazy man doing? But they started coming out."

Thirty minutes later the police arrived, first in one squad car, then by the dozen. The police matched the residents in numbers and separated them from the workmen. One lieutenant then took McKean aside and told him to make their fight legal and find a judge, fast. McKean knew one personally. He called him at home. The judge said he'd stay there until the protesters got some papers worked up. A couple of hours later McKean and a pair of attorneys knocked on the judge's door, only to find Helmsley's attorneys already there. "I guess they had spies in the crowd, 'cause we were talking about all this out there on the street," McKean said.

The residents got their injunction, but they still didn't trust Helmsley. A half dozen people slept in the park that night, and the very next dawn, on Sunday, the workmen and lumber were back, joined by a bulldozer. They also had a cute little trick. Just as the bulldozer pulled up, the residents noticed a woman unknown in Tudor City jump in a parked car and drive away, leaving an entry point for the bulldozer. The residents formed a human chain, and deepened their resentment toward Helmsley. They wrote messages to Harry and Leona on the plywood walls around their park—not profanity, but heartfelt messages about the value of trees and squirrels and peaceful quiet in a city that at times seemed as dense as Calcutta.

"I can't tell you how much anguish I felt," recalled Lowenstein, who would later take Mimi to picket Helmsley's headquarters three blocks away on Forty-second Street. She moved to the window of her apartment and looked down, through the spring blossoming, on one park. "Especially after we moved in and decided to stay. The parks were very important. We met most of our neighbors in the playgrounds. This community has a sense of oneness. There's no through traffic. It really is like an oasis in midtown, and the thought that this greedy person who certainly didn't need more income would just callously destroy a neighborhood, well, I've certainly had many hours feeling frustrated and angry toward Harry Helmsley."

On Memorial Day weekend 1988, eight years after the bulldozing incident, McKean sat on a bench in the north park and mused about Helmsley's motives and morals. McKean, wearing black work pants and a short-sleeved white shirt with its breast pocket stuffed with a notebook, pens, and a case for his glasses, held a thick notebook detailing the Tudor City fight. Said McKean: "Why did Harry do what he did? It's hard to understand. I think he always had in mind building here, and he looks at these parks and sees vacant land to build on. Why did he want more money? Why do the super-rich want to keep accumulating more? It's hard to answer. I suppose it's sort of a mania. They just enjoy making more money and more deals. With him it became pride. He was a proud man, and the fact that he was being frustrated just plain annoyed him."

Tudor City residents stayed involved, but the battle for their parks shifted to new ground as city officials realized they had better do something. Several land swaps were proposed in the early 1980s, but only one came close to consensus. It involved trading the Tudor parks for a city playground nearby, just south of the United Nations, and Helmsley gained a new formidable enemy in the form of a pack of teens who belonged to the East End Hockey Association.

Nobody thought anyone used the playground until John Caulfield stood up at a neighborhood planning group meeting in early 1981 and explained to the adults on the commission what roller hockey was and how he and his friends used the playground regularly. Phil Howard, a young Manhattan attorney, who was later named one of the city's ten most socially conscious citizens by the weekly *Village Voice* for his work on urban-planning issues, was the group's zoning specialist. Howard recalled Caulfield's testimony.

"Here was this red-haired Irish kid with bad complexion and a terminally bad stutter, and when he spoke, at the first of our meetings, he would have to go way beyond the three minutes allotted each speaker because he could only get out three words in that time," Howard said, laughing. "Roller hockey. I had never heard of it. The first time I saw him I thought, well, this is cute. Now let us get down to the serious issue of land-use planning before us. But he showed up again, and again, and I came to admire him greatly and got interested."

For Caulfield, who was actually twenty-six at the time, fighting Helmsley's swap was nothing short of a turning point in his life. Since he was older than most of the hockey club's 107 members, Caulfield was volunteered as the leader. He held strategy sessions in his apartment, banged out press releases and letters, and then reluctantly agreed to speak out at the meetings. And what Caulfield discovered was nothing short of miraculous, especially since he'd been whiling away his adult life convinced his stutter kept him from his dream of becoming an attorney. As Caulfield stood up, again and again, and as the crowds got larger and larger, his stutter went into hiding.

"The thing was, it was something I had to shelve concern about," Caulfield said, his voice clear and steady. "I wasn't self-conscious. I was conscious of the fact that people depended on me. No else could do it. And I had to get people's attention. Interestingly enough, I discovered that it's easier to speak to a group of three hundred than it is to three. You can command attention more easily. You don't have to compete. And more than anything else, it was the experience of speaking during that controversy that convinced me it was not such an absurd idea that I could be an attorney." Caulfield went to law school and in 1988 was clerking his way to a legal practice.

Helmsley had to scramble against this new assault, and he did two things that he had failed to do in San Francisco. One, he hired a politically connected attorney by the name of Samuel Lindenbaum. And two, he put his public relations representative, Howard Rubenstein, to work. Neither man did terribly well.

Rubenstein, who began his image-making career in the early 1950s writing press releases for an old-age home, quickly became the Manhattan real estate community's main man, representing a Who's Who of skyscraper-building and -owning clients. He could do his share of publicity stunts, but Rubenstein was better known as a soft-spoken conciliator. He could walk fences between rival factions like a cat.

Rubenstein never caught on to the Tudor City fight, which probably did more damage to Helmsley's public image than any other dispute. Indeed, at one point Helmsley agreed to debate a panel of Tudor City residents, ranging from a teenage girl to an elderly woman. The program aired on local TV and Harry was slaughtered, in McKean's judgment. Helmsley may have recognized how much Tudor City hurt him in public relations. Certainly Leona did. Though Rubenstein continued to work for Helmsley-Spear, Leona let him go. When their tax-fraud problems came up, they hired a far more aggressive public relations specialist.

Samuel Lindenbaum did even worse than Rubenstein on Tudor City. He made a tiny mistake that galvanized his opponents.

A specialist in zoning law, Lindenbaum was for a long time the attorney whom developers would hire if they didn't want to bother showing up at public meetings. His clients included Donald Trump, who inscribed a book—"Sandy, you are the greatest"—after Lindenbaum won him a $56 million tax break for his Grand Hyatt Hotel next to Grand Central Station. Lindenbaum, when asked what he charged, would merely quote others who called him the highest-paid attorney in New York.

His clout ran deep. In 1981 Lindenbaum represented Helmsley before a city panel that doled out a huge tax break to Helmsley's hotel on Forty-second Street. The panel's chair, Karen Gerard, ended the very brief session with the words: "Don't tell me this will be your entire visit, Mr. Lindenbaum?" He replied: "I am sorry for both of us, but happy for my client." He could move in and out of meetings just like that, pocketing huge sums for those clients.

Lindenbaum did fairly well for Helmsley through the early stages of the playground swap. To the eventual amusement of the community group and commissions hearing the swap idea, he would even refrain from mentioning Helmsley by name. It would always be the "group of investors" or the "assemblage company," leaving it to the swap critics to ensure that Helmsley's name stayed in the air. He also noted that the "investors" were willing to donate $1 million to the city for recreation if the swap was allowed.

But at one meeting Lindenbaum was asked point-blank about another possible swap, involving an unused public school site ten blocks to the north of Tudor City. And Lindenbaum said, according to one witness, "That wouldn't be acceptable to my client because the school at Fifty-first Street is not waterfront property."

The room fell silent as brains quietly clicked and lights went on. Aha, the entire hockey club realized, so that's the reason Helmsley wants our park! In short order, another politician began poking into the matter of what this hard-dirt playground just south of the United Nations and a ball's throw from the East River was really worth to the city.

His name was Andrew Stein. Stein would later be elected president of the New York City Council, the city's second-highest elective office. During the Tudor City fight he represented the borough of Manhattan on the Board of Estimate. The Board is to New York City what the Senate is to Congress—a smaller, in some ways more powerful elected group of officials representing larger geographical districts than members of the City Council.

Stein had moved into city politics from his seat in the state assembly, where he represented Manhattan's posh East Side. Assembly colleagues recall seeing him grow professionally from a brash twenty-three-year-old womanizer into a street-fighting reformist of sorts. Stein the Young Turk had to be tied to his desk. Stein the reformist won nursing-home protections and mental-hospital cleanups. He exposed subway-car scandals and pushed Mayor Koch to fight drug dealers on Manhattan's Lower East Side. In later years he wrote long and eloquently on the economic crisis enveloping the city's huge numbers of poor children, warning society, as has U.S. Senator Daniel Patrick Moynihan, that it will pay for their economic suffering. And while he is criticized for taking large sums of money from developers in the form of campaign donations, and being very chummy with some as a result, he tallies a "Ten Biggest" list of city slumlords, naming names in the best tradition of populist reform.

Property value, the intangible thing that it is, in this case worked against Harry Helmsley. He had told Mayor Koch that the parks and the playground were worth about $12 million each. But Stein, who had sided with the hockey players—and against the Tudor City residents at this juncture, since they supported the swap to save their parks —was suspicious.

He got on the phone and called around to other developers, including Donald Trump. Recalled Stein's aide at the time, Marty McLaughlin: "We went to the mayor. He listened attentively, and Andrew said the right buzzword: 'I do not want to turn over a piece of city property to give a developer a windfall.' Well, that hit the right button, because Koch said, and I can remember just how he said it because it's the way he talks, 'We are not in the business of giving windfalls to developers at the expense of the city, but you have to document this to me. Set up a meeting and follow this through.'

"So we left the meeting with Koch and I said to Andrew, 'You're halfway won on this issue.' We then called Donald and asked if he would mind coming to Stein's office, to have a meeting with some of Koch's aides. He came, and they questioned Donald, who was young and flamboyant and full of piss and vinegar, and Trump said he valued the property at $45 million to $50 million. And then to reinforce himself he whipped out his checkbook and said, 'This is good. You can call the bank to find out.' And everybody laughed and said, 'No, Donald, that's not necessary.' That was Friday. On Monday, the mayor announced that the swap was off."

Helmsley gave up with that defeat. His name was so bad around Tudor City that he had to sell the property to another condo conversion specialist, who managed to sell the apartments to the tenants only after agreeing to deed them the parks.

Leona had been quiet through the Tudor City affair, letting her husband take the hits. But now she erupted.

Every spring, New York City's politically powerful gather in a Manhattan hotel for a party called the Inner Circle. It's much like the Washington Press Club's annual dinner. The tables cost small fortunes. The food is bad. The skits are variously entertaining. The lampooning can be fierce. For the past decade in New York, Koch has provided ample literary fodder for the Inner Circle stage, from corruption in his administration to his on-again, off-again diet. "Porky 'n' Bess" was a big hit, chronicling him and his indicted former Cultural Affairs Commissioner, Bess Myerson.

In March 1981, the Inner Circle party came off much like the rest. A Who's Who of elected officials and their monied constituents mingled in a Manhattan ballroom with the City Hall press corps, a noble, decidedly fun-loving breed.

When Stein bumped into the Helmsleys at the affair, it was not surprising they were something less than chummy. Still, the encounter shocked Stein. And more than any of the dozens of anecdotes about Leona and Harry, the incident, as recalled separately by McLaughlin and Stein, explains the couple's very different attitude toward their business and toward fighting and losing.

"I was performing," said McLaughlin, who now runs his own public relations firm. McLaughlin's Irish brogue is light, and he spoke slowly, precisely, choosing his words like a public relations veteran. "And I was backstage. And Andrew came back laughing, with a kind of shocked look on his face. He said to me, 'Well, I was at my table and Harry and Leona come walking in. Harry was very nice. He said, "Hello, Andrew. How are you?" And we kind of chatted. And she was kind of walking behind him and she turned to me and, sort of sotto voce, leans over and says, "Fuck you, you cocksucker." ' And he said he was like, uh, he couldn't believe it. His mouth dropped open. And, of course, we had a big laugh at it, at Harry's expense."

"She was very nasty," Stein said.

Stein said he could not confirm, but he did not doubt, his former public spokesman's recollection of Leona using those precise words. More importantly, he said he remembered they were impressively vulgar, and he drew from them the same import as did McLaughlin. "Harry, he was cold, but always a gentleman. He knows as a professional that you win some and lose some, and that it's a small town. But she took it personally."

Said McLaughlin: "The bitch couldn't let it go by."

Leona Helmsley had never let anything in her life go by. Especially not the Palace Hotel.

## CHAPTER 10

# THE DEAN,
# THE CARDINAL,
# THE GOLD ROOM

LEGEND HAS HARRY HELMSLEY STROLLING DOWN MADISON AVENUE ONE fine day in 1974 when he is seized by a vision.

He is sauntering alongside St. Patrick's Cathedral, the story goes, when he looks up at the crestfallen Villard Houses, with their brownstone walls in sad decay. And suddenly, out of the Manhattan skyline, the Palace appears. And it is beautiful. And he casts open its golden rooms for the world to enjoy.

But that's only part of the Palace myth, tossed into press releases for literary effect and dished by up Harry and Leona for its promotional value. The real story deserves a place in American history, not legend—if only for the extraordinary meeting of minds that occurred to bring it off and for the fortunes they made at the public's expense.

[ 160 ]

It was a dance as much as it was a deal cut by two powerful people: the head of the Roman Catholic archdiocese partnering the master of real estate. They had an exquisite gentlemen's joust, the cardinal and Harry. Then they signed their names to a cunning pact that left both sides counting their take—in millions of dollars. And yet, to varying degrees, it became a devil's bargain for both.

Twenty years earlier, Harry Helmsley was moving ever so cautiously into hotels. Indeed, he backed into the business, as if he foresaw the trouble they'd bring him eventually, along with the pleasure in profit.

The person who tickled his interest was Steve Brener, who became Helmsley's tough specialist in hotels and motels—brokering sales and acquisitions, advising management, charting the market trends.

Helmsley mimicked the strategy he applied to the office buildings brokered by Helmsley-Spear. Occasionally during the 1950s and 1960s, he bought the hotels and motels that Brener spotted as particularly good deals. A few were stately: the Senator in Sacramento, the Taft in New York, the Ambassador in Palm Beach, the Colonial Plaza in Orlando, the Sand Castle in Sarasota. Other acquisitions were nondescript, and to none did Helmsley take a great fancy. "Those were the first blushes," said Brener. "But Harry didn't like hotels too much."

Neither did Larry Wien, though he joined Harry for at least one hotel deal. In 1961 they formed a syndicate to buy the St. Moritz, a luxury 700-room hotel in Manhattan that forms part of the masonry cliff that stretches along the south side of Central Park, anchored by the famed Plaza Hotel to the east. It was an exceptional boulevard then, as it is now, lined with horse-drawn carriages along one side and stretch limousines on the other. Central Park South is the place to see limos that have an extra set of wheels underneath a six-foot-long baggage trunk. It's also been the place to be seen, and people pay dearly for café tables by the picture windows so passersby can note their presence. With the Moritz came two famed eateries, the Café de la Paix and Rumpelmayer's, as well as boardrooms and ballrooms. Wien and Helmsley could play host to parties and corporate meetings.

But the Moritz was not so much a hotel to Wien and Helmsley as it was another of their real estate investments. They limited themselves to collecting the annual returns. Others handled the checking in and out and the more elaborate and messy tasks involved in running a major hotel.

Helmsley had trouble with several motels. The Cape Colony in Florida, developed by the first team of seven astronauts, had to be closed in bankruptcy when the space program stalled and tourists stopped coming. But generally, the preceding years had been good to motel owners. The late 1960s, in fact, were boom years. From 1966 to 1968, the number of motels in Florida expanded by almost one-third. The growth "undoubtedly reflects the shift in purpose of the motor hotel, from the by-the-road overnight lodging for travelers to a facility serving the complete needs of business executives, commercial travelers and vacationing Americans," Brener said at the time.

Then came the 1970s, opening as they did with a walloping recession. Helmsley's trepidations about wading deeper into hotels were washed away by loud pleas for help from his financier friends. The cries were such that Helmsley must have felt some déjà vu back to the Great Depression. A good many motel and hotel operators, it seemed, were no different from other building owners when it came to struggling with a downturn in the economy. The management weaknesses they were able to mask in good times came right to the surface as glaring flaws. Red ink flowed across the country, bankruptcies flourished, and the financiers were stuck holding the door.

Said Brener: "It seemed like every insurance company and bank and so forth called us and said, 'Will you take over the management of these hotels we suddenly have on our hands?' "

Helmsley owned thirteen or fourteen hotels in the early 1970s when the economy hit the skids. "All of a sudden, Helmsley was managing forty hotels, and we had over eighty key employees. That's when we got into the hotel business in a big way. In fact, we quickly became one of the biggest Sheraton franchisees."

Helmsley then made a milestone decision. He concluded it was dumb to manage hotels and motels unless he owned them. Unlike maintaining the Empire State and other office buildings, running and cleaning hotels is very expensive. It requires trained professionals. And even when things go well, the profits from mere management don't merit the investment of capital and anguish. The real money to be made, he figured, is in actually owning the things. So he switched tracks. He bought up the best deals he had going, adding to them an entire chain called Hospitality Inns. At the same time he winnowed, dumping those properties he didn't want. And Harry Helmsley pulled together a good-sized profitable chain of lodges, encompassing three dozen or so establishments in major cities. They all looked to be little moneymakers.

Meanwhile, Helmsley took what he learned from building office towers in Manhattan and developed the Park Lane Hotel on Central Park South, just east of the St. Moritz.

It was a gutsy move. At the time, the market for luxury hotel rooms in Manhattan was considered to be saturated. No one had opened a luxury hotel in years. Indeed, no one was even thinking about luxury hotels, except Harry Helmsley. When he opened the Park Lane in 1971 it broke a seven-year drought in new hotels, and his timing appeared to be awful. The 1970 recession was followed by New York's near bankruptcy, and both seemed to bruise Manhattan hoteliers as it did other businesses. Average occupancy rates that year fell from the high 70s to 68 percent, and they had farther to slide. "The hotel business has not been the greatest in the last year, and we're in there competing with a unique league of luxury hotels," said John Mados, who opened the Park Lane as its vice president and first manager.

But the Park Lane was not thrown to the wind. Helmsley was taking a personal interest in it, and his carefully laid plans figured not so much on tapping a new guest market as they did on luring wealthy visitors away from the St. Regis with its Salvador Dali suites, the Pierre, and even the Plaza, just down the street, where F. Scott Fitzgerald had lived and Eloise skated through the halls in children's storybooks. They were tough competitors, but Helmsley was going into hotels having played four decades of musical chairs in the office-space business, where he and his savvy brokers never waited for new tenants to appear. They lured them. And now Helmsley figured on luring those guests who had the biggest purses, according to Mados: "visiting dignitaries, business executives, diplomats, heads of state, and fine tourists."

"This place has been specifically designed to please a high class of people who want the ultimate in luxury and personal service, and we think we have a chance," Mados said of the Park Lane, whose brochure spoke of an "understated world of rich marbles and wood," as well as velvet brocade wallpaper, French provincial furnishings, and telephones in the bathrooms.

Helmsley had a little trouble with his own penthouse. Not long after he moved in, and just before Leona joined him, a friend stopped by to see his new digs and instead marveled at the mess. The apartment was dripping. Rugs were soaked. Chairs were standing in puddles. His pool had overflowed, and all Harry could do was laugh it off. But on his marketing ploy for the Park Lane he was right on the money. The Park Lane broke the drought, stole away guests, and made believers of any who doubted Harry could do hotels. In terms of the industry measure, occupancy, or the number of rooms rented out on average, the Park Lane—after a three-year buildup—has stayed well above the city average.

For many of his hotel empire-building years, Helmsley looked at hotels as he did other real estate. It was either a good or a bad deal, depending on the price, the expected return, and whatever fancy tax work he could muster. In 1978, for example, he applied his Real Estate 101 to a hotel he bought in downtown Orlando. The lodge is moderately priced, catering to salespeople on tight budgets, and actually looks more like a motel except, being downtown as it is, the parking is in a sunken garage. A bewildering set of wings and annexes stand around an ordinary motel swimming pool. The only distinguishing mark is a gaudily decorated cocktail lounge called the Monkey Bar. Helmsley attended the ribbon-cutting press conference set up by Joe Ash, who ran the Helmsley hotels outside of New York for much of the 1970s.

"Mr. Helmsley, why did you buy this hotel?" asked a young reporter from the *Orlando Sentinel*.

"There are two main reasons," Helmsley said, rattling off a few Chamber of Commerce-type factors: Orlando was coming back. It was going to be a vibrant city. The climate was good for pink flamingos and humans alike. Then he stopped and the reporter asked, "What's the second?"

"Helmsley looked at her," recalled Ash, "and got that silly little grin on his face, and said, 'Because it made a hell of a real estate deal.' " In short, he was able to buy it for less than he figured to get in returns.

But at some point Helmsley started to see something else in hotels, and he liked very much what he saw. In fact, his enthusiasm grew by leaps when he realized that overnight guests were even better than permanent Empire State tenants, for one key reason: their rent could be adjusted nightly. There were no locked-in ten-year leases in the hotel business. What one night was a $160 room could be $190 the next. Helmsley, the office-lease king, had been used to following long cycles measured in years or decades. Hotels were much more fun. Now he could speed everything up into cycles as short as the year's seasons, raising room rates just before business would get good, lowering them to boost the slow times. He started to read occupancy and room-rate reports the way others read the stock-market charts, and his larger hotels began capturing more of his time as he realized there were hefty profits at stake.

And then along came the Palace.

~

The Roman Catholic Church is a major New York City landowner, as are several other churches, in large part by virtue of having accumulated land for nothing when Manhattan was a mere village. Now and then, too, a church member wills a deed. The Catholic Church does not volunteer any figures, and there are no public records since its holdings are exempt from taxation. But real estate analysts routinely rank it among the top institutional landowners, behind Columbia University and Harry's old friends Met Life and Equitable.

In 1948, an arm of the Catholic Church, the Archdiocese of New York, obtained the land underneath the Villard Houses on Madison Avenue. Through the early 1970s, the Villard Houses served the church as both annex and income-producing property. The church leased the northern half of the houses along Fifty-first Street to Capital Cities and to another firm. It retained the southern half along Fiftieth Street for a church residence and office space. But then the church moved its residences across town, and it decided to unload the property, through a 100-year lease. The church had two good reasons: the city was going to yank the tax-free status it had enjoyed there, and there likely was a good deal of money to be made if someone developed the site.

For months there were no takers. Johnny Reynolds, a well-known New York real estate man, was the broker. He put out flyers and did a good bit of cold-calling on prospects, but no one was interested. It was, after all, a time of economic uncertainty in New York, what with the recession and local fiscal woes. Then Reynolds went to Harry Helmsley, an old friend. Helmsley was open to suggestions. The initial idea, possibly offered by Reynolds, was to do a fifty-plus-story high-rise tower that would be half office, half hotel.

They were extraordinary sessions, the talks that ensued between Terence Cardinal Cooke and Harry Helmsley. Their staffs put together the detailed minutiae—all the little things that go into making leases as thick as magazines. The lawyers and brokers held meeting after meeting, in rather ordinary fashion. But the cardinal and Harry retained the biggest and trickiest points, as well as the bottom line, the actual price. And theirs was a tussle rarely—if ever—seen in the real estate world.

With social etiquette on his side, the cardinal seized the negotiating advantage. "This was not as if Mr. Helmsley was buying any other piece of property on Madison Avenue," recalled Kevin McGrath, an attorney with the prestigious law firm of Shea, Gould, Climenko & Kramer, which represented the church. "Cardinal Cooke did not go to the Lincoln Building. The meetings did not start at 9 A.M. promptly. You made an appointment. You went to his residence. He didn't wear robes, but he had on his formal garb." The sessions were steeped in cordiality. Helmsley was formal to a tee. Every sentence was punctuated by or otherwise adorned with "your eminence."

Moreover, Cardinal Cooke was no pushover. He was head of the largest and richest Catholic congregation in the country. He knew what his site on Madison Avenue was worth. And, of course, he stood for a higher purpose than mere profit, though it was never expressed in so many words. Cooke did his homework on the debating points. "The cardinal had a price and he wasn't coming off that price," said McGrath. "He wasn't going to give away the store."

On the other hand, the cardinal also knew, as did Helmsley, that the property had not moved. He knew that under the Wagner administration the façades of the Villard Houses had been officially designated as a historic landmark, meaning the housefronts—as far back as 100 feet from the street—could not be demolished. Whatever was done legally had to fit snugly behind those brownstone walls.

The cardinal also had the church's canons to consider. Helmsley would serve liquor, of course, and that was fine with the cardinal; Catholics are no teetotalers. But the cardinal did have concerns about other possible businesses or retailers any landlord might install. After all, it wouldn't do for someone to be selling certain books or professional services on church land, right across from St. Patrick's. Those restrictions were the equivalent of covenants, and they tipped the balance of negotiating power toward Helmsley. As McGrath pointed out: "Landlords usually don't want to be restricted in any way."

For all the cardinal's grace, Helmsley was in his métier. It was as if he had practiced for fifty years for the moment he would sit at the cardinal's dining-room table and negotiate a multimillion-dollar deal in extraordinary style and class. There was no haggling. There was no open debate. They met three, possibly four times at the residence. It's also likely they bumped into one another at social affairs, where a word or two might have smoothed out some wrinkle. "Cardinal Cooke calls us the best team in Manhattan," Leona Helmsley said of her and Harry on the ballroom floor. "And we're not even Catholics."

Harry and the cardinal danced through the Palace deal the way professional gamblers might play a hand of seven-card stud. Terribly calm, without expressions, and the cards held ever so close.

No one who knows will say if the cardinal came off his price. Reynolds has died. So has Cardinal Cooke. The attorney McGrath said he is sworn to professional secrecy. But undoubtedly both sides went away feeling good. That was Helmsley's style, to be tough but fair at the same time, letting everyone involved gain something. That leaves a little momentum for the next deal, and who knew when Helmsley might want to go back to the church again. "Neither was trying to drain the last penny out of the other," McGrath said.

Indeed, there were no pennies in the agreed-upon price. The final figure for leasing the Madison Avenue frontage was a flat annual rent of $1 million. Helmsley will pay the church that sum until the year 2001, at which time the rent will shift to a percentage of the property's appraised value. The deal was signed and sealed July 1, 1974, with the payments to start in 1978 after three years of token one-dollar rents. Harry threw in some free parking in the hotel's underground garage for the cardinal and church staff.

Leona's direct involvement in the hotel wouldn't begin for several years. The cardinal and Harry had much left to do together, as they abandoned their sparring and joined forces to get the project underway.

Their pact was made contingent on Helmsley getting the necessary city approvals for his development—no permits, no lease. And at the cardinal's dining-room table they came up with a clever scheme to get those approvals.

Harry Helmsley was the developer. He would be putting together the investors, hiring the architects, directing the construction, invading and changing the neighborhood, and darkening Madison Avenue, which in those days was far more open and sunlit than it became after a cluster of towers followed his project. Harry Helmsley would be making every key decision. But Harry Helmsley would not seek the city permits to do all that. Nor would anyone else in his name. Not his aides, or his attorneys. In fact, no person at all would ask the city for permission to build on the site. The Catholic Church would ask for permission.

The cardinal and Harry settled on that ploy for one very good reason: the church would be far more persuasive. And they had some persuading to do. Indeed, only the church could get what Harry Helmsley had in mind.

The fifty-two story office-hotel tower Helmsley wanted to build on the 200-by-200-foot plot was far bigger than zoning law allowed. It also had none of the angled setbacks that had become a standard in city planning after the Equitable Building darkened the Wall Street area fifty years earlier. Helmsley was bent on having his engineers use every square inch of air over the million-dollar-a-year site that was technically feasible. Hundreds of windows in adjoining buildings would go dark. The streets would be cast in shadow. And Manhattan, by planning standards, would be just a little less livable.

But the cardinal, acting for the master of real estate magnates, had one fact of development life on his side. City zoning law was made to be broken. Indeed, much of the energy expended by planners is in deciding how much of the law to let developers break. In New York, the bestower of legal exemptions is a panel called the Board of Standards and Appeals, which decides when to favor private gain over the community interest.

Harry Helmsley could not have gone to the board with his hat in hand. One of the five tests the board puts to developers is financial hardship. There was no way Helmsley could persuade the board that he would suffer unduly if the tower was not built as big as he wanted. But the not-for-profit church could make that pitch. No permits, no lease, no million dollars a year for the church. Wasn't that the agreement the cardinal and Helmsley made? That their million-dollar-a-year deal would die if he was not allowed to break the zoning law? The board bought it.

No one who knew Harry Helmsley should have been surprised by the speciousness of that argument. It was a variation of the disingenuousness wielded by Helmsley time and time again over the years. He routinely tied himself up in his private deals, so that later in public he could claim to be bound by the very thing he designed for himself. There was nothing illegal about it. Other savvy developers use the same trick to get by an obstinate board or a misguided law. It was good hardball business. It was the *t* in the word "tough." And Harry's biggest admirers labeled him tough. It's just that for outsiders, from elected officials to interested citizens, the warm, friendly demeanor of a man nicknamed "Chuckles" put Helmsley above suspicion. He was too cute, too humble to make a good real estate ogre. And so he'd soon use the ploy again, personally, in building the Palace. But he'd first have to deal with the preservationists.

While the church went to bat with the city, Helmsley was struck from a blind side. He couldn't have guessed anyone would care for a few run-down brownstone houses. But someone did, and an uproar developed over their fate.

Jim Morgan, an urban planning professor living in midtown Manhattan, had just joined his neighborhood planning group in 1974 when Helmsley's first office-hotel scheme for the Palace site came up for review. The group, called a community board, is the grass roots of New York government. There are dozens of boards in the city, encompassing whole or parts of distinct neighborhoods. Each has up to fifty volunteer members, appointed by the chief elected official of each of the five city boroughs. They meet. They discuss. They advise elected officials and city planners. But their opinions, however cogent, aren't binding. Collectively, their reputation has grown to be anti-development, though many board leaders prefer to cast even their most biting commentary as constructive criticism. At any rate, they tend to be run roughshod over by more powerful forces.

Morgan's board promptly voted to recommend that the city reject Helmsley's plan as being entirely incompatible with the Villard Houses and Madison Avenue. The board's involvement might have ended there. Morgan and others had no idea what really was inside the Villard, which the church had kept closed to the public for decades. Then, in early 1975, another board member, a citizen activist and writer, Darcy Lewis, got somebody to let her into the Villard and she was astonished at what she discovered. The Gold Room was a mess. There were pigeon skeletons on the floor. But the gilt and the gilded were basically intact, needing only restoration.

"I was transferred to a time of gentleness and beauty and grace that I thought didn't exist anymore in the city," Darcy Lewis recalled. "And when I found out it was going to be demolished, that the Helmsleys were going to build right over it, that's when I vowed to fight them and beat them. It was cool out, the sunlight was fading, and as I walked down Madison Avenue, I asked myself, 'How dare they do that?' And, I guess because I'm a born and bred New Yorker, I got mad."

Morgan got a look at the preliminary plans Helmsley had done for the project, which still called for a tower with offices through the twenty-second floor. The plans clearly called for gutting the Gold

Room and the rest of the Villard interiors behind the protected 100-foot line. The problem with the Gold Room, Morgan recalled Helmsley's people as saying, was that it interfered with an area on a level below where Helmsley wanted to put the office space behind the hotel desk. The ceiling heights, it seemed, would be too low if the Gold Room stayed.

Lewis and Morgan were galvanized by what they saw and a community task force was organized, with Morgan as its chair. A year passed. Then another. There were dozens of public meetings, ranging in size from a few people to hundreds. Lewis, especially, proved the firebrand. "She was a walking bad cop/good cop routine," Morgan recalled. "She was a small woman with a big voice. And she taught me how to approach the city boards. I used to be nervous until she explained that when she stood up to speak she envisioned the board members as little tiny insects sitting up on their chairs."

The New York Landmarks Conservancy, a private advocacy group, also got into the act, though Lewis, among others, feels the group did far more compromising than was called for. Lewis wanted all of the Villard Houses turned over to a public entity such as a museum. The Conservancy only challenged Helmsley to preserve the Gold Room. Its members were mainstream, and included Kent Barwick, a director of the blue-blood Municipal Art Society of New York; Brendan Gill, critic for *The New Yorker;* Ada Louise Huxtable, a member of *The New York Times*'s editorial board; and former mayor Bob Wagner, who had become Harry's friend and ended up staying in the Palace for half a year when his Manhattan town house burned down.

Finally, there was a second Palace deal. Helmsley agreed to preserve the Gold Room. He agreed to get a good insurance policy that would pay for full restoration if one of his cranes should happen to drop a big ball and destroy the Gold Room. (The insurance was demanded because such an event had destroyed another New York landmark deemed to be saved.) He also agreed to devise and pay for a plan to restore other Villard rooms, and he promised to let the public in to see them. There could even be group tours six times or so a year. In return, Helmsley got their support for his tower.

Some of his former opponents don't fault him for being slow to see the economic value in preserving the Villard Houses. "It was absolutely natural for him as a developer to want to knock down some buildings," said Fred Papert, then president of the Municipal Art Society. "They weren't landmarked behind that one hundred feet. And I think it was fair for him to assume that since they weren't landmarked they could be knocked down. To just build from new was the easy way. It's a lot easier to just clear the site, move all the trucks in and out and not worry about preserving things."

McGrath, however, has added a footnote to the Palace history. When asked about the memories and written record that showed a Gold Room demolished, the attorney said the "plans" were merely inexpensive line drawings that Helmsley had had done far in advance of making up his mind on the matter. McGrath chooses his words like an attorney. "I can say this, that never in any of my discussions with Mr. Helmsley, did he have any statement as to destroying that Gold Room," McGrath said.

But then he added this curious remark: "He never had any intention of ripping it down. That was the war cry of his critics. What he did when all that came up was, he said, 'O.K., let them yell and scream about it.'"

Did Helmsley float the line drawings out in public to divert his critics, so he could then corral them by agreeing to preserve something he intended to save all along? McGrath wouldn't say. His critics think that unlikely. "It just couldn't have been," said Lewis. But the same sort of thought came up during the Tudor City park fight. Stein's former aide, McLaughlin, had just a suspicion—nothing provable by any means—that Helmsley never really wanted to build on the Tudor City parks. Or at the least, that he changed his mind about wanting the parks when he realized the alternative city-owned site had that nice full river view his attorney Lindenbaum spoke of. Some involved in that fight even thought the Memorial Day bulldozers were a mere ploy to stir up public anger and thus push the city to make the swap. Those line drawings showing a demolished Gold Room would have been Harry's bulldozer in the Villard fight.

Later events would force Helmsley to testify before a panel of judicial arbiters, and his account of his intentions for the Gold Room is ambiguous. However, he made it clear that not until 1978—three years after he sought his permits—did he decide to restore the Gold Room and the rest of the southern wing of the Villard Houses to the shape they're in today. It's also clear that Harry Helmsley had no idea what the project would cost him, in dollars and in reputation.

If Helmsley's critics were duped into funneling their fury into the Gold Room, it was because Helmsley wanted his zoning permit to slip by without a flutter of public concern. And it did. And it was beautiful. The permit obtained by the church gave Helmsley a huge exemption. The law said Helmsley's tower could total 729,500 square feet. The Board of Standards and Appeals gave him 890,000 square feet, more than one-fifth the extra height and bulk that planners had deemed appropriate for that Manhattan block. Measured in hotel rooms, it gave Harry Helmsley an additional 205 rooms to rent out every night (given the Palace's final configuration with 1,143 rooms). At the $140 minimum rates in the opening months, and an anticipated occupancy rate in the 75 percent range, the permit meant the following extra annual revenues to Helmsley: $7,856,625. And that's not counting room-service charges, phone-call surcharges, parking, dinner in the Trianon Room, and extra sales of the $15-a-deck playing cards bearing Harry's and Leona's images as the Kings and Queens.

McGrath, for the Catholic Church, had one final card up his legal sleeve to consecrate the deal the cardinal cut. Helmsley needed a liquor license to sell the $9 drinks the Palace would offer. And there was a problem. Within the Palace courtyard, to the right as one walks through the iron gate, is a main door leading directly to one of the cocktail areas that Helmsley built into the Villard Houses. From that door, across Madison Avenue, to the nearest doorway into St. Patrick's is something less than 200 feet.

Enter a New York State law that prohibits barkeeps from setting up shop within 200 feet of schools, churches, or other houses of worship. McGrath, for the church, had hired a liquor-law specialist to get Helmsley his license. "We were getting nowhere fast," McGrath recalled, until he took a close look at a historical book the cardinal had given him. It showed that the Madison Avenue entrance to the cathedral was meant to be private, built for only the priests to use, and thus did not technically qualify as an entry into the cathedral. Or so Mc-Grath argued. A sign was even hung near the church door indicating its exclusivity.

The church got Helmsley his liquor license. But Helmsley does not test the legal bridge McGrath built to get him there. The courtyard door into the Palace at issue is kept shut, and a guard stands there more or less permanently to keep people from using it as an entrance.

However cunning, the Palace bulk and the liquor license were mere court-jester tricks compared with the move Helmsley pulled off next. It came time for him to go to the city and talk taxes, and Helmsley squeezed hard to get himself the biggest break he could.

Osborne Elliott, the Harvard-educated former editor of *Newsweek* magazine, took the post of deputy to Mayor Abe Beame in 1976 to help New York redevelop its ailing economy. Those were the days of near bankruptcy and a stubborn federal laissez-faire toward the Big Apple's finances—"Ford to City: Drop Dead," became the *New York Daily News*'s most famous headline ever.

"There was no building going on at that time," said Elliott. "I remember going to Houston. We were taking Abe Beame down to make love to the oil companies because they were drilling off the coast of New York, and their rigs were the only cranes in the sky at the time."

Elliott took charge of a new city panel called the Industrial and Commercial Incentive Board, whose mandate was as its title said: incite business to do business in New York. The board compiled a number of ways to assist, but the big enticement, especially for real estate developers, was a colossal tax break. Typically, developers were allowed to forgo much of their property tax for a period of ten years. Sometimes, then, the tax would be repaid. More commonly, the city would just let the debt wash away.

Beame, and subsequently Ed Koch, have defended the giveaway on simple grounds: the ten years act as an incubation period, without which development wouldn't likely hatch at all. Besides, they have argued, eventually the developers start paying truckloads of taxes that more than make up for the loss. Theirs, however, is an unprovable argument. It assumes developers would not have proceeded to build without the tax breaks. Said Elliott in conceding the point: "I will never know how many, if any, of those projects that got tax abatements would have gone ahead without them."

As the city moved into the late 1970s and one of its greatest real estate booms ever, the public grew increasingly suspicious that Koch had simply given the city away. But even in 1976, there were skeptics who didn't assume all developers were thwarted by the city's economic problems. Harry Helmsley, for one, had learned long before that bad times can be the best times to sink lots of cash into solid buildings. He also had learned how to play the tax-break game better than most, so well that no one questioned him on that point. "The city was pushing to get building done," Helmsley said later.

In September 1977 Helmsley went to Elliott's board, represented by Lindenbaum, the attorney who also was helping him fight to build on the Tudor City parks. By now, Helmsley had altered his plans to eliminate the office space, since he felt a glut would soon develop and tenants might be hard to find. He would make a hotel of all fifty-two floors of the tower. Lindenbaum paraded a few witnesses to build up some points.

The architect, Richard Roth, Jr., showed some pictures. Then a pair of hotel industry experts said that city had lost lots of hotel rooms since 1946 and that the market showed "a need for construction of this hotel." Before anyone could ask, "Why, then, does Mr. Helmsley need help from the taxpayers if the market is so ripe?" they moved on to all the jobs and sales taxes the Palace would generate. For example, they said their studies showed the Palace would be able to claim credit for $22 million a year in "outside" spending—such as a guest who stops in a Madison Avenue boutique. (Added up, those are the little nuggets that allow mayors and all sorts of elected officials to regularly claim that such-and-such boondoggle development will boost the local economy with untold trillions of dollars in "outside" spending.)

Then Lindenbaum stepped into the murkier waters of occupancy rates. Although the city makes annual guesstimates, hoteliers refuse to make their exact figures public, so everyone hems and haws and speaks in generalities. Developers use high guesses when they're arguing the city needs another hotel because the existing rooms are full. They low-ball it when they're trying to get the city to give them a bigger tax break because the competition for guests is so fierce. Helmsley's team had to fly over the facts that 1976 and 1977 were stellar years for hoteliers.

But then came the one-two punch, and Harry Helmsley got up himself to throw them.

"I don't want to use the word 'redlining,'" he began, the way a presidential candidate might launch a debate by saying, "I don't want to call my opponent a communist . . ."

Helmsley continued: ". . . but New York City is very, very diffi-cult to get a large mortgage commitment, because of its problems, so that I think that we went to every large institution who would be capable of lending what we were looking for in lines of $55, $60 million. It really was only through my personal efforts that Metropoli-tan Life was willing to take the lead on giving a $50 million mortgage.

"Then I had to go find another institution who would take the other half, which I did. I am in the middle now of trying to work out a mortgage commitment for the hotel. Part of that mortgage commit-ment is that if I don't get a tax abatement they will not meet the loan. They will not feel secure. It is in the mortgage commitment. I have tried to get it out. They will not take it out. That is the only way I can proceed with the hotel and these are the only two institutions that I have found and I think I can do as well as anyone."

Then Helmsley took his last shot. Fine, the board said, bring Met Life to us and we'll ask them about this redlining. Nothing doing, Helmsley replied. There would be no statement from Met Life on the record that it required Helmsley to get a tax abatement. "We have no control over them," Lindenbaum said. "They do not want to be in a position of publicly inducing or requesting or testifying in a manner which would cause the city of New York to grant tax abatement, so they have said, 'If it is granted, we will make the loan, and if it is not, we will not, but we won't appear and testify.'"

Not only was Harry Helmsley, the man who could get a $78 million loan just on his signature, saying he was being redlined by all his banking friends except Met Life and a smaller institution in Massachusetts. He was saying that they refused to deal with him at all unless he got himself a tax break from the city. Again, he was claiming to be hamstrung, bound by his private, secret deal. And he ended his presentation with almost a whimper. "It is a gamble," he said of the Palace, for which he had just won nearly $8 million extra in annual revenue. "I have gone through seventy-five hearings and I have almost had it, but I am so deeply involved I cannot stop."

Helmsley was met with some healthy skepticism. At least one board member questioned him on the stubborn absence of the bankers. After all, she pointed out, this was a substantial deal for them. But Helmsley got his tax break, as did Donald Trump and every other real estate entrepreneur-turned-hotelier in the great hotel rush of the late 1970s.

No one can fault the city for what happened after Helmsley left the board with this courtesy from Elliott: "Mr. Helmsley, good luck to you." All of his numbers, all of his arguments, all of his rationale for getting taxpayers in New York to subsidize his Palace were destroyed by one of the most amazing booms in hoteling the city has seen. Occupancies rose from the 1975 average of 67 percent to 83 percent in 1979. And then, no surprise, room rates soared, more than doubling in just one year, from $31 in 1978 to $68 in 1979. Hotel after hotel went up. And Helmsley and other gleeful hoteliers were slipping almost nightly into their rooms to mark up the required price signs on the doors.

Helmsley had told the board he hoped to get $65 a night for singles, $200 for one-bedroom suites, $75,000 a year for one of the sixteen leased two-bedroom apartments. The Palace single opened at $140 and has been rising ever since. And Helmsley told the board he hoped to get a 60 percent occupancy. He's been 10 points and more above that.

"It's hard to remember what people thought about New York just a few years ago," Edgar Madsen, a real estate analyst, said in 1980. "The magic mark in the hotel business is 75 percent occupancy, and when it rises higher than that, everybody's eyes light up and there's a flurry of refurbishing and building."

But while the boom couldn't have been predicted, at least one former city official now sees a flaw in the program he helped to create. "You must go back to a time, to 1974, 1975, when not two bricks were going up. Literally, nothing was going on," said Henry Gavan, now a private-practice attorney who advised Osborne Elliott's panel after helping to write the legislation creating the tax-break program. "But realistically, it was an impossible job to determine whose need was legitimate and whose was not. Oz Elliott is a brilliant guy. But what you are trying to do is look into people's minds and figure out what they are doing."

Besides occupancy rates, the panel had to guess what room rates would be. "Figures don't lie but liars figure. I have heard so many conflicting stories concerning hotel-room charges that my head spins," Gavan wrote in May 1977 in an internal memo evaluating yet another Helmsley hotel on Forty-second Street in midtown Manhattan that followed close on the heels of the Palace.

No, the city can't be faulted for not seeing the boom. Even Helmsley didn't "see" it, really. But he smelled it. He felt it. He had to. This is the man who had seen cycles come and go for fifty years. He was the master of real estate magnates, who had always—with but one exception—been just ahead of the wave. He may have complained to the board about taking a gamble, but Harry Helmsley did not gamble.

Helmsley's ten-year tax break: $3.67 million, which otherwise would have gone to city safety and health programs.

Said Gavan matter-of-factly of the board's work, not judging it either way: "We subsidized millionaires."

Not in Helmsley's case. In his case the city subsidized a soon-to-be billionaire. It wasn't long after he approached the tax board that Harry Helmsley topped a billion-dollar net worth, managing property worth five times that much.

Adding insult to injury, the tax board later was snubbed. In 1978, after the Palace tax deal was done, the Industrial and Commercial Incentive Board's staff director wrote Lindenbaum a pointed letter, bristling at the fact that the board was left out of the subsequent celebrations and press packets. "As you know, this office has done an enormous amount of work on the Palace project," the director, Roman Ferber, wrote. "As a matter of fact, Mr. Harry Helmsley publicly stated at the ICIB meeting that were it not for the City's tax incentive program, this venture would not have been undertaken."

Harry Scanlan, a Helmsley aide, wrote Ferber back and politely told him Helmsley could not control press accounts of the Palace, "and, therefore, I am sure you will not infer that if your fine work is not always mentioned, that it is not appreciated."

With the lease, the bulk permit, the liquor license, and the tax break all sewed up, Helmsley next turned to developing the Villard Houses into the Helmsley Palace Hotel. The biggest chore was rounding up other investors to help foot the bill. Another was finding guests. He hired Wolfgang Haenisch, a renowned manager of ultra-luxury hotels in Europe, to bring the Palace on line. His assistant, Mal Seymourian, traveled the country setting up cocktail receptions where he would sell the idea of staying at the Palace to likely clients.

And as the steel went up, and the walls were emplaced, and the penthouses topped it all out, there was the devil for each to pay.

For the cardinal the price was a bit of the heavens. Every night a Palace employee throws moonlight on St. Patrick's Cathedral by beaming lasers down from the hotel. Harry is pleased by the resulting glow. He's mentioned it with apparent pride. Good as the real thing, he concluded. But it isn't. It's artificial, and it looks artificial. And it was the predictable consequence of the church's getting the city to let Helmsley block out so much of the Manhattan skyline. For its million dollars a year, the church gave up a piece of the real moon, not to mention the rising sun, that used to shine on the cardinal's cathedral.

The cardinal's price may have been small. He may never have noticed, or cared. Not so with the bargain Harry was to consummate with the devil in short order after the hotel operations got underway. The price he would pay was the thing he valued perhaps most in his life: his reputation as an honest man.

But first, Leona would move into the Palace. Already, she was getting excited, ordering up new gowns from Julia, her seamstress. "I can't wear these slacks anymore when we move to the Palace," she told Eboli. "I'm going to have to walk through the lobby and meet everybody."

## CHAPTER 11

# FIREFIGHTS ON THE FIFTH FLOOR

NOW AND AGAIN, THERE'S AN EXTRAORDINARY GATHERING OF POWER brokers in Manhattan. It's a traveling road show of sorts. And on September 12, 1980, a warm Friday evening, it came to the brand-new Helmsley Palace Hotel.

A queue stretched through the marble courtyard from Madison Avenue. It passed under the Romanesque arches, through the glass doors with their double reflections, up the glittering gold staircase to where Leona and Harry stood in greeting under a fourteen-foot-wide chandelier. More than two hundred of New York's illustrious were on hand—the governor, the cardinal, the mayor and three of his predecessors, a gaggle of movie stars, assorted chief executive officers, and other people in enterprises important to the Helmsleys.

Attendance was select. A former state official recalled standing in the reception line behind a couple dressed in something less than black tie and gown. They'd obviously been living on the street. They reached the Helmsleys, but before they could shake hands the hotel guards swooped down and hauled the crashers to the front gate. No charity at this ball.

Inside, a society-page reporter wandered about, catching bits of the conversation. The guests seemed duly impressed with the Palace. "*I* only go to hotels that are forty dollars a night," Ed Koch said, his head swiveling around in the Gold Room.

"*I* can't afford to stay here," insisted Hugh Carey, then governor of New York.

Former mayor John Lindsay chatted with Bob Tisch, then head of the Loews Corporation and a former Leona Roberts apartment client. Lindsay recalled visiting the Villard Houses when they were still private homes. "My brother and I used to slide up and down the banisters," he told Tisch.

Harry Helmsley confided to friend Douglas Fairbanks, Jr., that he had "cannibalized" his other hotels to staff the Palace. But at least four footmen that night were professional actors. They were earning some money since they were out on strike. "If you were in [office], we'd be working," Skip Lawrence, who played Danny the bartender in *All My Children,* told one of the former solons.

Harry stood straight and tall in his tux. He grinned and squinted behind his glasses at the same time. Leona, who had just turned sixty, looked something younger, though not quite the low fifties she insisted on to friends and reporters alike. She wore a silver-lace gown. It was designed and sewn by her private dressmaker, the Cuban-born Julia. "She's fabulous," Leona had remarked the previous day. "She has the taste of a Paris designer. I want her to be recognized. I'd never wear anybody else's clothes. You wouldn't believe the problems I've had with . . . a big name, I won't mention who . . . his clothes pucker, they stretch, they don't fit. But Julia! Her gowns move! They're feminine." The "big name" did not make the guest list.

There were others who did not attend. One was Sarah Tomerlin Lee, who designed and decorated the Palace interiors. Harry was still trying to calm Leona, whose feud with Lee was detailed in a long feature story that morning in the *Daily News.* "Don't talk to reporters, darling, you'll only get in deeper," Harry said.

"I can't help it," Leona replied with no hint of sarcasm. "I like people."

For inexplicable reasons, just before the party Leona had turned on Sarah Tomerlin Lee, disinviting her from the formal opening of what, in large part, was Lee's creation. The decorator was shocked, then hurt, and finally puzzled by Leona's action. Even eight years later she couldn't sort it out.

Lee's husband, Tom, was an interior decorator of international renown. Before World War II, he directed the Bonwit Teller displays. Then he designed Broadway shows. He did floats for the city's parades. He crafted the interiors of luxury hotels. Harry and Eve Helmsley hired Tom Lee to design the Park Lane interior, which won rave reviews for its stately, sophisticated decor.

In 1971, Tom Lee died in an automobile crash and his wife, Sarah, took over the business. A Tennessean who retained all her Southern charm, Sarah Lee had come to New York thirty-three years earlier. She was working as a copywriter at Bonwit when she met Tom. She wrote a series of Prince Matchabelli perfume ads and invented the line "Wear a smile and a Jantzen." She edited for *Vogue* and *Harper's Bazaar,* becoming editor-in-chief of *House Beautiful.* Lee had never decorated, but when Tom died she threw herself into the project he left undone, a forty-story hotel in Toronto, and she continued the business. (Thirty-seven hotels later, Sarah Tomerlin Lee was called on by Donald Trump in 1988 to help redesign the Plaza Hotel.)

Harry Helmsley was fond of Tom Lee, in part because he was very good at what he did and because he was his own person. "Tom got a telegram once from Harry," Sarah Lee recalled. "He was doing the Four Seasons in London, and Harry sent a telegram saying, 'Be back immediately or you're fired.' Tom was a funny guy. He wired back, 'Sorry!' with an exclamation mark. He wasn't worried a bit."

Not only did Harry not fire Tom, he called Sarah in 1978 when the Palace interior was ready to be designed. Sarah Lee was reluctant at first because she had been a member of the New York Landmarks

Conservancy, which had interacted with Harry over the Gold Room. "I was a little shy about taking on the project at the Villard. We had a chat about that. And Harry said when I saw him, 'I admired your husband more than any man in the business.' That warmed me."

Harry even got into the architectural restoration and decorating action, sometimes in earnest and sometimes in jest. He balked, for example, at an original scheme to have nine steps leading into a bar. The entry to any bar should be level, he stated, with personal-injury lawsuits on his mind. A platform arrangement was devised to replace the steps. He also insisted that the Palace cocktail lounges be shuttered so passersby wouldn't see people drinking. That may have been his own conservatism. Harry was never a big drinker. A scotch now and then he would have, never mixing it with work. But it's more likely that the shutters were at the cardinal's insistence. Harry was not much of a prude. One day he saw a nude that Sarah Lee had chosen for one Victorian-styled room. Harry picked up the painting, clutched it to his chest, and declared, "I'm going to buy this for myself."

In addition to enjoying Harry's enthusiasm for her work, Lee said she had no financial pressures whatsoever. "I have no idea what the overall cost was," she said. "We didn't see the purchase orders. [Harry] never questioned our budget. We bought seven paintings for the oval ballrooms for $37,000, just like that." Indeed, Lee at times was too fiscally conservative. She suggested making the brass-and-glass marquees over the hotel entrances just a single voluminous tier. But when Harry asked how much that would cost, and she replied $100,000, he said, "I'll take two." A double tier it was.

Lee also had free rein to scout area shops for things that had walked out of the Villard Houses in the transitional months between the church's and Harry's occupation. "A lot had been stolen in the shift," Lee said. "We found sidelights, five feet tall, Villard 1903 originals, in fine antique stores and we bought them."

But Harry's involvement in Sarah Lee's work was secondary to Leona's. And from the start, it was clear that Lee and Leona Helmsley had some fundamental differences in taste and in attitude toward old things.

"I met Leona on the second meeting we had on the Palace," Lee said. "We walked through it together and she said, 'Tell me what we can throw out.' Now, 1905 wasn't an especially nice period. In fact, it was ugly. But I said the Villard Houses were a landmark and I didn't think we could just throw things out."

"She was not difficult. She didn't even change a chair," Lee said of Leona. "We hadn't battled at all." But at some point friction began to build.

First there was the rug. Lee had ordered a custom-made carpet for the lobby whose design and colors were approved by Leona. The rug came. Leona changed her mind. The rug went. "But that turned out all right," Lee said. "We sold it to the Sheraton in Hartford, Connecticut, for $27,000. They call it the Palace Rug."

Then came the guest rooms themselves. Leona felt Lee's colors were too bright, so she held an audition—with Harry as judge. Lee decorated three bedrooms. So did Leona, spending lavishly. And Harry, to no one's surprise, picked his wife's beige, mint green, and apricot pastels. "I went a little kinky with the beds," Leona later said. "But in a hotel, it's fun to be kinky. If you want to describe them, I'd say they're sculpted wood, rococo gold and silver, upholstered."

And then there was the Palace library. Lee describes it as their most distinct difference of opinion. "I crossed up with her on the books," Lee said. "I wanted real books in the library, which is sort of a super-duper meeting room. [Leona] said, 'I don't want real books because no one would dust.' And she was insistent the hotel be kept immaculate." Leona got her way, and today the hundreds of "books" lining the library shelves with their classic titles are indeed clean, as well as completely and obviously fake.

Leona also informed Lee that she was disturbed by her other hotel projects, which kept her from being at beck and call. It had a familiar ring. Other professionals retained by Leona were expected to suppress all urges to do any work for others. Leona demanded exclusiveness as well as perfection. All told, the rug, the guest rooms, and the fake books added up in Leona's mind to a huge default on Lee's part. She simply disinvited Lee from the opening party as, Lee said, "I was screwing in the last light bulb." The *Daily News* article before the opening party exposed the decorator's hurt.

Considering the circumstances, Sarah Lee was relatively civil in print. "She should be called 'Leona the Magnificent.' She really wants total opulence . . . and I think she's gonna have it. She's been at all the meetings, and has had to approve everything. In the dining room, she insisted that the walls be covered in Florentine silk. I didn't think of that. And that the woodwork be rubbed in silver."

"Listen," Leona was quoted in reply. "I'm not a decorator at all. So I do the things I want to see when I go to a hotel. I care. It's our hotel. It's not just the Palace. It's the Helmsley Palace. And *we* have to live with it. . . . Look, let's just say Sarah Lee and I don't have any love for each other."

Said Lee later: "I didn't like her or dislike her." But the thing that likely hurt most of all, the thing that might have started Lee wondering about the Helmsleys, as others began to wonder, was the fact that Harry never called to apologize, or to explain, or to even yell at her a little more. No call. No letter. Nothing. It was as if her husband, Tom, had never existed and Harry had never asked for her help three years before.

Sarah Tomerlin Lee was not the first of Harry Helmsley's staff or contractors with whom Leona did battle. Indeed, if Harry's entry into hotels was reluctant, Leona made a swift dive and she came up for air with a furious breaststroke.

It was not long after they were married that Leona began itching to go back to work. After all, she was every bit the business machine Harry was, and when their European honeymoon tour ended, she wasn't about to stay home alone. Harry, for all his second wind, certainly was not forsaking his long hours behind the desk. Leona offered a plausible explanation for her prompt reentry into the working world. "I love my husband," she once said. "I love to be with him. So I work. That's why I do it." But those close to her felt that she burned with another need: to prove to the world she was a good catch for Harry on financial grounds. If Manhattan society presumed she was merely after his money, she would show them she could make *him* money.

In 1972, the Palace Hotel was not yet even a gleam in their eyes. But the existing Helmsley hotels were a natural place for her to start— for two reasons. One, her career as an apartment seller was all but sold out by the Sutton Place affair. Second, even Leona, as did Brener, would have found it tough going in the heart of the Helmsley-Spear empire dominated by Harry's closest aides, Schneider and Schwartz. They and Leona developed a truce of sorts over the years, maintaining a discreet distance that benefited them all.

Harry seemed amenable. Within the first year of their marriage, he gave her stock in his hotel partnerships and named her a senior vice president of his subsidiary Helmsley Hotels. Later, he listened to her when she suggested calling the chain outside New York the Harley Hotels—not after a motorcycle, but from a contraction of their first names. Both she and Harry later came to regret the name Harley, but changed only one marquee in the chain, renaming their Forty-second Street hotel the New York Helmsley. It took a huge advertising budget to assure the public that management hadn't changed too. She set up a small office in the St. Moritz. And it wasn't long before she battled one of Harry's aides.

That first encounter was with John Mados, and bitter it was. Mados, along with his wife, Suzanne, dated their relationship with Harry Helmsley back to 1966, when they began helping to manage his Manhattan hostelries—the St. Moritz, the Carlton House, where Eve Helmsley lived for a while, and later the Park Lane. The Madoses described theirs as "a close, personal and confidential relationship." For nine years, until 1975, they also had a tight business pact. Harry treated the Madoses the way he did his top brokers. He gave them a piece of the action, in part to minimize their salaries, in part to give them a vested interest in keeping the profits up. John and Suzanne went partners with Harry, splitting the shares fifty-fifty, on two smaller hotels behind the St. Moritz and Park Lane on Fifty-eighth Street, the Wyndham and the Windsor.

The Madoses continued to help manage the bigger hotels, as well as the Wyndham, for which the partnership gave them an apartment in the Windsor and a small annual stipend of $7,500. Their main income flowed from the hotels' profits. Then in 1973, and again in 1975, Harry began transferring some of his stock to Leona's name, and she took a more active interest in the Windsor and Wyndham, as she did with Harry's other Manhattan hotels. In May 1975, the Madoses were fired from the Helmsley hotels and their partnerships with Leona and Harry fell into disarray.

According to the federal lawsuit filed by the Madoses against both Leona and Harry Helmsley, the problem stemmed solely from Leona. They accused her of waging, "with increasing intensity, a campaign to discredit and demean [them] and to diminish and ultimately eliminate the close, personal and confidential relationship" they had with Harry. They accused her of "forcing" their termination and with "obstructing" their partnerships. They also claimed to have gotten along fine with Eve. In fact, they used the same law firm she did to settle her divorce from Harry.

The Helmsleys took a different view in their countersuit to dissolve the partnerships. They conceded that a "bitter dispute and controversy" had arisen between them and the Madoses. But they accused the Madoses of "blatant and wasteful mismanagement." Among other things, they said the Madoses insisted on operating a restaurant at the Hotel Windsor that in three years lost $73,578, when the Helmsleys thought it better to lease the eatery to a third party. The Helmsley action, which had to show cause for wanting to dissolve the partnerships, also charged that the Madoses had purchased "uneconomical" furniture and that they improperly maintained the hotel. Moreover, because the Madoses lived in the Windsor rent-free, they derived a benefit from the partnership the Helmsleys did not, the action charged. "Many personal items are charged by the Madoses to the hotel, such as food, tips and personal services. No such corresponding benefits are received by the Helmsleys."

People who knew both the Helmsleys and the Madoses at the time could only marvel at the bitterness and wonder how it grew. John Mados is deemed to have been a penny-pinching, hard manager—a trait the Helmsleys should have welcomed—by Herbert Peters and other former Park Lane staff. After some legal wrangling, the matter was resolved by splitting the two hotels. The Helmsleys took the Windsor. The Madoses took the Wyndham, which they continue to own and run, stepping out the front door to stare directly across West Fifty-eighth Street at the curved-back entryway into the Park Lane. A midblock pedestrian walkway runs from Fifty-eighth Street to Fifty-ninth, or Central Park South, alongside the Park Lane. It's a convenient access to the park and the boulevard for Wyndham customers. Not long after the Madoses took the Wyndham, Leona had the passageway locked shut, but she lost her little jab at the Madoses when the hotel union raised hell because the employees could no longer use the walkway to get to the subway on Fifty-eighth.

Several years after that bout, Leona saw the man who brought Harry into the hotel business leave his side.

Company rumor and industry assumption have it that Leona gave Steve Brener a big shove. Not so, said Brener. "Did Leona push me out? No," he said. "Did Leona ever say anything to me directly? No. But would I *not* be a good employee of Leona Helmsley? That became very clear toward the end." Still, he added, "she didn't beat me over the head."

Rather, Brener, then fifty-five, said he got the itch to try his own entrepreneurial hand. "Harry Helmsley offered me a terrific amount of security, but I think I became concerned that I never had an opportunity to earn a living on my own. I saw myself becoming more and more of a broker in my own office. I remember reading *Death of a Salesman,* and that's really what pushed me out." Brener did well. His firm now is nationally recognized by the hospitality industry for its expertise in brokering and managing hotels.

In one other way it was easy to see how Leona Helmsley and Brener could clash on a philosophical level. In 1969 he penned an article for *Real Estate Weekly* urging hotel and motel owners to stop "spoiling" their guests. "All the extras, such as stereo, color TV, bathroom scales, room service, remaining open 24 hours a day, seven days a week, and so forth, are great sales features. They have become things that people staying at hotels and motels—especially those at the hostelries getting higher rates—seem to want. However, isn't it possible hoteliers and moteliers are not analyzing the true cost of spoiling guests?" Brener then laid out a vigorous case against room service and for weekend closings when the business trade falls off.

It was a novel idea, much to Harry Helmsley's liking. In fact, years later Harry would urge newcomers to the hoteling business to "sell sleep," not elaborate and costly amenities. But service—exquisite, perfected service that spoils the guest—is what Leona Helmsley came to offer the world in rare style. When she was named president of Helmsley Hotels in June 1980, just before her birthday and the opening party for the Palace, Leona told a business reporter that she considered it her duty to ensure, firsthand, that service is provided. "I walk the hotel," she said. "I go to rooms, to public areas, to the kitchen, to the lobby. If the coffee isn't boiling right, you have to see that the coffee is boiling right."

She made a point of putting comment cards in every Helmsley hotel room. And when she got them back, she would respond to every one. A letter dated August 2, 1988, was typical, according to staff:

"Thank you for taking the time to share your thoughts with me regarding your stay at The Harley of Orlando. Please accept my apology for any inconvenience you incurred. The exposed wires and peeling wallpaper were caused by the installation of a smoke detector system throughout the hotel. The gift shop proprietor is a lessee of space in the hotel, and returned to Germany for 10 days because of a death in the family. The hours were curtailed while others filled in for her. However, there was a sign posted listing the alternate hours. As you may be aware, there are many other Helmsley/Harley Hotels situated throughout the country. In the event that we may be of service in providing accommodations to you in the future, we enclose a directory for your convenience. Please do not hesitate to contact us if we may be of service to you at any time. We value your patronage and look forward to having you as our guest at a Helmsley/Harley Hotel often in the future. Cordially, Leona M. Helmsley, President."

The Orlando hotel manager, Doug Stevens, also replied three weeks later, apologizing profusely and thanking the comment-maker. "It will help us to become your Favorite Hotel!" He copied "L. M. Helmsley" into his note.

A flattering 1984 profile of Leona in *New York* magazine, which Leona reprinted and places in every hotel room, states that she receives and personally dictates responses to 2,000 cards or letters a week. That would average out to a staggering 400 responses every weekday, or 50 per hour in an eight-hour day, or one every 70 seconds or so. Not so, her longtime executive secretary Maryann Eboli said. Not long after

Leona hired Eboli in 1979, the comment-card campaign was begun and they flooded into the office. Leona was at a loss on how to handle them. Eboli devised a system to group them by complaint and handle a good many with word-processing machinery borrowed from Harry's brokerage firm. Leona was briefed on but did not author the responses. An automatic signature machine was purchased to handle the volume. Her legal signature was altered to fend off any would-be, albeit amateurish, forger.

Leona, however, was not shy about occasionally telephoning a displeased guest. It was part of what she did best: marketing the hotels by selling them as perfect and herself as the enforcer of perfection. "There are times I pick up the telephone, I say, 'This is Mrs. Helmsley,' they don't believe it, and they are mine forever when I do that," she said once in a legal deposition.

Her influence grew. She concentrated on the Helmsley hotels, making periodic inspection tours to Cleveland, Orlando, Atlanta. She put her brother Alvin in charge of the Carlton House, where Eve lived for a time until, according to guests and hotel staff, she had to leave because of some discomfort caused by his presence. Leona had Harry hire her son, Jay, to run Deco Purchasing, the hotel-supply company Harry and Brener had set up in Orlando, Florida. She started to build her own staff. And then the Palace Hotel came along, and swept her full force into the business.

Leona developed several managerial traits that Harry scoffed at. She demanded, for example, strict formality where he preferred the informal. For years Harry instructed aides to have his employees call him Harry if they happened upon him, say, in the Lincoln Building elevator. Leona insisted on being called "Mrs. Helmsley" or "the President," and her hold over her staff was such that even in private conversation they would shorten it only to "Mrs. H." Aides learned to grow wary when on rare occasions she invited someone to be informal. Disaster usually loomed. Even Jay was no exception. "I was amazed by it," said Eboli. "In conversation outside of work he might refer to her as his mother or Mom. But in work situations it was always 'Mrs. Helmsley' or 'Mrs. H.' "

Leona and Harry also differed somewhat on wages. Harry in all of his sixty-odd years as a manager has been excruciatingly tight with salaries, causing many an employee to fear, if not resent, his negotiating powers. Harry would even discolor the year-end holidays by haggling over a $10 raise. The employees typically win the pittance, but the process ruins their mood and degrades them.

"Negotiating a bonus with Harry Helmsley is the very toughest thing imaginable," Seymour Rabinowitz said. "It was just like negotiating my annual salary. I considered myself to be an important cog in doing some very successful building conversions [from rentals to condominiums]. So I would always say to him, 'Harry, I cannot say to you what my value to you is, only you know that. And I know that you are going to be fair and I'm not going to have to argue. But just remember that I am a professional.' And he would come back and say, 'Sy, I recognize the job that you do and that you are a professional and one of the best. But I have to think of my salary scale and the whole organization. I can't treat you, as much as I'd like to, any better than anyone else, 'cause then I would have a revolution down below.' He'd always get me with that revolution."

Leona too would squeeze her personal staff, whether it be salaries or expenses. Limousines were a major point of contention, and Leona fought with everyone from Harry's longtime aides to her own sister Sandra about limo bills. She routinely had Eboli pore over expense accounts submitted by the pilots of the Helmsley plane when they had been on a trip. Pennies over their allotted meal money and Leona's radar sounded. But with some of her hotel staff she became almost free and loose with the salaries she paid. "Nobody ever has to ask me for a raise. I love to pay high wages—it means I've got top people on the staff," she told a hotel-industry magazine. Of course, the union keeps salaries for its workers in line. In 1988 pot scrubbers earned a minimum $353.54 for working a thirty-five-hour week, no less, often more. But even some of the non-union hotel professionals did quite better than industry averages, and Leona hasn't always begrudged them their earnings. Chef Andre René, for example, was working for the Pierre in 1981 when he was called to Leona's office to interview for a job at the soon-to-open Palace. René recalled the encounter as cordial, friendly, to the point. "I told them what I wanted, the salary, the suite, the space in the garage."

"I went back to the Pierre and I was barely back when a woman called," René said. "I didn't know who it was. She said, 'You got what you want.' And I said, 'Who is this?' And she said, 'This is Mrs. Helmsley and you got what you want.' " René got his parking, and his suite on the thirty-ninth floor, and his starting salary above $70,000 with escalators leading to $96,000 in four years. "I like to get a day's work for a day's pay," she said once, but she could have as easily flipped that around.

On the other hand, any generosity Leona had with wages ended with her top managers. They never quite earned what other hoteliers paid. Or, at the least, many came to feel, their salaries never met the demands of their jobs. To manage a Helmsley hotel was to sweat and toil and fret, and survive, maybe, three or four seasons. That most didn't last longer helps explain what union officials believe is the main trouble the hotel workers' union has with Helmsley hotels: their managers.

Vito Pitta, head of the Hotel-Motel Trades Council of the AFL-CIO in New York, was on the phone to a union leader at the Park Lane Hotel, where the Helmsleys have their penthouse.

"What?" Pitta growled. "Yeah? Well, then," he said, "get everybody down in the lobby."

Dispute was flaring into crisis. The Park Lane manager had ordered eight hotel staff to paint, plaster, and wallpaper some rooms. But he refused to give them additional pay for the extraneous tasks. The workers balked, citing their contract. "What contract?" the manager replied, and fired all eight on the spot.

Pitta put down the phone, exasperated. "This is not your typical grievance resolution," he said. "Ordinarily, we would sit down and talk this out."

So the white-haired Pitta, whose union formerly had ties with the Teamsters, pulled the next-best thing to an all-out strike: a hotel lobby meeting.

Lobby meetings are to hotel workers what the American Express card is to consumers: clout. They're also rather fun, except for management or guests in a rush to get in or out. All the staff—the bellhops, the barkeeps, the dozens of maids, and the chefs in their tall white hats —halt their work and gather in the lobby to hear and discuss what has happened. The union representative speaks, as do the shop stewards. The wronged employees bear witness. The lobby becomes a packed courtroom, with the hotelier presumed guilty until proven otherwise.

It's a testament to Pitta's strength that every major hostelry in New York City is unionized, but for one. The exception is a huge hotel near Times Square whose archconservative owner, Bill Marriott, has proven to be a match even for the Norma Raes of hoteling. It's also a testament to union-management relations that lobby meetings are invoked only occasionally. At the bigger Helmsley hotels, however, especially the Park Lane, they tend to erupt at least once a year.

The trouble does not flow directly from Leona Helmsley, said Pitta, who discreetly speaks approvingly of most New York hoteliers. "Every time I've met Mrs. Helmsley," Pitta offered, "she's been a gracious lady." Rather, he said, the union's inordinate fighting with Helmsley hotels stems from the high turnover rate in people who run their hotels. "Every year they get a new manager," said Pitta. "He doesn't know the contract. He hasn't worked with any union. And he decides he wants to show how tough he is."

Every new boss likes to settle into the job with a good union tussle. Some fuss for months before they accept the worker protections in New York City. But the manager on Pitta's mind that May day in 1988 decided with unusual speed that he'd made a bad move.

Fifteen minutes after Pitta hung up the phone, eight men in white painter outfits were in the Park Lane lobby shaking hands with the dark-suited manager and his assistants. A flock of guards dressed like presidential Secret Service men stood to the side, looking relieved. The lobby court was called off. The manager wouldn't say what changed his mind, but hotels hide few such secrets. Several union officials came to hear that Leona informed him—with a few indiscreet words—that this was not the time to pick such a public fight.

Pitta's cordialness notwithstanding, Leona's management has a lot to do with the attitude of her managers. Simply put, the Helmsley hotel managers have come to be known as one tough lot to an excess.

Besides wages and formality, Leona has differed from Harry in the very essence of her managerial style—in everything from the way she hires and fires to the way she walks through her offices.

When Harry comes out of his office in the Lincoln Building, he moves slowly through the center of a large, open, and noisy work area. Secretaries sit left and right. Along the sides are two rows of executives in their cubicles. A quiet frenzy is in the air. Yet Harry passes with nary a thought about disturbing those around him. He peers straight ahead, not even turning his head to intrude. And if he does pop into somebody's work area, it's to casually invite him to lunch.

Leona bolts from her office, and rarely passes by someone without interacting. Often the interaction is with good intentions. Indeed, the effusive charm with which she often moves around staff and social friends alike can't be overstated. Her business lunches are flush with her gushing mannerisms. More than one professional retained by Leona has had the lunch date Joseph Forstadt did.

"She's very gracious, makes you feel like a part of the family," said the attorney. "I remember she was concerned about what I was eating, that it wasn't good for me. I had ordered a mixed grill, sausage or salami or something with high cholesterol, foods she thought were clearly not in my interest. She was very maternal. Not in an old-fashioned Jewish mother way, but clearly she was concerned about my health. If I was going to be her lawyer I had to be in healthy condition.

"She was very warm," he continued. "She would take my hand, and be very gracious. I was going with her to some meeting, and she arranged to have the chauffeur take me back afterwards." Similarly, Stephen Kaufman, a criminal attorney Leona later hired, was typically seen with his hand held. Leona liked to touch, to pat, to caress. It wasn't sexual. It was matronly.

Her courtesy extended to Harry's friends and associates. Phil Blumenfeld, Harry's broker and partner in some deals, recalled one trip to Miami in the Helmsleys' private plane. "I asked Mr. Helmsley, 'Should I bring lunch with me? Is there going to be lunch?' And he said, 'Don't worry. Leona will take care of you.' When we were on the plane, she took out lunch and in a very motherly, Yiddish kind of way, said,

'Here, I have some great crabmeat-and-shrimp salad for you,' and I almost heard my mother saying, 'Here, Phil, ess,' meaning eat."

Her doting carried over into her social life, though intimate friends describe Leona as relaxed and fun to be around. "Time flies with them," said Robert Wagner, who, with his wife, periodically dines with the Helmsleys at their Connecticut house. "She sets a good table. You enjoy their company, just having a nice dinner, talking generally."

Leona could even charm reporters brought by Rubenstein to her office door for a profile. Her former advertising agent, Joyce Beber, recalled several journalists "coming in ready to kill, just ready to tear into her, and they would be absolutely bowled over. She could be into wringing ten people out all at once, and if a reporter came in, she would be like Dr. Jekyll and Mr. Hyde."

Wring people out? Dr. Jekyll? This same person who gushed with affection? Time and again, those who have spent time around Leona—from fifteen minutes to fifteen years—speak of Leona's dual personalities. And most, like Forstadt, came to believe that only one of her sides was real. "She is an extremely charming lady, when that suits her," he said.

There is good reason to discount some of the stories about Leona's tirades. She has fired a lot of people, legitimately and not. Many feelings are hurt. Moreover, Leona worked in a man's world, and a brash, arrogant man's world at that. "I suppose when she started it was sort of unusual for a woman to be running a hotel chain," Wagner suggested. "No one considered that a spot where a woman should be. And I suppose a lot of men, particularly in that business, don't like to be bossed by a woman."

Also, at least one of her former aides claims to have sold his reminiscences of the Helmsleys for $15,000. The aide, Jerry Kadish, represented by his attorney son, Scott, said his four-year stint as a Helmsley hotel director gave him "great insight" into both Harry and Leona Helmsley. Kadish said that Harry came to consider him an "adopted son." And that Harry confided to him his "most intimate thoughts." But executive aides who were close to the Helmsleys at the same time doubt Kadish's claims. "He was never close to Leona or

Harry. He may have wanted to be," said Maryann Eboli. Even if true, Kadish's words are inherently tainted by his price for talking.

Many who spoke freely about their experiences with the Helmsleys expressed guilt, because they knew the truth might hurt the very people they knew or worked for, and in many cases continue to know and work for. "Despite all we went through, I have a soft spot for her," said Beber, who became an intimate of Leona's as well as her ad agent. "And I know I'm betraying her."

If Leona ever attempted to hide her tirades, in most cases she failed. "If something is wrong," she told a hotel-industry magazine, "I tell them the first time the situation is not right and needs changing. The second time I ask an octave higher. The third time I ask the person if they want me to do it. And the fourth time they're fired." Notwithstanding that reasonable managerial self-description, Leona in fact tended to skip the first, second, and third steps and move right into the fourth—at octaves higher than people guessed she could muster. The accounts of her explosions are so many that nearly everyone who knows her has at least one to tell: hotel employees, hotel guests, high-ranking executives, contractors and vendors, the man who did her nails, the woman who took her notes. "You can't imagine what she sounds like," one former employee was quoted in describing Leona throwing a fit. "It's like an animal. She turns purple . . . and she growls." Her rages have astounding depth. Heated and hostile intimidations. Threats. Near blackmailing in at least one case. Split-second firings of longtime, trusted employees. "She would turn up the pressure until you couldn't take it anymore, and if you did take it, then she was more direct, but only then," said Eboli, who was both recipient and observer of countless beheadings. In some cases the acts seemed entirely inexplicable.

Leona with the trucker's mouth could even face down real truck drivers. In 1983, long before public opinion began turning against her, Leona had just such a confrontation on a Manhattan street. She had been visiting her dressmaker, Julia, in Harry's Graybar Building, alongside Grand Central Station. She emerged, heading to yet another dressmaker's shop for a fitting. There was no hurry. But that didn't matter when she discovered her limo was blocked by a truck, which belonged to a company renting space in the Graybar. The driver refused to budge.

Said one man who was with her: "She got out of the limo and goes right up to the driver and starts shaking her fist, screaming and yelling at him, saying that she'd have Harry kick his company out of the building. I couldn't believe it. Right there on the street. And she was wearing this bright pink wool suit and ruby earrings. But the funniest thing was that people were walking by, they recognized her, and they started cheering for her, saying, 'Come on, Leona! Get him, Leona!' "

The most explosive episodes occurred in her inner offices at the Palace Hotel, where her closest aides bore the brunt.

A royal red color shouts at the visitor getting off the Palace Hotel's elevators at the fifth floor. Just a few feet ahead is a floor-to-ceiling glass wall, behind which sits a receptionist. On the red walls hang the signs that are scattered throughout staff areas in the Palace and Helmsley hotels nationwide. "If you weren't the best at what you do, you wouldn't be here," says one. "Don't forget, remember this is a Helmsley Hotel," reads another.

To the right of the receptionist is a small corridor leading to a set of offices. Several are occupied by secretaries. At the end is a round vestibule area serving two doors. The left leads to the office that Harry uses when he visits the hotel, typically for only a few minutes in the late afternoon. Harry's office is done in his favorite color, red. The upholstery is red, as is a wall covering. The wall is padded with a thin material. His desk is massive.

Leona's office, to the right, is done in pastels: the wall fabric in rose and green shades; the upholstery in a rose-colored damask. On the walls are pictures of Harry and one of her son, Jay. There's a watercolor of a masquerade ball that looks like it's taking place at the Palace, but that's only a guess. The painter appears to have been fantasizing. On a mantel is a fifteen-inch-high clock with gold leaves and diamonds on the pendulum. One very large window looks out on Fifty-first Street.

Her office is small, measuring twelve by fifteen feet at most. And the furniture takes up most of the room. Her desk is kidney-shaped, with the top done in rosy-pink leather. Her thickly padded chair, too, is done in a dark rose hue. There's also a love seat, and two side chairs. Visitors sit. Leona does not. She does anything but remain seated and still. She hovers. She stalks and prowls the room. "I almost never see her sitting," one current aide said. "She likes to stand when she works. When you're showing her plans, she's back and forth, across the room, around her desk."

Her constant movement was another distinction from Harry. He sits, for long periods of time, stirring at most to lean back in his chair and stare at the ceiling. Leona literally runs through her day, on her feet, creating and feeding on the chaos around her. "She would be on the phone, going through the mail, calling her secretary, and somebody would be showing her soaps and she would be smelling them," marveled Beber. "That's how she worked best, in that tumultuous environment.

"She liked to have an audience around," Beber continued. "This is a woman who shined with people around. She would conduct a meeting, and someone would come in and say, 'These are the hangers.' So you had to have resilience, and wait your turn, and know you'd be interrupted. It was sort of fun. You sort of rolled your eyes. One of my staff once said that working for Leona was exciting to him. And once you said to yourself, 'It's not me, it's her,' you could relax about it."

People came to marvel at the resilience of Maryann Eboli, as in this interaction described by one of Leona's longtime financial aides who later testified before the grand jury that brought the tax-fraud and extortion charges against Leona.

"One day I was there, sitting with Maryann, and Leona was asking me to find out some information from a bank, and she wanted me to call them," the aide said. "Leona was very pleasant, very cordial. She said, 'Do you think you could call the bank for me?' "

Leona wanted information about someone's account, and Maryann said, "But the bank won't give him that information."

"So [Leona] screamed like you can't possibly believe," the aide continued. "She screamed, 'SHUT UP.' At the top of her lungs. Just looked at her secretary and screamed, 'SHUT UP! I'M NOT TALK-ING TO YOU!' At the top of her lungs. And then, just as quickly, she turned back to me and put on her pleasant face."

Those new to Leona's explosions are taken aback. They sit in shock as she lets loose with a stream of "bastards" and "fucks" and "shits." But those who became familiar with her explosions enough to detach themselves came to notice something else.

"The manager [of a Helmsley apartment complex] was spending substantial amounts of money doing tenant investigations, to see if there were any illegal tenants, and our audits showed there were no written approvals by Mr. Helmsley of the audits," said the financial aide. "And I was trying to establish a procedure where that was done. But rather than look at the recommendation I was making, she picked up the phone and started harassing him, screaming at him, instead of dealing with it in what could have been a constructive manner. She did that so many times that it seemed like she did it for effect, not to intimidate them, but to intimidate me or whoever was in her office. She routinely picked up the phone and hollered and screamed at somebody while you were in the room, never asking you to leave, and it had an effect. On a couple of occasions when she called me [on the phone] to scream and yell, I always suspected there was somebody at the other end in her office feeling what I felt."

Joseph Forstadt agreed there was something purposeful about her tirades. "I always sensed that a lot of it was playacting," he said. "She used anger and charm to achieve a result. Oftentimes the anger was turned on for a purpose, with a purpose, and she thought that would achieve a result. I think it was a business judgment she made, and she could turn it on or off when she felt it was necessary. In the same conversation she would turn to you and be charming."

"She would try to intimidate people any way she could," said Eboli, who became not so much a lightning rod as an early-warning signal for Leona's tyrannical visits or eruptions. Many employees, from Helmsley-Spear brokers in Florida to the Park Lane Hotel staff, speak lovingly of Maryann for giving them advance warnings of her visits. And a call from Maryann with a summons to see Leona was invariably met with a frenzied "What does she want? How bad is it?" But if her office assistants grew to receive the brunt of her force, the hotel staff got the whip of her tail.

The staff does its best to get out of the way. The dreaded "Leona

Alerts" are fast and furious. "The Queen! The Queen!" or sometimes
"The Queen Bee!" a security guard or doorman calls out when they
learn Leona is in her limo and on the way. Tranquil scenes dissolve into
frenzy, with the hotel staff either slipping out of sight or dashing for
the lobby to stand at attention in their crisp white gloves. There is
reason for what guests on hand might view as madness. The woman
soon to arrive is a walking vial of nitroglycerin.

A cigarette butt on the carpeting: "Get that up! Now!"

A spill on the kitchen floor: "Listen, sweetheart, gorgeous, puh-
lease wipe that up."

She'll venture upstairs to a room, and erupt at the housekeeper if
there is a spot of dust or a quilt laid to something less than perfection.
"That maid has to go!"

Again, all that is the image Leona doesn't mind for the world to
see. She displays it, and even puts on special shows for feature writers.
In March 1981 a *Forbes* magazine reporter was interviewing Leona over
lunch at the Palace. Leona called for the check, which arrived, but
without the compulsory embossed-leather case. "Find that or you'll be
looking for another job," Leona was quoted. Her spokeswoman later
explained that Leona's intentions were good, in that she meant to
"instill in him that you can't be slipshod at the Palace. When he found
it and presented it properly, she complimented him."

Leona even ambushed the ambush specialist, Mike Wallace, of *60
Minutes,* who thought he was catching her with her guard down. What
he caught was Leona playing the Queen guard. "I'm tough, but I'm
fair. I'm very fair. If you lie to me you're through. I won't do business
with you."

Actually, Leona's style is attractive to some managerial pundits.
She doesn't win high marks from professors at the reputable Cornell
University School of Hotels (Helmsley is one of the few chains that
don't recruit their coveted graduates). But in a business where employee service is often horrendous, and a corporate world where the
top bosses often fail to show any hands-on interest, Leona's intentions
get good marks from many. Even Steve Brener hands her a compliment for her attention to service. "She was a real stickler for doing
things in a very precise manner," he said. "She would be aggravated

about things. But she's a difficult person to work for because she likes things done right."

Also, her instincts about guest services are shared by other hoteliers. A 1988 survey of 659 hotels in the country showed that seventeen of the twenty-two most popular guest services were offered by more hotels than in the year prior. The survey showed four in five hotels offering bathroom amenities, if not the huge fluffy towels Leona does; over half had a gift shop, though not with Harry and Leona playing cards; and almost half claimed a multilingual staff, as do the Helmsley hotels and most others in New York. "Hotels are fighting for people, so they're offering more goodies," said Laventhol & Horwath, an accounting and consulting firm specializing in lodging.

But as Leona worked her way deeper into the hotel business, it became clear that her style and manner were getting in the way of her business-smart intentions. Indeed, her whole mind-set about interacting with employees was a warped version of the corporate standard for making forays into the working parts of a business. If McDonald's Corporation executives all spend one day a year bagging fries behind the counter to feel what it's like, Leona spends an hour a day in her hotel kitchens and guest rooms kicking asses to see if *they* like how it feels.

Leona prefers to speak more serenely of her hotel wanderings, as she did in a legal deposition. "Well, with reference to the Palace Hotel, I usually arrive there at eleven, I will probably go downstairs and have lunch [at] one, when it starts to crowd up, walk through the dining room, see that everything is all right in the kitchen, see who I know, who I don't know. I introduce myself, and go back to my office. Go through the letters, make telephone calls if there are any complaints. I call the people themselves, and it could be anywhere until eight, nine o'clock that I'm there.

"I walk the hotel," she continued, "the restaurants, kitchens, tearooms, there are times we go into Harry's Bar, after another function, and we mingle with the guests. They love it, and they stay longer and spend money. One night we brought Frank Sinatra in and the place was empty and all of a sudden they came out of the woodwork, they came, I don't know where the people came from, you couldn't get into the bar and he never sang a note and—I like people."

Even her wardrobe is geared toward her forays, she said. "I have had to, truly, increase my wardrobe enormously since I am at the hotel, because I am Mrs. Helmsley, I am the president, and when I walk through that room I have to be dressed properly. I can't come in in a little pair of slacks. I don't anyway."

She's open about her involvement in personnel matters. "In the course of making inspections if you find anything out of order or any defects do you take any action?" she was asked. The terse reply: "I take a lot of action. It is corrected." Later, she elaborated: "It isn't for myself. [It's for] the guest [who's] coming in. They want what they are paying for and by all means if I have anything to do with it, they are going to get it."

But her input lacks thought or attention to the value of a chain of command. "I was with her at the Park Lane for lunch one time, and a porter came by and he clearly was not dressed properly," said Forstadt. "Part of his suit was unbuttoned, or maybe he didn't have a tie. And she called him aside directly. One would expect she would talk to the manager and the manager would talk to the maître d' and the maître d' would talk to the personnel director and it would flow down that way. But she did not. She called him over directly and told him he better shape up or he would be out of a job. She was quite pointed about it."

Other times she would get the manager involved. But in trying to kick-start a chain of command, it would dissolve into the cries of people in a panic. Once she happened upon a cigar butt on the Park Lane floor. "She freaked," recalled a hotel employee on hand. "The manager was in the lobby and he runs down to housekeeping to find the porter. But it wasn't his fault. He'd been by just five minutes earlier and in the meantime along came some businessman who doesn't know how to use an ashtray. There were half a dozen assistant managers in the lobby and she could have asked anyone to pick it up. But she has everyone so intimidated, the manager just ran off. It's disgusting to see grown men act like that."

The most telling flaw in Leona's hands-on approach was that she never saw the great majority of her staff unless she happened upon a

Harry Helmsley began his career by collecting rent in Hell's Kitchen. He became known as a "clean dealer" who would close a transaction with a smile and a handshake, although one writer dubbed him "Hungry Harry," because of his thriftiness concerning the upkeep on his buildings. *(New York Times)*

Mayor Edward I. Koch and the Helmsleys sing the famed "I'm Just Wild About Harry" that Leona frequently requests at Harry's birthday parties and other celebrations. Koch's presence was tolerated at this 1981 opening of the New York Harley. Later his presence at Harry's birthday parties was routinely banned by Leona after a falling out. *(Wide World Photos)*

Leona and her daughter-in-law Mimi Panzirer seemed to have a wonderful relationship until Jay Panzirer died of a heart attack at age forty-two. After the funeral, Mimi was served with an eviction notice and a flurry of lawsuits followed. *(Mimi Panzirer)*

Leona and the Panzirers on board the Helmsleys' BAC 1-11. To get an idea of the plane they wanted, Harry and Leona toured one decorated in gold that was ordered for King Hussein. But even the Helmsleys thought that was excessive. *(Mimi Panzirer)*

The Helmsley Hotels experience occasional lobby "meetings," in which every union worker in the hotel—maids, barkeeps, chefs—will pour into the lobby area to stage a protest. Amidst the startled and curious guests, the workers discuss their grievance. *(Ken Brooks)*

Blaine and Robert Trump share a laugh at a 1987 New York Hospital benefit. But brother Donald Trump's feud with Leona began when he bought the St. Moritz Hotel from the Helmsleys—and Leona wanted him to pay for the stuffed animals in Rumpelmayer's, the hotel's ice cream parlor. *(Ron Galella)*

One of Harry's favorite moves with reporters is to go to his office window, sweep his arm over the Empire State Building and the Manhattan skyline, and comment on how he is taking inventory. *(Kirkland/Sygma)*

The twenty-six-acre Dunnellen estate in the new-money section of Greenwich, Connecticut, has had a string of owners with one thing in common: Their time at the Tudor mansion was marked by misfortune. For Leona and Harry, who purchased the estate in 1983 for $11 million, their first years at Dunnellen brought them a series of fights with painters, gardeners, and contractors. *(New York Newsday)*

Twice the Helmsleys were dragged into court to answer allegations that they had defrauded the state and federal governments of taxes, and other charges. They surrounded themselves with bodyguards wearing little golden "HH" pins as if they were Secret Service. *(New York Newsday)*

Although the court was still deciding whether Harry was mentally and physically fit to stand trial, he and Leona were discovered in Hawaii. Their embarrassed attorneys then had to go to court—after the fact—to seek permission for the couple to travel out of the continental United States. *(Ron Galella)*

The usually flashy Leona dressed in gray and appeared disheveled in December 1988 as the Helmsley lawyers prepared their defense. *(New York Daily News)*

lobby meeting. Hotel staffs are huge. The Palace has 17 people in the accounting office, 13 in the garage, 15 keeping the engineering working, 298 cleaning the rooms, 19 answering the phones, 14 keeping security, 92 in the kitchen, and 94 handling other food and drink service. Nor did her random inspections seem to serve as example to others. The code of survival in Helmsley hotels is not so much to be good as it is to avoid being caught in Leona's sight.

Aside from her managerial style, it was unclear to her associates just how many business smarts Leona acquired. Some of that suspicion stemmed from Leona's general manners. She and Harry did the crossword puzzle in *The New York Times* most Sundays, keeping it around throughout the week as they would compete to fill in the blanks. But she rarely read that or other newspapers. Her taste in music ran to Frank Sinatra and Julio Iglesias. She despised classical music, and when she received opening-night tickets to the opera, she threw them away. Moreover, to Joseph Catania, her interior decorator, Leona seemed most at ease when she ditched her limo to do simple, pedestrian things —window shopping, walking through the park, stopping to buy a hot dog from a street peddler.

Some who know her said she has a sort of natural, unschooled street smarts on par with her husband. Bill Kimpton recalled meeting with Harry and Leona in the late 1970s about a hotel project. As they pondered some architectural drawings Leona jumped on them in a flash.

"She looked at the plans and saw all the flaws," said Kimpton. "I'm sure he did too, but he didn't say anything at the time. She said, 'This and this and this isn't going to work.' She looked at the design, and saw all these problems in the shape of the hotel, and the layout of the rooms. She saw about ten items, just like that. And sure enough, she was right. I ended up firing the architect and ended up in a huge lawsuit over the whole thing."

Harry would boast of his wife to reporters. "She can do a lot of things that I am not geared for," he said once. "She likes detail. She is very observant, and she is more of a perfectionist than I am. I like to do things with a broad brush, and I like to see the bigger scope, and I hate the details. So we mesh pretty well."

There's some question, however, about how capable Leona Helmsley is in running, not just one, but a whole chain of hotels. She certainly is no studied corporate executive of the sort who could define the most basic terminology. During a deposition in a legal proceeding, she could state her own investment in the hotel without pause: a flat one million dollars. But she couldn't distinguish among the several entities involved, Helmsley Hotels, Inc., the Palace Co., Harley Hotels. "I don't know, that is not my forte," she told the three-member arbitration panel hearing the proceeding. To another question, about her title, she remarked, "I don't know, I really don't. I don't look at the papers, I really don't."

Leona even had trouble defining herself.

Question: "Are you the chief executive officer of the Palace Hotel, do you understand what that means?"

Answer: "No."

Her attorney: "No, you don't understand?"

Answer: "No."

Question: "Do you have the chief operating responsibilities for the Palace Hotel?"

Answer: "I don't know if I have the responsibility, but I do it. Whatever has to be done, is done. I don't know about titles, I really don't."

Then, after a succession of similar questions and answers, she was asked: "So when you say you are president of Helmsley Hotels, you mean you are president of an entity, as you understand it, that runs or controls, supervises those hotels. Is that what you mean generally?"

Answer: "There is no entity that supervises. I'm a person, I'm not an entity. I—my title—this gives me authority, my title, to go in and do what I deem necessary."

Occasionally she conceded, even overstated her naïveté. "I did not know anything about the hotel business," she told Anna Quindlen, then a deputy editor of The New York Times, who went on to describe Leona as the Joan Collins of the hotel business—"all tough talk, big jewels and no nonsense." Continued Leona: "I still don't. It's like running your own house. I try to do a good job for my husband. I love the whole thing. It's action. I love picking a pickle. I was at lunch yesterday downstairs. I said to the people at the next table, 'How are the pickles?' They're half-sours. I picked them. They're good pickles. People are grateful."

Once she said in an interview, "If I had to explain and justify every decision, if I couldn't use instincts to run these hotels—just as any woman runs her house—we wouldn't be where we are today. I'm smart but I'm not brilliant, and he is. He fixes the tough stuff when I'm at my wits' end. When I need to hide, Harry is my hiding place."

"Leona is not bright. She does not know numbers," said Eboli, who suddenly found herself handling all of Leona's personal finances, as well as her corporate work.

The result, some of Leona's aides came to believe, was that she had a great sense for trees but completely missed the forest.

"There was a problem at the Palace Hotel, not too long before I left, where a guest had been allowed to overstay his welcome," an accountant recalled. "He ran up $70,000 in unpaid charges, and they are now in litigation with attorneys, and we were trying to control the situation. The guest was bouncing checks, and the credit department wasn't aware that the checks were bouncing, and the guest was continuing to charge. There were a whole series of weaknesses in the system and we wrote a report about that, and it went directly to her, and my feeling is that a copy of it went to the controller before she ever got it, because by the time she got the report, he already knew. And she called me, and rather than address the points, which were very valid, she called me, screaming at me, and asked why I was attacking the controller. She said he's a good man, and that he's staying, and while I tried to indicate to her this had nothing to do with him personally, that I liked him and I thought he was capable, she didn't listen. She just screamed that he's staying and that was that. She just got emotional about the situation, thinking that I was attacking someone who in that week was in her good graces."

Perhaps the greatest pitfall in Leona's style is the wrath it draws from her staff. She came to be hated to an astounding degree by some. Later, it would manifest itself when government prosecutors would be able to boast about having a line out their door of disgruntled employees willing to go before the grand jury. But much smaller incidents occurred regularly that might even shock Leona if she ever learned of them. At the Park Lane, for example, the kitchen came to be dominated by a group of raucous, gruff waiters of Greek descent. They came to be known as the Greek Mafia, on account of some of their business dealings with other staff. On more than one occasion they would rescue their pride after a Leona inspection tour by unzipping their pants, pulling out their genitals, and dunking them in glasses of water, which they would then serve to the Queen.

She alienated the best around her. Other associates marvel at how long Maryann Eboli was able to last as Leona's secretary. "I was never yelled at," said the ad agent Beber. "But she screamed at Maryann like I couldn't believe. And yet you had these tremendous double signals going on all the time. It would be 'Maryann, you need an operation. I want you to have my doctor. I'm going to call seven doctors for you,' and 'Maryann, you're ill. Have chicken soup.' Then it would be [Beber slips into a growl] 'Maryann, you sent something to the Palace cleaners. You're a thief.' All of that would happen in a two-day period. From worrying about Maryann, and coming on like a loving, caring person, to saying she was going to have Maryann jailed because she spilled something on herself and sent it to the Palace cleaners."

"People would say, 'God, how do you stand for it?' " said Eboli, who shrugs it off. "I guess it's because I've never been afraid of her. It's not my style, though my stomach did pay for it." But like so many others, Maryann also left Leona's side with a storm swirling around her. The day Eboli turned in her resignation to take another job as executive secretary with a Manhattan designer, Eboli met Leona in the dressing room that Leona had built in Harry's Park Lane penthouse. Leona began throwing things at her. "She just started pulling things out of the closet, one after another," said Eboli. She ducked, as did Leona's decorating assistant, who was on hand.

Leona worked the world like a one-woman volleyball team, faking a soft shot to relax her opponents and then hammering one down the middle as they stand off guard. "She would have an immense hold on you," continued Beber, who also was fired after a long relationship with both Harry and Leona. "Anyone would who came on that strong. You drop the layers of defenses you put up in business. You get close.

You think it is real. And then you're dumped. She seemed to do that more to women than to men."

The hotel staff turnover, especially at the Palace, was extraordinary. The first manager, Wolfgang Haenisch, left within a year. "Haenisch, once he left it all fell apart, or started to fall apart," said Karl Hofer, a veteran hotel executive who was part of the Haenisch team. "We had a damn good team. The turnover when we opened, it was like 40 or 50 percent, a ridiculously low number because in an opening you have a lot of turnover. I checked it about a year after we left, it was 200 or 300 percent, meaning every position in the hotel turned over two or three times a year."

Leona later acknowledged the problem, but looked elsewhere for the reason. "In the beginning I had a lot of turnover, but if I were a man, they'd say I was a good executive. The only ones who really like it are my guests. They deserve it."

Leona felt slighted because she was a woman working in a male-dominated industry. "I'm not a tough cookie," she told a reporter who suggested as much. "If I were a man, they'd say I was a great executive. I'm a woman, so I'm a tough cookie."

Some of her staff with a few years' hindsight feel her intentions were good. "I don't think she knows that she is doing it," said Hofer. "I bear no personal resentment. I think she hurt many good people. Again, though, I don't think she meant it."

Mal Seymourian, also part of the opening team, said, "She wanted to bring the best out of everybody, but didn't know how to do it. Motivation is a difficult thing, how you bring out the best in people. Sure, she brings out something in some people. I'm not sure it's the best thing. For Haenisch, I would kill myself. He worked me hard, but he also knew how to take care of you."

Certainly a good number of Helmsley hotel employees did not feel taken care of, in many ways. One was the Helmsley policy on staying at hotels in the chain. Many big chains give their employees discounts at their hotels when they're on vacation. Not so with the Helmsleys. Like some hotel owners, not only do they not give discounts; they forbade employees from staying at their hotels altogether. No one understood why. Possibly it was because New York was unionized and many of their hotels, such as those in Florida, were not.

Leona fought with others besides her employees. Some are forgiving. But two episodes in the mid-1980s are especially revealing, and at least one of those on the receiving end of her tirades will never forget or forgive.

There was a general, citywide hotel strike in June 1985, and for its duration the royal gate into the Palace courtyard was locked shut. The courtyard is superfluous to the hotel. But it's used as a main entrance for several nonprofit groups that work out of the northern wing of the Villard Houses.

Chief among them is the Municipal Art Society, to whom Harry Helmsley rented the wing at a very low rate. It's unclear why he did that, but the reason is presumed to be linked to the role that the society and its offshoots, the Landmarks Conservancy and the Landmarks Commission, played in the restoration matter. The society in turn collects rents from others, including the Parks Council, to which the Helmsleys contributed $50 once.

To get into its offices during the strike, the society used a side entrance and hired a private security guard to keep it safe. The bill came to $2,167 and the society promptly sent the bill and a letter of explanation to Leona Helmsley.

"I never heard. So I wrote again," said the society's accountant, Gloria Froy. Froy never did hear from Leona. But the society's president, Kent Barwick, did. Leona telephoned him, and Barwick—a rather discreet, conservative person—was unable to recount her words verbatim except to say they were filthy and slurred and out of control.

The society's chairman decided to pay the guard bill, and the staff was able to joke about it. Kent's secretary asked him, "Whose head is going to roll?" and he replied, "Gloria's."

Froy in turn chuckles about how Leona addressed Kent. "She kept calling him Mr. Barhead. Kent Barhead." Barwick is noticeably balding.

Donald Trump will never laugh about Leona Helmsley. Nor will he speak of her for quotation, though he will wax at length and admiringly about Harry—the old Harry, the pre-Leona Harry. Leona's and Trump's first encounter was pedestrian to the point of being silly.

When Trump bought the St. Moritz from the Helmsleys and booted Leona out of her office there, Leona held on to the stuffed bears and other animals in Rumpelmayer's, the hotel's ice-cream parlor—not for sentimental reasons, for money. She wanted Trump to pay extra, and he laughed her to the door. The animals disappeared.

Until that point Donald Trump had been a mere rival to Harry Helmsley's real estate dealings. But soon Trump's own wife, Ivana, would take control of the Trump hotels as Leona did the Helmsleys'. And a natural, competitive rivalry grew between the two women as it had between the men.

The feud was, for the most part, subdued and unstated. In the offices of several Helmsley-Spear executives there are cartoons on the walls referring to the Trumps. One shows the skyline of Forty-second Street in Manhattan and the word "Trump" is plastered over a dozen buildings—except for the Helmsley Hotel, which is labeled "No Trump." Aides and relatives alike knew not to bring up the Trump name during dinners. Leona and Ivana courted both the hotel industry and the same new-rich society circles, and their very different styles and tastes clashed.

But eventually it was Leona and Donald who seemed most at odds. For Trump's part, it showed itself not in what he did, but in what he failed to do. In 1988, Donald repeatedly failed to comment publicly about Leona when the Helmsleys' tax troubles arose, even though he praised Harry to no end as an honest, evenhanded real estate dealer. And that year's Fourth of July weekend, when Trump paraded the $30 million boat he purchased from the international arms dealer Adnan Kashoggi, the extensive invitation list excluded the Helmsleys—even though it was Leona's birthday. Her aides said she fumed, and covered up any hurt feelings by waving around a letter of courtesy Donald had sent to her and Harry expressing his regrets about their indictments.

## CHAPTER 12

# PALACE PLOY

THE HELMSLEY PALACE HOTEL BEGAN CHECKING IN GUESTS AS SOON AS the spilled champagne from the party was mopped up. And it seemed, to some on hand, an inauspicious start. The lobby was gilded enough. But upstairs, the hotel remained a shambles. Bugs needed working out everywhere.

"My God, it was a messy opening," said Mal Seymourian. "Those first days! The guests were crawling over debris in the lobby. We would do manager-on-duty tours, eight or ten of us [on rotation]. On one of my nights, I think the fire alarm went off fourteen times. It was impossible to get a good night's sleep."

It's not uncommon for hoteliers to open early, with work still in progress. Usually there is financial pressure from the lenders to start the revenue rolling. But Helmsley had a mere 231 rooms ready when he threw open the Palace doors. Four in five rooms were still being worked on, as were the cocktail room, dining room, and ballroom.

Workers competed with guests for the elevators. The first arrivals were not impressed.

"It can set a very bad image," Seymourian said of early openings. He told many of his personal customers—corporate and personal friends whom he'd enticed to start staying at the Palace when in New York—"to wait a time before coming."

Olen Earnest of Beverly Hills wasn't tipped off. "Shortly after its much-ballyhooed opening, business colleagues and I decided to stay at the Helmsley Palace," he wrote to a magazine editor. "When we checked into the still-unfinished hotel, I was taken to my room, where I discovered only one towel in the bathroom, a pair of panty hose draped over the sink, and a rumpled bed. I had no time to change before rushing out to a business dinner, and I requested that my luggage be moved to a clean room while I was away. When I returned, I was told that my original room had been cleaned. In fact, nothing had changed—except the night maid had turned down the dirty, rumpled bed and left a 'good night' chocolate on the pillow! It took five phone calls and two and a half hours until I was finally moved, at 2:30 A.M. Two nights later, I was preparing for dinner when the toilet overflowed. I was unable to use the bathroom until a maintenance man unclogged the toilet, and I was over an hour late for my dinner appointment. The hotel's consolation prize was a slight discount on the room rate. My letter of complaint was answered by a letter addressed to Jeeves of Belgravia, thanking me for my interest in providing a dry-cleaning service to the Palace. But, they regretted to inform me, the service had already been contracted. I am still waiting to hear from the Queen."

Helmsley never explained why he rushed to open in 1980. It wasn't his lenders. Met Life and Mass. Mutual gave him an extension until June the next year. He hinted that he felt he was in a race with several other hotels underway, including Trump's eight blocks away on Forty-second Street. He may simply have wanted to start collecting those nightly rents he'd become fascinated by. In any event, he complained to his investors about construction delays, and he blamed the building industry for slowing him down. Indeed, builders of all sorts were enjoying the late 1970s construction boom in Manhattan, thanks perhaps to the city's generosity with tax breaks. There was a rush by office and hotel developers alike to get their projects up.

"The big problem was the skin," Helmsley said, referring to the outer shell of the fifty-one-story hotel tower that went up behind and over the Villard Houses. "Everybody in the city was having trouble getting the skin put on their buildings. There weren't enough laborers to do it. And those that were working didn't do any work. So that everything was delayed. It was incredible, no matter what you did. Carl Morse [the builder] fought with the contractor, but there was nothing he could do. He was stymied. He had taken too much work. He couldn't deliver."

But there was another problem Helmsley was having, and this one lay within his own board of directors. In short, the Palace restoration —all the gilding, the chandeliering, the brass plating and picture hanging—had gotten out of hand. Change orders started coming in left and right. Earlier cost estimates doubled, then tripled, then quadrupled.

It's unclear at what point exactly the Palace slipped away from Harry. By 1978, however, he had become uncharacteristically loose with the purse strings. This was not the same frugal multimillionaire who, before meeting Leona, owned only two suits. Nor was it the same penny-pinching real estate magnate who once, in buying the New York Central Building with the requirement that he rename it, chiseled only two letters—the C and the t—to make it the New York General. When asked about that move, he replied, "I'm cheap."

If he was the same frugal person, he didn't let it show. There was nothing cheap about building the Palace. Helmsley let a rare emotion surface. "His true love was the Palace," said his former ad agent, Joyce Beber. "It seemed like in other things in his life his pride didn't count. He wanted to make money. That was his scoreboard. But with the Palace he dropped his pragmatism, his seeming pragmatism. The Palace itself gave him pride."

Helmsley may have winced now and again, but he let himself and the budget go. His jubilation over the Villard Houses shows in a somewhat rambling narrative he gave under oath.

"No one really knew what a gem we had until we took a look at it and found that it was covered with probably fifty years of dirt," he said. "Then when we did start to clean it, we found that we had a clock which dated back to the original date of a hundred years ago. There are these marvelous fireplaces, Saint-Gaudens. The marble in the stairway. So that I suddenly realized this could be the best hotel in the whole world, not just another hotel.

"To give you another example, in the Madison Room, which is the room facing Madison Avenue, I looked at it and I figured we'll order carpets. . . . When we got to the point of laying the carpets, by that time we started to clean the floor, sand it, and came up with this beautiful parquet floor which no one had ever known was there. The same with the dining area, the Trianon Room, and the bar. These are so much better than anything you find in today's hotels. So I just didn't go ahead and say, well, all right, these are the plans, build it as cheap as you can."

But the lavish restoration and decorating costs weren't the only thing that got out of Harry's hands. When the September 15 gala party was cleaned up and the Palace opened on the sixteenth for paying guests, it started leaking money like the champagne that had flowed at the bash. Fountains of cash streamed out the door as operating expenses towered over the income. Helmsley had expected some red ink during start-up, but the numbers were far worse than he ever imagined. "Little did I know," he later would say with a sigh. And when the bills started coming due, Helmsley, for the first time in his life, faced a pack of investors who were both very angry and very capable of expressing themselves.

The financial magic that created the Palace was typical of the real estate syndicates Helmsley and Larry Wien learned to use in their later years. Instead of mass-marketing $5,000 or $10,000 investment chunks as they did to buy the Empire State Building, the duo, and then Helmsley on his own, evolved into using small groups of big investors —people each with a million dollars or so to risk. Helmsley turned to a Californian to put the Palace pool together.

Bill Kimpton is the archetypal successful San Franciscan. He has a deep tan, accentuated by his swept-back silver hair. He looks and acts extremely healthy. He dresses casually on Friday afternoons, which he regularly takes off—year round—to play golf. Kimpton owns a chain of hotels in the City-by-the-Bay that he remodeled into low-amenity, high-value suites. "I learned from Harry to sell sleep, not fountains," he said.

In 1976, Kimpton, then a corporate investment banker, was marketing a hotel and condo project on Maui, when Steve Brener introduced him to Helmsley. They flew to Hawaii, stayed at the Manakea Hotel on the Big Island, and in the negotiations Kimpton got his first look at Helmsley's financial prowess. The landowners, a venerable Hawaiian family organized into the Maui Land and Pineapple Company, had never heard of Harry Helmsley. So when it came time in the agreement where he would have to buy them out for $400 to $500 million, Harry simply said fine. "They were quite surprised," said Kimpton. "They didn't believe there was anybody around who could write that kind of a check."

Helmsley's role in the deal fell through when the family decided to use conventional bankers. "Nothing materialized but we became very good friends," Helmsley later said of Kimpton, who would stop in to see Helmsley in New York. He made the "Wild About Harry" party list. One night, Kimpton was dining at the Four Seasons restaurant with Harry and Leona. "We were talking about the Palace Hotel and she said to me, 'Well, why don't you raise the money.' I was like Sam Spade at the time, between projects with nothing to do, and I thought that might be fun. That changed my life, that dinner."

Kimpton went to the Lincoln Building for more formal discussions. "It was interesting because he had offers from Merrill Lynch, Goldman Sachs. They had long memorandums detailing how they would do it, and here I was with a small firm in New York City, basically by myself, and I had one little piece of paper." Kimpton's firm was called Lapercq, French for "little pear."

The big investment houses all wanted to syndicate in the traditional $5,000 and $10,000 units. Kimpton suggested doing it in one-million-dollar units. So he and Harry had a typical deal-making dance.

"That's never been done with hotels before," Helmsley said.

"I'll go abroad and do it. Here's my airline ticket," replied Kimpton.

"Well, I'm skeptical," countered Helmsley. "Here are all these huge firms."

"I can do it," said Kimpton.

"Well, go do it," said Helmsley.

Kimpton learned later that he was Helmsley's only choice. Met Life and Mass. Mutual, who were lending Helmsley the $50 million, insisted on having no more than twenty-five investors putting up the additional $23 million needed to complete the project. That was only the start of Kimpton's good fortune. He modestly ascribes to "pure luck" his rounding up of the foreign investors.

"It was all by accident. The Germans came through because a friend of mine, a broker on Wall Street, was sitting on a train next to a guy from Germany, and the guy said, 'Yeah, I'd be kind of interested.' My friend found me in a bar in Kansas City and said, 'You've got to talk to this guy.' And out of that came the German investors." Beteiligungsgesellschaft, their entity, was in for $4 million.

Kimpton's next overseas score reads like a sitcom. "I was going to Paris, and this guy called me and said, 'I've got a Saudi investor for you. Can you come over and see him?' And I said, 'Well, I'm on my way over anyway,' and he said, 'Well, can you come a day early?' So I agreed, but I said to myself that I didn't believe anything is going to happen. I've met so many Saudis and none of them are ever going to invest in my firm. So I go to this guy's office in Paris, but I've already gone to a restaurant and made my reservation for bouillabaisse, and I'm much more interested in the bouillabaisse than I am in talking to this Saudi. It turned out there's a line down the street to see him, a mental line, so I said to him, 'Look, I've only got about an hour here 'cause I've got my lunch, and you Saudis pretend to invest, and you never do invest, and I'm probably wasting my time.' He was insulted, but he also was so amused by my abruptness that he didn't hit me. And before I left I had his letter." The Saudis, through their French and Netherlands Antilles companies, were in for another $4.5 million.

"It was all on Harry's reputation," said Kimpton. "He was such a draw." Several American investors also joined in for a million apiece, including Barbara Sinatra; Gordon McDonald, a California shopping-center magnate; and Jack Massey, an industrialist from Nashville, who owned Kentucky Fried Chicken and founded the Hospital Corporation of America. For Massey, Helmsley waived the customary letter of credit that would certify he was good for a million. For his share of the profits, Helmsley contributed the mortgage loan and the development and management expertise. He also agreed to absorb any additional costs above the estimated $73 million total price tag, and, conversely, would reap the windfall if he could bring the Palace on line for less than that sum. It was a classic Helmsley setup: he traded in his sweat and expertise for a hard-dollar position.

One benefit to Helmsley and the banks in using such a small group of investors was that it kept things all in the family. There was no need to file all the usual basketloads of internal documents with the federal Securities and Exchange Commission, where outsiders could snoop. But there was also a drawback for Helmsley should a problem arise. Small investors don't pay close attention, but big people do, especially when they're the business professionals and astute investors Kimpton rounded up. It was a sophisticated lot who received Harry's ominous "Dear Friend" letter in early May 1981, and their reactions were keen.

"I am sure all of us are proud of the critical acclaim given to our hotel and of the appreciation of our efforts by our guests," Helmsley began, warming up to the matters at hand. ("Yes, indeed," the investors may have mused.) The upper-floor apartments were due to be completed that month. The mortgage closing would occur the next month. Then, almost with an audible sigh, Harry informed them that there were $9.5 million in excess development costs. Also, the operating losses had passed $8 million. All told, Harry said he would have to swallow unexpected costs of $17,575,000. ("Too bad for Harry," the investors may have thought, "but that was the deal.")

Then Helmsley threw his pitch, and it was clocked at ninety-five miles an hour.

"In order to create what we believe is the finest hotel in the United States, and perhaps the world, and, of course, in order to secure a greater income as a result, we made many changes to the finishes and efficiency for the operation of the hotel, which were not reflected in the plans of our architect at the time when we entered into our partnership agreement on Nov. 1, 1978."

For one thing, Helmsley explained, the Villard Houses became more than he bargained for. "The preservation of the Villard Houses, whose uniqueness gave birth to the idea of the Helmsley Palace, has grown from a simple preservation of the condition of those buildings at a cost of some $2,300,000 to the re-creation of these mansions as they were when completed a hundred years ago and the integration of new and exciting public rooms and amenities, plus the installation of administrative offices in the basement and attic. The façade, which most experts said would disintegrate if a cleaning were attempted, has not only been cleaned, but restored to its former soft beige limestone, new and exciting courtyard gates, trees and greenery, lit from the 55th floor roof, plus authentic 19th Century street lampposts are all being added. When you see it all, you will agree that the additional $6,750,000 is worth it." ("But isn't that what we expected for our investment?")

Helmsley wasn't finished. "Another $7,350,000 was added to costs for such things as the enhancement of the grandeur of our public rooms in the new hotel, improvements to security systems, fire safety, air conditioning and lighting, the magnificent furnishings and decorating of the apartment suites for greater income, and a host of other new and previously unconsidered improvements." The sum total of unexpected costs, including $5,300,000 in additional furnishings: $19,377,800. A $73 million Palace had become a $110 million Palace, and Harry wanted the investors to foot the larger bill. Otherwise, he argued, the investors would be "unjustly enriched" by the Palace "improvements."

The investors were outraged. They threatened to sue. And Harry was forced to invite them over to the Palace for lunch, where he accused them of stirring trouble and he blustered, "I won't be had."

Deciding to press the issue was not easy, said François Letaconnoux, managing director of Lapercq. "I was intimately part of the decision to go after him. In the beginning, there were some sleepless nights. We saw it as David versus Goliath. How could we go after Harry Helmsley? we asked ourselves. We hesitated. But we had no choice because we were representing these investors. It was scary, but it was the thing to do."

A public fight was avoided by having the matter privately arbitrated by a panel of three illustrious Manhattan attorneys. The chair was Robert Patterson, Jr., of Patterson, Belknap, Webb & Tyler. The hearing lasted several weeks. Extensive testimony was taken from both Leona and Harry Helmsley, under oath.

The investors hired Manhattan attorney Gerald Fields, who presented their case in four main arguments. One, they said the hotel that Helmsley delivered was no more than what they paid for. "The limited partners were promised a turn-key job, that is, a fully-equipped luxury hotel (inclusive of any improvements or amenities Helmsley deemed desirable), for the fixed investment bargained for, regardless of the final cost of construction to Helmsley." The arbiters spent hours poring over pictures in the original Palace offering brochure, which had been approved by Helmsley financial aide Joseph Licari and by Helmsley's longtime legal representative in creating syndicates, the law firm of Wien, Malkin & Bettex. The brochure undercut Helmsley's recollections. There were a few changes, such as the envisioned courtyard fountain that Helmsley scrapped because keeping it clean would involve too much labor. But generally, the artist renderings of everything from the façade to the banisters compared closely with photos of the final result.

Similarly, the investors rejected Helmsley's contention that the Palace had evolved—from being an ordinary hotel into being a model of luxury—after the investors got on board. Helmsley had gone on at length in his testimony to make that point. "So I went ahead and hired the best artisans we could. And it was a little heart-rending to see them take their toothbrush and clean each mosaic tile on the ceiling at $20 an hour. That hurt me. But anyhow, it made the building what it is. The Gold Room, which we only had to maintain, it's all covered with gold leaf now." But Fields rolled out the Palace feasibility studies done in 1976, immediately after Helmsley won the Landmarks Commission support and before the investors signed up, to show an original Palace concept not unlike the final result.

Two, the investors took issue with Helmsley's contention that they had, indeed, gotten one of the world's best hotels, his glowing descriptions notwithstanding. "You are familiar with the rooms, the public rooms that we have built, the—I think we call it the Regency Room, but at any rate, it's the room that we use for banquets," Helmsley testified. "You don't find, as you would in a Hilton or someplace, where it's all a square block. Everything is curved, even to the ceiling, which is a domed ceiling. It's the most beautiful of the ballrooms in the city. I think there are some leading hotels in the world, and probably ten of them all told. And I wanted to be in that class and I think I'm the best, not only are we in the top ten but I think we are No. 1. At least everyone tells me and I'm modest enough to accept it."

"It appears that Helmsley has fallen short of this goal," argued Fields, producing evidence that it was not even one of New York's best. They cited the Ziff-Davis *Official Hotel Resort Guide,* which classified the Palace as a "deluxe" hotel along with Trump's Grand Hyatt, the Plaza, the Regency, the Mayfair Regent, and the Waldorf-Astoria. That was a notch below the "superior deluxe" awarded the Carlyle, the Pierre, the Waldorf Towers, and the United Nations Plaza Hotel. Similarly, the Exxon and Mobil guides gave a five-star rating only to one hotel in the city: the Carlyle. The Palace got four stars.

Leona Helmsley later would trumpet a five-diamond rating given to the Palace by the American Automobile Association. But more than one hotel guide has been critical, as in this narrative from Gault Millau's *Best of New York:* "Above all, the Palace is an exercise in conspicuous consumption. Bewildered-looking tourists roam the halls, as there is virtually no public seating (no doubt to discourage loitering by any neighborhood bag people). The rooms are housed in the Erector Set structure looming over the neophyte *hôtel* decorated in Queen Leona's regal style." Tim Zagat wasn't much kinder with his 1988 *The Zagat United States Hotel Survey.* New York City as a whole did terribly, ranking thirty-fifth out of the thirty-eight cities included. And within that grouping, the Palace fell behind four or more others in every category: rooms, service, dining, cost. Discriminating Palace patrons wrote to Zagat complaining that it "provides only Leona's copywriters' vision of perfection."

For the third argument, Fields charged that Helmsley informed neither the investors nor the two financial lenders that any substantial changes were being made in the plans.

Finally, the investors took issue with Harry's contention that the changes were all to their partnership's financial good. The Palace was not any more profitable than they had anticipated. Indeed, despite all the gilding, or perhaps because of it, the bottom line had seemingly slipped. Helmsley had projected income to all the partners of $7,118,000 for the first fiscal year ending June 1982. They actually received $318,000 less. But the overall picture was far grimmer. Back in 1979, before the cost overruns became apparent, Helmsley, by his own testimony, suggested to investors that the year ending June 1982 would show a net profit of $25 million—free and clear, after paying the lenders.

The three arbiters met, and on December 21, 1982, they decided against Harry Helmsley. They flatly rejected his bid to charge the $20 million in unexpected expenses to the partnership by taking out a second mortgage. Helmsley was stunned; he had to scramble. The investors turned the tables by laying down a series of counterclaims against Helmsley. In short, they charged him with double-crossing the syndicate, and their offensive laid bare Helmsley's way of doing business as no previous challenge to him had done.

Fields hired accountants to pore through the Palace financial records. What they learned—a few thousand invoices later—astounded the investors. To Helmsley's credit, many of the extra costs in restoring the Villard Houses or building the hotel tower were due to mere incompetence of the sort that might beset any developer. The glue holding 534 toilet-paper rollers to the bathroom walls proved inferior and had to be replaced. Cost: $2,625. The coat checkers couldn't keep up with the system they'd been given and three mechanical conveyors were added. Cost: $3,193. A glass door had to be rehung to reverse its swing because people coming out of the Palace vault tended to hit it. Cost: $3,211. The investors showed that those were Helmsley's mistakes to bear, and there was nothing sinister about them.

Also, they questioned the good business sense in paying $2,675 for a door to prevent a draft in Leona's fifth-floor office, and in paying $2,273 for a window in her office and one in Harry's office. But again, as long as Harry bore the cost that was fine with the investors.

But then they started to notice that Leona was behind many of the additional expenses, and that when Helmsley said "we" in his testimony, he was actually referring to her. It was Leona, for example, who decided the plastic light switches in the ballroom should be replaced with brass. Cost: $2,750. It was Leona who went into the public bathrooms after they were done and ordered all new lights and chandeliers. Cost: $42,381. It was Leona who wandered into the Trianon dining room and two other rooms after they were done and added embellishment on top of embellishment. Cost: $112,714. Helmsley staff working on the Palace later said that Leona was constantly changing orders, as she would do on other Helmsley projects during the 1980s.

Also, the investors found that some of the purchase orders were misapplied to the Palace. A $4,000 painting of Queen Anne in the lobby, for example, was originally purchased for the Doral Hotel. Harry had wanted the Palace investors to foot the bill.

The invoices, however, were only part of the investors' case against Helmsley. They raised half a dozen fundamental issues that went to the very essence of the way Harry Helmsley had come to do business in his private syndications and how he had amassed his fortune. For one thing, Helmsley did not buy the telephones, computers, televisions, and refrigerators that went into the hotel; he leased them, from his own companies. "Self-dealing" is how the investors termed that ploy, and Helmsley reaped untold profits in fees and tax benefits.

Helmsley, the investors also discovered, paid something far less than the market rate for the space he rented on the fifth floor for Leona and at least two of his subsidiaries. Leona had complained about the deal the nonprofit Municipal Art Society was getting. But she was paying at least 50 percent less than others would for her fifth-floor office.

And finally, the investors—especially the German group—discovered that Helmsley was making considerable sums at their expense by buying hotel supplies through his subsidiary Deco Purchasing & Distributing Co., Inc. at inflated prices. Helmsley argued that Deco made up in efficiency what it lost the investors in price. But experts were called in to testify that Deco's charges were far and away higher than the charges of other, comparable supply firms, and the investors showed that Deco's rates, like Leona's rent, were arbitrarily set.

Deco struck a sensitive chord in Helmsley. Deco was to play a key role in the tax-fraud charges filed against the Helmsleys five years later, as would the mystifying way the Helmsleys handled invoices. But already, it seemed, Harry Helmsley was very concerned about the firm, which was being run by Leona's son, Jay. After a blistering round of questions and answers that raised untold questions about Deco and the Palace, as well as about other Helmsley properties not at issue in the arbitration, Helmsley fumed, "You are not supposed to be in my books! What are you doing in Deco anyhow?!"

At another point, Helmsley was asked by chairman Patterson: "What troubles me, Mr. Helmsley, is the—I think what has concerned the limited partners is that you may be using Deco as one means of gaining income from Helmsley Enterprises, and taking a profit there, at the expense of a profit in the hotels or in your . . ."

Helmsley cut him off. "You have to make [a] supposition then. You have to suppose that I'm a crook, which I am not."

On December 14, 1983, a year after rejecting Helmsley's claim for the $20 million, the arbiters found that Helmsley had effectively stolen from his investors. The arbiters ruled for the investors on three main points: the leased equipment, the space rental rates, the Deco charges.

The investors lost their bid to remove Helmsley himself, having charged him with "gross negligence and bad faith" in managing the hotel syndicate. "The evidence established that Helmsley has run the partnership as his own fiefdom with little or no regard for his fiduciary obligations and the rights of his partners," Fields had written in conclusion. But the arbiters did order the removal of his accounting firm, Eisner & Lubin, which the investors said allowed the Palace books and records to fall into "disarray." The firm, the investors had argued, had become so extensively involved in Helmsley affairs over the years that it could not produce an impartial analysis of his books.

Feelings still run bad in the Palace investor case.

"Here's a man," said Fields, "who turns around to his limited partners, as we read it, who didn't put any of his money into the project, and says, 'You owe me another $20 million.' How do you explain that? It's a guy taking a shot. But he met his match."

Bill Kimpton is perhaps the most impartial observer of the case in that his allegiances are balanced. "For a period there, I was like a big piece of Swiss cheese," he said. "Everybody who shot a bullet had to go through me. It was a very painful period. The investors were my friends. The Helmsleys were my friends. In some ways I thought both sides were right. I knew the hotel that Harry and I negotiated to build, sitting on his deck in his apartment in Palm Beach, where we would spend $73 million for this hotel and he would be responsible for all overruns. But the $73 million hotel that I sold my partners was one thing, and the $110 million hotel that was built was another. Harry didn't have any rights to ask them to pay. But on the other hand, the partners ended up getting a much better hotel than he and I had talked about building. So they were both right. But the country being as litigious as it is, everybody held right to the rules of the document.

"Why did he do it?" Kimpton continued. "When I asked him afterward, he said, 'Well, I had to try it.' He said, 'Right is right, and I shouldn't have to follow the rules here.' "

All told, the arbiters awarded the investors $757,616, to be paid by Helmsley. Helmsley's defenders point out that the investors' legal fees —estimated by Lapercq to be $500,000, including their hired accountant's charges for roaming through Harry's books—absorbed much of that winning. But Fields said that future savings to the investors from the accounting changes Helmsley was forced to make gave them effective winnings of more than $3 million over several years.

Letaconnoux said he would like to let it all pass. "My intention is not to belabor this whole process. It was unfortunate. It happened. We corrected it and now let's bury the hatchet," he said. The Palace has since proven to be a good investment, he said, earning the investors a return between 17 and 23–24 percent a year. Each year's profits are split this way: The investors get the first $2.3 million. Harry gets the next $2.3 million. And everything over $4.6 million is split fifty-fifty. Also, the hotel management company, owned entirely by Helmsley, gets a $250,000 annual fee, which increases substantially when profits exceed $4.6 million. Thereafter, the management entity gets 25 percent of the net return.

Letaconnoux said he was relieved in 1988 when government investigators probing the separate Helmsley tax-fraud matter didn't call on him to help put it into context. Leona's secretary, Maryann Eboli, said Leona carefully avoided any extraneous billings to the Palace after the investors' dispute. "She felt that the investors were all over her back," said Eboli.

But there was something in the invoices the investors dug out that would have been of interest to the government.

There, amidst the bills for gold leafing and silver rubbing, were invoices for things no one could find. Among them: a mysterious item costing $138,337 paid to Zwicker Electric, "with a notation that at the direction of Leona Helmsley it was to be paid from the current operations in fiscal 1982."

"However," the investors' legal charges went on, "no invoice could be found by the Palace staff for this amount and no explanation has been provided as to what it is for and why it was paid from operations."

Again, from the investors' charges: "A mysterious $1.7 million payment was made by the Partnership to Morse Diesel (Helmsley's construction supervisor for the Palace *and* the Harley [on Forty-second Street]) in July 1981. This amount was subsequently repaid to the Palace. No adequate explanation has been given for this transaction." (Their emphasis.)

Helmsley also tried to bill the partnership for $3,100 paid to Morse Diesel for duct work on the upper floors, but no invoice could be found and the work could not be traced.

At an early stage in the proceeding, Helmsley quickly withdrew some $5 million in charges that he sought to lay on his partners when they challenged the invoices. And in the end he lost on all $20 million. But perhaps the most startling aspect of the investors' investigation is what they did not find, because they did not look. The investors only studied a sampling of the Palace accounts. Hundreds upon hundreds of invoices were passed over because they were for amounts less than $2,000.

Thereafter, Leona was more careful with Palace invoices, Eboli said. Not so with the other Helmsley properties. The same year Harry Helmsley lost to his investors, he and Leona bought their estate in Connecticut and they began using a very complex, incoherent, and inconsistent procedure for billing the home repairs and furnishings. At the minimum, they showed a confused, albeit innocent, system of accounting. At the maximum, the billings were crafted to avoid paying income tax.

But first, before the state and federal investigators began poring through their accounts with the latter motive in mind, Leona would make hers a face as familiar to the world as the Palace itself.

# CHAPTER 13

# THE QUEEN
# CAMPAIGN

It was only May, and still morning at that. But the heat already shimmered off the streets. The air was sodden. An early summer —Manhattan's sultry, humid, smog-choked version of summer—had caught the city off guard.

It was hotter still inside the Fifth Avenue offices of Taylor-Gordon, Aarons & Co. The president, Elaine Taylor-Gordon, was on the phone to the building manager, furious. Construction workers had knocked out the air conditioner ten days earlier. And one endless heat wave later, her advertising agency staff was sagging.

Taylor-Gordon fumed into the phone, refusing ambiguity. "I want to know why and I want to know when," she said, at the same time waving a visitor into a seat. A sign in her office quoted Walter Lippmann: "Only a mediocre person is always at his best."

But for all that duress, a much bigger problem for Taylor-Gordon had just walked through the front door, in the hands of a bicycle messenger dressed in black tights. He gave the receptionist two large, flat envelopes from *The New York Times Magazine*—proofs for the latest Helmsley hotel ads.

Taylor-Gordon and client were at a critical juncture. Leona Helmsley was getting trounced in public. Almost weekly there were news headlines about the tax-fraud charges pressed against her and Harry. Gossip columns flared her latest feuds with a fur-coat cleaner. Magazine cartoonists turned up the volume of their lampoons. Even rival hoteliers smelled blood. "Palace with Queen: $210," a competitor's ad in the *Times* said smugly in the summer of 1988, showing the Helmsley Palace brass-and-glass birdcage marquee, and then: "Palace *without* Queen: $130," it countered, with a shot of its own more sedate hotel front. "We wouldn't settle for an overpriced hotel room, why should you?" read the text. "We'll only charge you for the palace, not the Queen."

If ever an ad campaign had bestirred a negative reaction, Queen Leona took the satirists' prize with her fuming and fretting over the comfort of her paying guests, with her pompous "I wouldn't settle for skinny soap, why should you?" and with her self-revealing "When I married Harry . . ."

But the Queen could not simply be dumped like a drug-doped Ben Johnson or a crazed Mike Tyson, who were banished from the Madison Avenue promo scene overnight. For one thing, the Queen ads had always suffered at the hands of critics while at the same time accomplishing their mission: sending occupancy rates sky high. Somehow, they worked perfectly well on the people who stay at Helmsley hotels, and it was not at all clear that the negatives were starting to spoil that success.

For another, more obvious reason, Queen Leona was safe where other fallen stars would have been snuffed. This was a Queen no one cared to inform she no longer wore clothes. The beheadings she ordered for far lesser offenses were by now well known.

Nine years earlier, the person who gave the world Queen Leona was driving up Florida's seaboard coast to West Palm Beach. She was going to see a man named Harry Helmsley about a job. Joyce Beber, based in Miami, had been referred to Harry by the real estate agent handling sales for his new Miami condominium tower. "He's looking for a new agency," the realtor told Beber. "Talk to him. But pay attention to the wife. She's very strong and I think she'll be a part of the decision."

Beber carried an agency portfolio up to the Helmsleys' West Palm Beach penthouse. Harry was somewhat removed during that first encounter, Beber recalled. He was interested, and polite, but he was not totally there. "He seemed more of a bricks-and-mortar kind of guy at that point," she said. Leona, though, as the real estate agent had guessed, was riveted to the more artistic matter at hand. Barefoot, wearing shorts and no makeup—"naturally pretty," said Beber—Leona pored over the ads. She won Beber's respect by picking the ones that Beber also thought best.

"[The ads] were for the Boca Raton Club and Hotel, and they had themes like 'At Boca Raton, we never forget that you're the guest.' They showed the payoffs for good service," said Beber. "One of the ads she liked a lot had a picture of a little boy in a big glamorous dining room with a vaulted ceiling, and this little boy, who looked a little petulant, had ordered a peanut butter sandwich and he got it on a silver tray. Another ad showed an umbrella being held over a golfer."

Leona almost cried out, "That's what the hotel business is all about: service." (Indeed, the silver tray came to life at least once at the Palace. A Manhattan executive was entertaining his young daughter with brunch before a Broadway matinee. The girl left behind her dental retainer. They fretted during the show, rushed back to the Palace. The headwaiter bade them wait but a minute, went into the kitchen, and came back out with a silver tray holding the retainer wrapped in cellophane.)

Leona told Beber to send "Mr. Helmsley" a letter of agreement. "She was very deferential to him at that point. Very polite and respectful," said Beber, whom the Helmsleys then hired, at first to advertise the Miami condos. That campaign did very well, helping to sell out the apartment-house tower even before it opened. Beber also got a firsthand look at the Helmsley sales technique. As is typical of other amenities in condo projects, the poolside cabanas were selling separately for $20,000. At one point someone suggested giving a cabana to a buyer of one of the million-dollar penthouses—a very expensive apartment by Miami standards in 1980. It was meant to be a "closer," like a car dealer handing a toaster-oven to someone who couldn't quite make up their mind. But Harry Helmsley said no to the cabana idea. It was not because he was cheap so much as it was his calculation that the freebie would cheapen the apartment and prompt the buyer to start chipping away at the million dollars.

The Helmsleys then brought Beber, and her creative director, Tad Distler, to Manhattan to work on the Palace when it opened later that year. The first ad was a pre-opener, recounting the six years of effort by thousands of people that went into its creation. Of course, they used the revisionist account of the Palace creation. The second ad heralded the actual opening of the hotel by trumpeting the employees. Beber used the lines that became Leona's motto: "If you weren't the best at what you do you wouldn't be here." The Palace was the best hotel in the world, and so it hired the best, the ad said.

The Helmsleys, meanwhile, had opened the less grand, 800-room New York Harley on Forty-second Street, and business was bad. Occupancy rates couldn't get above 24 percent, compared with city averages in the high 60s. The problem in large part was location. Harry liked to say the hotel was "just around the corner from the United Nations." But the city hadn't yet beat out the vice crowd that dominated that eastern end of the boulevard, and Harley guests were better off driving up on motorcycles by the same name than in taxis or limos. They had to step over pimps and prostitutes to get in the door. Leona asked Beber to take a shot at the Harley, and out of Leona's own frenzy a campaign was born.

"We went to the Palace for a meeting," Beber recalled. "She was conducting several at the same time, looking at towels she was thinking of buying for the Harley, big towels, and looking at big coffee cups. She would pick them herself. Her meetings were always tumultuous, a lot of people coming and going. She's a restless person, and likes to be coming and going all at once. She actually was reading all those comment cards, and if something was wrong she would track down what was wrong and would wring the person out who did it. And she would apologize to the guest. One time, she called somebody on the phone and said, 'I'm sorry the air conditioner was noisy. I hope you'll come back again.' " Awaiting their turn with Leona, Beber and Distler took it all in and it produced an image immediately.

"I thought, this is an amazing thing," said Beber. "You've got a lady here who is not just a very rich lady because she married Harry. She's a lady who is very customer-oriented. And I realized this was the thing that could differentiate the hotel—this lady who is actually watching over the hotel this way."

At first Leona was reluctant. She said it might cause a security problem for her to show up in her own ads. Beber persisted. Leona consulted with Harry, who said, by all accounts, "Do it." And the next day Leona told Beber, "O.K., show me what you mean."

Leona rejected Beber and Distler's first proposal, whose copy read something like "I hate skinny soap." She said it was too harsh, and she balked at the word "hate." "I would never use the word 'hate,' " Leona said. And so was born the theme: "I wouldn't settle for . . ." Week after week, Leona popped up in the Sunday *New York Times Magazine* in a business suit saying things like "I wouldn't drink from a plastic glass. Why should you?" and "I insist on excellent service. Why shouldn't you?" and "I wouldn't get along without a magnifying mirror. Why should you?" Several paragraphs of ad copy fleshed out the headlines. "You don't have to settle for an ordinary Manhattan hotel room and ordinary bath," read one. "For the same price you can stay at The Harley, New York's finest hotel. I've made sure that the baths of all 800 rooms have a two-sided extension mirror, and the kind of lighting you need for shaving and makeup, so you can look your best for any meeting. And, if you think I just got you a mirror, wait till you see your toothbrush, shampoo, shower cap, clothesline, scale and bathroom phone." And usually there was a kicker: "We're going to be your favorite hotel."

The ads worked. Nothing else changed about the Harley marketing, but occupancy went from 24 to 80 percent. And Harry underwent a remarkable transformation. For the preceding four or five decades, he had limited Helmsley Enterprises to the driest of dry industry ads. He would take, for example, the coveted top left corner of the centerfold in an annual *New York Times* real estate supplement. Three paragraphs of tiny print talking about "dynamic real estate markets" and "revitalization and growth" ran next to a tiny black-and-white photo of Harry B. Helmsley in one of his two business suits. But overnight, after seeing the occupancy rates soar, Harry became a believer in what must have seemed to him the kind of advertising only Procter and Gamble did. And Beber got her second lesson in business the Helmsley way.

"Instead of being ecstatic, the first thing he said was: 'Raise the room rates.' And we were reluctant. We gave him a little argument on that, 'cause the ads had a tag line that said a great hotel doesn't need to be expensive. We felt sure the occupancy would fall. But he said, 'No, raise the price.' It went from $80 to $90. And we did lose occupancy, but it came back. And he raised the rates again, to $100, and the occupancy fell and then came back again. And each time he made more money. He was into the bottom line like nobody I had ever met all the years I've been in business."

Not long after that, the Harley began selling gift certificates, and Beber got another look at the more irrational Helmsley affection for profit. The certificates worked like any other: prepay for a room and present it to someone as a gift. The certificates were advertised in a separate magazine campaign, and when the accounting came in it was clear the ads were not generating a big enough response to merit the cost. Beber suggested dropping them. Leona and Harry both disagreed, adamantly so.

"It was absolutely amazing how much they loved the idea of those certificates," said Beber, "and I couldn't figure it out. Then she told me, 'But you don't understand. We get to hold their money. And some people never even use the room.' "

Beber and Distler—now heroes to Helmsley Enterprises—turned their attention to the more stately Helmsley Park Lane Hotel. They put Leona into a different character role to fit the setting. They sat her down at an antique desk-table, with Central Park in the background, penning replies to her loving guests. Distler insists the letters were real, though a gossip columnist discovered eventually that the names at least had been concocted—to protect the privacy of the real letter writers, Helmsley's publicity agent quickly reported.

But some of the responses were so gushy, sickly sweet, or bizarre that many readers questioned their authenticity, if not their style. A man from Boston wrote to bless the hotel concierge for helping him get Broadway tickets, and Leona wrote him back to tick off her favorite plays—all having the words "Park Lane" in their title. A Mrs. Emily Peterson, writing to compliment the hotel, mentioned that she was a sky diver from Los Angeles. So, Leona responded, she must be an expert on finding good views. "Mrs. Peter Stetson," Leona addressed one guest who had written to say she enjoyed getting rolled around in her Park Lane sack. "Congratulations and thank you for the birth announcement. I doubt, however, whether I can attribute the conception of your baby boy to the amenities in your suite as you mentioned in your letter. This time Mother Nature deserves the credit. May I humbly suggest that you name the baby 'Lane' to celebrate a night you'll always remember." Again, the ads worked in terms of drumming up business. Industry analysts who get their hands on occupancy rates say the Park Lane has continued to do well in the face of mounting competition.

After those two campaigns, the Palace itself came easy. And the image of Leona as Queen just rolled out of the imaginations of Beber and Distler. They merely had to watch Leona in action. She walked right into the Palace ads, regally dressed and sweeping her arms across the grandeur. "It's the only Palace in the world where the Queen stands guard."

Getting Leona to model was easy, said Distler. "She's a ham. She loves to get in front of the camera," he said. Even Harry was game. In 1986, as a favor to Beber, both Harry and Leona modeled clothes for a Miami client of Beber's. Harry, understandably, was "not terribly comfortable." But Leona lapped it up, slipping into a low-cut, provocative gown and playing the part of a temptress against a posh pink backdrop. "It was a wonderful feathered gown with a long stole," said Distler, whose arm appeared in the photo holding the boa.

Leona also seemed better able to refrain from her explosions when the cameras were on her. Only once did she lose control. She was in front of the Harley on Forty-second Street, which was partially blocked to traffic. And down from the bluff came the Tudor City residents with their picket signs. They'd gotten under her skin once before by setting up a small picket line outside the Palace on opening night. Take your signs and shove them, Leona now effectively told the tenants Harry was battling. She had to be taken inside the hotel.

Leona did differ from her ad agents on the matter of supporting roles in her ads. She insisted on using the hotel staff. It was not, as she said now and then, for authenticity's sake. She flat out refused to pay modeling fees, or even the lesser amounts charged by mere moonlighting actors. Distler once had to sit at the piano himself because everyone in the hotel looked stiff at the keys. As a result, the staff in her ads generally look terribly pained, standing rigid and keeping their eyes off the Queen. Pity the poor peons, is the most immediate reaction in seeing them with their tails between their legs.

Aside from that, both Beber and Distler said they found working for Leona a joy. "It was our only agency where we worked directly with the chairman, so getting a decision was sort of a pleasure. If she said, 'Yes, I want it that way,' that was enough," Distler said. They were disappointed, then, when Leona gave them the boot in 1981, just as they were bringing all three campaigns to a head. But Leona flipped ad accounts almost as often as she flipped hotel managers.

Beber and Distler were let go when Leona was convinced by an aide, Bill Dowling, that he could do the advertising job in-house. Dowling freaked when new ads started coming due, and he hired his friend Jane Maas. "Handmaiden to the Queen," Maas titled the short chapter in her autobiography that deals with Leona, and she spoke of the same blissful experience with Leona as her predecessors had had, initially. She wrote glowingly of her first meeting.

"We met at the Park Lane for lunch. Leona swept toward the dining room with Bill Dowling and me in her wake. She stopped short and beckoned to a staffer stationed near the door. 'You. Yes, you with the dirty fingernails. Come here.' The little man recoiled. Leona looked down in a fury. 'Get those fingernails clean or don't come back tomorrow.' She started away then turned back. 'I'll be here to check on you.' Greeting the maître d' in the dining room, Leona turned from tigress to pussycat. No one I have ever met is more gracious than Leona at her most gracious. I was charmed. All over the dining room, heads turned as guests realized who had just entered. They were charmed. Waiters and busboys snapped to attention. I thought most of the staff looked scared to death. Later I learned they were."

Leona threw Maas her usual low-budget offer: "Do a good job for us, sweetheart, and I'll help you get lots of other clients. You can be a big, successful agency." She put Maas up in Harry's Graybar Building, introduced her to her dressmaker, Julia, invited her to a few "Wild About Harry" parties, and then, a few months and a few fights later, Maas too was fired. Maas said of her former boss, "She comes on as extremely forthright, but that turns into brutality. She's icy, without compassion. She is remorseless and pitiless."

Paul Elson figured much the same, but he can shrug off his interaction with Leona because his attorneys handled it. Elson, a professional photographer and a friend of Maas, was commissioned in 1982 by Leona to shoot the New York Harley on Forty-second Street. Elson had built both a good reputation and a specialty in hotel advertising. His portfolio included brochures for the Marriott and Sheraton chains, as well as the Helmsleys' St. Moritz, for which he won the best brochure of 1981 award from the Hotel Sales Management Association. Elson and an assistant moved into the Harley for four days. They concentrated on between twelve and fifteen scenes, slowly and methodically shooting a roll at each scene. The hotel executive staff hovered, but otherwise Elson enjoyed the shooting. "It was a nice hotel. The decor was nice. The people were very nervous about having us around, especially the general manager. I don't know what had been said, but he was an excitable type."

The best of some eight hundred slides were submitted. Maas thought they were fine. Leona did not. She rejected them, sending them back to Elson through Maas. "I never did find out what she thought was wrong with it, but she didn't like the photography, I guess, and decided she would not pay," said Elson, who was left holding his bill for approximately $10,000. Maas wrote that later Leona said, " 'That bedroom was a mess. It looked cluttered. I like bedrooms *without* people.' I have been turning that remark over in my mind for several years."

Elson offered to correct any technical irregularities in the photos. Leona agreed to meet with him, then changed her mind. "Tell him to sue me," Leona told Maas. "Tell him to stand in line." He did. And the state Supreme Court judge found he was entitled to his entire fee. "The judge was thoroughly inappreciative of Leona Helmsley's point of view," Elson said modestly. Actually, the judge called his work on the Harley "lush and beautiful."

Beber and Distler were rehired. They revived all three original ad campaigns, and lasted four years this second time around. They again had a falling-out—this time over none other than Donald Trump. In short, Leona claimed that they had taken on a Trump project in Palm Beach that was inherently conflicting with Helmsley Enterprises. Beber said there had been only preliminary talks when Leona fired her. Both sides sued: Beber asked Leona for $1 million in alleged unpaid fees; Leona countercharged Beber with stealing from her. The suits were scheduled to go to trial in 1988, but were delayed.

Enter Elaine Taylor-Gordon and a new honeymoon phase. She, as do Beber, Distler, and Maas, speaks highly of Leona's strengths, especially her decision-making abilities. "I prefer and my partner prefers working with clients who have a sense about where they want to go," said Taylor-Gordon, who, with partner and creative director Larry Aarons, took over the Helmsley advertising account in late 1986. "Otherwise you're hunting in the dark. Mrs. Helmsley has a very strong sense of self and she has a vision of where she wants her hotels to go."

"And that's a positive thing for a client," said Aarons. "Because there are those who will say, 'Just show me, just show me, and then I will see what somebody else thinks.' But when they are very definite about what they want, and know exactly how to attack the problem and how to solve it, it works."

"She knew exactly what she wanted, and she wanted something head and shoulders above everybody else," Taylor-Gordon said. But doesn't every client want that? Yes, she answered, "but not every client can articulate that. She knows what is going on in the field, in terms of other people's advertising. She knew what she liked and didn't like. She knew what she wanted and she could tell you that. And you always know where you stand with her."

All told, Beber and Distler are pleased with their work. "Whether you love her or hate her, I think the advertising was impactful, memorable," said Beber. "The Queen was mean-spirited, but it meant that she ran a tight ship. We hoped that people would be responsive, and see it was all for the public's benefit. The big soaps. The coffee cups. Hangers that come out of the closet. Nobody would not check into a hotel because the hangers didn't come off, but it made you think she paid attention to all such details. It titillated. It triggered. It made people curious. It didn't necessarily make them like her, but it made them feel that somebody out there was very tough for the customer's benefit, and that the guest would benefit."

They also defend themselves from critics who believe the ads cost more than the business they drum up. They have been prolific—running in the *Times, The New Yorker,* and sundry in-flight magazines, often three or four ads to an issue. Some guessed the annual cost was $20 million, but Beber said that's ridiculous. She said the campaign cost only about $3 million annually, sometimes less. The only year the budget went much higher, more than doubling, was in the early 1980s when the Helmsleys admitted their mistake and changed the name of the Forty-second Street Harley to the New York Helmsley, said Beber.

Many an advertising competitor liked the Beber-Distler approach. "If you asked me to name one campaign for a hotel or a chain of hotels, I couldn't do it," Manhattan ad executive George Lois told the trade magazine *Madison Avenue.* "Out of the dozens and dozens of hotel campaigns in the last ten years, this is the only one that I can think of that's really made an impression. They've created a strong image of hotels where there's a guardian *yenta* who watches over everything." Said another: "Most of their hotels are still relatively new, and the best way to get people in is to make the kind of promises Leona makes. It's a good trial-getting device; her ads are very specific, and they hit the emotional chords of business people who travel."

And if the staff is plainly made to suffer? "The employees in the photos look at her as if they're scared to death," Lois said. "It doesn't seem funny at all—it seems deadly. Her message is, 'Fuck up once and you're fired.' But that wouldn't necessarily bother the upper-middle-class people who go to her hotels. Her attitude fit right in with the mood of the Reagan administration: It's okay to chew out the little guy."

An *Adweek* magazine columnist agreed. "The ads worked, perhaps because the signs of raw money and power clicked in the middle of the Reagan age, when the flaunting of wealth and status became not only correct but enviable," wrote Barbara Lippert. "No doubt, with a decline in general standards, the message of an insane attention to hotel detail struck a chord. The cult of personality worked, too. As with other owner-endorsers, the ego had landed, but so had the message of intense dedication to business."

Others seemed more struck *by* than struck *with* the ads. One industry magazine columnist blustered that Leona "couldn't sell Pepsodent, not to mention hotel rooms." Said the hotelier Seymourian: "The theory is good behind the ads, but her position in the ads overshadows it. It's just an ego trip for her." Lampoons, from cartoons to columns, were merciless. One magazine reader seemed to capture the negative reaction the ads produced. "Dare I hope that in the future I may be spared the sight of an offensive woman on a monstrous ego trip? For years, I folded back the pages of *New York* [a weekly magazine] to avoid looking at Leona Helmsley when her ads were placed next to what I was reading. Do you know of anyone who likes these ads?" wrote Patricia Joralemon of New Jersey.

Some hotel pundits, though, considered the ads brilliant from the vantage of occupancy rates. "If a hotel can house many, can it also care for one?" asked Bunny Grossinger, a columnist for *Lodging* magazine. "The Helmsley Hotels are one of the best examples I know of where the owner-operator projects the image of not only caring but also of being directly involved. If you are one of the many who grit their teeth at the frequency with which Leona Helmsley's countenance is exposed in the media, remember that a major law of advertising is, 'Repeat, repeat, repeat.' And the first law of hotel-keeping is, 'This is my home, and you are a guest in it.' "

But in 1989 Elaine Taylor-Gordon faced the challenge of selling a home where the proprietress had become widely ridiculed, was known for mistreating her staff, and was in danger of going to jail. And yet, the solution was not to out and out dump the Queen, even if that was politically possible, said Taylor-Gordon.

"We talk about USP around here, unique selling proposition. In any product you look for a USP, something to set it apart. And with the Helmsley hotels, that's Leona herself. She is the spokeswoman. She stands for something to the public. She's their brand identification. And I frankly don't believe that you should walk away from that. . . . I just came back from the Motel Hotel Association convention, where I talked about something else, and many, many people mentioned the ads and how effective they are."

On the other hand, she continued, "any advertising campaign continuously needs to be changed. Even Cutty Sark moved away from its ship in the bottle. Advertising loses its punch if it stays the same. You try to evolve." And how to evolve away from the Queen without seeming to be dumping the client?

"Elaine and I sat down and said to ourselves: What else is going to differentiate the Palace from other hotels?" said Aarons. "And after our first interview with management, we just figured it was the landmark status, that this was the unique way to position the hotel. Everybody can talk about how they have softer towels, better food, greater service, how they are there when you need them. That's all a parity product. What we had to do was find something that makes this hotel superior to the rest. And something that shows the customer is treated as if there is none more important in the world than them."

To the rescue came the Japanese and the Germans and the French and everyone else who ever built a true monument to ostentatious wealth. Taylor-Gordon, Aarons settled on a series of full-page glossy ads showing the Matsumota Castle, Versailles, the Linderhof Castle, and the Taj Mahal. "In New York," the ads all say, "it's the Helmsley Palace."

"These are stops on any tourist's itinerary," said Taylor-Gordon. "We did some research, and we discovered that the Palace was right up there with them, because the Villard Houses have had that kind of cachet. The ads say it is beyond comparison, as far as other hotels.

There is no other comparison. In New York, it's the Helmsley Palace. That's a statement of fact. Very definitive."

And Leona? She is relegated to a small, inset head shot. Only her broad grin and the significantly shrunken subtitle—"The only Palace in the world where the Queen stands guard"—are remindful of the old Queen ads.

For her part, Leona has said that the Queen campaign was entirely a put-on. "I didn't do it to be the queen," she said. "I know I'm not a queen." The campaign was all "tongue-in-cheek of course," she said.

Leona may never have realized just how strong her image had become fixed in the American mind. Maybe it was because she never took commercial air flights and flipped through the in-flight magazine of nearly every carrier to find herself alternately smiling or goading someone. Maybe it was because she couldn't get past her insecurities to see that she had indeed become famous, if not yet infamous. Joseph Catania recalled that Leona was forever surprised at being recognized on the street, and genuinely so. "Everywhere we went people would instantly know who she was and come up to say something to her," he said. "And she never seemed to understand that would happen. We would go places in a hurry and I would suggest maybe taking another door to avoid having to stop and talk to people and she would say, 'No, no one will recognize us,' and then of course they would."

But those around her knew the Queen campaign was all too real, and there was a downside to the Queen ads that neither ad agent nor publicist could fix. Two types of people in Leona's life came to resent the ads as they resented her. Some were hotel staff. Others were contractors, or retained professionals, or suppliers. And more than one of those who would tip off the state and federal prosecutors would mention her ads with the taste of venom still in their mouths.

It could be that the Queen Leona campaign brought her enemies to her door. But what is certain is that both she and Harry were racking up enemies like bowling pins.

---

## CHAPTER 14

# WRESTLING
# THE WORLD

ON DECEMBER 13, 1984, VINCENT SCLAFANI AND SIX OF HIS MEN PULLED up to a New Jersey warehouse with a very large truck. They were met on the loading dock by Gerald Dubin.

The encounter was not friendly. Dubin was being sued by Leona Helmsley and Deco Purchasing, the Helmsley hotel supplier for which Sclafani worked. They exchanged a few curt words. Dubin brought out a pallet of cartons. Sclafani and crew opened one box, turned it upside down, counted the 392 plastic vials that spilled out, repacked and weighed it. Then they loaded the truck with sixty cases, making sure each was the same weight. Now and then, one of his men furtively stuffed his pockets with loose vials.

Sclafani went off to make a telephone call, and came back in ten minutes with news for Dubin. He would take only sixteen of the sixty cases. No way, Dubin replied, they were Sclafani's now. The accounts differ as to what happened next. But it's agreed that Sclafani, after making another call or two, unloaded all sixty cases and left the warehouse empty-handed.

Six days later Sclafani was back. This time he and his crew merely opened a series of cases to inspect the contents. Dubin made them all crowd into a six-by-six-foot area, upsetting Sclafani by drawing an imaginary line across which he forbade anyone to step, especially the pocket-stuffer. Sclafani took two vials from an untold number of cartons and drove off again in a huff.

Several weeks later, attorneys for both sides were back in court complaining bitterly to the judge about the warehouse sparring. They pointed fingers. They bluffed motion and countermotion. Leonard Sand was fit to be tied. As a federal judge in Manhattan, Sand had seen some silly fights and tortuous legal maneuvering. But here were grown people driven to utter childishness, fighting over a few thousand tiny plastic vials with all the vigor of drug dealers beating their brains out for cocaine. This bunch merited a little scolding, the judge figured, or this case would never go away.

"Let me very frankly tell you my perception of this whole litigation," Sand fumed. "It has been totally blown out of proportion, of which this application is a further symptom. This was a relatively simple commercial dispute with respect to some soap. I think it involved $170,000. The amount of counsel time which has been expended in this matter has got to have been a multiple of the underlying amount in dispute."

Soap? Judge Sand did not misspeak. The warehouse and courtroom sparring was over liquid soap, and some shampoo, bath gel, and hand lotion, all given a chemical coconut scent and shot by machine into tiny opaque plastic vials. They cost Leona at most 40 cents apiece and as little as 15 cents. They were the freebies her housekeepers rolled around in their carts, making sure each bathroom had a full supply each night.

But this was no mere tussle over coconut soap that landed on Sand's docket. Three of the four attorneys before him that day were representing Leona Helmsley. She was furious at Dubin, whom she had accused twice by then of trying to cheat her. And as a growing number of people were coming to discover, she never, ever let anything go by. Neither has Harry, very often.

~

Not all of the Helmsleys' disputes wind up in court. Harry has worked hard to keep his syndicates from seeing the light of litigation. He will settle the rare investor complaint, even if he thinks he is right, just to keep from opening his records. By having privately hired arbiters hear the evidence and arguments behind closed doors, even his fight with the Palace investors was structured to keep it all in the family. Records of that case were released by the investors for this book only at request.

Other times, the people Leona and Harry fought were too weak to battle back in court, or they found other means. Stuart and Ruth Landau were fortunate to have a buildingful of friends and a newspaper columnist take their side in a lease dispute with Harry Helmsley and Irving Schneider, his partner in a large, nondescript office building in the garment district of Manhattan. The Landaus had fully expected to renew the five-year lease on their newsstand when it came due in April 1988. They had agreed to redo their floor, paint the walls, and to tough out a more than doubling of their monthly rent, from $700 to $1,500. Then came the eviction notice. They were stunned. So were their customers. From throughout the building tenants swarmed down to the defense of Stu and Ruthie. "I am quite frankly outraged," Jeffrey D. Roth, treasurer of Vivanti Sportswear, Inc., wrote to Helmsley management. "Not only do the Landaus provide a much-needed service to this building, but they create a pleasant atmosphere for all those employed here. Above all they are hard-working people who run an honest business."

A petition gathered dozens upon dozens of signatures. Columnist Dennis Duggan happened onto the scene and recognized their shop as an oasis. "These candy and cigar stands are to many New Yorkers what the pot-bellied stove in the general store is to Vermonters—a place to visit and to schmooze," he wrote. "In a city where the ability to rush from one place to another head bent to avoid eye contact is respected, these stands are tiny redoubts where some form of civility can be shown without danger." The Landaus enlarged the column and posted it next to their display of the current *People* magazine issue with Leona in Harry's arms on the cover, next to the screaming headline: "Greedy, Greedy, Greedy." They beat the eviction without having to sue.

More often than not, however, the Helmsleys seem to end up in court. Perhaps that's inevitable, given the huge number and range of people they've done business with over the decades. But Leona and Harry both have been extremely litigious even for people of their working pace and financial stature. According to some sampling of records, they have rushed into court far more often than other property managers and landlords. They also seem to have been sued at a far greater rate. One 1988 tally by a weekly business paper found the recent litigation involving Helmsley Enterprises to number about 110 lawsuits, compared with a mere nine for the likes of developer William Zeckendorf, Jr., who was putting together some very spectacular and difficult apartment developments that could just as easily have spurred litigation, but didn't. Several other busy developers scored equally low.

A more accurate search would be immensely time-consuming. Sometimes Harry and Leona use their own names, but often their lawsuits are filed under the title of a subsidiary or an obscure corporation set up only for one venture or property. However, even their most obvious cases have left a trail that is long. The Helmsleys have sued or were sued in four of New York City's five boroughs—Staten Island being the exception. There's extensive litigation in Florida and California. In New York, they appear on docket sheets and archives records through the full spectrum of courts—from Small Claims, where the ceiling on judgments is $2,000 and the typical plaintiff plunks down the $5.50 fee to convince a Judge Wapner that they lost $168 to a slipshod rug installer, to U.S. District Court, where civil complaints routinely are adorned by claims in increments of a million dollars.

Of course, much of the Helmsley litigation has undeniable merit, such as several suits brought against guests who failed to settle their bills upon checking out. Both Leona and Harry have also fought off a long string of personal-injury suits that are common to property owners, and at times are more than a little suspect. Just months after the

Palace opened, two men from Hawaii asked for $2 million after alleg-
edly cutting their hands on a windowsill in their penthouse bedroom.
Mary Washington, forty-six, was trapped in a lift for an uncertain
amount of time and then passed out when she was finally freed. She
asked for her lost wages, $400 a week, saying she was unable to work
because of head trauma, poor concentration and forgetfulness, para-
cervical neck spasm (whiplash), and a "severe blow to her self-esteem."
Washington lost her case, as did several others who filed suits like hers.

Once, Harry Helmsley sued to defend the usurping of his own
good name. In 1977, a firm by the name of Helmsley Real Estate Co.
set up shop in a small New York State town called Liverpool. The
Helmsley Real Estate Co. proceeded to buy, sell, and otherwise broker
and manage parcels of commercial land and buildings. Things went
well for the firm until 1981, when Harry got a few calls by mistake
from people who wanted the Helmsley Real Estate Co. of Liverpool.
Harry tracked the firm down and promptly filed suit to force it to
change its name. He even went to the extent of paying someone to go
through three dozen metropolitan phone books to prove that in all
those areas no more than one other Helmsley unrelated to Harry existed.

Harry most frequently, perhaps, is wearing his landlord hat when
he goes or is taken to court. In the New York borough of Queens, for
example, there is case after case—dozens of them—filed against his
Fresh Meadows apartment complex entity, for everything from racial
discrimination to excessive rents to harassment. Harry the broker has
also been a frequent litigator. When he feels cheated out of significant
sums of money, he hammers back fast and hard.

In 1986 he took on a pack of West German financiers—Deutsche
Anlagen-Leasing GmbH, DAL Multinational-Leasing GmbH of
Mainz, and Westdeutsche Landesbank Girozentrale of Düsseldorf—
alleging that they failed to pay him $1,065,000 in brokerage fees for his
role in selling the Gotham Hotel on Fifth Avenue. That case against the
West Germans is particularly revealing of the way Helmsley conducted
his brokerage business in a very tough world.

The hotel was built in 1905, with an ornate beaux arts architectural
style enwrapping its twenty-three stories and 254 rooms. In 1979, a

hotelier named René Hatt bought a long-term lease from Sol Goldman, an infamous New York landlord who left a legacy of embattled tenants when he died later. Hatt planned on creating a world-class luxury hotel. The money was provided by a consortium of West German banks, all named in Harry's suit. In 1984, the whole thing came apart. Hatt, hit by cost overruns and disagreements, bailed out, and the banks hired Helmsley to dispose of the property. They signed a broker's agreement on August 23 that was to give Helmsley six months to sell the lease. He got a monthly retainer of $50,000 and a minimum $600,000 fee upon sale, with additional sums in increments of $100,000 depending on the date of the sale and the price the lease fetched. In November 1984 the lease was sold for $45 million to an investment group called Imperial Holding Corp., headed by Arthur Cohen, a prominent real estate developer. But problems arose to hold up the sale's formal closing—problems that Helmsley claims the West Germans did not tell him about, including their own legal feuding, a clouded title, a claim by Goldman that the leases were in default, and a third mortgage, or loan, on the property for $15 million held by Banque Worms SA in France. The contract signing was delayed beyond the deadline for Helmsley's delivering a seller. So on July 10, 1986, when Harry sent the West Germans his balance due of $900,000, the investors effectively told him he had his facts wrong. Harry sued and the case is still pending, even as the hotel lease was resold in 1988 to a Hong Kong-based chain for $127 million.

While Harry has tended to fight mostly with tenants, business associates, and tax assessors coast to coast, Leona has wound up in court in a good many battles with her hotel staff. And many would kick up some potentially embarrassing dust.

Ralph Schwing, for example, said he was hired as a security guard at the Park Lane and Palace hotels on July 14, 1980, and then fired unfairly three weeks later. He sued for $12,250 in pay and $350,000 in damages, charging he was harassed because of a mixed racial ancestry. Schwing settled, but not until he began to tell the court about an incident in the Palace in which his security chief fired six shots from a pistol into the walls and floor of the office space being created on the fifth floor. There's no police record to substantiate the claim.

Avner Shakarov, for another, settled his case in December 1987 after charging racial discrimination (he is a Russian Jew). Shakarov was hired in October 1985 to serve as assistant chief engineer at the Palace, and was dismissed a year and one month later. But in the course of the litigation, he charged that he was dismissed in part because he complained to a superior that the Palace fire safety sprinkler system was partially inoperable and that it "created a substantial and specific danger to the health and safety of the public." Shakarov told the court that management had no interest in his determinations. Again, there's no city record to substantiate the claim, but fire department inspections in New York are many years behind schedule.

And when Leona fired chef Andre René, the entire workings—or misworkings as they might be—of her Palace kitchens came out in court.

Papers Leona's attorneys submitted to the court lay out a two-day Palace diary that reads like a comedy of errors scene from a *Masterpiece Theatre* episode. It certainly raises some questions about René, but more than that it challenges Leona's image as a hands-on, in-the-kitchen, behind-the-scenes instiller of efficient perfection. In a 1985 memo, Paul Wolman, the hotel's food and beverage director, presented the following synopsis:

• Mr. and Mrs. Gutman Party—refund of $2,600 due to poor quality food.

• Wed., Dec. 11th, Reuben H. Donnelley Dinner. No vichyssoise was prepared. A last-minute substitute with chilled cream of cucumber was offered.

• Thurs., Dec. 12th. No chef was scheduled for Ortho Pharmaceutical Breakfast. The Room Service Chef was not advised of any special party.

• Chef René has lost control of the stewarding department. When it was brought up to Chef René that more whipped butter was needed for lunch in all of the food and beverage outlets, he blamed the stewarding department for not providing enough butter crocks.

• Wed., Dec. 11th, Trianon Room. Mr. Nevins, Hotel Guest, ordered a lamb chop rare and it was cooked well done. Guest was upset and maître d' replaced it with a roast sirloin special.

• Wed., Dec. 11th, Trianon. Mr. Bernstein, table of six visitors, ordered his meal at 8:30 P.M. and it came out at 9:45 P.M. The kitchen forgot to fire a sirloin ordered by one of Mr. Bernstein's guests. When finally the entrees were served, the food was cold, and Mr. Bernstein complained about the "Duck Normande—inedible." Mr. Tom Fennelly had to comp. dessert and coffee, he also took the duck out of the check.

Maybe Leona was out of town. The memo went on to blame René for everything. René is now the executive chef for the Rainbow Room restaurant atop Rockefeller Center. In an interview at his office, he sighed and went through the memo's charges item by item. "The vichyssoise, I agree. I had it prepared, but it was not there to service. It was misplaced or something, but it is a fact that it was not there," he said in a French accent as thick as his sauces. "The convention, I was not advised about. The stewards, I did not control. I had nothing to do with them. The sirloin, I don't know about that. The duck, well, from the guest's perspective, he is always right. But you roast every duck like every other duck. Some are tough. You don't ever know, and now and then you get complaints."

René, a soft-spoken man, was stirred by the whipped-butter complaint. "That's a lie. We had them. The problem was that there were not enough empty crocks. We ran out of crocks because the busboys kept putting them in the garbage. I mentioned that in our meetings, that I had no butter crocks, no butter crocks, but nobody listened."

Leona, ironically, tried to disavow any knowledge of disorder in the Palace kitchen—disorder René had conceded, faulting circumstances beyond his control.

So René's attorney excerpted a memo from Wolman to Manfred Braig, the hotel manager, to show she indeed knew what was going on. The memo also is typical of the formality Leona insisted even her key employees maintain in referring to her. "Our President, Mrs. L. Helmsley, shared with me her desire to see some changes in the food quality and presentations," Wolman wrote. "Our President wishes, and has asked me, to hire back Mr. Joel Huchet, whose professionalism is well known. My task would be the implementation of new specials, more in the taste of our President, and more to the liking of our guests."

René believes he was caught in a power struggle and ousted to make room for someone's ally in that game. Regardless, René said he would not have taken Leona to court had he been dismissed with anything close to politeness or respect. "If they would have just said something to me, anything, fine, I would have torn the contract up. Instead, I get this, this telegram," he said, waving the mailgram that read in full: "This is to inform you that as of today your services are no longer required at the Helmsley Palace Hotel, sincerely, Manfred Braig." (Braig himself later sued Leona when he too was fired.) To make matters worse, René had been on vacation when the mailgram was sent.

Harry battling his tenants and business associates. Leona battling her employees and the professionals she retained. They make a very writ-happy couple. But the picture of the Helmsleys in court is more intriguing than that. The ways they became similar people in life are many. They both are excruciatingly tough business machines, extracting the most from every situation, whether the payoff is immediate or is saved for the next deal. But in one way they did not quite blend. Faced with a no-win, no-gain situation, Harry will read the bottom line and pull back. Leona will not.

No complete picture of their legal fights even in New York is available, since records prior to 1970 generally are discarded or shipped off to archives closed to the public. But there is one very telling, albeit narrow, glimpse of their presence in Manhattan Civil Court, a medium-level court where judgments can range up to $10,000. Prior to marrying Leona, Harry Helmsley filed suit in that court five times in 1970, seven times in 1971, and five times in 1972. In 1973, the first full year they were married, Harry Helmsley sued seventeen times—as much as the previous three years combined. And thereafter, the number kept rising until lawsuits pressed by Harry or Leona or both show up in that or another court almost every week.

Coconut soap was by no means an isolated case. But it is one of the more vivid illustrations of the emotion that Leona let seep into her business judgment, of the way she dealt with suppliers and contractors, and of her belief, deeply held, that the whole world was out to steal from her.

No one faults Leona for being a tough buyer or a tough negotiator. If they did, she certainly could cry discrimination, because Harry was the toughest and she tried to emulate him, as in this exchange caught by *New Woman* magazine:

> The toothbrush salesman holds up three brushes in different colors. "These are the new brushes," he says nervously. "We hope you like them."
>
> She takes one and begins to brush some fish from her teeth. "Too hard and too expensive," Leona replies, "but I like the way it looks and feels in my hand."
>
> "If we make them softer and cheaper but keep the original design, will it be O.K.?" he asks.
>
> "Yes, but don't forget the cheaper part," she warns. "If I save one penny on one item, I save $12,000. Multiply one piece of soap seven thousand times for seven thousand rooms we stock and you'll see we're heavy purchasers—*and heavy purchasers who pay on time can be fussy.*"

No, it wasn't her tough negotiating that spoiled her relations with vendors. It was her disregard for the trust on which business relationships are built and the obligations inherent in agreements once they are reached. For more than four years, Gerald Dubin, president of Cococare Products, Inc., had done business with Helmsley Hotels. Cococare acted only as a distributor. It had the shampoos and other soap products manufactured in Dayton, Ohio, shipped to its New Jersey warehouse, and then sent out to buyers, including the Palace and other Helmsley hotels in New York.

Then, in April 1983, in the midst of a large contract, Leona called Dubin and asked him to knock 20 percent off the agreed-upon price. Furthermore, Dubin testified, Leona "suggested that Cococare make other payments to her on pain of losing the opportunity of doing further business with the Helmsley hotel chain." In other words, Leona was proposing he pay up or move on, said Dubin.

"I will not dwell on the displays of arrogance and abuse to which I was subjected at the hands of Leona Helmsley," Dubin told the court. "Suffice it to say that, at her deposition in this action, Leona Helmsley testified that she felt free to disregard a prior contractual commitment with a supplier if she could get a different product elsewhere for a few cents cheaper."

Indeed, Leona's testimony was plain. She'd been asked to explain her attitudes about renegotiating an existing contract with vendors in general.

Leona: "They get a lot—when they get a Helmsley hotel they get a lot of additional business all right. Now, they have the opportunity of saying, 'All right, I will meet the price,' or 'Perhaps I have been too high and, therefore, I will give you a discount all right.' . . . If the man is fair, I'd just as soon stay with someone that I had done business with before than to start with a whole new ball of wax. If it has to be done, I do it."

The attorney: "You do what?"

Leona: "I will change my vendor."

The attorney: "What happens to the outstanding purchase orders? . . . Let's say you have a purchase order to purchase a thousand, a million washcloths. The guy has delivered 500,000 of them. You say, 'I can get these for a penny and a half cheaper elsewhere. Could you match my price?' "

Leona: "I will call him in and say, 'I can get the exact identical for a penny and a half less. Will you absorb it?' "

The attorney: "Say he says no."

Leona: "If he says no, I say, 'Then I don't have to be robbed because you tried to hurt the Helmsley.' "

The attorney: "And what happens to that outstanding purchase order?"

Leona: "If he wants to meet the price, I will take it. If he does not want to meet the price, I see no reason in this whole world why I should be subjected to paying more money for the same pencil or the same pen or the same piece of paper."

The attorney: "Even though Deco had previously or the hotels previously agreed to that price?"

Leona: "You know, what you are talking about seems to be a one-way street. In other words, because the Helmsleys are respected, honor-able people and pay their bills, they are the target for a lot of this nonsense that goes on. It's a one-way street. The Helmsleys are the targets. We have to be punished for taking somebody's word as to a price. I don't think that is very fair. And if they're going to be unfair, well, that is up to them. That is exactly what happened."

Leona herself may have felt pressured to lean on Dubin. The Palace operating bills were starting to roll in and everybody, Harry included, was shocked. When Harry was asked by the panel of arbiters hearing the Palace investors case about precalculating the Palace expenses, Helmsley replied, "Well, it wasn't quite that scientific. You see, the thing is—when we opened the Palace, I had no idea what all these amenities would cost. So I was—I did it by the seat of my pants, if you want the truth of it. I figured—I didn't figure there to be any $5 million of purchasing after the hotel was opened, but the fact of the matter is, it came out that way."

Dubin was in a tight spot that day when Leona asked him to meet her new price. She owed him $177,000 for soaps already delivered, and the contract balance called for her to buy $550,000 more, over half of which was already made and waiting to be shipped. But Dubin refused. Leona stopped payment. Dubin sued.

To make a lengthy hearing before a magistrate short, Dubin won hands down on the 20 percent issue. The court had rarely heard some-thing so silly as Leona's view of doing contract business. She was forced to pay him the full agreed-upon $177,000. But then things got rough. Dubin was still suing Leona for much of the contract balance when she had her attorneys throw what in the legal world is a full-force body block. They threatened to depose, or interrogate, all of his suppliers and customers in an effort to determine if anyone else got a price lower than did Leona. Maybe some did, though it's not at all clear how that would have helped Leona's case since her contract said nothing about her getting the best deal in the world. But the question-ing would have hurt Dubin very badly, in time and effort expended alone, and he agreed to settle for about $400,000.

Leona's attorney, Joseph Forstadt, recalled that point in the case. It was the only time he saw Harry step into one of Leona's matters to make a decision. "It was not that he overrode her," said Forstadt. "She refused to make a decision and left it up to him. Why? I think she felt that she was too emotionally involved with the case. There was a lot of name calling, and when the question of settling came up, ultimately she effectively washed her hands of it. But Harry made the decision [to settle]."

Dubin, however, was to have the last laugh. Since shampoo and other creams typically last no more than one year on the shelf, the settlement expressly disclaimed any guarantee that the soap was still good. So by the time Leona was ready to pick up her soap, it had lost much of its stuff.

She sued Dubin, charging he had broken the settlement. That case went back and forth, from warehouse to Judge Sand's courtroom, and finally another federal judge in early 1985—two years after Leona first called Dubin—ended the whole mess by ruling against Leona. "In my view," the judge wrote, "it is absolutely clear that Helmsley was to take the goods 'as is.'"

Was Leona angry? "I suppose she held me responsible for creating the settlement," said Forstadt, who continues to represent Harry Helmsley on several matters. "She chose not to have further contact with me."

But she wasn't through messing with coconut soap yet. Right after her initial falling-out with Dubin, Leona contracted with another supplier, Marietta Packaging of Cortland, New York, for more than two million one-ounce bottles of coconut shampoo and lotion, and yet another legal battle erupted when Leona charged the firm with deviating from an agreed-upon formula. Not so, said Marietta; it was Leona who ordered that the fragrance and color be altered in midstream. That case is pending.

Leona also soon would wage war against a series of contractors who worked on their Connecticut house. But first, before the government came knocking, Harry and Leona were to have the most unbelievable of their court battles. Not with a supplier. Not with a tax collector. Not with another shrewd real estate player. With their very own daughter-in-law. And the pettiness and viciousness with which they pursued her would shock even their friends.

# CHAPTER 15

# A SON'S DEATH

ONE DAY EARLY IN MARCH 1982, LEONA HELMSLEY WAS HAVING LUNCH with her son, Jay Robert Panzirer, at the Park Lane. They dined in the public restaurant.

Panzirer was a familiar sight around the hotel. He lived in Florida, but stayed in a Park Lane suite on his frequent trips to New York. Sometimes his wife, Mimi, and three boys would be along. They had the run of the hotel as though it were their own home, and the staff was instructed to treat them well. That wasn't considered a chore. The family was liked. The bald and bearded Jay was jovial. He had a softer version of his mother's broad smile.

On this wintry day, though, the forty-two-year-old Jay Panzirer looked weary. Inwardly, he had been a sick man for much of his life. He suffered from a terminal heart disease. He had had one bypass operation and once spent an entire year in a hospital bed.

Not long after this particular lunch with Leona, he had gotten more discouraging news from his heart specialist in Boston. Jay, according to Mimi, was taking an experimental medicine and recent testing had shown some irregularities. The doctor wanted him hospitalized immediately for further testing. Jay demurred.

Jay spent part of the lunch with Leona arguing with her about taking some time off from work, recalled the waiter who served them. "He was saying, 'Mother, I'm tired. I've been working hard. I need a vacation.' He was begging," said the waiter, who has asked for anonymity for fear of reprisal from Leona. At least one other person sat at their table, and Jay looked embarrassed.

Leona rebuked him, for reason unknown. The restaurant noise swallowed that fine point of their conversation. The time off might have included the day in early May when she wanted him in New York for the annual real estate industry dinner. She might have had something for him to do in Orlando. Or she may have simply been grousing. Leona liked to remind Jay of the things she had done for him as a grown man. She persuaded Harry to hire him when he needed a better-paying job, as she did for other men in her family. Then she pushed Jay, against Harry's instincts, to the helm of Deco Purchasing. Finally she prodded Harry to expand Deco so it supplied not only Helmsley hotels but all of the office buildings and warehouses owned by Harry or managed by Helmsley-Spear. Jay rode the Deco shooting star with its $22 million annual volume. But it was not Jay Robert Panzirer former salesman without college degree who ran Deco. It was Jay Robert Panzirer the son of Harry Helmsley's wife. Leona expected appreciation of that.

Mimi, when asked about the lunch conversation, recalled that she and Jay had planned a vacation to the northern California wine country in April, the following month. Leona likely knew of that trip, she said, and in any event did not chastise Jay in general for taking vacations from work. "Our problem was she always wanted her and Harry to come along," said Mimi. Nor was Jay a Milquetoast to his mother. But Leona did hound Jay. He and Mimi had a lost weekend once and came back to fifty-eight phone messages from his mother.

"You have business to take care of," Leona told him, according to the waiter's recollection. "I did not give you this business to take a vacation. Be a man. Go down there, and after that you can take your vacation."

Jay did go to Florida, and before the month ended he was dead. He fell ill during a meeting at the Harley Hotel of Orlando, and then, after lying down on a bed, he was hit by the third and final heart attack of his life. The jolt was so strong it knocked him off the bed. His heart literally consumed itself. The coroner found only a cavity in his chest where the ailing muscle once was. Jay died on the floor of the Helmsley hotel.

Leona got the news, oddly, flying to Florida with Harry in their private jet. They just happened to be on their way to West Palm Beach when Mimi reached them in the air. Leona shrieked, and broke down as never before. For two weeks her face was bright red from crying. She would continue to dissolve into tears at the mere mention of Jay's name by anyone—friends, staff, Mike Wallace. Leona, in fact, never stopped crying about Jay's death. And her outbursts are such that some of those closest to her wonder how much is grieving and how much is guilt.

Few knew of the last lunch. But there have been other, more public displays by Leona that exhibit an emotion other than the naturally deep lament of a Jewish mother for a lost only son. One such outburst came during the post-funeral gathering in New York, when Leona suddenly wheeled toward one of her grandchildren and accused the fourteen-year-old boy, inexplicably, of "killing" his father. Another was her subsequent treatment of Mimi over the course of many months. If it were mere grieving which Leona pulled from within herself to hurl at Mimi, then it manifested itself in a viciousness that only Leona Helmsley, the Queen, could muster.

Jay Panzirer spent his life like a person with a terminal but insensible disease. He lived for whatever day it was, and he lived well. There was no sense in squirreling away a retirement account or, on the more personal front, in sustaining any untoward emotional sacrifice for some payoff down the road. Jay married three times. He had four children altogether. He treated his boys, especially, more like buddies than like kids. People typically underguessed his age by five or six years.

Born in 1940, Jay attended lower schools in New York City, the

Cheshire (Conn.) Academy, and then the Philadelphia College of Textiles and Science, according to family-approved records. The college has no record of his graduation. At some point, possibly after his first marriage, Jay moved to California, where one of his former wives now lives. He worked as a salesman, then as a hotel supplier, probably using contacts from his father's hotelier family. Jay never spoke much of Leo to friends, and by some accounts they weren't terribly close after Leona divorced him, but Jay did check in with his father now and then. It was in Los Angeles that Jay spent an entire year in the hospital.

Not long after Leona's marriage to Harry in 1972, Jay was hired by Helmsley-Spear in California. Harry then put him to work for Deco in Orlando. Jay was known as a partier around the Disney World town. He was the kind of guy who would walk into a bar, pull out his wallet, and hand it to the bartender to buy rounds of drinks. Jay made lots of casual social friends. He also won the community's respect for the charitable work he did. One of his last achievements was raising $10,000 for the American Heart Association.

"He played the role of a wealthy young man with a lot of dollars to spread around. He was a real sport. He would buy for everybody," said Phil Blumenfeld, the real estate broker who developed projects for Harry in Florida. Said Joe Ash, whom Harry put in charge of his hotel chain outside of New York: "Jay was very friendly, very likable." Deco's landlord—Harry didn't own that office building—was Charles Turner, a Maitland dentist and friend. "Jay was trying to make a name for himself here," said Turner.

Mary "Mimi" Doyle had moved to Florida in 1972 after divorcing her childhood love. She was born to a New England family and was raised in Englewood, New Jersey, and in Meriden, Connecticut. Her father had been the New York manager for a national construction company. In 1979, Mimi was selling ads for an FM-radio station in Orlando when the Harley opened there. Her boss gave her his invitation to the press party that christened the Harley, and that's where Mimi met Jay.

Mimi is chatty, very attractive, and friendly. That evening Jay was at his best, and he spotted Mimi across the room. "The waiter came over to me, knowing my name, and said, 'Miss Doyle, the gentleman over there asks if there is anything you would care for,' " recalled Mimi. "I said, 'Well, yes, since you mentioned it, I would care for a bottle of Dom Pérignon, but I'll settle for . . ." Too late. Jay sent her a bottle of Dom P. '66.

"I remember I said, 'Wow.' He certainly got my attention. I was impressed," said Mimi.

The hotel manager asked her to stay for a private dinner. She did. Jay asked if he could call her. He did. Mimi and Jay dated, though somewhat tenuously. Less than a month after they met, he proposed, she accepted, and then she backed off. Mimi said she was scared of his illness. "My father died when I was ten of a heart condition and my mother told me, 'The worst thing you can become is a widow,' and I didn't want to become a widow."

But Jay was fun to be around. And Mimi makes no bones about seeing success in his eyes. Having tasted of failed relationships, they both were quick to sense that this one might click. Mimi gave in to Jay and her own intuition. She called him at Thanksgiving, and they married in Orlando on January 12, 1980, making the social pages of the *Orlando Sentinel*. They honeymooned in Europe, then Mimi moved into Jay's large ranch-style house on Lake Maitland, in an affluent suburban area north of Orlando. Jay slipped her into his social life. They played in a tennis league, attended charity balls, made most of the major galas. "They were at the parties we covered all the time," said Lee Yost, founder of a local society paper, *La Femme*.

If Jay felt very open and comfortable in Orlando, he showed the complete opposite personality at the parties his mother and Harry threw in New York. Suddenly, Jay the extrovert was shy, reclusive, hesitant to sidle up to a Gregory Peck or a Sonny Werblin or a Cliff Robertson or any of the mayors and governors attending the soirées. Maybe it was simply a son succumbing to a mother's dominance when he moved in her circle. But people with Jay sensed that he felt totally out of place for other reasons.

"Very often we would be the youngest people there, so we would sit together," said Bill Kimpton, the San Francisco hotelier. "[Mimi] was terrific. And Jay was very nice, and very shy. He was ill at ease in the groups that [Leona] would have him involved in. Harry was very nice to him. Attentive. But Jay just seemed overwhelmed. He just wasn't used to hanging out with the powers of the world like that."

That was understandable, said Seymour Rabinowitz. Jay was not the only one to look around in awe at the pocketbooks Leona and Harry gathered on one dance floor. "At Harry's birthday parties, especially, I would say that within the room there was $10 billion worth of money," Rabinowitz said.

Similarly, Jay never quite grew comfortable with running a business like Deco either.

Deco was, at first, of little consequence to Harry Helmsley. Almost every big chain of motels or hotels—Westin, Hilton, Sheraton—has its own supply firm. They typically provide everything from toilet paper to beds. Deco was set up by Steve Brener in 1974 to serve the blossoming Helmsley chain. Then Deco grew, in two giant leaps. The first expansion came when Harry bought the Hospitality Inns from Sohio in 1979, and the second was when he decided shortly thereafter to start using Deco to supply all his commercial buildings. Harry's reasoning, on record, was based on volume: Deco could do better than, say, many individual purchasers for each property, because it was handling huge amounts of supplies.

"When you go in to buy a million, you can buy it a lot cheaper than if you are buying just a few, for a particular hotel," Harry told his investors, rejecting their contention that the Palace would be better off with its own in-house supplier. "Not true," Harry said. "That's the trouble. Deco can kill you with their volume. They buy cheaper than anybody, and what I find is that as we get more and more volume, we get more and more manufacturers that want to come in and negotiate direct. They don't go through a middleman anymore. They come and we buy direct from the manufacturer." Previous Helmsley suppliers like Cococare were squeezed out of the picture.

Harry had other, private reasons for cherishing Deco, however. For one thing, Deco charged a fat service fee, but only to some of those it served. The fee varied widely depending on Harry's investment in the hotel or building being supplied. Helmsley officials and others familiar with Deco said Harry routinely reduced Deco's fee for properties he wholly or mostly owned. Conversely, he increased the fee for properties he only managed or had a small part of. Mimi, who came to know Deco's operation through her husband, recalls the ratio being a perfect direct inverse proportion.

There was nothing inherently illegal about that rate structure, since Deco itself was wholly owned by Harry, but it did fuel the Palace Hotel cost-overrun case when the investors charged that Deco's "service fee" of 20 percent was excessive, relative both to other hotel supply firms and to other Helmsley hotels. Harry fumed and protested, but the special arbiters found for the investors and knocked Deco's fee down to 5 percent. Other aspects of Deco's financial arrangements exposed in the Palace fight would later pique the interest of government prosecutors. For example, a good portion of Deco's business—as much as $7 million a year in the early 1980s—was not showing up on its books because the hotels being supplied paid immediately through wire transfers of funds. That gave them what is known as an agency relationship, as compared with a supplier-client, and the secrecy gained from avoiding paper invoices accorded Helmsley Enterprises all sorts of accounting possibilities.

At any rate, Deco grew from a five-person, $1 million affair to a company with fifty-five to sixty staffers and an annual volume above $22 million. Harry, at some point, became concerned about Jay's handling of the rapidly expanding Deco. Possibly he was hearing back from his trusted aides. "I liked Jay. But Jay was naïve in a business sense," Rabinowitz said. Ash agreed. "I don't think he was particularly bright. He ran Deco very poorly."

"Jay took care of Jay," said Blumenfeld. "Jay was the son of the multi-multimillionaire mother whose husband was not attentive as to how Jay handled the business's money. . . . Jay was the beneficiary of that opportunity. Anyone who questioned his business aspirations or machinations in a way that might offend Mrs. Helmsley was not likely to remain in the company."

Leona knew the expert business opinion weighed against her well-liked son, and her own attitudes were mixed. At times she tried shoving Jay toward the dedication that she had toward work. Other times he was coddled. "Jay and his mother were constantly battling," said

Blumenfeld. "She wanted him to achieve. She wanted him to also get into real estate in his own right."

Leona and Harry had fights over Jay's involvement in Deco, and one of the few times Harry erupted in visible anger toward Leona was over what Harry believed was Jay's mistake. Jay had discovered the Best Western hotel chain was looking for a supplier, and he put together a proposal. He intended to present it to Harry. But then he left for Europe on his honeymoon with Mimi, and while he was gone Harry sent down his internal auditing crew, who discovered Jay's plans. Harry fumed, thinking them signed and sealed behind his back.

"It was shortly after we were married," Mimi recalled of the ensuing encounter. "I thought it was just a power thing, but, of course, [Harry] didn't want the outside world bringing attention to the books and records of Deco, and that would have done it." Leona, Mimi, Harry, and Jay were all together, and Harry yelled at Leona and Jay, "That's it!"

Harry then said, "One more time and you're both out on your asses!" It was also a rare foul word from Harry, whose tongue was sweet by real estate industry standards.

"It was a very rough time," said Mimi. "Jay was ready to walk after the blowup. He was incensed that they pulled an audit and he asked what I thought of it. I said, 'Look, you're forty. You've had two heart attacks. You don't need this, but basically they leave us alone, and it's the best game in town.' I can look back in twenty-twenty hindsight and know I was in no position to have given that advice. Perhaps Jay would have been happier if he had walked."

Harry thought about moving Deco to New York. But there were two nagging problems with that, he told the Palace investors. Rent was much cheaper in Orlando. So were salaries. So Harry did the next-best thing: he put people he trusted close to Jay. Later, when Jay started to get an itch to expand his horizons and develop some real estate, Harry told Blumenfeld to go help.

"That's one of the reasons I met [Jay]," said Blumenfeld. "He was going to try to convince Helmsley to do a real estate deal in Palm Beach, and Harry said, 'Phil, meet Jay, and get involved.' I love development, and he and I hit it off well. It was important for Jay to trust me, and know I wouldn't turn him in to Harry, and that I would give him credit, even though Harry knew I was behind it. But Jay had good instincts about development. I think the deals he was seeing would have worked."

For Mimi and the Helmsleys, time is basically measured: "Before Jay's Death" and "After Jay's Death."

After the Best Western rift healed, Mimi said she was quickly made to feel part of the Helmsley family. She certainly came away with an intimate glimpse, the pieces of which others confirmed. "Everything was extremely cordial," said Mimi. "We crisscrossed back and forth between our home and theirs for holidays. Easter was in Palm Beach with them. July Fourth was either Palm Beach or New York, wherever they were, to celebrate Leona's birthday. March was to celebrate Harry's birthday. The entire first week of November was in New York for the hotel show, in addition to celebrating Jay's birthday. Then we'd spend a week or ten days out of every month in New York. Not continuously, but whenever we arrived, we would have dinner with them the first night."

Leona would go out of her way to make it a personal family dinner. Jay and Mimi would sleep in a Park Lane suite reserved for them, but they'd hang out in the Helmsleys' duplex, and they would dine there. Leona and Harry have their own cook. Other hotel staff would be called up to serve. After dinner, if they weren't going out, they'd often do what normal families do: rent a movie and watch it on TV.

"Leona was very chatty, open—normal is the word I keep coming back to," said Mimi. "This is someone Jay would talk to every day in terms of business, and I would talk to three times a week, and we'd exchange notes. You tend to see in-laws you're involved with more anyway. There were discussions of business over cocktails, since the object of Jay being up there was business."

Often business in general would linger over dinner. "Inflation was probably a very important subject for everyone at the time, and it's fascinating to hear Harry's views on business and the economy. Harry could explain to me in fifteen minutes what economics professors had tried to drone into my head many years earlier. He felt we needed a 4 percent inflation in order to function in our economy. I can recite it now. It was something he obviously spent a great deal of time thinking about. He talked about the stock market, and gold. Harry didn't like gold; he felt that you were betting against yourself. We talked about a number of things like that. He really loves his work. He really had fun."

There was even the typical family-type tiff now and again. Leona's brother, Alvin Rosenthal, fancies himself knowledgeable about wines. The only trouble for Mimi is that Alvin makes a point of it, and as she retells the story, she was at a family Christmas dinner shortly before she and Jay were married. "He picked a fight at our dinner table with a very close friend of mine over a wine selection. That was a *fun* family dinner," Mimi said with sarcasm. "But he was all right. He did whatever Leona told him to do, and I imagine he still does."

There were, however, some differences from the average American family get-togethers. A few subjects were taboo, like Donald Trump, who seemed to be closing in on the Park Lane with his various Manhattan hotel and condo tower projects. Kids, too, were kept very tame, as was Mimi's dog, when the Helmsleys visited them in Orlando. Jay and Mimi understood Leona and Harry's reaction. "People who aren't used to pets and kids don't like dogs sitting on the couch slurping on the velvet, or grubby kids coming in from the basketball court or football field and giving you the odd hug or kiss. They like clean, well-mannered kids that don't smell bad," said Mimi. "But that's just typical of people who don't have kids. My tolerance level for little babies these days is almost none, especially wailing little babies. That didn't strike me as particularly odd. They were a little cold to the children, but mainly they just weren't used to kids." Actually, Harry did pretty well with some children. He had learned to remember a little communications trick that most people forget. Kimpton, for one, recalled that Harry knelt down when talking to his young son so they could meet eye to eye. Both Kimptons were left impressed, and feeling closer to this white-haired giant.

The Helmsleys and Panzirers went on trips with the kids and adult trips on their own—to Sea World, about which Mimi marvels at how

Leona and Harry seemed just like regular people, gawking at the killer whales and cheering on the porpoises, and to Las Vegas.

Harry felt awkward at Vegas. If he wasn't a big risk-taker in real estate, he certainly wasn't going to gamble at games he didn't understand or where he knew too well that the odds were against him. He had another quirk. When he did gamble, he didn't like to gamble with others. So Harry loitered in the casino, and then when he played, mostly blackjack, he bought all the seats at the table so he could gamble alone.

They flew in a BAC 1-11, which Harry refitted from a 125-seat airliner into a very large corporate jet—a soaring penthouse of sorts. The remodeling itself is a typical Harry B. Helmsley story. He bought the plane for some incredible bargain, and then shopped around for someone to tear out the innards and rebuild the plane. What Harry found was a specialized service industry where the demand far outstripped the supply. Harry figured he could buy an entire aviation remodeling company for nearly the price of redoing his own jet, so he did just that, and Georgetown Aircraft Services, Inc., of Georgetown, Delaware, was added to the list of Helmsley subsidiaries.

The BAC 1-11 was given a living room and a master suite with a full bath. But it's not any more lavish than a mobile home in its layout. The TV is wedged above the microwave, and three people will crowd the center aisle. They gold-leafed the interior, but conservatively and modernly, not with gilt or rococo. To get an idea of what they wanted, Harry and Leona toured other planes being done, and one on hand was ordered for King Hussein—in total gold. Even Leona and Harry thought that too much. Meals were served on china, the Helmsley china: blue with a gold band.

Mimi also got to know Leona alone, as a mother-in-law, a businesswoman, a socialite. Mimi does not agree with the lampooning Leona has received for having several dozen pairs of shoes and two or more closets of dresses and gowns. "You read a lot about her closets," said Mimi. "But they are not extraordinary, not for people who traveled in the circles that they did. I'm quite sure Harry has two or three dinner jackets."

Mimi and Leona had similar tastes in everyday clothing. "We

didn't go in for flowing skirts and all that," said Mimi. "Loads of times I would wear something that she just absolutely adored, and I would try to get her something like it. She was a ten, and I was a ten." Leona liked Bill Blass, especially when he brought out a line of longer-length jackets that flattered Leona's figure. They gave her a sporty, casual look. Leona, in fact, most times leaned more toward the sporty side of fashion rather than the frilly kind. She came up with very feminine-looking things when the occasion demanded. But Leona was not a prissy dresser in private, and she wasn't terribly fussy about what she wore anytime. Her secretary marveled at the chunks of time Leona spent with discount clothing mail-order catalogues, leafing through them and picking out two of this kind of slacks and three of those sweaters, as if she was swept up by a bargain-basement sale with no eye to quality.

Both Leona and Harry's favorite clothing color is red. "He had one red cashmere robe that he was fond of. We gave it to him one Christmas. I wore a red velour outfit, and Leona commented later how much Harry liked it. There was a picture of me in his dressing area, of me in a red dress," said Mimi.

Mimi also got to know the Helmsley household routine, though Leona never showed Mimi her shrimp-eating trick in the pool. The Helmsley cook in those years was Mikito, a woman of Japanese descent with a light touch with the oils which Leona detested. There was a regular maid. Louis, Leona's hairdresser, came in every morning at nine. He did her face and hair, and he traveled with them on most occasions, though not always. Louis was young, very chatty, and came to Mimi's assistance as a critical eyewitness.

Mimi was exposed to Leona's remarkable acts of seemingly selfless generosity. Mimi's brother, John Doyle, a former top aide to Connecticut senator Lowell Weicker who later started his own political consulting firm, lived in Virginia with his wife. In 1981, the Helmsleys invited them to a business group where Leona was honored as "Woman of the Year," and they stayed at the Harley Hotel on Forty-second Street. After the dinner, Mimi's sister-in-law stayed on. She suspected that she had a tumor and wanted to have it checked out at the Sloan-Kettering Institute for Cancer Research in Manhattan. Leona made all the arrangements so she could be seen right away. There was no cancer. "It was a very, very kind thing. Leona was capable of extreme kindness, in things maybe she didn't think were important but were extremely important to me," said Mimi.

Mimi got to know Harry too, though once it was in a bizarre sort of way that she can't make sense of. In the only other retelling of the incident to a newspaper reporter, Mimi described it as a pass. In subsequent interviews she hedged, more unsure. "To categorize it as a pass is pushing it," she now says. When it came out in *New York Newsday* the story shocked Leona and Harry, as well as their friends, further embittering them toward the New York press. But she tells it simply, and certainly with no visible malice toward Harry.

"We were invited up for cocktails, and for some unknown reason I got there early. I am always late. I mean always late. Leona wasn't there either yet, or had been delayed in traffic. Whoever let me in, maybe the maid, said, 'Mr. Helmsley is upstairs,' and I was to go right up, so I did. I was supposed to be there. He knew I was supposed to be there. He had left word that I was supposed to come up. So no, he wasn't surprised." Harry stood by the pool stark naked.

"It's quite possible he was off in a little world of his own and never even thought about it. I don't know. It never happened to me before, and nowhere in my Amy Vanderbilt is it mentioned."

Mimi guessed what Amy might say. She nonchalantly turned away, and Harry put on a robe. "The first thing I did was to tell Jay. He just registered the information, we kind of had a chuckle over the thing, and there was never anything more. Later I asked my mother and she said, 'You did exactly like you should have, ignored it.' "

Mimi also got to know them together—the loving, touching, kissing, caressing, hugging, arm-hanging, "Oh, my gorgeous," and "Isn't he lovely," and "Look how strong" Leona and Harry. She had the same reaction as did many others. "Coming from a fairly staid New England background, I found that kind of peculiar. Then you have the odd thought that maybe they're right and we're wrong. That maybe we should all be a little more affectionate. It was not my style, but it was kind of easy to get used to."

They played a parlor game one evening. More than the two couples were on hand. Alvin Rosenthal and his wife were there. So were some nonfamily friends. The game went like this: Everyone in turn was asked to describe themselves in one sentence. There had been some drinking, and hosts and guests alike were feeling loose, a little playful. Yet it was early in the relationship Mimi was building with her in-laws, and her response caught everyone by surprise. "I'm the best sales-man you will ever meet." Mimi didn't know that Harry had heard that line before. Leona slipped away with something like "I'm just wild about Harry." But the group never quite recovered. "It got a little dicey," said Mimi. "You know, you hit people with that after cock-tails. I don't think Harry forgot what he learned from everyone that night."

Of course, Mimi grew closest to Jay. And if her recall paints too perfect a picture of their relationship, there are two likely reasons: time sweetens the memory; and Mimi took some big hits to her ego and self-esteem after Jay died. "Jay had a very clear sense of his own mortality and lived every day," she said. "I can't find a picture of him where he's not grinning broadly. The only picture the press has is one where he's scowling. It doesn't look anything like him at all. He was a very happy man. He gave great happiness to people, not because he gave them things or gave them money. He was just a fun person to be with.

"But if you ever wanted to make Jay angry, do something to upset me. And that included everybody, from his children to my mother to his parents. If you wanted to get him mad, that was *the* way to do it. It was a little uncomfortable at first, frightening to realize you're that important to somebody else. It had never happened to me before. I married a best friend in Jay. He made it very clear how important our relationship was. It was kind of frightening to know if you're having a bad morning, he's having a bad morning, and could jump on three or four suppliers and tear their heads off before breakfast, if you want to carry it to the extreme. And he's still my best friend. I was raised an Irish Catholic, and I can believe in life of the soul after death."

There was, however, precious little life for Mimi left in the Helmsley house after Jay died.

Leona and Harry landed in Orlando minutes after Mimi reached them in the sky. They came to the house. Harry took charge of making arrangements. A company secretary fielded calls for Mimi all day. Her brother phoned every hour all day and all night to talk to and reassure his sister. Mimi was dazed.

The first inkling of something going wrong came the very next day. Rabbi Larry Halpern of Orlando's Congregation Liberal Judaism, a close friend of Jay and Mimi's, came by the house and they began to make plans for the funeral and burial. Mimi wanted to bury Jay's body in the Orlando area. Harry said no. Leona wanted Jay to be interred at the Helmsley mausoleum in the Bronx—a tomb sporting a stained-glass skyline of Harry's Manhattan buildings.

The funeral in Florida was uneventful. There was a slight stir when Jay's brass casket wouldn't fit through the cargo door of the Helmsley jet. Harry arranged for shipping the casket by commercial air freight. A second memorial service was held in New York City, where the guest list ran past 2,000. It was, some attendees said quite frankly, the kind of affair where many people felt obligated to be seen—contractors, brokers, politicians, all made a point of signing their names to the guest books. Harry's associates remember getting pressured to donate thousands of dollars to a fund Leona set up after Jay's death to build a memorial heart clinic in Orlando. Leona's former husband, Leo, showed up, easily spotted in the crowd because, oddly, he wore a red, not black, yarmulke. Leona threw him out, but not for a breach of etiquette. The grieving mother seemed to hurl her own guilt feelings at Leo, said Maryann Eboli. "She yelled at him, 'You weren't ever there when he needed you.' "

After the service, the family went back to the Park Lane for a Quaker/Jewish version of a wake. Leona's two sisters, Sandra and Sylvia, were there. So was Mimi's brother, Rabbi Halpern, and Jay's oldest child, Craig. Mimi recalled seeing Bob Wagner's wife, Phyllis, perhaps Leona's closest friend at the time. Out of the blue, Leona turned to Mimi and erupted during the refreshments and quiet conversation. "Leona looked me right in the eye and said, 'I will destroy you.' There was no warning. And then she turned to Craig and said, 'You killed your father.'

"Craig went bananas," said Mimi. "I was on the other side of

Craig, trying to explain to him that in times of grief people say things they don't mean, and my brother came dashing over from wherever he was and said, 'Come on. It's time to go home.' "

A week later Mimi got an eviction notice. Their house, it seemed, was owned by Deco. The household staff was provided by the Harley Hotel of Orlando and paid for through the hotel's accounts, said Mimi. "The gardener, live-in housekeeper, day maid five days a week, a pool man, an all-purpose work person. I never thought about it at the time, but all our household staff was paid by the Harley. I hadn't known the house was owned by Deco either."

Harry was staying at the Harley, and Mimi called him to ask why. He came to the house. "I asked him, 'Why are you doing this?' And he explained to me, quite in detail, that the house was worth X amount of dollars and he could sell it for X dollars and realize such and such a profit. He could no longer amortize the cost of leasing the house to Jay against Jay's salary. And the final line was, basically, 'I need the money.' And I thought, Harry Helmsley is standing here telling me, 'I need the money'? And I said, 'What about Craig? Craig is in Maitland Junior High School. He graduates this year, in the latter part of May. We're already in April.' " Harry gave them six weeks. Then they were out.

Meanwhile, Leona and Harry began unleashing what can only be described as a legal barrage. They sued Mimi and Jay's estate more than six times. They sued to recover the air-freight bill for transporting Jay's casket. They sued to take back Mimi's 1982 DeLorean automobile, with its Florida license plate, "Le Toy." They sued for cash—$100,000 Leona said she had loaned Jay to let him purchase an investment share in the Helmsley Palace. And they sued for gold—an 18-karat ring containing one precious topaz and 136 diamonds.

Leona claimed that she had only loaned the ring to Mimi. But Leona's own hairdresser recalled a different event. On November 7, 1980, J. Louis Rodrigues testified for Mimi, Leona went to the closet in her Park Lane apartment where she stores her jewelry. She took out the disputed ring, and handed it to Mimi, saying, according to Rodrigues's recollection, "I'm giving this to you as a present—an early gift for you for Craig's bar mitzvah. Now, listen to me, get this on your insurance right away. I bought the ring at Buccellati over on Fifth Avenue. Take the ring to them and get it appraised and sized, as it's too big and you will lose it." Mimi did not insure the ring, thinking it was worth far less than the $18,000 Leona claimed. But the clincher for her in that suit came when she discovered a newspaper photograph that she said showed Leona indicating the ring had indeed been a gift.

The other litigation had mixed outcomes. Mimi and the kids also beat Harry's coffin ploy—he had to foot the bill. But they lost on the $100,000 claim when Leona produced a promissory note dated June 16, 1981, for that amount, signed by Jay, and due "on demand." She also lost the DeLorean, though a friend bought it for her at the sheriff's auction.

There was more, however. Leona and Harry claimed in another lawsuit that Deco had mistakenly credited Jay's account one day after he died with his normal periodic compensation of $37,500. Jay was paid in advance, however, and after losing in a lower Florida court, the Helmsleys triumphed on appeal. Then they sued Mimi again, charging that she had forged Jay's signature to transfer $67,000 from Jay's Shearson–American Express account to a joint account.

Indeed, the transfer was made one day after Jay died. But Shearson executives, the notary who approved Jay's signature, and others testified that he had arranged for the transfer one week before he died, after hearing the bad medical news from the doctor in Boston. This time Mimi lost in the lower court and won on appeal. "It was a Pyrrhic victory," said Mimi, "because the funds were all depleted. By the time the $37,500 paycheck was paid back, and the attorneys were paid, there was nothing left." Mimi estimates her legal expenses at over $40,000. The Helmsleys may have spent a large multiple of that.

"They had an absolute unwillingness to negotiate. Everything had to be litigated," said Frank Finkbeiner, one of Mimi's lawyers in Orlando. "It was so bitter, they were so petty."

After Mimi moved out of the Deco-owned house, the Helmsleys took inventory and claimed some things were missing: various paintings and wall hangings, a Betamax with remote control, a silver set for sixteen, a backgammon table. Mimi returned the items. There was one final slap. Mimi sold Jay's share in the Palace to restore the estate. Leona offered $115,000—only $15,000 more than Jay paid for the share three years earlier, and only half the money the share was earning each year. Mimi's attorneys shopped around and sold it for $175,000—to Paul Newman.

Jay had died without leaving a will, and under Florida law, Mimi and the four children would have split the estate, half to her and the remainder to the children. And that's just what happened. After Leona took her loan and other claims, and the attorneys took their share, the $231,438 estate was left with $3,354.68. Mimi got $1,677.34. Each of the kids—Craig Stuart, David Bevan, Meegan Jill, Walter Keith—got $419.33.

Mimi had a rough time in the local press. "Where I come from, your name is supposed to appear in the paper three times," she said. But these were no social announcements. "I was accused of stealing, looting the estate. One headline said, 'Wife accused of stealing priceless art objects.' What they didn't print was that the judge threw [the matter] out when I showed up in court with what they said was an original oil painting and it was a painting-by-numbers picture done by our daughter."

The experience awakened Mimi to the issue of pretrial publicity and fairness, and she felt sorry even for Leona and Harry when, in 1986, the New York Post began blaring headlines like "Helmsley Scam Bared" and "Leona's Loophole." Said Mimi: "I'd be a hell of a hypocrite to say Harry and Leona are not guilty until proven guilty. It's up to the prosecutors to prove them guilty, not Leona and Harry to prove their innocence. On the other hand, I also believe in—I suppose karma, if you want to call it that. I believe that what goes around comes around."

Mimi was contacted by the government prosecutors pursuing the Helmsleys for the tax-fraud allegations. After all, she came to understand Deco's way of doing business fairly well. But she was not called to testify before the grand jury and she was not made a witness. "I told them that if I knew anything, really, I would have used it six years ago on my own behalf."

There's no mistaking that Mimi remains embittered toward both Helmsleys. On the one hand, she would like to forget them. "It's surprising enough to all of you folks," she has told the reporters who knocked on her door for interviews over the years. "But I'm really not interested in what happens to Harry and Leona, what they're doing, who they're doing it to, or why. They were a part of my life, for longer than they should have been. They are no longer a part of my life, and other than idle curiosity, I really don't care. It would be different if they were still family, or anything like that. But it's an embarrassment to have ever been associated with them."

On the other hand, she talks about having a different perspective in hindsight about much that she did with and felt about the Helmsleys. "Let me put it like this," she said. "I've seen it work. I've seen the plan. I've been in the room, in the meeting. I've watched it. I was taught it. Harry and Leona do the best act I have ever seen. You've heard 'dog and pony show,' 'good cop/bad cop routine,' 'velvet glove covering iron fist.' That's exactly it. I've seen the act so many times.

"What people don't remember is that she wouldn't be anything without Harry's money."

Mimi has thought about Leona in another sense—the Leona who she says once sent her a love note that read: "If I could pluck a star from the sky, I would give it to you, because you made my son so happy."

"The kind part of me wants to say, 'She just lost her son. Children are not supposed to predecease their parents. It's not the normal course of events. It's not the way it's supposed to work. That she just snapped.' The realistic part of me says, 'Her son loved something other than her. I was the focus of taking that modicum of love away from her, and she hated me for it.'"

Leona Helmsley pulled together the Helmsley friends' money to build the Jay R. Panzirer Memorial Heart Center at Marks Street and Highland Avenue in Orlando. Later, she and Harry gave a fistful of millions to New York Hospital in Manhattan, which dedicated a wing to them.

They did not, but perhaps should have, received a dedication in the regional courthouse at Stamford, Connecticut, for all the legal work they brought in. Like a loose cannon, Leona suddenly began knocking holes in Helmsley Enterprises that the best attorneys couldn't patch up.

# CHAPTER 16

# ACCOUNTS PAYABLE

SHORTLY AFTER THE HELMSLEYS PLUNKED DOWN $11 MILLION IN EARLY 1983 to buy their Tudor estate in Greenwich, Connecticut, Leona began to spruce up and remodel. A $130,000 sound system here. A grove of $57 hemlocks there. For $1 million they raised a marble dance floor over one of the outdoor swimming pools. Then the bills started coming due, and coming due, and a good many remained due.

Brian Marlowe was left with outstanding charges of $147,100 for the work his firm did to restore the marble floors and columns. Landscaper John Fahey figured his account payable at $6,600. The Post Road Iron Work, Inc., totaled its unpaid bills at $8,631.99. Sheldon Feinstein at the Bergen County Cut Stone Co. had receipts for limestone work at $85,686.23. Nick Vasileff, nurseryman, needed two dozen pages of invoices to tabulate his unsettled billings of $9,448.37 for the acres of sod, the King Alfred daffodils, and the other greenery he planted. Vincent Falcioni figured he was still owed $7,725 for installing underwater lighting and foot-grab railings in the pool. Painter Jay Nichtberger estimated his unpaid-for work at $88,000. Bronx carpenter Virgilio La Pietra just wanted his old Helmsley office-building job back after he was loaned out to the estate to perform a little custom TV cabinetwork; he got paid, but his old job was axed in the interim.

All told, the accounts payable came to $353,191. And that sum, in a golden hand basket, is the bad debt that bought Leona and Harry Helmsley their tax-fraud troubles.

Not only did all eight contractors take the Helmsleys to court. Some of them went to the press, and then to the grand jury, where they testified with abandon about the accounting procedures the Helmsleys were using to cover the bills they did pay. Several, including Marlowe, later joined the list of seventy-eight witnesses for the federal government against Leona and Harry. In the end, the shrouded twenty-six-acre Helmsley estate in Greenwich with its thick stone walls, electronic black steel gates, and German shepherd guard dog lay exposed to the world.

It's as if someone rolled a Trojan horse through the gates in the form of the Maytag repairman and out sprang the tax man. But what's remarkable about the war that broke out in Greenwich is that all of it —the lawsuits, the press tips, the ratting to prosecutors—is extraordinary by comparison with the way contractors and artisans generally interact with the rich.

For one thing, they do not, as a matter of routine, sue. Court records in Stamford, where Greenwich cases are filed, and in Manhattan show very few other lawsuits filed by the contractors the Helmsleys hired. Similarly, there are few lawsuits filed against the contractors by their other clients. If they were getting into fights with others, the differences of opinion were being resolved without stepping before a judge.

Indeed, it seemed that several of the contractors may have been fighting their first legal battles. One out-of-towner assumed the Helmsleys were Connecticut residents, and wasted considerable time and money filing in the wrong jurisdiction. The Helmsleys recruited their best corporate attorneys. The contractors' lawyers were kept a step behind the Helmsley ploys: rotating law firms, aggressive counter-suits, threatened wholesale deposition of the other people the contractors did business with. Attorney Alfred Zullo even had trouble serving his client's papers on the Helmsleys. They were simply refused by the guard. One police car came. Then two. Finally a lieutenant from the Greenwich Police Department had to make the seven-mile drive from the town jail to the Helmsley estate before Zullo's papers were accepted by someone with authority to sign for the Helmsleys. Requests to question Leona directly in legal deposition were put off or rejected out of hand.

Also, for contractors to run to the press or the government is even more unusual. Disputes are almost always settled in private. Having names splashed in the papers and on the six o'clock news does nothing for business or reputations. Something drove the Helmsley contractors to talk, even against their attorneys' advice.

Certainly one possible explanation for all the unpaid bills was that the Helmsleys were being overcharged. There may indeed have been some price gouging. Regardless of the facts, perception was more important. Leona certainly felt cheated. She "knew" she was being cheated. By everyone. And in every case, she urged her attorneys to counterclaim that the contractors didn't deserve to be paid. "There was no question she felt that she was prey for just about any supplier or service who would try to rip her off," said her former attorney Joe Forstadt, who handled several of the estate-related suits.

But something else was afoot at the Helmsley estate. Their neighbors with multimillion-dollar last names—even the new-money types like Tom Seaver, Ivan Lendl, Alice Cooper, Donald Trump, or Tom Watson, Jr., of IBM—use the same nurserymen and painters and they don't end up in public fights. Harry, especially, should have known the ropes. If a price seems too high, cut it down with volume by promising the contractor other work in the future. In one case, Harry let Leona use a major and trusted Helmsley Enterprises contractor, Remco Maintenance Corporation, Brian Marlowe's firm. But even in that instance relations dissolved into a bitter furor.

The something afoot, it seems, was none other than Leona, according to the contractors. Working on the Helmsley estate was unlike anything they had done before. It was as if they were back in the army, where a drill sergeant ordered a hole dug, then filled, then dug again—except the language was more foul. Colors were chosen, then rechosen. Plans were drawn and then redrawn. Degrading wasn't the word. Several spoke of losing face. "She made me stand on a hill and sent a gofer back and forth between us to carry information," said Feinstein the quarryman.

"I'd work for the bag ladies before I'd work for someone like that again," John Fahey told a reporter. He didn't. Nor did the others. They did something else, said Feinstein. "People decided they wanted to get even with her."

In Manhattan, meanwhile, Leona was having her first brush with the tax collector. It seems that she had discovered the Fifth Avenue way of bargain shopping: don't pay sales tax. Or so said the government.

The relevant law in New York State is rather simple. Sales tax on goods can be skipped if the item sold is not for "use" in New York. Of course, even basically honest people would be tempted to make that claim falsely. So the state requires that the item actually be delivered to a legitimate address out of state. No ship, no skip. The practice, however, is something else. With the combined city and state sales tax at 8.25 percent, cheating is by no means unusual. Retailers typically will entertain suggestions from steady customers, such as shipping items to a friend or relative across the Hudson River in New Jersey. That at least satisfies the shipping component of the law. But what happened in Leona's case was a little different. She and a host of other celebrities were accused of having a store ship empty boxes to their second or vacation homes. They would then walk out of the store with their purchases in hand, the state's social service programs be damned.

"It's a particularly heinous crime . . . because we're talking about people who can obviously afford it," said an indignant Abraham Biderman, then city Tax Commissioner. The case broke in 1983 when the state unveiled the fruits of its investigation. All up and down Fifth Avenue, stores were busted. Cartier, Bulgari, Carimati, Ben Thylan, and Christie Brothers all pleaded guilty to sales-tax scams. Van Cleef & Arpels, the jewelry shop Leona frequented, eventually was ordered by the court to pay more than $5 million after the firm and its seventy-four-year-old president, Claude Arpels, pleaded guilty to fifth-degree conspiracy and fifth-degree offering of a false instrument for filing.

Funny thing was, though, only the stores got hit. "The object of these prosecutions is not to embarrass prominent people," a deputy to the state attorney general said at one press conference announcing a $1.9 million settlement with Bulgari. "It was and is to encourage compliance with the tax laws and to collect back taxes." But some observers cried foul when, several years later, the list of prominent people who got off the hook began leaking out.

Those named in the government's cases as having escaped paying sales tax included George Steinbrenner, Henry Kissinger, Donald Trump, and Frank Sinatra. They had awkward company. Others named included the former Philippine First Lady Imelda Marcos, who apparently did considerable shopping when she came to town and stayed at the Helmsley Palace. Another big spender and sales-tax evader was deposed Haiti President Jean-Claude Duvalier, the case papers showed. Some observers smelled the flow of dirty money too. "They're just laundering their money," said Richard Kestenbaum, a former senior trial attorney for the IRS. "It's no different from when they talk about organized crime. There's a tremendous amount of evasion going on—at every level."

Marianne Arneberg of *New York Newsday* reported on the government's decision to punish only the stores, and was told by an unnamed source on the state investigative team that Chrysler Corporation chairman Lee Iacocca wrote to the state attorney general implying that an investigation into Bulgari Jewelers was a "waste of time." The letter was not obtained, and Iacocca declined comment. The probe, though it netted $10 million in unpaid taxes, paled compared to just New York City's loss in uncollected sales taxes, which city officials guesstimate reaches $400 million every year.

Also among those named but not charged was Leona Helmsley. Store records showed she bought ten items from Van Cleef's for which there were no taxes paid, the prosecutors said. In 1981 and 1982 her purchases included a $375,000 diamond necklace and a $105,000 platinum-and-diamond clip, with a tax due of $40,000 that went unpaid.

Empty boxes were shipped to the Helmsley penthouse in Palm Beach, prosecutors said, and Leona walked out of the store and rode back to the Palace with jewelry in hand.

Leona claimed that she bargained with jewelers like she bargained with everyone: hard. She said she presumed the jeweler was including the sales tax in his asking price. Her attorney at the time, Steven Hayes, who would continue to represent her through the earlier stages of the subsequent tax-fraud charges, said his "understanding" was that she "fully believed that the price she was paying for the jewelry was inclusive of sales tax—she had no idea at all that they were not paying any taxes that were due."

But someone popped out of the woodwork to dispute that account, much the way Leona's hairdresser testified that she had given, not loaned, the bar mitzvah ring to her daughter-in-law. After Van Cleef's was busted, its salesman was fired, and he talked. "She was the one who said, 'I don't have to pay sales tax since I have a residence in Connecticut,' the fired salesman, Daniel Issert, said later in sworn deposition in a separate suit he filed against the store claiming he was dismissed because of the ensuing battle the store had with Leona. Leona could not have said that prior to June 1983, when they bought their Connecticut address, but it's possible her purchases at Van Cleef's continued beyond 1981 and 1982 when she bought the necklace and clip. Issert declined to comment on his sworn statement or say how his suit was settled.

At any rate, Leona was not prosecuted. Like many others, however, she did testify before the grand jury, in secret. It's not known what Leona said, but she was given immunity from prosecution for her sworn account. Later, she would try using that immunity to extract herself from the subsequent income-tax case against her.

Just as the state was beginning to look into the empty-jewelry-box scams, the Helmsleys began hunting for a Connecticut estate. It's a common move among New York City's wealthy. Greenwich, especially, is an attractive place since it's the first town over the state line—a Tijuana, of sorts, for land barons. The old-money families have estates down by the water. The new money heads for the hills. But in either direction, the area is wooded, peaceful, and altogether lovely.

And the property taxes are very, very low. The residents have always been able to pay as they went, so there's never been a school or sewer bond to burden future citizens with debts.

Still, there were some inauspicious signs that all would not go well for the Helmsleys in Greenwich. First off, the house they chose seems to be a bearer of bad tidings. It sits on a hilltop, less than an hour's drive along a beautiful parkway from Manhattan. The view of Long Island Sound is not at all bad, though it's no match for the sweeping Hudson River scene Harry had from his house with Eve north of Sleepy Hollow. But the estate's history is anything but placid.

The house—really a mansion, with twenty-one rooms, counting some very small ones—was completed in 1918 at a cost of $1 million. Daniel Grey Reid, a banking-and-steel magnate, had ordered it built as a gift to his daughter, Rhea Reid Topping. She named it Dunnellen Hall for her mother, Ella Dunn, but some locals still call it the Topping House. Her two sons were regulars in the social pages and gossip columns for their parties and successive marriages. The next owner was a steel fabricator, Loring Washburn, who bought it in 1950. He ran into financial trouble and sold it thirteen years later to a financier as an investment. A partnership bought the vacant house in 1966, broke off some of the land, and sold the remaining eight acres of land and the mansion for $212,500 to Gregg Sherwood Dodge Moran, a show girl and former wife to a Dodge automobile fortune heir. Her next husband, Daniel Moran, was a New York City police officer who later shot himself to death in Florida. In 1968, the house was used for the movie *A Lovely Way to Die,* starring Kirk Douglas, in which the body of the house owner is stashed in the freezer. And that same year Moran sold the estate for $1 million—a Greenwich record—to Jack Dick, a financier who was indicted in 1971 on charges that he stole $840,000 by initiating an improper loan.

"The house has seen some unbelievable things," said Marjorie Rowe, founder and president of Preferred Realty, a fourteen-office regional realtor based in Greenwich. Rowe sold Dunnellen twice, the first time to Moran. "When Jack Dick had a party, five hundred people came, in Camelot style, with menus on parchment and French '75s in a silver bowl at the entrance. They were the most lavish parties Greenwich had seen in many years." Dick turned the basement into a wine cellar and stationed a wine steward there during his soirées.

Dick died before his case went to trial. In 1974, Ravi Tikkoo, an Indian-born oil-supertanker magnate, bought the mansion for $3 million. Tikkoo was forced to sell when the tanker market sank. Then along came the Helmsleys. But they weren't the first to look it over. Another person of wealth did so just before the Helmsleys, and rejected it as too insecure. "I showed the house to the Shah of Iran's widow," said Rowe. "Well, not the Shah's widow herself, of course, her representative and one of our country's ambassadors. But the problem was security. You see, it's surrounded by public roads on all sides. You can get very close to the house. And someone could land a helicopter there on the grass."

Rowe does not subscribe to the haunted-mansion theory, but she does note one thing about the estate's name itself. Rowe said she recalled that the deed Gregg Dodge had obtained stated that she could not call it Dunnellen Hall. Presumably, that covenant has passed down through the years, yet the Helmsleys use the name Dunnellen, posting it on the gate along with a coat of arms. Rowe has another thought about the estate: that the Helmsleys paid several million dollars too much. A mansion down the road that might appear more attractive to many buyers than the stone Dunnellen, which seems out of place among its white-boarded Yankee neighbors, was not selling fast in 1988 priced at $5 million. Nothing in all of Greenwich has sold for as much as the $11 million the Helmsleys paid for Dunnellen.

The Helmsleys could make up with a little effort what the estate lacked in refinements. Attorney Rabinowitz recalled an incident to illustrate how business contacts Harry made accord him some of the simple pleasures in life, like getting his home telephone to work. The Friday afternoon before the weekend that he and Leona moved into their Greenwich estate in 1983, Leona discovered that the seller had disconnected the phone. "People do strange things, you know, it's not just the Helmsleys," Harry's in-house counsel, Seymour Rabinowitz, said with a laugh. "I guess they thought Harry was going to make a long-distance call." Trouble was, as Leona pointed out to Harry at 5 P.M., they were planning to use the house the next day and it was not the kind of neighborhood where one could go next door to use the phone. Recalled Rabinowitz: "He finished talking to Leona. Punched another button on his phone. Called Ceil and said, 'Ceil, get me so and so, please,' the chairman of the board of the phone company. Ceil found him at home having cocktails, this being late Friday, and the next morning Harry and Leona had their phone."

But then, of course, there was a lot of work to do.

Joe Forstadt, one of Manhattan's heavier legal hitters and a specialist in corporate law, was a little surprised to find himself sparring with the out-of-favor contractors Leona brought to his door. "We were usually involved in corporate matters," he said, "but when you have clients as important as the Helmsleys, sometimes their personal matters are as important as their corporate matters, if not more so."

Individually, the contractor suits are difficult calls to say who is right. Several have been settled in the contractors' favor, but the parties involved declined to state the exact terms. Several are pending. Doris Elliott's dispute, at $60, was so small that she couldn't really go to court, but she considered it a matter of principle to fight for it. Elliott is president of the Help! Domestic Employment Agency in Weston, Connecticut. She founded the firm in early 1983. Four years later, Leona's new personal secretary, Marty Goldstein, who succeeded Maryann Eboli, began contacting Elliott for estate help: butlers, housemen, chefs, couples. "I was never able to place someone," Elliott said. "Either they wouldn't pass muster in the interview or they wouldn't take the polygraph or they wouldn't pass that. Finally, I was able to place a maid there, and she was fired in two days."

Her help hunter's bill for $60 went unpaid. Elliott wrote to Leona, suggesting that she might not know what's going on. Leona's attorneys wrote back. "Don't bother suing," is how Elliott characterized their response. "The Helmsleys didn't hire the maid, the Five Twenty-one Corporation did." Indeed, on February 14, 1986, the Helmsleys had ridden down to the town clerk's office in Greenwich to hand the estate over to a corporation they set up in Delaware, called, unimaginatively, the Five Twenty-one Corporation, after the street address on Round Hill Road.

Elliott was finally paid by the Helmsleys, with a "521" check. But not until she gained a decided opinion about whoever was running the Helmsley mansion, whether that be the Helmsleys or their aides. "I never met Leona, so I don't know if it was her or someone in charge. But I've interviewed a lot of help that have worked for her, and they're like battle-scarred veterans. You ask how it went and they say, 'Please don't ask.' The Helmsleys are one big revolving door, in and out," said Elliott, adding that she had only one other such problem with a client of their means.

Forstadt remains convinced that in one of his cases, involving a stereo installer, the Helmsleys stood on particularly high ground.

"There was a dispute over the final payment because it was not installed in her dressing room" in a cabana near the pool, he said. "The speakers had to be installed into the walls, so in order to wire the dressing-room area it would be necessary to break open the walls again." That was a major expense the installer didn't feel was his to bear. Leona bore down on the installer. "She was quite put out over it," said Forstadt.

Justified or not, the Helmsleys took the hardest swing at Remco, Marlowe's firm. Remco is the largest office-building cleaner in the New York City area, if not the country. Its crew of 600 services hundreds of commercial buildings, running around in their green uniforms and hanging from scaffolding all over town cleaning walls and logos, as well as the stone surfaces of plazas and sidewalks. Harry Helmsley was a big customer. Remco had twenty-eight accounts with Harry, including the St. Moritz Hotel, when Leona invited the company up to Greenwich to restore Dunnellen Hall. Remco billed her $147,100 on February 21, 1984, and Leona refused to pay. Leona claimed the work was defective. Remco sued, claiming she was asking them to eat the bill and do the work for free because they were doing so much business with Harry. In any event, before Marlowe could bat a legal motion, he was staring at thirty-five to forty lawsuits she threatened to hurl against him, charging that the work the contractor had done for the other Helmsley commercial buildings was faulty. Even Forstadt concedes it was a calculated maneuver in a legal fight he describes as a "bloodbath."

"I can't say this was solely retributive, because there would have to be some basis to the legal claims. I had to be satisfied there were witnesses who would testify that the work was not up to standard," said Forstadt. Of course, those testifying for Forstadt would be Helmsley men—the dozens of managers who run the buildings the Helmsleys own or manage. "But clearly," Forstadt continued, "it was a defensive maneuver in connection with his lawsuit against her, to seize the initiative as a legal strategy." Marlowe settled his suit. But he'd have the last laugh, as would the other contractors when they discovered that some of their invoices for work at the mansion were being billed to other Helmsley properties.

It's unclear who decided to call the *New York Post*. The tabloid, with its screaming blood-and-guts headlines ("Headless Body Found in Topless Bar," adorns the paper's souvenir coffee mugs), owned then by Rupert Murdoch, has a distinct and loyal readership. Ransdell Pierson said he was working the overnight rewrite desk when the tip came in shortly before Christmas 1985. Almost a full year later the *Post* unleashed the first article under the headline "Helmsley Scam Bared." The article said the *Post* had obtained "stacks of invoices initialed by the Helmsleys" that indicated millions of dollars in renovation bills for the mansion were falsified as business expenses and charged to the Helmsley office buildings. Oddly, unidentified attorneys at Steve Hayes's law firm of Parcher, Arisohn & Hayes decided to talk at length about their clients, the Helmsleys, and with incrimination. Yes, the initials were real, the law firm said. And yes, the Helmsleys had ordered the mansion billing be disguised somehow. But it was done only to protect their privacy, they were reported to have said. "The Helmsleys are extremely private people, especially so with what she spent at her home," the lawyers at Hayes's firm said, according to Pierson. There was no elaboration, leaving the explanation somewhat implausible. The article extensively quoted the mansion's former construction manager, John Struck, who had been fired the year before—during the same month the *Post* got its tip. Struck named two other recently fired Helmsley aides, Joseph Licari and Frank Turco, as having managed and reported the invoice alterations to the Helmsleys.

The Helmsleys either had just left for the Caribbean island of Barbados or went shortly after the news story ran. The *Post* tracked them down and gave them the old Murdoch tabloid ambush. "For sure, they would like to forget their legal problems," said the news story, under a huge photo of Leona and Harry on the beach. The reporter prodded them for a quote, any quote at all. " 'Forget it,' Helmsley bellowed when he and Leona were approached on the beach by this reporter seeking their comment on the investigations. . . . When I asked Mrs. Helmsley, 'How about you, Leona? Do you care to comment?' she replied: *'Leona!'* [emphasis the newspaper's]—apparently in outrage at my inadvertent familiarity."

On their return, the Helmsleys, especially Leona, began circling the wagons. Leona found less talkative attorneys. And she began hounding those on her staff who remained at all friendly toward the dismissed Turco and Licari. To outsiders, it might have seemed plausible that Leona was merely protecting herself and Harry from a couple of staffers gone bad. But many inside Helmsley Enterprises knew Turco and Licari well, and they believed them to be two of the empire's most loyal aides.

Licari, especially, had won the respect of many associates. A 1958 graduate of St. John's University, he worked for the predecessor to the firm of Ernest & Whitney before joining Helmsley Enterprises as a staff accountant in 1965. Shortly after Jay died, Licari began working more for Leona than for Harry. She fired him ostensibly for exceeding the car-for-hire expense limits, and there's no question but that he was bitter. "After twenty-one years, I don't even get a watch," Licari said.

Licari, like some of the contractors, spoke out when asked about the invoices and his falling-out with Leona. "She made me fire a whole department—eight people—right before Christmas in 1985," he said. "She felt they were stealing from her. When I started questioning why she felt that way, she said simply, 'Well, can you do it or can't you do it?' She gets this obsession that people are ripping her off, and that's how she feels."

But if there is any hint of vindictiveness in those words, Licari was not always that way, said his associates. Licari was the smiling, friendly, helpful, and always polite boss to his staff of eighteen accountants. "He was a cherub," said one affectionately. "He is a kind of small person, five feet six inches, and you'd never, ever think he was in the position he was in by looking at him. He didn't hold any airs. It wasn't until I worked there that I realized he was the chief financial officer and Harry Helmsley's right-hand man. Nothing was done financially without him."

One of Leona's assistants, who became one of the government's witnesses but asked not to be identified, said Leona turned on him and other friends of Licari. "She was looking to blame him for the entire situation she was in, and was implying if I didn't show my allegiance to the company, and not associate with him, that I'd be in association with a guy who stole or was criminal or whatever."

The assistant played cards with Licari, who lives in Oyster Bay, Long Island, about an hour's commute from the city. They played pinochle, with the kind of stakes where if someone won five or ten dollars it was a lot of money. Leona found out about the games once and rebuked the players. "I never understood it. I think she got the impression that these were five-dollar hands of poker with lots of heavy cigar smoke," one of the players said.

One day in January 1987, Leona called the assistant up to the Helmsley Park Lane apartment to discuss a theft at the Park Lane Hotel. Harry sat on the couch. Leona had taken a chair. They talked about that for ten minutes, then spent the balance of the hour discussing Licari. "She didn't really pull any punches," the assistant said, describing the discussion as a near monologue by Leona blasting Harry's former trusted aide Licari.

Harry was very quiet. He didn't say much at all. He had just come home from the hospital, having had patches removed from his eyes in an operation that eased the squint he had all his life. "Only once when she had interrupted me did he interrupt her to say, 'Let him finish,' which was a little unusual in itself because there were many times I've been in conversation with her where she'd be going on ranting and raving and he would just sit there and be oblivious and not want to get involved," the assistant said.

Yet Harry was very much present in the room when, earlier, the theft was discussed. "He was paying attention then, because there were some substantial dollars involved," said the assistant. "That was during the business conversation. During the rest, he didn't say a word. It was like her own personal vendetta."

Leona's last comments to the assistant were: "You have a family. You have children. Be smart." It is possible that Leona was merely trying to protect him from what she felt was a dangerous relationship. But the assistant, to whom it's unthinkable that Licari is a danger, felt that Leona was nearly blackmailing him, telling him to stop seeing Licari or the bad news would be coming from her.

Spurred by the *Post*, the government prosecutors launched an investigation into the Helmsleys. They had only to pick up their ringing phones and answer the front door. People literally came out of the woods of Greenwich and the halls of the Palace. Within weeks it was clear that several dozen people were willing to risk the Helmsleys' wrath by testifying against Leona, and Harry as well.

It's unclear how deeply the prosecutors went. Much later, there were those involved who felt the prosecutors had become overwhelmed by the amount and complexity of the information they had gathered. Several of those who spent hours testifying before the grand jury said they were not asked about things they had deemed important. Some tried to guess the grand jury's particular interest in any one line of questioning. In one case they asked a Helmsley financial aide a series of seemingly innocuous questions: how tax returns were sent out, who signed them, who kept copies. "I figured out later that all had to do with the mail-fraud charges," the aide said.

"There were many things they could have asked me about and didn't," said one of those who testified. "If the state went in and really looked hard, they could have accumulated their tax records going way back."

Then, on April 14, 1988, one day before the annual income tax filing deadline, the state prosecutors unloaded their charges, followed by the federal prosecutors a week later. The indictment reports were thick. The respective grand juries had indicted the Helmsleys, along with Turco and Licari, on as many as 188 counts of tax fraud. In short, they were accused of evading personal income taxes by sloughing personal expenditures onto their business accounts. In effect, the government charged, the Helmsleys were treating their estate as a business enterprise. Over the course of three years starting in 1983, the prosecutors said, they directed some $3 million in remodeling and furnishing bills to be paid by sundry corporations set up for their commercial properties.

Much of the money in question had to do with the various contracting work done on the estate. But the prosecutors said the Helmsleys also billed numerous furnishings to nearly a dozen Helmsley subsidiaries. The list read like a Park Avenue auction house haul: a $210,000 mahogany card table, a $150,000 cherry-wood highboy and a set of carved walnut chairs, $80,000 in side chairs, a $60,000 side table and musical clock, four pieces of jade that the Helmsleys had bought in San Francisco for $500,000. The furnishings went to the Greenwich estate. The jade, for example, found a home in the vast foyer. But the billings, the prosecutors said, went to one of their businesses—the Park Lane Hotel, the Graybar Building, the housing complex in Queens.

Moreover, the government said, bills for personal items were also made to look like business expenses. The Park Lane Hotel was billed $2,000 for "uniforms" that turned out to be a white lace and pink satin dress and jacket set and a white chiffon skirt, the government said. There were only two innocent explanations: either a Helmsley maid was getting invited to one of Harry's parties or Leona figured she could designate the clothes she wore on her hotel forays as her uniform.

The prosecutors amassed boxloads of documents: memos between Harry and Leona and their aides; memos between Licari and Turco and their aides; invoices for the things the Helmsleys bought; instructions for billing the purchases; corporation records of all sorts. Some of the paper is rather innocuous, if not humorous. One memo noted simply that yogurt-making jars would cost $28.39—Leona made her own yogurt? But the bulk of it, the prosecutors were convinced, would prove two things: that Harry and Leona knew full well what was going on and that what was going on was nothing short of deliberate financial deception. In May 1984, for example, Turco wrote Harry to say the pool enclosure job would cost $1,056,022. Harry responded. There was another exchange that detailed some redesigning that might save money. Harry initialed them just as he initialed every property lease transaction that his Helmsley-Spear brokers conducted.

Harry would get involved in actually deciding how to pay for expenses. On February 10, 1984, for example, Licari was asked by an aide how to log in the accounting books a $9,498.37 expense Harry had paid for with Park Lane Hotel checks written to the Mauna Kea Beach Hotel. Presumably the check paid for a vacation the Helmsleys took, unless Harry had happened upon a fire sale and picked up some cheap furniture. Licari apparently consulted Harry, because nineteen days later Licari wrote the aide back, attaching a note from Harry saying the check was to be designated for "furnishings."

Many of the invoices are scrawled with the initials LMH. Deco, which Leona continued to control after Jay died, appears to have been a major supplier of the Greenwich estate. Charles Hunter, president of the Manhattan custom-furniture company Cavallon Associates, reported to the prosecutors that he received five orders from Deco in 1984 and 1985. They totaled some $70,000 worth of ottomans, Lucite lounge chairs, and dining-room chairs. But only two of the five orders went to the Park Lane Hotel. The rest of the furniture was shipped to Dunnellen, Hunter said.

The federal charges differed only technically on the tax-fraud charges, but there was one key difference in the federal case. Leona and her personal aide, Turco, also were charged with conspiring to commit extortion. The indictment accused them of "demanding and receiving free goods and services from various contractors and vendors doing business with the Helmsley organization, and, in some cases, cash payments, and that certain employees in the Helmsley organization were allegedly instructed to prepare false and fraudulent travel vouchers to general cash, which was then given to Leona M. Helmsley."

The bottom line, as Harry might see it, was that the government figured they had failed to report income in the years 1983, 1984, and 1985 totaling $333,443, $1,273,147, and $1,068,836, respectively. The additional tax due was somewhat more than $1.2 million. If convicted on all counts, the Helmsleys would face 162 years in jail and fines reaching $2 million.

But all that was only the *public* assault against the Helmsleys. Privately, they faced what could be much bigger trouble for the Helmsley empire. Harry and Leona, it turned out, were only part owners of the Park Lane Hotel. They held only 78 percent of the stock. The remaining shares were owned by an entity called Realesco Equities Corp., and Realesco had minority shareholders. Ironically, Realesco was formed years earlier from the dissolution of a company that went bankrupt because the owners were charged with bribing a local official to win a zoning change.

Given that, the government charges take on a very different light. Leona was not only avoiding income taxes by billing the Park Lane Hotel for fancy "uniforms" or a $45,000 silver clock designed in the shape of the Helmsley Building, as the prosecutors charged. If true, she also would have been billing the minority shareholders in Realesco. Those might be viewed as minor perks for the wife of Harry Helmsley, willingly suffered by any investor. But there's something heftier in the government charges. They say that Leona billed the Park Lane, and thus the Realesco minority stockholders, for fake monthly consultant fees totaling $88,333.34. The period of time is unspecified, but could total hundreds of thousands of dollars in lost revenue for the Park Lane partnership. Should the Realesco minority shareholders make a public fight of the matter, the ramifications for Helmsley Enterprises are far greater than the government cases against the Helmsleys. It was one thing for Harry to be charged with cheating the IRS, and quite another for him to be accused of cheating his own private partners. Suspicion would grow and spread to the other Helmsley properties, and untold fights resembling the Palace investors case could arise. The very delicate Helmsley syndicates—syndicates built and dependent upon mutual trust—could crash like so much crystal.

For the time being, however, the prosecutors made the most of their case. And their timing was exquisite in bringing the Helmsleys to court for indictment on April 14.

The government conceded that the Helmsleys were not alone if they did indeed cheat on their taxes. The IRS estimates that the 1987 cheating totaled some $130 to $140 billion, enough to rub out the federal deficit. On the other hand, honesty still abounds. No small number of Americans would be trooping down to the U.S. Post Office the very next day and standing in long lines to mail out the tax forms that would settle their annual accounts with the government, fair and square. And the prosecutors were primed to make that point at a press conference after court. The state attorney general's staff had pushed themselves hard to bring their case out on the day they did, and now the attorney general unloaded his tax joke on the Helmsleys with force —just in case anyone missed the point. The next day was April 15, Tax Day, he told the reporters at the press conference following the Helmsleys' indictment in court. Tax Day, when all good citizens would be paying theirs.

"I've made criminal tax enforcement a high priority," the attorney general said, boasting that the state in the previous three years had hammered tax dodgers for 241 convictions that gained the state $14 million in restitution. "You're going to be caught if you don't pay your fair share or fail to file a return."

"The Helmsleys were treated as any other indicted defendants are treated," he added. "The state means business."

The Manhattan-based regional U.S. attorney spoke with equally robust indignation. "There's very little the government asks for the tremendous blessings we receive in this country," he said. "The government asks two things: pay taxes and obey the law."

Leona and Harry Helmsley said little to the press on April 14, 1988, when they were forced from their private protected world into the hands of their enemies—the government prosecutors, the media, and anyone who might inquire of their affairs or question their ethos. They were the rich and indicted. The public was intrigued. But the Helmsleys were not about to hold a press conference.

In regal defiance they moved, encircled by their guards. Leona, sixty-seven, wore a strained royal red smile. Harry, seventy-nine, held his back straight, chin level. They walked separately, but still wrapped themselves around one another to fend off the world and their own troubled thoughts.

The Equitable Building near Wall Street in downtown Manhattan was just waking when they arrived at 7:36 A.M. and climbed out of the dark gray limousine that brought them to a side entrance. Office workers were starting to pop through the revolving doors. The cigar stand had a short queue for morning papers and coffee. The normal contingent of three or four security people soon had their hands full watching over the lobby—a long-bodied and high-ceilinged expanse, decorated with ornate turn-of-the-century relief.

A few reporters had been ambling about the lobby, nervously realizing that the Helmsleys could enter through any of the doors leading to four streets since the building filled an entire block. The betting favored Nassau, where a couple of television crews gathered on the sidewalk.

The Helmsleys chose Pine, cutting away from the assemblage. A television camera crew spotted their limo just as it turned away off Nassau and swept onto Pine. By the time Harry was helped onto the sidewalk, the other crews came on the run lugging their gear.

It was a gentle pounce, that first interaction. There was a lot to be gained merely from watching the couple move through the lobby. Harry, especially, drew hard stares. His face and his movements were scoured for signs of health, and for whether he knew just where he was and what was happening. He had aged rapidly in recent months. It had been rumored in the days before their appearance that Harry suffered from Alzheimer's. Indeed, his associates later whispered that his mind seemed to slip in and out. One day he would recognize his longtime business pal and onetime heir to the Helmsley Enterprises throne, Alvin Schwartz. Another time he would not.

Harry moved first through the Equitable lobby, looking straight ahead, and now and then down at his feet. He walked very slowly, taking tiny steps alongside—though not clutching—a nurse. The stature of this grandfatherly man in his long cashmere coat was remarkable. Harry Helmsley stood as tall and straight as the Equitable. His glasses rode high on his nose. His white hair stayed brushed back off his face. And at six feet three inches, he towered over most others.

Still, he seemed frail, even faded a bit in the way the sick or tired appear. He'd be overlooked in a crowd were it not for his height. His friends later observed and fretted that he was badly torn by the government's charges. After all, this was a man who had forged his fortune on integrity, honesty, and the multimillion-dollar deal sealed with a handshake. While it was only the government's tax collectors who had called him a cheat, a cheat, nonetheless, it was. Rarely in his long life had he been called that, and when he was called just that by the Palace investors, he didn't take kindly to the notion.

Leona Helmsley walked through the Equitable lobby a few yards behind Harry, surrounded by her own set of private Helmsley guards. Incredibly, she strolled right out of one of her hotel queen ads. Her colors were all-American, with a dash of New York. Her conservative coatdress was in her husband's favorite color, red. It had a blue collar, and she wore a white shirt and white medium-heeled shoes. The dash —a black purse, which hung from her left shoulder. Her face was well kept, astounding, really, for a woman who would turn sixty-eight that summer. Her motions were neither fluid like a younger woman's nor frail like her husband's. She was definite.

In fact, Leona, unlike Harry, would not be overlooked in a crowd. Her gaze was commanding. Powerful, though not intense, it seized attention. To look away, at her feet to note her shoes or to her husband to see how he was proceeding, required a conscious effort. She drew the focus. And when she spoke, it was directed with such force that it was as if she and the person she was speaking to were alone at two ends of a visual tunnel. Such willfulness, and yet her thoughts must have been swarming with the preoccupations of the legal battle at hand.

The entourage made it into the elevator without incident, and with Harry's wink the door closed, leaving the media on the ground to wait. They would awaken, swell in ranks, and grow more feisty as the morning progressed.

The Helmsley party stopped at the twenty-sixth floor, where the state attorney general had his offices. It was there that the Helmsleys had their appointment to be questioned before being taken to court for the formal arraignment on the state's indictment against them. But they were so early that no one was there to greet them.

They waited in a sterile reception area—no carpet, no art on the institutional blue-gray walls. There was only a pair of seats. Leona and a guard took a two-seat wood-frame bench with faded purple cushions. Harry sat on a three-seater, same color. On a low pine table before them sat a spider plant and three small stacks of single-page advertising flyers. One was a short-order menu. The others dished up little nuggets of irony. "The buck stops here at EGI Check Cashing," blared the headline in a vivid yellow ad for a money broker—buck stopping and checks, grist in the government's case. The skills of a tax preparer were pushed in the other, urging everyone to be done on time and within the law's prescriptions.

In five minutes the Helmsleys were ushered into a set of offices, passing through a door locked with a five-digit code. It proved amusingly effective in barring their own staff and friends. A stray Helmsley guard arrived six minutes later and knocked to get in. After a while there was a muffled response from inside, and the guard outside boomed back, "I don't have a password."

Three minutes later another guard raced down the elevator for coffee. He rushed back with ten cups and a container of milk and then waited for five minutes—alternately knocking and pacing the waiting-area floor—before he was let in.

The locked door halted another entire Helmsley group in its tracks. There were four men in this second party, and they arrived on the twenty-sixth floor half an hour after Harry and Leona passed into the inner offices. Two were former Helmsley aides. Charged with assisting the alleged tax-evasion scheme, they were in no better spirits than their former employers. The other pair was their legal help. The attorneys were considerably more at ease, and one chuckled when a reporter wondered out loud about the odds in blindly breaking the five-digit code on the doors. "That's just what I was thinking," said the attorney. No one else laughed or said another word until the group was admitted into the offices for its round of formal questioning with the state prosecutors.

The questioning dragged on. Attorneys call it "pedigree," in which defendants are asked to affirm their presence in the world: birth date, parents, education, property.

For two hours they were held, and then the pedigree ended. They were taken down an elevator, through the lobby crowded with reporters and onlookers, and out to the street, where they were packed into state cars and driven to the courthouse a short mile away, where the real legal action would start.

Downtown Manhattan was in full churn when the Helmsleys arrived at the New York County courthouse. Everywhere, people stopped to watch. Harry spoke to a reporter who, close at his side, asked how he felt about the ordeal. "It's just starting," he said softly, matter-of-factly. Again, his movements were scrutinized for how well he fared in the crowd and for how keen his mind seemed to be. At one point, someone stumbled. But it wasn't Harry. It was a rushing photographer less than half his age. "He's gonna trip," Helmsley whispered to the aide at his side.

Now three hours into their ordeal, Leona and Harry reached their assigned courtroom. They took the first bench on the right, followed by the guards. The press veered to the left. A few courthouse regulars wandered in. The house became packed, but many were there for the other scheduled cases posted on the wall outside.

The routine of the state courtroom must have seemed slightly bizarre to the Helmsleys as they sat—she on his left—listening to the judge, Carol Berkman, harangue a series of drug dealers and thieves. She is a loud, tough-talking justice who interrogates more than she presides, and the cases preceding the Helmsleys' drew a few chuckles from the reporters on account of her alternating tone of incredulity and outrage.

"How much money did you take?" she boomed out at a woman in her early forties accused of stealing from the nonprofit social service group that employed her. "Approximately $12,000? How did you steal it? And the other $6,000?" The defendant cowered, whispering answers only the judge could hear. Leona occasionally looked up at the judge.

Harry and Leona whispered frequently. The media had received permission to put cameras in the court for the Helmsley arraignment—one a still, the other a video, with their pictures to be shared by newspapers and the television news. The pool photographers stood twenty-five feet from the Helmsleys, clicking off shots when Leona turned from her husband to look them straight on.

Their attorneys entered the courtroom. Leona had hired Steve Kaufman, a fifty-six-year-old former chief of the U.S. attorney's criminal division in the district of New York, who had since distinguished himself in private practice. He sat next to Leona. His co-counsel was Gerald Feffer, a leading tax-fraud attorney at the Washington firm of

Williams & Connolly, which specialized in white-collar cases. Feffer sat next to Harry. The former Helmsley aides had quietly entered the court and sat on the left side behind the reporters, unrecognized.

Just before 11 A.M., the judge turned toward the Helmsleys and started the arraignment. The prosecutors had wheeled up to Judge Berkman's bench several dozen sets of the state's thick indictment, covered in baby-blue-colored paper, and they now handed them out to the four defense attorneys as they too approached the bench.

The judge was visibly fuming. Publicity over the Helmsleys had been thick all week, with the city's four daily papers each carrying similar stories that day about the preliminary secret grand-jury proceedings, the subsequent indictment, and the Helmsleys' scheduled appearance in her court—something, it seemed, the press had discovered before the judge herself found out. She wasn't about to let that go by.

"The major reason I had all of you step up here without your clients is that I received applications from the media to take film and moving photographs of the proceedings," she said to the four defense attorneys and the prosecution team. "It would appear that someone, I don't know who, is giving out information which should not be disclosed and there is a good possibility that a crime has been committed. I am quite upset that this information appeared in the press, information which I in fact was not privy to.

"I was fascinated to read how many witnesses testified under a grant of immunity, absolutely fascinated. And I think this is a very serious problem which puts the criminal justice system in a very bad light. So I think it is very important that this be investigated and that the sources of this kind of behavior be uncovered and brought to justice."

The judge stopped with that blast, and invited the Helmsleys and their former aides to approach the bench. The camera clicked. The video ran. There was utter silence as Leona and Harry stood before the state judge and pleaded. Leona's voice was the loudest—a clear, resonant "not guilty," impressive enough to be mentioned in most of the press accounts of the indictment. Harry's identical response was much softer, and their former aides spoke their "not guilty's" more softly still.

The judge wasn't done yet, however. An assistant state attorney general asked the court to require the Helmsleys to put up a $1 million personal recognizance bond, and their attorneys cried foul.

Harry's attorney accused the prosecutors of hunting for headlines in the next day's papers that might read: "Helmsleys Forced to Put Up One Million Bucks," while the attorney Leona hired argued that both Leona and Harry were good bets to show up in court.

"On behalf of Mr. and Mrs. Helmsley, there is not a couple in this city that has greater roots, ties, and commitment to this city. It can't seriously be considered that Mr. Helmsley won't be here when required," he told the judge.

The judge seemed to agree, but got her own name high up in the news stories by sniping, "I'm sure if the Empire State Building and Helmsley Palace are on the block, we'll hear about it." A week later when they were arraigned in federal court the Helmsleys were handed a far greater insult. They were forced to relinquish their passports and give up their cherished trips to Barbados.

The defense had its work cut out for it. First, there were heated denials to be made to the press. In written releases—the Helmsleys never spoke directly—they called the federal indictment "part of a broad attack on them that is so unfair and so groundless it has never been attempted before. The indictment represents the first time that the state and federal government have ganged up on any American citizen to jointly prosecute them on charges based on their income tax return." They went on to say the charges were "motivated by the prominence of the Helmsleys and the interest they attract from the media."

"The Helmsleys have more than paid their dues to the city and country in which they consider themselves fortunate to live and work," the attorneys continued. "They have probably paid more taxes to the government over the years than any other individual in this city. In the past five years alone they have paid more than $270 million in taxes and given over $35 million to charity. The Helmsleys will fight the charges in both cases because they are false and malicious and they will struggle to protect their good name and reputation for honesty and integrity."

Most quoted by the press as an excerpt from the statement's kicker: "They will fight these allegations tooth and nail."

Then there was a change in attorneys. Kaufman left the case. He said later it was by mutual agreement. Others familiar only with the way Leona did business said he most likely had simply given her advice, or a reading of the situation, that she did not like. He was replaced by John Wing, a fifty-one-year-old graduate of the University of Chicago Law School and former assistant U.S. attorney. Both he and Feffer said they felt optimistic about beating the charges, unless Leona's persona got loose in the jury's mind. "Hopefully this trial will be one of tax evasion rather than personality," Wing said.

To further counter the negative publicity, the Helmsleys passed over their longtime public relations man, Howard Rubenstein, and hired Douglas Hearle, a burly former reporter who's been described as the Red Adair of the public relations business for flying into corporate messes as though they were oil-rig fires. Hearle represented Pennzoil, RJR-Nabisco, and the Occidental Chemical Co. when the Love Canal toxic-waste disaster broke into the open.

Hearle first turned his attention, as did the lawyers, to the question of whether the Helmsleys could get a fair trial given the volume of pretrial publicity. But such defense moves never go far in New York. A ploy to change venue to Philadelphia because of pretrial publicity fell flat. The federal judge hearing the case, John Walker, Jr., also turned down motions to extract Leona from the case because she was given immunity in the jewelry-tax case.

But doctors examining Harry succeeded where Leona's attorneys failed. Five physicians with expertise in neurological disorders, including one appointed by the court, found Harry's memory to be insufficient to assist in his own defense. In December, he was removed from the trial. Those and other delays pushed the trial back from a September 15, 1988, start to late April 1989.

Perhaps the most damning report about the Helmsley case was published by *New York Newsday*, which two weeks before the mid-April arraignment reported that Leona had turned down a plea bargain offered by the prosecutors. According to the story, prosecutors told Leona she could spare her husband all legal grief—they would grant him immunity from all charges. All she had to do was plead guilty to one felony count of business fraud. The story was significant because it implied Leona was deep-sixing poor old Harry to save her own skin.

There's some reason to discount the story, which was based on unidentified "law enforcement sources familiar with the case." The prosecutors later flatly denied the report. Indeed, the timing alone would have made this a highly unusual procedural move. Prosecutors have rarely made such an overt gesture to a big-name, high-visibility defendant *before* an indictment occurs and the charges are formally made.

One witness heard that Leona was offered a plea bargain in the summer of 1988, after the indictments.

The deal was this: Harry would get off completely free, and the charges of conspiracy to commit extortion would be dropped against Leona. In return, she would have to do six months at a prison farm. It's unclear what, if anything, the two Helmsley aides were offered. Observers most typically thought that the prosecutors eventually would grant Licari and Turco immunity from prosecution in exchange for their testimony against the Helmsleys.

In any event, Leona said no to the offer. She dug in her heels. And the word around Helmsley Enterprises in late 1988 was this: Now that her Harry was safe, Leona was going to fight the case all out, with every tool and trick she could muster.

Meanwhile, more turmoil stirred through Helmsley Enterprises.

## CHAPTER 17

# CRUMBLINGS

ON WEDNESDAY, JUNE 22, 1988, CARMELLO LIUZZO, A THIRTY-FIVE-year-old advertising executive, checked into the Helmsley Windsor Hotel in Manhattan. His wife, Cheryl, twenty-eight, was with him. They had reserved a $120-a-night room. But by the time they arrived all the rooms at that rate had been booked. So they were given a $200-a-night special on the top floor. Suite 1628 had a bedroom, a sitting room, a pantry—and a killer ceiling.

The following day, Cheryl checked out and flew back to Greens-boro, North Carolina, where the Liuzzos lived with their fifteen-month-old daughter, Cassandra. Carmello stayed on to wrap up his business. He had only recently moved to Greensboro from New York and was closing out his affairs in the city. The Windsor, just a block away from the Helmsley Park Lane, was conveniently located for his work.

Built in 1926, the Windsor is a quiet, almost cozy 304-room hotel. "A lot of charm and service for the money and location," says one discriminating critic. The lobby is chandeliered and paneled. There's a restaurant and bar. And, of course, all the bathrooms have the Helmsley freebies: the coconut soap, the mending kits, the shoe-polishing cloths, and the very thick towels. Harry Helmsley bought the Windsor in 1972, the year he married Leona, and promptly cut her into his 50 percent share. The Madoses owned the other half and ran the hotel for several years before their bitter falling-out with Leona. The Helmsleys acquired their shares in 1975, and since then there has been a succession of managers directly under Leona's control.

Before dawn that Friday, at about five-fifteen, other hotel guests near Carmello's room were awakened by a loud noise. But no one notified the hotel staff. Ninety minutes later, the switchboard operator noticed that the phone in 1628 was off the hook, and hotel security went to check.

What they found was Carmello's body lying under an estimated two tons of concrete ceiling. Rescue officials were called, and it took them a full five minutes to dig out the body. "You couldn't even see him," one fireman commented dryly. The ceiling below Carmello's room cracked from the weight, but no one else was injured.

City officials had never seen anything like it, but it didn't take them long to figure out what had happened. Water had leaked from the Windsor Hotel roof into the layers of ceiling materials. And rather than rip out the entire mess and rebuild it, someone merely covered it over. Like painting over rust, it was cosmetic at best. Any handyman would know it was only a matter of time before the whole thing would seep through. Discovering exactly who did the work and when has proven difficult for city building inspectors, but they didn't take long to fix the blame. Legal responsibility, the city said, rested with the Helmsleys, and they were charged with failing to maintain a structurally sound building. A conviction could bring a $5,000 fine and ninety days in jail, but there might be some first-offender sentencing. The hotel has had a clean record with no prior code violations.

"It's clear they were aware there had been some deterioration," the city Buildings Commissioner said. "The false ceiling is that evidence. It would indicate they wanted to cover up a badly damaged ceiling. I can't see how you could miss it." Leona and Harry had their public relations man issue a terse statement expressing regrets. They did not visit the scene, just half a block and a long elevator ride from their penthouse. Nor did they scramble to contact the wife. One newspaper reported that she telephoned the hotel that Friday morning to speak with her husband and was told point-blank by the operator that the person in 1628 had, regretfully, died.

The Helmsleys can trace their combined public image and corporate troubles back to when they were first married and Leona started clashing with Harry's aides—the Madoses especially. But Harry was not immune to trouble in his prior life.

There was the time in 1963 when a congressman charged that tax-exempt foundations set up by the wealthy were being used illegally to finance stock purchases for their friends. Listed with five others was the Harry B. Helmsley Foundation, established by him in 1959 to wash some of his profits through tax-exempt donations. Then there was the time in 1972 when Helmsley was discovered to be the landlord of a Times Square sex shop. The timing was bad. The city was hell-bent on clearing the area of such trade, and Harry looked rather sheepish. He barely missed buying a real live whorehouse in Manhattan when he acquired the huge IFC bankruptcy holdings. The house was sold off by the bankruptcy administrator before passing into Harry's hands.

More recently, he was named in a *Wall Street Journal* story about the unmeasured influence that real estate firms have over elected officials through their campaign donations. Helmsley seldom gave directly to electoral campaigns. He gave through others in his firm, especially Irving Schneider, who also doubled as Ed Koch's mayoral campaign finance chief in the years Harry was receiving his tax breaks.

Plain old business deals also fell through for Harry over the years. The master of real estate was not completely safe from mistake or misfortune, and sometimes got bricks knocked off his shoulder when he spoke too soon. In 1973, the business press was aflame with word that Helmsley was buying the Plaza, the city's most prestigious hotel. Helmsley had it all figured out. He was going to pay $18.5 million for the hotel—$7.5 million cash on top of an $11 million mortgage. But then the deal suddenly fell apart, for unexplained reasons.

Harry had said he wanted the Plaza because it "represents the best of New York and I believe in its future." Fifteen years later, Donald Trump said much the same thing when he bought the hotel—for $410 million. If Harry felt any consolation in the fact that Donald paid a good deal more than anyone else thought it was worth, he would nevertheless have grimaced at the changing Monopoly board along Central Park South. Suddenly, Harry was surrounded by the Casino King. Trump and his hotelier wife, Ivana, already had the St. Moritz. They now had the Plaza Hotel. And wedged between them were Leona and Harry in their Park Lane.

Another big loss for Helmsley was the Pan Am Building, a fifty-nine-story curved monolith that went up in 1963 between Grand Central Station and the much smaller New York Central Building, which later became the Helmsley Building. The Pan Am, designed in part by the modernist Walter Gropius, inspired groans from the architectural crowd. Its shape was supposed to have given it the appearance of flowing from one of Pan Am's airplane wings. Instead, it merely brutalized the skyline with an aesthetic crash landing. Harry, however, had his own special interest in the Pan Am—an interest bordering on the emotional, since there was no direct dollar computation. Buying the Pan Am would have given him the satisfaction of owning all four corners around Grand Central Station—the Graybar, the Lincoln, the Helmsley, and a pair on the Forty-second Street–Lexington Avenue corner.

Leona, too, was thrilled at the prospect of sharing in a real-life monopoly. One evening at a charity ball she happily told a friend that Harry was very close to buying the Pan Am. But the very next day the deal fell through. Bill Kimpton was in Harry's office and heard half of the conversation. "It was fascinating," said Kimpton. "Pension funds were coming onto the market then with lots of money and [the pension-fund administrators] outbid him by $100 million or so. But his bargaining position up to the end was this: 'Pan Am is in the building and it has a big lease and very low rent and thus the building is only worth X amount, so I'll offer you that.' That all occurred in five minutes, and that influenced my life, because I saw him as one person making the decision, just like that. And when you have one person making the decision you have a lot better chance of making things work. You can't take time to think. You have to move. And you *can* think fast. You can think very clearly once you train yourself."

Harry's timing was bad for another reason. The Pan Am had been owned by a business friend of his who died and left it to his widow. She did not know Harry in the same way as her husband. Even at Harry's level of doing business, deals often jell or do not jell for reasons as simple as that.

Whether because of that loss or simply because the Pan Am overshadowed the Helmsley Building, Helmsley shortly thereafter spent $30 a square foot to gold-leaf the Helmsley Building. The work was done by Douglas Leigh, an exterior design and lighting consultant who invented the smoke-ring-blowing Camel cigarette billboard on Times Square. It was a meticulous process. Artisans would stand on the scaffolding and wait for the slightest breeze to pass before applying sheets of gold. They were the thinnest of thin and had to be brushed on—too fragile to be put on by hand. The refinishing worked. To observers standing on Park Avenue looking south, the Helmsley Building is now visible against the taller Pan Am. Yet the gold is not gaudy, or excessive, compared with other lavish gildings in the city.

There were other losses for Helmsley. He was an early proposed developer of Battery Park City, a collection of apartment and office towers that finally went up on the 100 new landfill acres in lower Manhattan. Before all that happened, however, a stall in the project pitched Helmsley overboard. In 1980, he had big plans to build a $100 million movie studio on the West Side of Manhattan for his old pal Frank Sinatra. But the studio idea collapsed into a bitter lawsuit when the development of an adjoining property blocked his access and light. And in 1982 Helmsley joined the long list of entrepreneurs who at one time or another laid plans to build the world's tallest tower. His 112-story skyscraper would have edged out the World Trade Center as well as Chicago's 110-story Sears Tower. He didn't have a site, Helmsley said then, but, he added, "I'm serious. We're the greatest city in the world, so we should recapture the honor in skyscrapers too."

Harry Helmsley's biggest loss, perhaps, came to a head in 1985. But loss is the wrong word. Harry rarely let any of his net worth slip away. When he lost money, it was in terms of lost potential profit, not lost dollars in hand. Harry Helmsley missed out on a lot of calculated potential profit in Miami.

Phil Blumenfeld, the Met Life real estate veteran whom Harry recruited to do some of his Florida dealing, was on hand for the entire episode. "The Florida market, when I got there in 1979, was absolutely indescribable," he said. "It was a skyrocketing boom. You could do no wrong. It was a sure thing. You could throw a dart anywhere and where it fell there was money to be made."

Harry's first project was the Miami Palace, a $35–$40 million condo tower on Brickell Avenue overlooking the shimmering turquoise waters of Key Biscayne. Construction began in August 1979. By November, all 254 units were sold, for a total of $80 million. Harry was looking at a $40 million gain from the three months' work by Blumenfeld and others.

The tower was not duck soup for Blumenfeld, however. Leona became Harry's emissary, and she dug into the Miami Palace with nearly the enthusiasm for detail she had for the Palace Hotel in Manhattan. Leona didn't trust Blumenfeld's taste in decor, and she started spending time at the site looking things over. If Leona did for the Palace Hotel what she tried to do for the Miami condos, said Blumenfeld, it's clear in his mind how Harry was stuck with $20 million in cost overruns.

"You can go around to a construction site and opine and say what's wrong and make numerous suggestions, and, in effect, you are saying to the staff, 'You better do it.' " said Blumenfeld. "And if you go and do all those things, and you don't have a cash register in your mind— and I'm sure she didn't add it all up—then you don't realize that all these changes have real dollars attached to them. I'm sure this happened on an ongoing basis at the Palace. I know the people who worked on that. And when all was said and done, Mr. and Mrs. Helmsley looked at it, and . . . they blamed everyone else."

In Miami, Blumenfeld discovered a way around Leona. He remembered her bristling, for example, at the shape of the pool. Three times it was redesigned until she was pleased. But the elevator doors were too much for Blumenfeld. "She didn't like the color," he said. "It had gone through the approval process. She saw the color before they were painted. It was an acceptable blue. And then she just didn't like it. Well, there are six elevators in the building, or maybe eight, per floor. And there are forty-three floors. So do you repaint them all?" Not if you're Phil Blumenfeld and you're counting every penny spent like it was your own money. Leona never realized he simply balked at her order, said Blumenfeld, who was acting on Harry's cautionary advice. "Harry told me to never put him between me and her," said Blumenfeld. " 'You do what she wants,' he said, 'and if what she wants is contrary to reason, you don't do it. Tell her you did it, and let me know what is going on.' "

Blumenfeld believes that he survived in Helmsley Enterprises as long as he did because she came to appreciate his diligence with the dollar. "I think everyone knew that Phil Blumenfeld was a stickler for bargaining, and I assured her, and this is how we eventually made peace, that we got every nickel, dime, and quarter of every bill that I approved," he said. "We got the best value for a buck, and I was there on the site to make sure, personally. The cost overruns we had in the Miami Palace were nominal compared to the Palace Hotel."

Even as the Miami Palace was going up, Blumenfeld spotted another deal for Harry, and a deal it was. What may well have been the best undeveloped site in Miami was for sale—a parcel of land right on the water. And it sat on a point of land that gave it a 240-degree waterfront view. Blumenfeld pitched it to Harry, who was contemplating another site in booming Miami at the same time. But Leona made the choice, since Harry wasn't willing to do both at once. "Mrs. Helmsley had looked at both sites," said Blumenfeld, "and we were at some real estate function when she came up to me and said, 'Philip, which one would you rather do? Which one is the safer project?' And I said no question, this is the safer project, and she said something like 'I trust you. This is the one we'll do.' "

"I was very turned on," said Blumenfeld, "and I caught Harry in one of those relaxed moods where he would be open to my ideas." Harry bought it. He authorized Blumenfeld to dicker with the land seller, the Mutual of Omaha company. Then his architects got busy. And off their easels sprang the Helmsley Center, a glittering $200 million, fifty-five-story hotel and office complex that was the tallest and most spectacular thing Miami had ever seen. It even had the world's highest sky bridge linking two towers at 350 feet above the ground. A bubbling newscaster called it a landmark, Miami's version of Manhattan's colossal Rockefeller Center. "Helmsley Enterprises is not new to Miami," the newscaster continued. "He built the Palace condominiums. And with the Palace complete, he's going to start building his kingdom."

And then came the Miami bust.

Not even Harry could have foreseen it. He may have developed a sixth sense for economic cycles in the United States. But it was the crashing peso and other South American currency, not the dollar, that knocked Miami's socks off in 1981. And as the formerly rich from Rio went home to batten down their affairs, Little Cuba scrambled.

Harry did pretty well on the Miami Palace condominium tower. Many of the units had sold in multiples of two to ten units, picked up by foreigners for investment and not personal homes. But a good many of those investors suddenly couldn't meet their payments, and fully half of the 254 units did not formally close. The Miami Palace opened half empty. Blumenfeld innovated. He rented the unsold units, with options to buy. He fiddled with owner financing. Eventually the units were resold, and Harry, who bought a few for himself, even made money on his own apartment sales. "He did quite well, really, on the Palace," said Blumenfeld. "He made out quite decently."

There was no such luck with the Helmsley Center. Blumenfeld pleaded with Harry to hold on to the site. But Harry said no. Arguing against it was his financial accountant, Joseph Licari, who later testified that he "saw no light at the end of the tunnel" Miami had driven into. Harry stopped making payments on the land, which he had purchased for $22 million. Mutual of Omaha sued him. And Harry, possibly for only the second time in his life, went into Chapter 11 bankruptcy.

Just how deeply the bankruptcy affected Helmsley is unclear. "Mr. Helmsley was totally shocked to see how fast values fell apart in the Miami market," said Blumenfeld. "And, after the fact, he said he had always distrusted it, he never liked it, and considered it ephemeral." Helmsley lost an estimated $6 million on the abandoned Mutual of Omaha site project.

Still, it's unlikely Harry regretted his time in Miami. As he did when losing to Andrew Stein on the Tudor City park swap, Helmsley never let his losses eat into his mind or emotions. They were losing deals, but they were deals nonetheless, and he blended them in with his winners, of which there were many, many more. That attitude streamed through his empire, carried by aides like Alvin Schwartz, who loved to stop by the desk of a broker about to buckle from stress and say soothingly, "If you don't have any problems, you're not doing any business."

But the loss rubbed Harry personally too, as the succession of names for the project shows. Early on, it had been called the Imperial Palace. That name was abandoned when it occurred to Blumenfeld and the Helmsleys that it sounded a little too much like a Chinese restaurant. In fact, there was an eatery in Miami with the same name. They changed it to the Helmsley Center, and it was the Helmsley Center that got all the grand press and television coverage. But then, right before the bankruptcy was filed in late 1984, Helmsley ordered the name changed back to the Imperial Palace. "Didn't want the name Helmsley associated with the bankruptcy; is that what he said?" Joseph Licari was asked during the ensuing legal battle in the bankruptcy case. "Yes," Licari replied.

In that same February 1985 proceeding, Licari came the closest anyone ever has to putting Helmsley's net worth on written record. Helmsley's worth has always been a matter of speculation. *Forbes* magazine, which annually ranks the world's wealthiest, can't be trusted. In general, net-worth figures made public by *Forbes* and others are distorted in that the truly rich downplay their net worth, whereas the wanna-be's lobby hard to get on the most-wealthiest lists. Helmsley most likely qualified for the first category. "He never walked around boasting about how much money he had," said Harry's friend Robert Wagner.

Still, there are parameters: the size of the entire Helmsley empire, the amount he funnels every year through his private foundation, the tax information obtained in the tax-fraud proceedings. One Helmsley Enterprises accountant who was privy to Helmsley's tax records said that, as of 1987, reports putting his net worth between $1 and $2 billion, and closer to $1 billion, were accurate. In late 1988, *Forbes* pegged it at $1.7 billion. Licari gave a somewhat different number under oath. Mutual of Omaha's attorneys were interested in establishing Helmsley's worth as a matter of course in arguing that he could handle the Helmsley Center losses. A lengthy exchange occurred in which they basically took inventory of the Helmsley properties and subsidiaries. There were some surprises. Licari, for example, divulged that Helmsley once owned a fast-food chain. He was hesitant about pinpointing Helmsley's net worth, which he deemed not within his authority to reveal. But after a lengthy exchange, Licari did answer one question. "Let me restate it. Do you put his personal wealth at $500 million to $1 billion; is that statement generally correct as of December 1982?" Licari: "Yes." He refused, however, to say if in the meantime Harry's worth had gone up or down.

Meanwhile, Helmsley Hotels began losing more than its ceilings. As president, Leona began to let some other things slip. Perhaps the worst case is the Harley of Orlando, where her son, Jay, died. It's possible Leona never stepped foot in the hotel again. Jay's widow, Mimi, never has. But the people Leona sent down periodically from Manhattan should have seen the things that would have driven Leona mad.

In July 1988, at least one of the $60-a-night rooms offered to guests was a far cry from the advertised claim of perfection. All the coconut soaps and other freebies were there. But the hot- and cold-water knobs in the bathtub were reversed. The radio was broken. Large pieces of wallpaper were peeling, and there were cracks and stains on the walls. Pictures were hanging crooked. Outside in the halls, room service trays were left sitting, untouched, with leftovers on them, for at least twenty-four hours. Perhaps the most obvious sign of neglect was in the front lobby, where the Helmsleys hang huge posters of their Manhattan hotels. There was the Park Lane, and the Palace, of course. And alongside them, a glossy poster ad for the St. Moritz—Donald Trump's St. Moritz, the one he bought from Harry three years earlier. The Harley became—by anyone's measure—just another ordinary, run-down motel, with a higher room rate. Management at most of the Harley chain is currently suffering one of the highest turnover rates in the business, industry sources have said. In the past several years the Helmsleys have tried unsuccessfully to sell the entire Harley chain outside of New York City.

One 1980s crash that Harry did manage to escape was the depression in real estate syndicates. When Congress finally altered the tax codes in 1986 to tighten up sundry loopholes, the bottom was knocked out from under the tax-oriented real estate syndicate market. But for people still in the deals on which Harry had built his fortune, 1988 was a torturous year. The torment was deciding whether to stay in or cash in.

A gambling frenzy tinged the air. The volume of shares in existing partnerships that were sold off to other investors jumped by 50 percent through June from the year-earlier period, soaring from $300 million to $450 million. Share owners were bailing out, and at fire-sale prices to boot.

At the same time, purveyors of brand-new limited partnership deals were having a hard time finding investors. In fact, the number of new shares that were sold in 1988 fell just as dramatically as the used-share market rose. "I'm seeing a lot of confusion," said Jerry Clevenger, president of a Florida-based brokerage firm that handles second-hand real estate syndicate shares.

That investors were baffled was understandable. Limited partnership syndicates are complex animals. They can be tossed into two large groupings, but really, every deal is different. They're not easy to decipher when they're sitting still. They're harder to sort out when any variables start to stir. And by the end of Ronald Reagan's stay in the White House, several extraneous economic and legal matters that affected real estate syndicates were in a hard spin.

By contrast, many of the people who created real estate syndicates were cool and collected. And therein lies the magic in syndicates.

There are two kinds of players: the investors and the creators. And by and large, the investors have been in over their heads. They're gambling at a table where the rules are too many, the strategy is too complex, and the amount of time that it takes to learn and stay on top of everything is too great. As in shooting craps, investors could often ride with a winning creator if they were lucky in picking a good thrower. But they'd have to know when to get off and find another table.

The limited partnership involves the selling of shares in a building, as stock involves shares in a company. But no limited partnership deal was done to make a bundle of profit when the shares were finally sold. It happens that many did rise in face value, some even spectacularly. But profit at the end was mere icing. The main attraction was something of more substance along the way.

The real money, and the real reason the country went absolutely wild over real estate syndicates, stemmed from either the tax-shelter benefits or the hefty annual dividends plucked from the profits gained from operating the building. For comparison, if a syndicate owned taxis—and it could, under the government's very loose regulatory hand—the profit would roll in from the fares collected, not from whatever the battered cab would bring in at the end on the used-car lot. Real estate syndicates often would reap both operating profits *and* a good resale price on the used-share lot. But that was pure bonus, and only further stirred investor passions.

One breed of limited partnership syndicate seemed a good bet in 1988. That was the deal based solely on equity—that is, on the money to be made from operating the building, and secondarily on the building's value itself. Geography played the big spoiler. The equity syndicates formed around those shiny new steel-and-glass towers in Houston weren't worth much more than the oil-soaked dirt on which the buildings stood when the Texas market went bad. Starved for tenants, some syndicates went belly-up, leaving the investors with the equivalent of battered taxis that couldn't even be sold for parts. But overall, equity syndicates have done well on both scores. Annual profits rolled in as expected, with double-digit dividends up to 25 percent. And the property value rose as well. Many deals cut on the coasts—apartments in Los Angeles, office towers in Manhattan—soared.

Not so for another major breed of limited partnership syndicate, which was formed mainly to shelter investor income from taxes. All went well until 1986, when Congress decided finally to reform the tax law and destroy the breaks that the wealthy had gotten for decades. By the time investors saw the reforms coming, it was too late. A share in the average tax-based deal purchased for $1,000 before the 1986 reform could be sold on the used-share markets for a mere $120 in 1988, down 50 percent from just the year before. Worse, their practical value as tax shelters had completely evaporated. They became the gold-mine certificates of the 1980s—mere pieces of paper born of some bad-luck greed.

Between those two syndicate types was a mixed-bag deal, crafted to get both some tax breaks and some equity profit. Many of these have done well, if they relied on one or more of the tax breaks that Congress spared and if the geography played out right and rent-paying tenants were found. Many others have stalled out, leaving the second-hand market flush with investors anxious to sell but short of buyers. Analysts were urging everyone to look extra hard at what they had sunk their savings into. "Many people are in for a rude awakening," securities analyst Robert Mills said in mid-1988. "We all knew real estate had some bad problems, but what's happening to these partnerships is a real shocker. If things don't get better for another two years, you're going to see a bunch of them go bankrupt."

An even better gauge of the looming danger was the trend in sales of brand-new limited partnerships. New issues were almost 40 percent off in the second quarter of 1988, compared with the year-earlier period. And the dollar volume, some $1.3 billion, was less than half the sum of three decades earlier—when $3 billion in real estate syndicate shares were sold in 1959 dollars. The smart money had gone elsewhere, or was waiting to see what would shake.

Had Helmsley been doing syndicates in 1986 when Congress acted, there's no question he would have been the first to jump. But, of course, Harry was no longer doing new syndicates. The ones he was involved in were already made, and he was merely managing their fruits—the offices and warehouses and hotels of the $5–$6 billion Helmsley-managed empire.

Harry Helmsley liked to joke that if dealing in real estate was so brainy he would have found something else to do. But he knew better than anyone else that the real profit lay in management. Others could put their money into the actual property. Harry would be content reaping commissions for finding the tenants, cleaning the offices, insuring the buildings, and even providing telephone service. The extent to which Helmsley played the commissions game is best illustrated by the Empire State Building.

In 1982, one of Helmsley's staffers at the Park Lane Hotel picked up the downstairs telephone that sometimes mistakenly rings when someone in the Helmsley penthouse makes an outside call. The staffer realized it was a false ring. But when he heard Harry's voice, the employee listened. Harry was telling someone that buying some stock in a certain company might not be such a bad idea.

It's not likely that Harry himself bought the stock. He didn't play the market. He rightly considered that to be gambling on someone else, and there was no one better than Harry himself to bet on. The eavesdropper told his own mother, who dabbled in stocks, and she did quite well. In short order after that call, the stock's value soared from a third quarter 1982 high of 7$1/8$ to a fourth quarter high of 14. It then rose to a first quarter 1983 high of nearly 18. Then, just as quickly, it plummeted to below where it started six months earlier. The eavesdropper's mother, however, had cashed in her profit just as it started to dip and was quite pleased by the whole matter.

The company Harry mentioned was Telesphere International, Inc., a long-distance phone service company based in Illinois. There were two likely reasons the stock jumped. One, in August 1982 the federal government announced it was cutting AT&T into little bits, opening the way for upstarts like Telesphere. And two, the company announced with much glee a little later that it had sold its long-distance service to the Helmsley hotel chain. Moreover, it had won an agreement with Helmsley to put a major switching station in the Empire State Building, giving it immediate and noncompetitive access to all of the building's hundreds of commercial tenants.

Thus, it was a very proud Telesphere that put the Empire State Building on the cover of its annual report for 1982. In the next year's annual it reported that its phone service had gotten to be very popular with Helmsley's tenants. "Our switching location in the Empire State Building serves over 1,200 business customers, many of whom are business tenants of the Helmsley organization."

In-house attorney Greg Casey and other officials at Telesphere refused to discuss the matter. They wouldn't say whether Helmsley bought any of the company's stock. But it's clear from the company's subsequent federal filings why the price of its stock plummeted: some innovative equipment had failed, revenues dropped, salaries and staffing rose. The young firm was struggling in a fierce market. And that wasn't Telesphere's only problem. In 1988 the Securities and Exchange Commission began investigating the firm's pricing structure, on the basis of complaints from consumer groups that its rates were too high. The state of New York, with more vigor, has launched a similar probe.

That was not an unusual charge, said the SEC staffer handling the case, Gregory Vogt, noting that the agency was getting hundreds of complaints from consumer groups that many long-distance carriers were gouging their customers. Casey and the company's filings indicate that the firm justified its rates by saying its quality of service was so high.

But what's interesting about the Empire State Building situation is that every time one of the tenants chose Telesphere for its long-distance service, Harry made money. In its 1983 filing with the SEC, Telesphere noted that its agreement with Helmsley gave him a commission on all of the long-distance calls placed through the switch. The reports did not indicate, and again Telesphere officials refused to say, how much Helmsley's commission has been. But in the competitive market, it would have ranged as high as 15 percent.

Commissions on telephone calls. Fees for cleaning the offices. More commissions for leasing space to the tenants. And a cut of the huge annual profits that exceeded the initial expectations. Helmsley got all that from the Empire State Building and his other Manhattan properties in exchange for virtually no dollar investment of his own. Even the small sum Helmsley was initially required to invest in the Empire State he was able to pay with his broker's fee of $500,000 for the original transaction with Robert Crown.

Whether the federal or state probes into the telephone matter will affect Harry's income remains to be seen. But there were other strange happenings in the Helmsley empire that spelled trouble. Not one, but two fires in the summer of 1988 forced evacuations of the Empire State Building. At least one fire appeared to be arson. And that year, too, seemed to bode ill for Helmsley-Spear's ability to hold on to its best and brightest brokers. Several bailed out, telling a business weekly as they closed the door that Helmsley-Spear was losing its stuff.

Certainly, neither fire nor attrition is new to Helmsley Enterprises. The Helmsley hotel on Forty-second Street caught fire in February 1981 on its opening day, just two hours after Mayor Koch and three hundred other guests celebrated the opening with an elegant buffet luncheon. Harry and Leona were in the hotel bar popping more champagne corks and had to rush out into the street. "This is just one of those things that go wrong," Harry told a passing reporter. "This was not arson. This was not vandalism. This was just something that happened." Still, he added: "There have been so many hotel fires lately— you worry whether this could be another Las Vegas. But it was not anything serious." Ironically, the fire scared yet another Greensboro, North Carolina, resident, who was staying on the seventh floor. "I paid no attention to the alarm," said Kathryn Shaver. "But then I smelled smoke and went out into the hallway. Then the door closed behind me and I couldn't get back into the room."

Still, it's with some melancholy that longtime Helmsley aide Steve Brener pulls out old Helmsley-Spear corporate reports and runs his finger down the list of the names of the top executives. "Walter Helmsley, he's dead. Maurice Spear and Leon Spear, they're dead. Earle Altman, he's still there. Newman, he's dead. Raff, he's dead. Kazis, he has his own business. Greene, I think he's dead. Luery, he's around but not there. Malloy is gone. Feder is gone. Sydney Wien, he died. Weiss, not there anymore. Wallach, not there . . ."

Socially, the Helmsleys began losing even more of their stuff— both in Greenwich and in Manhattan, where the new-money circles are finicky about things like criminal indictments. The Helmsleys never quite fit in in Greenwich. They gave money to the local police youth and public service funds and to a couple of charities. But the old-money crowd was put off by their gaudiness and social faux pas, as when Harry once failed to wear a black tie to a United Way fundraising event. The Helmsleys were not asked to sponsor one of the two dozen dinners that were held in the better Greenwich homes to raise money for charity. The last big party they threw was for Leona's sixty-sixth birthday in 1986. Among the guests were Barbara Walters, Norman Orentreich, a Rockefeller, the Trumps, Kitty Carlisle Hart, the Wagners, Jane Powell. But that was a mere superficial social affair, said one social-scene observer who was there. "I remember one of their neighbors commenting about something in the house being very tacky," he said. "I mean, how could a friend say that? These were not friends." Nor were they even liked by the country-store owners down the road. Of course, the Helmsleys never stopped in for a soda pop. But the staff and contractors did, and their stories are the stuff of oral history.

"Did you hear about the sheep?" the storekeepers' daughter asked. "The ones they showed on *60 Minutes,* where Leona had given them all names and when she called to them for Mike Wallace to see they ran the other way? They were all dead the next day. Slaughtered. They were put on the staff's menu." Not true, said a Helmsley friend, recalling that the sheep were sold because winter was coming on and Harry suggested that it might be a pain to feed them. But fact or fiction, it didn't matter. History was writing itself around the Helmsleys in their own neighborhood.

Leona's pretensions to know good food never ceased to astound those around her. The ad agent Jane Maas was privy to one scene involving Leona and her brother Alvin, who prided himself on being knowledgeable about food, as well as fine wines. Leona, or someone, had ordered Swedish smoked salmon for the Palace's restaurant, the Trianon Room. The day before, she had blasted the maître d' for slicing it too thin. "*This* type of salmon is meant to be sliced thick," Leona instructed. So the next day along comes Alvin. He picks up a piece, munches it a little, and shakes his head no. "It would be O.K., but it's sliced too thick. Way too thick."

So Leona beckoned to the maître d' and sent him back to the kitchen with a new scolding. "Take this salmon away, and learn how to slice it the way it should be. Paper thin." There were deep bows from the doubly chastised.

Similarly, Leona had a substantial change of mind once about some caviar from the Baltic Sea. She sampled. She ordered—a huge amount. And then when it came she ordered it sent back. What was wrong? The hotel manager never found out, but the reason was that Leona had reacted to the Chernobyl nuclear accident in the Soviet Union by banning a good many European items from the Park Lane and Palace, where she might eat. She also changed her bottled water to a non-European brand and even warned those around her against traveling to London, for fear of the radiation.

Palace chef Andre René tells another story, about how Leona worked hard to make someone pay for what only she could consider an error. She had come back to the Palace Hotel late one night from one of her balls, and she went into Harry's Bar. Diet or no diet, she wanted a sandwich. The only sandwich material on hand was corned beef. "Well, the beef was not the best, after sitting out in the heat all day," he said. "And she didn't like the sandwich. She said it was too fatty. So she didn't pay the corned-beef salesman's bill. It was about $8,500. There was nothing he could do."

The hotel staff felt sorry for the salesman. So after that, they made a point of cooking a fresh turkey every day, a fourteen- or sixteen-pounder, charged to the Palace expenses. They would have it ready and freshly roasted by 11:30 A.M. just in case Leona should happen to want a sandwich.

Leona won awards from people who appreciate fine food and wine. In 1985 she was recognized by the Culinary Institute of America in upper New York State. The Culinary Institute had received $100,000 from the Helmsleys that year.

Newspaper and magazine readers responded to the rash of articles about the Helmsleys, their hotel episodes, and their tax troubles. It was not the first time that articles about them spurred criticism. A 1974 profile of Harry in *The New York Times* prompted Joan Blackett Schlank to write the editor: "As a real estate broker I am embarrassed and as a New Yorker I am outraged at the picture I get of the ultimate real estate broker, Harry Helmsley. Mr. Helmsley's business philosophy of profit at any price, as drawn in the article, is grossly out of step with the desperate needs of his city and responsibilities that should certainly be felt by its business community. One no longer wonders at the sad quality of living that New York City offers to those of us who love the city and would like to live here." But such letters were as rare as the press on Helmsley until Leona's hotel ads and the tax troubles arose.

"What gonifs, what schnorrers, Harry Helmsley should be sent up the river, and Leona Helmsley should be placed in a federal prison where she can practice what she does best—housekeeping," wrote one Manhattanite. Said another: "There the Helmsleys stand, naked before the world. The saddest thing is they will probably never realize that without honor, their $5 billion might as well be 5 cents." Adding injury to the insult, running alongside that pair of letters was a stately full-page ad for Donald Trump's Plaza Hotel.

Leona granted only one interview after the sales-tax charges broke in December 1986—a long chat the following spring with Susan Mulcahy, *Newsday*'s gossip columnist. Also present were Harry and her attorney, Steve Kaufman, to avoid any deep probing of the tax matter. Leona said she felt cheated by the press's reliance on her anonymous critics. She found it difficult to believe the preponderance of negatives. "One must have said something nice," Leona chided Mulcahy. "One person had to say, 'She's a nice lady. She did something nice for me,' or 'He's a nice man. He did something nice.' No one?"

Alvin, her employee and only surviving sibling, eventually went to her assistance. "The *Post* is the garbage heap of New York," he said. "The Helmsleys are taking a bad rap. They really are good people and to run them down that way is just lousy. She is a very generous, very loving, very giving person. That's the way she has been all her life." Alvin refused to make any further comment. Even Howard Rubenstein tried to help out. When the *New York Daily News* voted Leona as one of New York's ten pushiest women, he charged sexism. "If she were a man, no one could call her pushy."

One Helmsley Palace supplier, Howard Brandston, wrote a local business weekly to say he had never been treated the way others had. "My company designs lighting systems, and provided those services for Helmsley hotels, as well as other projects. I was always treated with respect and open cordiality. Whenever I met either of the Helmsleys, I was greeted with a smile. I was also paid well and paid promptly."

But those tributes and mild protestations were lost in the storm. The professional lampoons were the worst, or the best, depending on perspective. And as the hotel ads continued to display Leona's grin, even as the headlines blared "Tax Scam," comedians all around town added Leona to their stand-up routines. Even the old-timers sensed Leona was good for a barb. An exception was Henny Youngman, who knew Leona personally from handing her his rent money years back. He did not pop off any one-liners during an interview and was asked why not. "She is not funny. All that is not funny," he said, in what must have been a rare pulled punch by the man who could poke good-natured fun at anyone. But comedienne Carol Burnett had no qualms when asked by a magazine whom she would be doing takeoffs on in 1988. Burnett named Fawn Hall and Jessica Hahn. "I would also be doing Leona Helmsley, definitely," said Burnett.

Cartoonists like Bill Griffith, creator of "Zippy," did frame after frame on Leona, featuring her special "You're fired" smile and her running feud with Ivana Trump. *Esquire* magazine featured her as "one of the women we love to hate," along with Barbara Walters, Maggie Thatcher, Shirley MacLaine, and Brigitte Nielsen. The magazine captioned Leona's picture with the words: Hotel Despot. "Bellman, call me a paddy wagon!"

In 1984, *The Wall Street Journal* reported on an avant-garde group called Salon Bon Ton and its debut of *The Trouble with Harry*, a lampoon operetta in which Harry and Leona waltzed around a skyline of brownstones while a Shakespearean bard in black lace regales: "Who but a monarch and his mate could lay whole neighborhoods to waste." Said one audience member: "He owns all of New York! I mean, how could someone like him? Really?"

*Spy* magazine began putting Leona in almost every issue in 1988, perhaps reacting to the following letter to the editors after the Helmsleys went to court and Donald Trump announced he was making Ivana chief of the Plaza Hotel, with the compensation of one dollar a year and all the dresses she could buy. "I'm disappointed in you, *Spy*," the reader wrote. "I recently picked up the April issue, and whom did I *not* see in a face-to-face feud on the cover? Leona 'I Don't Pay My Taxes, Why Should You?' Helmsley and Ivana 'One Dollar a Year and All the Dresses I Can Buy' Trump—the respective queens of The Palace and The Plaza. It's such a natural *Spy* cover. Shame on you."

Though Cardinal Cooke did his best to restrict the unsavory from the Palace Hotel, sundry guests and would-be guests provided more fodder for the gossips. The arms dealer Adnan Kashoggi rented out whole floors of suites for his bejeweled entourage. Imelda Marcos used one of the fifty-first-floor penthouses on her regular shopping forays in Manhattan when her husband, Ferdinand, was still in power in the Philippines. Muammar al-Qaddafi secretly reserved fifty Palace rooms in November 1982, placing a $75,000 deposit with the Helmsleys. But his plans leaked out and the visit was canceled.

In the spring and summer of 1988 there were more blistering profiles in *People* and *New York* magazines. And CBS's *60 Minutes* reran its fifteen-minute segment of three years before, updating it only by mentioning the tax troubles. This time Leona didn't grant an interview even to her "friend," correspondent Mike Wallace, who described Leona to a *Chicago Tribune* reporter this way: "She's a strange, capable, difficult, generous, mean-spirited, selfish—again, generous woman." Harry, too, lost ground almost overnight. The biographical blurbs on him in *Forbes* and *Fortune* magazines went from listings of such niceties as his being named the best-dressed businessman in 1983 to his being indicted along with his wife, the "Queen."

It was all beyond public relations wizard Doug Hearle's reach. Asked whether Leona ever considered spending the summer wrapping bandages or something else civic-minded to boost her public image, Hearle said no. Instead, Leona fought back, attacking the rash of news stories that erupted during their indictment. "It was straightforward from the beginning," he said of his effort on her and Harry's behalf. "We were trying to get across the injustices inherent in a system that was letting the press go into a frenzy. I took issue with the more than a hundred unattributed quotes, particularly in the *Post*. According to Journalism One, you're supposed to say who is saying what."

Leona, in fact, made it worse for herself by filing a couple of fresh lawsuits. She sued the company that altered her fur coats, charging them with a pair of misdeeds: mangling her $100,000 Russian sable and ill-fitting her into a $2,500 Persian lamb jacket. And she sued the interior decorator whom she had hired to do their new retirement home in Paradise Valley, Arizona, claiming the decorator misspent the $50,000 advance. To no one's surprise, Leona used brand-new attorneys for both cases.

By October, Hearle was off the account—his contract suspended because the trial was delayed until 1989. And the Helmsleys were on their own. Their passports suspended, they headed to Hawaii and were caught on the beach by some local photographer/reporter who supposedly got Leona to say that she and Harry might spend another night because it was free. The stereotyping had reached across the Pacific.

In late 1988, their public image seemed set only to plummet further. Leona, however, knows how to use what could be her greatest public relations ploy.

Time and again after Jay died, Leona has reacted with tears to the mere mention of his name. She cried for Mike Wallace and the millions watching *60 Minutes*. Her eyes become wet even if only one other person is present. What she does in private, of course, no one knows. But there's good reason to doubt the authenticity of the tears.

To be sure, they were very real in the beginning. The Park Lane Hotel staff confirm that she was a wreck after Jay's funeral. Her entire face was red for two weeks. She grieved for her only son. And she exacerbated the emotion with her own guilt over her role in his short life. But over time, Leona began noticing something about those tears. What she noticed was the way people responded. They reacted with sympathy, with caring, with love. When Jay died, Barbara Sinatra sent Leona a poem. It was the sort of thing you would send to a mother whose son predeceased her. The poem said everyone is a child of God, and eventually God calls everyone, some sooner, some later. Leona had the poem framed and put on a shelf in her office.

Years later, Leona continued to cry when his name was mentioned. She held on to the warmth and attention inherent in that touching gift from Sinatra—a gift unlike any the hardened, almost totally friendless Leona had ever received.

Joyce Beber has said, "I think she's come to use tears like she's come to use everything else in her life. To get something. And they get her sympathy."

If that's been Leona's motive, what happened in court during her arraignment with Harry may well have been a test run for what she could do to help her legal defense.

The judge having dismissed everyone, Leona turned to leave and halted just short of the doorway. Perhaps she was waiting for Harry, who was moving more slowly. When she turned around to face him, it was plain for everyone to see that the lioness, the iron lady, the hotel magnate who seemed to ask to be hated, was crying. One report called it a gushing. Others more accurately described it as a mere wetness around her eyes. Whatever, her mascara was smeared. And in the next day's reports there was mention of this apparent soft and human spot in a woman considered to be solid venom. Leona could gain much if society bestowed on her its sympathy.

Certainly Harry looked very sad to see her cry.

# CHAPTER 18

# BLIND TRUST

A LATE SUMMER'S DAWN BROKE WITH A HUSH OVER THE HELMSLEY estate in Greenwich. Autumn was just to the north. The leaves were starting to turn. The air was drier, though not yet tinged with any coolness. There was a slight stirring inside the mansion.

A limousine turned off the Merritt Parkway onto Round Hill Road and rolled up to the estate's southern boundary. It continued for another eight-tenths of a mile along the stone wall until it reached the employee entrance. The gate opened. The limo moved slowly through and stopped.

Out stepped a muscled young man. Moments later he was in the pool with Harry Helmsley, who proceeded to put his tall, straight seventy-nine-year-old body through laps. The trainer stayed by his side. They moved slowly at first, then picked up the pace to a steady, vigorous stroking. Leona Helmsley, who had just turned sixty-eight, joined them in the water, and not for a long while did they retreat to an athlete's breakfast. The limo carried the therapist back to Manhattan, to return the next day.

Thus the Helmsleys spent a good part of September 1988 awaiting their trial on tax-fraud charges. Harry's strength in the water was notable, given the equally vigorous efforts by his attorneys to extract him from the government's charges by arguing that he was in poor health—too poor of health to assist in his own defense. But it wasn't physical prowess the defense referred to. It was Harry's mental health. And over the summer, a series of neurologists tested him and found Harry mentally lacking. His memory had deteriorated, they said. He couldn't recall those invoices with his initials on them or the genesis of the corporate policy that created them.

Skeptics abounded. Those around him remembered the many times Harry would tune out of a fight Leona was picking in his presence with someone else. "I think he has faded in and out very, very conveniently," said Joyce Beber.

Phil Blumenfeld agreed that as a matter of routine Harry would turn away from an awkward personal situation. Any business matter he could handle and tackle head-on. But bring up something emotional, something that he couldn't easily appraise or categorize or stack against everything else by putting a price on it, and Harry was at a complete loss. "That was Mr. Helmsley's style. He never wanted to deal with an uncomfortable position. He certainly never wanted to talk to people who would make [Leona] unhappy."

Watching Harry swim, one Helmsley aide found it hard to envision him as anything less than a strong person headed with vigor toward his ninth decade. A professional in the Helmsleys' employ who stayed at the mansion commented, "He's absolutely fine." Seen at the Palace early that summer, Harry seemed almost youthful, puttering about the lobby or standing in patient wait for Leona.

The prosecutors, of course, were most doubtful about the defense claims that Harry had lost it. They pointed out that some of the doctors had links to the money Harry donated to New York Hospital. Moreover, it turned out that part of the $33 million that the Helmsleys publicly said they had given to the hospital in 1986 was only a pledge. The rest was to come, and it dangled like a jewel. In late October, however, yet another specialist in neurology, this time appointed by the judge from a hospital in Boston, also found Harry to be mentally lacking. Harry looked set to be freed of the charges. The prosecution remained skeptical, but anticipated the judge's ruling. Suddenly several things came clear: Harry's failing now and then to recognize his closest aides, his heavy donations to Alzheimer's and "Fountain of Youth" longevity research, his very slow, unsteady gait and the almost doddering look in his eyes, and maybe things even closer to the heart of Helmsley Enterprises.

Lending its own prognosis to the situation, *The New York Times* reported the final doctor's findings with a story that began on the front page of the local news section and jumped to the obituary page. "Twenty dead people and Harry," one reader joked. People began speaking of Harry B. Helmsley in the past tense.

What will happen to the Helmsley empire if Leona is convicted, or if Harry dies in the near future, is a matter of self-interest to more than their 10,000-plus employees. The real estate community, other hoteliers, the Religious Society of Friends and other charitable groups, Leona's own grandchildren, and even Donald Trump all have an economic stake in the fallout, as does the IRS. At stake is the $5–$6 billion gross, as well the $1.3–$1.7 billion net, of the Helmsley empire. Leona may have an inside track if she survives Harry. But many others could do rather well. Or they could gain nothing at all by Harry's death.

Alvin Schwartz and Irving Schneider were, for a long time, considered the heirs apparent of Helmsley-Spear, the brokerage concern. But it's unlikely either would want to run the company for long, or even at all. Schwartz reportedly had wanted to retire and only changed his mind when Harry got into legal trouble. Both men are sufficiently wealthy from the deals they have made as full partners with Harry. And while both have worked very hard in their lives, associates describe neither as the type of person who would devote his last years to someone else's company—especially not one whose leaders had foundered.

There are a few younger underlings with more drive and ambition. But Helmsley-Spear itself, some believe, is a rather bad bet to continue for long, or at least in its present form. To make that case, critics point to everything from the company's lingering reliance on Rolodex cards and shoe leather for tracking clients and office space to the deteriorating condition of Helmsley-Spear buildings themselves. Really, though, it's more that the nature of real estate itself is changing, shifting away from tycoons like Harry to the faceless corporate manager. Even young Trump is an anachronism, a throwback to the age of entrepreneurs who were able to move huge deals with their own individual or familial financial power. An expanding Trump is worth no more than his bank credit, and the vaporware that sells his deals long before they have any substance.

Increasingly, real estate is playing a key role in corporate mergers and acquisitions, in everything from the recent sale of the *New York Post* to a real estate developer, to the Canadian financier Robert Campeau's purchase of Federal Department Stores, to the buy-out of the Stop & Shop stores. The land underneath is rivaling the improvements above in value, or certainly it is playing a bigger part in the deals. Wall Street houses, in turn, are moving directly into the real estate business as brokers. Goldman, Sachs & Co. has already done so. Morgan Stanley & Co. and First Boston are pondering giving chase. "The entire industry is changing," said one Chicago-based consultant. "There are only going to be six or seven companies handling the real estate of the Fortune 500, instead of fifty." If Helmsley-Spear continues to vie for that business, it will face increasingly sophisticated, computerized competitors with instincts for the bottom line every bit as strong as Harry's.

That's not to say Helmsley-Spear would disappear all at once tomorrow. It owns or manages too much of Manhattan, not to mention much of the country.

In fact, in recent days Harry Helmsley has been brought to the verge of becoming the largest single personal owner of Manhattan—an accomplishment that just might tickle the fancy of the man who liked to take guests to his office window or penthouse patio and sweep his arm over the city, uttering some version of "Just taking inventory."

Just about half of Manhattan's 14,310 acres belong to the public or to nonprofit institutions, according to a recent real estate industry survey. The city itself owns almost 5,700 acres, of which 2,600 acres are used by the Parks Department, including the 840-acre Central Park. Roadways and streets consume another 2,500 acres; the city's housing, 500 acres; foreclosed property, 250 acres; offices, fire stations, and hospitals, 280 acres.

The state, the federal government, and a regional public entity or two hold about 180 acres for housing, post offices, and bus stations. The universities have about 190 acres. Utilities fall in next with about 90 acres. Churches are more difficult to measure because their land is tax-exempt. Only the holdings of one—Trinity Church near Wall Street—are vast, covering almost 33 acres of Manhattan. The Roman Catholic Church is thought to own far more than that, but declines to say just how much. It may be party to things even more interesting than the Helmsley Palace.

Of the for-profit corporations, Helmsley's old friend Metropolitan Life is at the top of the landowning list. Met Life sold Harry the expansive Parkchester housing complex in the Bronx, but it has held on to another in Manhattan, Stuyvesant Town, and still holds title to 140 acres. Equitable Life is next with less than 6 acres. Below that, in order, fall U-Haul, Prudential, and McDonald's, whose stores are growing though they are terribly out of place alongside the Russian cafés, Italian bakeries, and Puerto Rican bodegas that still dominate Manhattan's street fronts.

Measured in raw acreage, Donald Trump's holdings in 1988 put him ahead of other individual property owners. His name was on deeds to 78 Manhattan acres. But it's thought that he won't hold that place of distinction for long. All but a couple of those acres are part of an undeveloped site that he was looking to sell in late 1988. Trump had dreams of building his own little city and tower to the gods on that site, but the neighborhood was not willing to accept it. Ironically, Harry once wanted to use the same site to put up the world's tallest tower.

The landlord Sol Goldman was next with 41 acres when he died in 1987. Goldman left an estate totaling $1 billion, and despite his stated wishes in his will to keep the holdings intact, a huge battle shaped up in New York's Surrogate Court between his wife and children. There's little doubt that much of it will dissolve.

With Trump wanting to slice off the bulk of his landholdings and the heirs of Sol Goldman consuming his empire, the Helmsleys would rank first in Manhattan property holdings, carrying the deeds to an estimated 40 acres of land underneath dozens of buildings—double the acreage of even the Rockefeller family.

But, of course, Harry has to climb into his jet to survey all that he acquired. And beyond his direct holdings throughout the country, there are the dozens of pieces of property that he owns through his syndicate partnerships. How they will resolve upon Harry's death could vary. Most partnerships allow the inheritor of the deceased's holdings to carry on as a partner. Others would force the heir to make an immediate sale. In either case, untangling the Helmsley empire holdings would take years and a monumental effort by probate attorneys.

How charities will fare under a dissolution of the Helmsley empire is, of course, a matter of his will, which Harry could change at any moment. Harry's old friend Larry Wien, who died in December 1988, had developed a distinct philosophy about giving his money away, which he tried to share with his friends and associates. Wien believed that the best way to become philanthropic was to study a charity as one might study a corporate aquisition, and only then donate significant sums. Harry Helmsley's approach has been more haphazard.

A complete record of Helmsley's giving could not be obtained. It's significant that Harry's giving may not necessarily be charitable. Undoubtedly, a choice between handing over his income to the IRS or to a group of his own choosing has guided some, if not all, of Harry's giveaways. It's also clear that his brand of charitable donations is rather self-interested. For Harry, that's meant that the bulk of his donated dollars have gone to the hospitals in which he and Leona have been treated. Maybe he's simply been taking Wien's advice and giving to things he knows of firsthand. But there's no indication that he's a person who cares for the impoverished or the otherwise disenfranchised at large.

The donations he has made through his private foundation have increased sharply since the fiscal year 1981, when he doled out $130,065. In 1982, the sum jumped to $256,358, and in 1983, it again nearly doubled to $436,675. In 1984 the Harry B. Helmsley Foundation gave out $826,420. There have been a wide range of beneficiaries, but they can be grouped into local Greenwich causes, including especially the police department service funds; religious groups, including several Jewish synagogues and forums and the Catholic Church, as well as the Quakers; and medical organizations which are concerned with areas that trouble the Helmsleys themselves—eyesight, heart, and aging.

Other than hospitals, a big medical recipient has been the Orentreich Foundation, set up for the medical center run by Leona's doctor friend Norman Orentreich. The medical center specializes in a wide range of skin- and aging-related problems. Its foundation, in turn, funds research into Alzheimer's disease and various aging studies. IRS tax records show that other big donors in recent years include Doris Duke, Perry Ellis, Estée Lauder, Warren Beatty, and the Ivan Boesky Corp., which gave $10,000 in 1984. The Orentreichs refused to discuss the Helmsleys' donations, describing Leona and Harry as "patients" of the medical center. But records show the Helmsleys' donations ranged from $10,000 in 1982 to $200,000 in 1984 and $200,000 again in 1985.

Many of their donations earned the Helmsleys formal recognition and praise. In 1983, they gave $21,500 to the Boys Town of Italy, and were honored with the International Humanitarian Award at the thirty-eighth anniversary Boys Town ball for 1,200 guests at the Waldorf-Astoria. But none of their giveaways won them more good publicity than their $33 million pledge in 1986 to New York Hospital, which pushed them to the top of *Town & Country* magazine's list of the nation's biggest living givers.

In their comments, they made no bones about being self-interested. "I'm trying to make myself one of the more important people in New York and so I wanted to do something for New York," said Harry. "It is the size of this gift which is unusual for me. I have been having treatments at the hospital and they seem to handle things with heart and great skill. So the whole idea of giving to them seemed to strike a chord."

Nor did he disguise his joy in getting to put his name on a new hospital wing. "The nice thing about this is that the hospital is actually built and the residence will be open by the fall, so you don't have to go through the heartaches," he said. "I know how long it takes to build from scratch, and we're pleased that we can see it now."

Added Leona: "I trust these people."

But even the full $33 million donation to New York Hospital, if it all comes to pass, did not set any records. In fact, a larger donation was made in 1983 to the associated Cornell Medical College, and it was made completely anonymously, without regard to publicity.

Among those most likely to receive a large chunk of the Helmsley empire is the Religious Society of Friends. Contrary to his own statements, Harry is no longer officially a member of the Fifteenth Street Meeting House where he and Eve were active. Sometime after January 1985, Harry was dropped from the rolls—not for nonpayment of dues, as some of his former Gramercy Park neighbors believed, but for general inactivity after his divorce from Eve.

Still, Harry gained a deep appreciation for the fastidiousness with which the Friends handled their donations. In his years as treasurer of the Quakers' Murray Fund, the officers met regularly in Harry's own office, poring over tiny requests with all the care and attention he'd give to his major real estate deals. "The whole fund was worth only something on the order of $50,000 or $60,000," said James Wood, who succeeded Harry as treasurer. "We would disburse something in the area of $4,000 or $5,000, to a variety of enterprises, in $100 and $200 amounts. And here would be Harry sitting at his desk. And on his shelves behind him were notebooks on the Empire State Building, or the Lincoln, or other buildings that each were worth so many times more than that. And yet Harry would be giving the fund the attention and care that he gave to those buildings. He was familiar with many of the groups. He didn't want long answers. He would just want to know that whenever the monies were allocated they were going to be looked after and not squandered."

Several Helmsley-Spear executives have said privately that it's been Harry's intention to give the Quakers much of his empire. At one point it was reported that Leona was to get a substantial share of the proceeds. On the other hand, one news report quoted a rumor that they had a very strict nuptial agreement that would severely restrict her take should Harry die first.

At any rate, Harry could change everything at any time with a stroke of his pen, and the rudest cartoon lampoonists show Leona perched on his deathbed holding his arm so he can sign what appears to be a new will. In 1985, Leona's secretary, Maryann Eboli, was peripherally present during a massive rewriting that took place in the Palace offices over several evenings. Both Leona and Harry were present. "There were a lot of raised voices at times," Eboli said. She was never made privy to the will's contents, but she did see the document and describes it as thicker than the New York City white and yellow pages combined.

What Harry may have in mind for her grandchildren is another matter to extrapolate from past events. Harry, though he likes children in general, never took to them personally. Neither he nor Leona wanted to be called grandparents, said Mimi Panzirer. And Harry's work ethic is such that he would not likely make them suddenly rich.

Leona, too, is unlikely to vest them with unearned wealth. She had savings accounts in each of their names. But immediately after Jay's death she had Eboli send the three youngest a letter informing them they were being taken out of the will. The reason: "They didn't attend the memorial," said Eboli. Beyond that perhaps impermanent anger, Leona made it clear she would never be overly generous with the kids. She was not born into money, Leona told friends, and she thought children should work for what they get. The only photo of a grandchild that Leona kept in her Palace Hotel during the time Eboli worked for her was that of the youngest, Walter Keith Panzirer, born in 1976. Leona once remarked that she thought he looked like her.

Mimi Panzirer knows only that she must keep an official distance from her late husband's children. "The official line is that if the kids have anything to do with me, they can forget being remembered in any way whatsoever. And I won't do anything to disturb that," she said.

Regardless of what the grandchildren receive, if anything, the Helmsley name will die. Harry does not have a single blood descendant. He has no children, no grandchildren of his own. His brother, Walter, never had kids. The family mausoleum has a finite number of spots—one for Harry and one for Leona. The name Helmsley may pass altogether if Harry's own genealogical search a few years back is any indication of how unique the name is. Hemsley, without the first *l*, seems to be a more common name in the United States.

Public opinion on the couple is more difficult to assess. "The Helmsley name will always be good," Leona declared in the legal dispute with the Palace Hotel investors. But many are those who want to forget the Helmsley name as fast as they can. Few are publicly standing by Leona and Harry even in their time of need.

Leona and Harry were largely alone during their two court appearances in the spring of 1988, except for their hired staff and bodyguards. There was but one exception. Throughout the proceedings, a woman sat in the courtroom staring intently at the couple. She even looked a fair bit like Leona—wispy hair, red lipstick, conservative clothes. At one point she pulled a store-bought greeting card from her purse, wrote some words on it, inserted it into its white envelope, sealed it, and handed it to one of the guards to give to Leona.

Later she said that her name was Lena Hartley and that she had lived in one of the New York housing projects that Helmsley had forced into condominium conversion. It was a bitter fight, as were the other Helmsley conversions. But Hartley said she didn't fault the Helmsleys, especially Leona, directly. "I don't blame her," she said. "It was management that was trying to throw us out."

In fact, she said, Leona had written her a letter during the ordeal, wishing her well. That was something Hartley wanted to repay. "I'm here to support her like she supported me. She was very kind to me, and I just wanted to express my best wishes," she said. It may well have been the kindest act toward either Leona or Harry inside or outside the courtroom.

When the Helmsleys left the court, climbing into their limo for the short ride uptown to the Park Lane, some of their friends and peers spoke out. Some of the comments were touching. They were true friends who would stick by a friend in trouble no matter what the cause.

"I like him," said Charles Urstadt, the former state official who had known Harry Helmsley as a business associate and personal friend since 1957. He pronounced each word with force. A picture of Harry

Helmsley hangs on Urstadt's office wall, and he spoke fondly of golf games and dinners and just-with-the-boys joking with Harry. "I admire him. He hasn't stepped on people. I have a warm spot in my heart for him. It's a damn shame that this would destroy a lifetime of work."

Bob Wagner also admitted to becoming one of Harry's closest friends. "I really feel very close to him personally and I admire him very much," said Wagner. "The real estate business is a tough game and I have never heard anybody say an unkind word about Harry. He was always a good man, a man of his word. His handshake was his bond, and he made a great contribution to the city of New York in many ways."

There were also one or two overt gestures toward Harry. At a dinner hosted by a real estate charitable group that channels donations to needy brokers, Harry Helmsley was given a loud and vigorous ovation. Both he and Leona were applauded at a fundraising dinner for New York Hospital.

But as their critics rejoice and the lampoons flow, there is no public or even private counterattack from their peers, their friends, any of the dozen or so men Harry Helmsley made into millionaires, or the thousands of small-time investors who made money—substantial amounts —from his buildings. The Real Estate Board hasn't held a press conference to extol his good deeds. The Koch administration hasn't spoken up to tabulate all the value the city gained from giving Harry so many tax breaks. Koch lost face trying to get into Harry's parties. But now he is keeping his distance. Even the man perhaps closest to Harry, Larry Wien, had to be ferreted out by a reporter and coaxed to say anything at all. And then it was only these words, spoken shyly and without any elaboration: "I have known Harry for thirty-nine years, and he has been honest for those thirty-nine years."

Why Leona's friends are silent is obvious. Close friends are hard to come by. As she warned her son, Jay, once, according to Mimi: "You'll never have any real friends being a Helmsley. People who say they're your friends will only be after your money."

But the excuses from Harry's pals fall flat. True, there is litigation pending against the Helmsleys. And with the New York media's reputation for fierceness, their friends could by no means be certain their words of praise would be favorably presented. But there always will be litigation of some sort against the Helmsleys. And far more than their accounting with the IRS is at stake. Their entire standing in the world, everything Harry has built up and stood for, is being flushed down the drain with heaps of public scorn. There's no excuse for why Harry's pals say so little about anything in his life. No excuse, but there is explanation.

Something is causing the silence, and that something is Harry's culpability in letting Leona destroy everything he'd built. Among those who best express that common feeling is Bernard Mendik, a very successful owner and developer of commercial properties, who, when he entered the business in 1957, spent weekends and nights studying the way Harry Helmsley did business. The fact that Mendik has deeply admired and respected Harry only further underscores his feelings today.

"I happen to like Harry," Mendik said. "But I think the community is very, very hurt and disappointed in the indictment. I think they are saddened by it. We are all saddened. Here is a man who was on top of the world, the kingpin of our industry, and this is a very vital industry, with some of the great entrepreneurs of the world, and here is a man who is the epitome of them all, the one we all look up to, the poor guy who made good, came out of the Bronx, not very well educated, and commands the respect of everybody in the business, with a reputation for being a man of his word, for being of great integrity, and in his eightieth year is being brought down. He cannot even get old and die peacefully, and that's what is sad and so unnecessary."

Then Mendik got to the point. "For whatever reasons that is happening, one has to feel he is to blame for not watching. He may not be blamed for anything else, he may not be culpable in a legal sense, but he's culpable by omission. This is kind of like when a spouse loses a spouse maybe because they smoked cigarettes and got cancer. Along with the sorrow, you feel angry that they did that to you. Well, we all feel angry that he let this happen to him. It's a blight on the whole community. I don't think anybody thinks, 'There but for the grace of God go I,' because we all beat our own drum. It's just sad, just sad, and it's sad for Larry Wien too, who probably agonized and suffered more than anybody."

Phil Blumenfeld agrees. "I don't know what his obligations were with a loose cannon like Leona around," he said. "But you have to ask yourself why the silence and the passivity of not doing something when he had the total wherewithal of doing right. He remained silent in the face of vicious behavior, which he could have stopped."

Joseph Licari, abandoned by Harry after twenty-one years of service, speaks more directly. "He's a gentleman who doesn't want confrontations," Licari said. "Unfortunately, Leona started getting more authority and power and calling some of the shots. His ego said, 'I still call the shots,' but there was a question in my mind about who really was in control. In recent years, I would say to him, 'Do you want me to do it this way? That's not the way she wants it.' He would say, 'Let me think about it . . .' I know that ten years ago he would have said, 'Do it this way.' He would have given me his decision. He wanted to buy himself some peace."

Even people trained to find the best in everyone found themselves with little to say that was nice. Asked about the Helmsleys' tax troubles, Rabbi Larry Halpern, Mimi and Jay's friend, told a reporter over the phone, "I think a lot of people are pleased because Leona Helmsley is a very difficult lady. I don't feel that is a proper reaction for a rabbi to have." But, he added, "I had dealings of my own with Leona that were not entirely positive."

Such reaction—whether from rabbi or former employee—is understandable, given the fact that, for many, knowing the Helmsleys was not a matter of association but a matter of surviving. There's a mass catharsis underway as ex-survivors purge themselves of the association. Ad agents, real estate brokers, hotel employees, contractors all speak of being chewed up and spit out and of having to pick themselves up and start anew, egos bruised. "Once you leave there, you have to fight and claw your way back to reestablish yourself," said Blumenfeld. Said Jane Maas: "I had almost forgotten what it was like to have an enthusiastic client. Fresh from the sneers of Leona ('Do you call this an ad, sweetheart?') I suddenly had . . . applause." For Mimi, the road back to feeling good about herself was perhaps longest and most agonizing.

That Leona has attempted a coup on the Helmsley empire, and has perhaps destroyed it in the effort, is so obvious to many that there remain, in the end, only two puzzles: why Leona did it and why Harry let her.

The first is easier to guess at than the second.

Regardless of how the tax matter turns out—it is, after all, just the more visible part of the coup—Leona's motivation is clear to those closest to her. If she cooked the company books as her aides say she did, she did not cook them for money. If she screwed contractors out of their payments as they say she did, she did not screw them for money. And if she fired hotel employees willy-nilly without regard to justice or feelings as they say she did, she did not do it for her guests. Rather, she did all that for fun. For the mere pleasure of playing what she considered to be the only game in life.

True, like most wealthy people of his generation, Harry also became rich and stayed rich by paying as little wages and as few taxes as legally possible. Harry had spent his lifetime thinking up ways to cut costs and avoid taxes. As he said in a legal deposition when asked about one elaborate system he'd set up to that end, there was "not much sense in my paying myself the money so I can have Uncle Sam collect the tax on it." Indeed, much of the real estate world in which he toiled was built on money from others who were just trying to avoid paying taxes. They didn't care about land or buildings. They cared about depreciations and the latest IRS rulings.

Leona played the same game, but two things trapped her. One, she simply is not as smart as Harry. And with the IRS painting a very fine line between legal right and legal wrong, and one that frequently changed, she couldn't tell when she crossed the line. Said one former aide who worked on her books: "The one thing she lacked was good business sense. She didn't know when it was worth fighting. She'd fight over a dollar and lose sight of thousands. And sometimes when the most practical way was maybe to drop it, she couldn't see that. That was the most difficulty I had with her. Getting her to focus on the important things rather than on the personal things that she would pick up on."

Second, Leona suffered because of her emotions, her uncontrollable rages, her paranoia at thinking the world was out to get her, and her inability to trust anyone in her life. "Harry? Maybe he was an unwilling participant," mused her former financial assistant. "But it was a game for her. She would have done it for thirteen dollars, let alone millions. She thought she was better than anybody and anything, that her way was better than anybody's. And that carried over to everything she did."

And above all, she craved power and was consumed by it. "Power tends to corrupt and absolute power corrupts absolutely," Lord Acton once said. But there's a better version of that truism to fit Leona Helmsley, suggested one of her longtime attorneys: Power is delightful and absolute power is absolutely delightful.

And so, the other puzzle—why Harry let himself get swept away by Leona.

He seems to have had ample and early warning. In 1973, less than a year after they married, the Helmsleys were asleep in their penthouse in Palm Beach when they were startled by an intruder. "We were awakened by someone in the room leaning over my wife," Harry said a few days after the incident. The intruder was trying to cover Leona's mouth and nose. "So I struck out at the person—she did too—and knocked the person down. I'm not sure whether it was a man or a woman. Obviously it looked like a prelude to a robbery." Murder as a prelude to robbery? The story got stranger as Harry went on.

"When we chased her or him, we got stabbed—my wife in the chest and I got stabbed in the arm. The person fled and I called the switchboard and the girl got me an ambulance." Later, said Helmsley, police found the Helmsleys' own twelve-inch kitchen knife on the grounds outside.

Leona, indeed, was seriously hurt. She had been stabbed in the chest. One lung was punctured. She spent several days in intensive care and was described as near death by her doctors.

But several things are wrong with that official version of the episode. First of all, the building, the Palm Beach Towers, was the most tightly secured property in tightly secured Palm Beach. John Kennedy used to have press conferences there; its security staff was top-notch. "It's as secure as they come around here," said one local crime reporter.

Second, common burglars rarely break in with people at home, and if they do by mistake, they flee. Later, the Helmsleys added to the story by saying some items were indeed missing—which would mean the burglar, after struggling with Leona and Harry, walked downstairs carrying the knife and goods.

It's unclear why the police did not investigate further. The case was left open, and was then lost. News reporters in Palm Beach say that's not unusual. Privacy among the wealthy is highly respected.

However, at least two people think they know the truth of what happened. The Helmsleys weren't burglarized, they say. Leona was attacked by the boyfriend of a maid she had fired that day. That's what Leona later told her, said Maryann Eboli. "She said that they learned it was the boyfriend of the maid, who was mad because she had fired the maid," said Eboli.

Additionally, a former real estate associate and friend of Leona's received a late-night telephone call from Leona as she was recovering in the hospital. He couldn't recall her exact words, but it is clear in his mind what happened because he remembered his own words. "I told her, 'Leona, don't be messing with Harry's employees like that. It can only bring you trouble. Why do it?' "

And there's another piece of evidence to ponder. Afterward, the Helmsleys didn't install new locks or burglar alarms. They hired a personal bodyguard, Ed Brady, who has stayed with them ever since and goes everywhere, including the beach, with the couple.

It's a wonder that, of the countless employees she fired over the years, another didn't strike back with more than a lawsuit.

Why didn't Harry speak up then and there?

The answer goes back to why they married each other—she at age fifty-two, he at sixty-four—in the first place.

Right off the bat, Leona had to defend herself from the gold-digging charge. "I didn't need to marry for money," she would insist. "How much money can you spend? How many homes can you own, and how many clothes can you wear? After you have so much it just doesn't matter." But a million dollars, if that's what she had when she married Harry, is not a billion. Besides, what she coveted was not mere fortune. It was power Leona craved, and that's what Harry had.

What did Harry think about Leona wanting to marry him? Some of his closest friends feel certain that he must have thought like the pragmatic person he always was. Notwithstanding her endless emotional fondling of him, Harry knew he was not pretty—or certainly not as pretty as he was wealthy and brimming with power. "How would Harry feel about it?" Steve Brener was asked. "I'm just guessing. He's a realist. Did he say to himself, 'If I didn't have money, would she marry me?' Possible, but not realistic. I'm putting myself in his position. I don't know, but that wouldn't be realistic."

Helmsley himself dropped some clues. After describing his admiration for Leona, Harry was once asked to explain what he thought attracted her to him. The white-haired, squint-eyed master of real estate replied, "I don't know what would appeal about me to her, but I'm not so bad. My power? I hadn't thought about it. . . . I think women are attracted to men with power, like Kissinger. But he doesn't have power because he's been elected to something. He has power because he's smarter than the next guy. Same way with me. I don't think where I'm so attractive to women, and if I were and acknowledged it, I'd have my head cut off. So for my well-being, I'm telling you I'm not attractive to women."

And what did Harry see in Leona?

Joyce Beber has thought about their relationship, in part because initially she was so shocked by the way Leona gushed over him. " 'You're a genius! How smart! How good-looking!' That's how she would talk to him on the phone," said Beber. "And he was quite self-absorbed. In a way I don't think he was interested in her at all. Rather, he loved her interest in him."

And so Harry stuck by Leona, perhaps because she came to mean everything to him in that selfish, perverse way. "Joe," Harry once told his former aide, Joe Ash, in a still and happy moment not long after he and Leona were married, "I'm having a good time." Who else but Leona would never spend a night away from her Harry, even to the point of wheeling a bed into his hospital room, as she did when he took ill.

Finally, there is one other explanation for why Harry would have bound himself so tightly to Leona even as she knocked holes in his ship and dragged his name through the mud. Theirs was a marriage not unlike the syndicates on which Helmsley built his empire. Deals are defined by mutual gain. Then they are cut and soaked in interdependence. And they are made contingent on the partners remaining partners to the end of the game. The magic ingredient in all that is trust. Partner has to trust partner, and do so blindly in total faith, or the whole thing collapses.

Harry trusted Leona, even as she was building walls around them —walls behind which the empire would crumble. "Darling, as long as you're convinced," she said to Harry on the *60 Minutes* segment for millions to see, "then just let the rest of the world go by."

And Harry, to whatever consequence, has done just that.

The metallic whirring of black Nikons stirred the air as photographers pushed their motor drives for a front-page shot of the Helmsleys getting arraigned.

"Mr. Helmsley, your friends tell some amazing stories about the things you've done over the years," a reporter offered gently, hoping to prod a response.

"They're all true," his wife snapped back.

"Mr. Helmsley, then what do you consider your greatest accomplishment?" Harry was asked half a minute later as the couple stepped into an elevator, hemmed in by their guards. He turned back toward the doors, facing the floodlights and flashes.

"Marrying her," he said with the slightest wink.

It was a practiced response, both the words and the wink. Maybe Harry was acting on reflex. Or maybe he just never allowed himself in on the truth.

# INDEX